S0-BBX-152

VIRGINIA MAXWELL

İSTANBUL
C I T Y   G U I D E

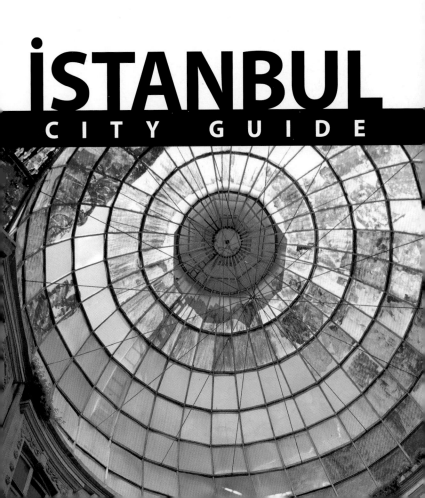

INTRODUCING İSTANBUL

Get hot at the Spice Bazaar (p82)

İstanbul is hot. And we're not talking about the weather. These days, there are more happening restaurants, bars, galleries and clubs around town than there are exquisite Ottoman mosques (and that's a lot)

The international fashion and design press have been talking up İstanbul ad nauseam, but the most significant thing about the accolade 'World's Hippest City' is that İstanbullus themselves have come believe it. The creeping sense of decrepitude that had fallen like a pall over their once-all-powerful home town has vanished, replaced by a sense of energy and innovation no seen since the days of Süleyman the Magnificent.

The city's over-abundance of important historic buildings and exciting new art galleries and museums provides visitors with more than enough to see during the day, but it's at night that the place swings into high-velocity, mega-stylish action. Locals are flocking to see and be seen at an ever-growing array of bars, clubs and restaurants, bringing with them an infectious sense of *joie de vivre* and a discerning ability to judge these places on their standard of service, drinks music and food as well as their position in the what's-hot-and-what's-not stakes.

That's not to say that the locals are turning their backs on much-loved city institutions such as the rakı-soaked meyhane (tavern) or tranquil çay bahçesi (tea garden), because they wouldn't dream of doing anything so foolish. They know, after all, that such institutions are one of the reasons that their home is – and always has been – rightfully dubbed the 'City of the World's Desire'.

İSTANBUL LIFE

This meeting point of East and West has rarely been as full of confidence and hope for the future as it is today. In its guise as Constantinople, the city was powerful and mysterious, but as the 21st century kicks off, modern İstanbul is poised on the brink of a total rebirth and is joyfully shouting this news to the world.

The biggest change on the horizon is, of course, tied up in the country's bid to join the EU. Official accession talks have started, but the outcome sure ain't in the bag. Spain, Germany, the UK and Italy openly back Turkey's membership, but the Scandinavian countries have reservations mainly to do with human rights, France is frankly antagonistic and Greece (traditionally a foe) is unlikely to actively intervene on Turkey's behalf. Though optimistic, the Turks are nowhere near certain of success. To be honest, İstanbullus aren't all that fussed about the situation. They know their city has a growing European flavour and they suspect that an EU membership isn't going to change its complexion or their lifestyles to a significant degree. Nor have they surrendered their pride in being inheritors of the glory of the Ottoman Empire, with its deep Islamic sensibility and self-conscious separation from the rest of Europe.

Some changes are inevitable as part of the bid for candidacy. Initiatives to bring the country into line with its European neighbours in the areas of human rights, environmental protection, economic management, freedom of speech and the introduction of democratic processes are already underway, but significant improvements – particularly in the areas of free speech and human rights – are essential if the holy grail of EU membership is ever to be attained. The infamous Article 301 of the country's penal code (see p41), which has seen internationally fêted writers Orhan Pamuk and Elif Şafak charged with 'insulting Turkishness' for raising the contentious issue of the alleged Armenian Genocide of the early 20th century, and which is thought to have triggered the assassination of Turkish Armenian journalist Hrant Dink in 2007, will have to be binned if the country is ever to have its candidacy taken seriously. Similarly, the national furore over the Constitutional Court's contentious legislation banning the wearing of the headscarf in the country's schools, universities, parliaments and courts (see p40) will need to be resolved if the country is ever going to be truly unified in its bid.

At the moment, the ruling Justice and Development Party (AKP) is at the helm both nationally and in İstanbul; this worries the city's intelligentsia and business community, who fear that the party's hitherto-checked Islamist ideology might be let loose as a result of the party's emphatic win in the 2007 national election and subsequent ratification of AKP stalwart Abdullah Gül as the country's president.

These weighty issues aside, the city is supremely optimistic about the future that it has in store, and so it should be. After all, its standard of living is rising; it is home to an ambitious transport infrastructure project (see p234); its monuments are being restored to their former glory; and its novelists, fashion designers and artists are building international reputations. It's one heck of a town.

Ortaköy Camii (p120) can be seen from many angles

HIGHLIGHTS

SULTANAHMET

The venerable heart of the Old City, Sultanahmet, once home to Byzantine emperors and Ottoman sultans, is now first port of call for most visitors. Here, all within walking distance of each other, are mosques, museums, hotels and cafés.

❶ Aya Sofya
Gaze in awe at the mighty dome and surrounds of Aya Sofya (p49)

❷ Blue Mosque
Escape the bustle of the city in the serene Blue Mosque (p54)

❸ Basilica Cistern
Enjoy the dim light and underground ambience of the Basilica Cistern (p58)

❹ Hippodrome
Walk through the Hippodrome (p56), where Byzantine chariots once raced

❺ Baths of Lady Hürrem
Breathe deep in the steam-free rooms of this historic hamam (p53)

❻ Arasta Bazaar
Get a taste of the city's mercantile possibilities in the Arasta Bazaar (p59)

TOPKAPI PALACE & AROUND

Sultan Mehmet cannily sited his palace on the headland overlooking the Bosphorus. Alongside the serene surrounds of Gülhane Parkı, the palace neighbourhood is a warren of cobbled streets, museums and Ottoman timbered houses.

❶ Topkapı Palace
Be sultan for a day wandering the pavilions and chambers of the Topkapı Palace (p62)

❷ Topkapı Harem
Follow in the footsteps of courtesans and concubines in the Topkapı Harem (p68)

❸ İstanbul Archaeology Museums
Delve into countless centuries of Anatolian history at the İstanbul Archaeology Museums (p70)

❶ Grand Bazaar
Haggle with the best of them at the Grand Bazaar (p76)

❷ Spice Bazaar
Head into the Spice Bazaar (p82) for fragrant and foodie delights

❸ Süleymaniye Camii
Savour the sea views and the spacious interior of this magnificent mosque (p80)

BAZAAR DISTRICT

İstanbul is the market city par excellence. The action is centred on the Grand Bazaar and stalls run downhill past the magnificent Süleymaniye Camii to the Spice Bazaar and the city's transport hub at Eminönü.

WESTERN DISTRICTS

Tucked within the city walls, the Western Districts don't see many visitors, but these neighbourhoods bustle with life and hide esoteric treasures and architectural curios.

❶ Chora Church
Step into the Chora Church (p93) for jaw-dropping mosaics

❷ Church of St Stephen of the Bulgars
Marvel at the Church of St Stephen of the Bulgars (p98), constructed wholly of cast iron

❸ Eyüp Sultan Camii & Tomb
Linger in the shade of great plane trees at the Eyüp Sultan Camii & Tomb (p99)

❶ Galata Tower
Look out across the skyline – and two continents – from the top of the Galata Tower (p104)

❷ Nargileh Cafés
Smoke up a storm with the locals at the Tophane nargileh cafés (p174)

❸ Kamondo Stairs
Stride up – or down – the distinctively curvaceous Kamondo Stairs (p104), an Art Nouveau oddity in this hilly neighbourhood

GALATA & TOPHANE

Just across the Golden Horn from the Old City, Galata and Tophane retain a bohemian edginess. Artists and students frequent its bars and nargileh cafés.

İSTİKLAL & AROUND

The pedestrianised strip of İstiklal Caddesi, pulsing with life day and night, is the main artery of Beyoğlu. Crowds flock here for clubs, bars, boisterous evenings in meyhanes and great shopping.

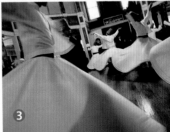

❶ Nevizade Sokak
Settle in for a night of revelry in a meyhane on Nevizade Sokak (p167)

❷ İstiklal Caddesi
Catch the antique tram along İstiklal Caddesi (p106)

❸ Galata Mevlevihanesi
Get giddy with the best of them at the Galata Mevlevihanesi (p106)

❶ Ortaköy Camii
Linger under the Bosphorus Bridge at the Ortaköy Camii (p120)

❷ Çırağan Palace
Gaze your fill at the neoclassical architectural extravaganza of the Çırağan Palace (p119)

❸ Dolmabahçe Palace
Get a taste of the grandiose at Dolmabahçe Palace (p116)

BEŞİKTAŞ & ORTAKÖY

With the imposing palaces of Dolmabahçe and Çırağan, and low-key waterfront cafés, these neighbourhoods combine the best of İstanbul: grandeur, village atmosphere and waterfront bustle.

THE BOSPHORUS

Splitting İstanbul in two, the Bosphorus is one of the city's defining features. A journey on its waters, busy with ferries and fishing boats, offers spectacular views and glimpses of everyday life.

❶ İstanbul Skyline
Ponder İstanbul's perfect composition of land, water and fabled skyline as your ferry carries you Asia-bound (p212)

❷ Ferries
Join the lucky local commuters who get to journey between continents every day (p231)

❸ Bosphorus Cruise
Head towards the fishing village and the ruined castle of Anadolu Kavağı on a cruise (p212)

CONTENTS

INTRODUCING İSTANBUL	**2**
HIGHLIGHTS	**4**
THE AUTHOR	**15**
GETTING STARTED	**16**
When to Go	16
Costs & Money	18
Internet Resources	18
BACKGROUND	**19**
History	19
Arts	28
Environment & Planning	37
Government & Politics	38
Media	39
Fashion	39
Language	40
NEIGHBOURHOODS	**43**
Sultanahmet	49
Topkapı Palace & Around	62
Bazaar District	76
Architecture	85
Western Districts	93
Galata & Tophane	102
İstiklal & Around	106
Taksim, Harbiye & Nişantaşı	114
Beşiktaş & Ortaköy	116
Üsküdar	121
Kadıköy	126
Other Neighbourhoods	128
SHOPPING	**131**
Sultanahmet	134
Topkapı Palace & Around	136
Bazaar District	137

Galata & Tophane	140
İstiklal & Around	140
Taksim, Harbiye & Nişantaşı	142
Kadıköy	144
EATING	**145**
Food & Drink	**149**
Sultanahmet	158
Topkapı Palace & Around	160
Bazaar District	161
Western Districts	163
Galata & Tophane	163
İstiklal & Around	165
Beşiktaş & Ortaköy	169
Üsküdar	169
Kadıköy	170
DRINKING	**171**
Sultanahmet	172
Topkapı Palace & Around	173
Bazaar District	174
Galata & Tophane	174
İstiklal & Around	175
Beşiktaş & Ortaköy	177
Kadıköy	177
NIGHTLIFE	**179**
Clubbing	180
Live Jazz	182
Live Turkish Music	182
THE ARTS	**185**
Art Galleries	186
Cinemas	187
Classical Music & Opera	188
Cultural Centres & Performance Venues	188
Dance	189
Theatre	190

Continued from previous page.

SPORTS & ACTIVITIES 191
Health & Fitness 192

Activities 192

Spectator Sports 195

SLEEPING 197
Sultanahmet 198

Topkapı Palace & Around 203

Bazaar District 205

Galata & Tophane 205

İstiklal & Around 206

Taksim, Harbiye & Nişantaşı 208

Beşiktaş & Ortaköy 209

EXCURSIONS 211
Bosphorus Tour 212

Princes' Islands 220

Gallipoli & Troy 223

TRANSPORT 230

DIRECTORY 236

LANGUAGE 245

BEHIND THE SCENES 250

INDEX 259

WORLD TIME ZONES 267

MAP LEGEND 268

THE AUTHOR

Virginia Maxwell

 After working for many years as a publishing manager at Lonely Planet's Melbourne headquarters, Virginia decided that she'd be happier writing guidebooks rather than commissioning them. Since making this decision she's authored Lonely Planet books to Turkey, Egypt, Spain, Italy, Lebanon, Morocco, Syria and the United Arab Emirates. Virginia knows İstanbul well, and loves it to bits. As well as authoring the previous edition of this city guide, she has also covered İstanbul for Lonely Planet's *Turkey* guidebook and for a host of international newspapers and magazines. She usually travels with her partner Peter and young son Max, who have grown to love the city as much as she does.

VIRGINIA'S TOP İSTANBUL DAY

After popping into a local *börekçi* for a breakfast of freshly baked *ıspanaklı börek* and a glass of tea, I saunter past the Blue Mosque and Aya Sofya, and up Divan Yolu to the Grand Bazaar. After assuring the good-humoured touts that I have no money to spend, I walk through the Old Book Bazaar and around İstanbul University to the Süleymaniye Camii so that I can marvel at Sinan's most wonderful creation. After this I join the sea of locals on the bustling streets of Tahtakale, making my way past the shops and street vendors down towards Eminönü, where I catch a ferry to Kadıköy in Asia. My first stop there is for lunch at the fabulous Çiya Sofrası, and then I wander for an hour or so around the vibrant fresh-produce market. Catching a ferry back to Eminönü or Karaköy, I recharge over a tea and a piece of the city's best baklava at Karaköy Güllüglu, before walking up through the narrow streets of Karaköy and Tünel to İstiklal Caddesi for an hour or so of browsing in the book and record stores. Then it's on to meet friends for a drink at Leb-i Derya Richmond or 360, followed by dinner at Sofyali 9 in Asmalımescit or at one of the rowdy places on Nevizade Sokak. Rakı, meze and good friends, all in the best city in the world – life doesn't get any better than this!

GETTING STARTED

WHEN TO GO

The best times to visit İstanbul are around spring (April–May) and autumn (September–October), when the climate is perfect. During July and August it is hot and steamy; a lot of İstanbullus head for the west and south coasts over these months. Biting winter winds and snow are common in winter.

Be aware that during the five-day Kurban Bayramı (see p238) banks shut and ATMs can run out of money. During Ramazan (Ramadan; see p239) business hours can be erratic.

Hotel rooms skyrocket in price and are often overbooked during the Formula 1 Grand Prix in May.

FESTIVALS

During the warmer months İstanbul is awash with arts festivals and music events, giving the visitor plenty of choice when it comes to entertainment. Most of the big-name arts festivals are organised by the İstanbul Foundation for Culture and Arts (☎ 212-334 0700; www.iksv.org/english; İstiklal Caddesi, Luvr Apt No 146, Beyoğlu 80070), though Positif (www.pozitif-ist.com) organises its fair share. Tickets to most events are available from Biletix (www.biletix.com). For a list of public holidays refer to p238.

March

NEVRUZ

Locals celebrate this ancient Middle Eastern Spring Festival on 21 March with jolly goings-on and jumping over bonfires. Cankurtaran (in the Sultanahmet neighbourhood) becomes one giant open-air party.

April

INTERNATIONAL İSTANBUL FILM FESTIVAL

www.iksv.org/english
The program features retrospectives and new releases from Turkey and around the world. If you're keen to see the cream of the latest Turkish cinema releases and a few local film stars, this is the place to do it. Venues are mainly on and around İstiklal Caddesi in Beyoğlu.

CHILDREN'S DAY

The national public holiday on 23 April is celebrated on Beyoğlu's İstiklal Caddesi with a morning parade. Children march, twirl batons, perform folk dances and make a racket with brass instruments, watched by crowds of parents and indulgent onlookers.

May

INTERNATIONAL İSTANBUL THEATRE FESTIVAL

www.iksv.org/english
Turkey's major theatre festival alternates every year with the International İstanbul Biennial (opposite), and is scheduled for 2008 and 2010. Big-name international companies share the stages with top local talent and the result is often inspired. Very few performances are in English.

INTERNATIONAL ÜLKER PUPPET FESTIVAL İSTANBUL

www.ulkerkuklafestivali.com
Turks take their puppetry seriously, and this one-week festival held at the start of May highlights Turkish karagöz (shadow) puppetry as well as international acts. Performances are at small venues and cultural centres throughout town.

ORTHODOX EASTER

www.ec-patr.org
The celebratory Easter Sunday Mass is the biggest event of the year at the home of the Greek Orthodox community in Fener.

June

EFES PILSEN ONE LOVE

www.pozitif-ist.com
This two-night festival features pop and electronic music. Up to 15,000 İstanbullus turn up to hear headline international acts such as the Beastie Boys and Nenah Cherry.

INTERNATIONAL İSTANBUL MUSIC FESTIVAL

www.iksv.org/english
The city's premier arts festival includes performances of opera, dance, orchestral

concerts and chamber recitals. Acts are often internationally renowned and the action takes place in Aya İrini (p188) in Sultanahmet and the Atatürk Cultural Centre (p188).

July
INTERNATIONAL İSTANBUL JAZZ FESTIVAL
www.iksv.org/english
This festival was once part of the International İstanbul Music Festival, but branched out on its own a decade ago and has subsequently gone from strength to strength. It usually runs for two weeks and programs a weird hybrid of conventional jazz, electronica, drum 'n' bass, world music and rock. Recent acts have included Norah Jones, Cassandra Wilson, Wynton Marsalis, Antony and the Johnsons, and Önder Focan. Venues include Cemil Topuzlu Open-Air Theatre (Cemil Topuzlu Açık Hava Tiyatrosu), the İstanbul Modern (p102), Cemal Reşit Rey Concert Hall (p188), the İstanbul Jazz Center (p182) and Nardis Jazz Club (p182).

August
ELECTRONICA GLOBAL GATHERING
www.electronicafest.com
This three-day festival features international DJs and live electronica acts duelling it out on eight open-air stages. A huge crowd gets its fill of trance, house and mashup.

September
INTERNATIONAL DESIGN WEEK
www.istanbuldesignweek.com/main_eng
This festival showcases the city's vibrant design world with exhibitions, workshops and loads of glamorous openings. Venues are offbeat – the 2007 festival was held on the Old Galata Bridge (Map pp46–7)!

INTERNATIONAL İSTANBUL BIENNIAL
www.iksv.org/english
The city's major visual-arts shindig takes place from early September to early November in odd-numbered years. An international curator nominates a theme and puts together a cutting-edge program, which is then exhibited in venues around town. In 2003 paintings, sculpture, installation and multimedia work by some 85 artists from 42 countries was on show in a range

of venues including santralistanbul (p186), the Atatürk Cultural Centre (p188) and the İstanbul Modern (p102).

ROCK'N COKE
www.pozitif-ist.com
Turkey's largest open-air music festival rocks for two days, with past headliners including The Smashing Pumpkins, Manic Street Preachers and Franz Ferdinand. Crowds can hit 50,000.

October
AKBANK JAZZ FESTIVAL
☎ 212-252 3500; www.akbanksanat.com
This older sister to the International İstanbul Jazz Festival is a boutique event, with a program featuring traditional and avant-garde jazz, as well as Middle Eastern fusions and a special program of young jazz. Venues include Aya İrini (p188) the Cemal Reşit Rey Concert Hall (p188), Babylon (p180), and Q Jazz by Les Ottomans (p182). Recent headline acts have included the Archie Shepp Quartet, Mark Murphy and the Phil Woods Quintet.

November
ANNIVERSARY OF ATATÜRK'S DEATH
At 9.05am on the 10th of November a minute's silence is held to commemorate the death of the nation's revered founder. Sirens blare and the city comes to a standstill, with people, cars and buses literally stopping in their tracks.

ADVANCE PLANNING
Two Months Before You Go If you're travelling in spring, autumn or over Christmas, make your hotel booking as far in advance as possible. The good places book up quickly!

One Month Before You Go İstanbul's big-ticket festivals sell out fast, and for good reason. Check the festival list above to see what tempts your fancy, and then book ahead.

Two Weeks Before You Go Book a table for dinner at Mikla (p165), Hamdi et Lokantası (p161), 360 (p165) or Changa (p165).

One Week Before You Go Sign up to the weekly email service by My Merhaba (see p18) for the latest openings and events in the city.

December

EFES PILSEN BLUES FESTIVAL
www.pozitif-ist.com
This two-day İstanbul event in October or November has been entertaining fans of the blues since 1990. Headline international acts have included names such as Long John Hunter & the Bad Blues Band, Philadelphia Jerry Ricks and the Zydeco Brothers.

AKBANK SHORT FILM FESTIVAL
☎ 212-252 3500; www.akbanksanat.com
Beloved by the black-clad Beyoğlu bohemian set, this artsy film culture event is held at the Akbank Culture & Arts Centre.

COSTS & MONEY

The Turkish lira has been going from strength to strength in recent years, and is now considered relatively stable. In this book we have given hotel and tour prices in euros, as this is the currency that hotel owners and tour operators work with. All other prices are given in Turkish New Lira (YTL), and reflect the reality on the ground at the time of research.

Though İstanbul is no longer the bargain travel destination it was in the past, it still offers good value for money. A three-star hotel room for two can cost as little as €45 in Sultanahmet and you can enjoy a decent evening meal for YTL15 to YTL30. Public transport is both efficient and dirt cheap, and many sights – in particular the city's wonderful array of historical mosques – are free. Others are relatively inexpensive, with the average museum entry being YTL10.

This isn't to say that everything in the city is cheap. If you decide to have a night on the town and hit the bars in Beyoğlu and nightclubs in Ortaköy you'll need to be cashed up – nightclub entries can be as high as YTL50 and a drink in these places will cost at least YTL20; a glass of wine in one of the glam rooftop bars in Beyoğlu will set you back YTL15. And shopping at the new generation of malls such as Kanyon (p143) is no different to blowing your budget in Knightsbridge or on Rodeo Drive – this is designer turf and is priced accordingly.

HOW MUCH?
Litre of unleaded petrol YTL2.90
Litre of bottled water YTL1-1.50
Efes Pilsen (bar prices) YTL4-7
Ticket on public transport YTL1.30
Fish sandwich YTL3
Glass of çay (tea) Around YTL1.50
Taxi ride from Sultanahmet to Taksim YTL8-10
Movie ticket YTL10-15
Nargileh YTL8-9
Copy of an English-language newspaper YTL1.50

INTERNET RESOURCES

ExpatinTurkey (www.expatinturkey.com) Expat's travel advice including jobs, working visas, classified ads, and eating, drinking and sleeping recommendations. The occasional cattiness makes for great reading.

İstanbul Şehır Rehberi (http://sehirrehberi.ibb.gov.tr) Online maps of the city.

Lonely Planet (www.lonelyplanet.com) Check out the Thorn Tree bulletin board to find out what city discoveries are being made.

Ministry of Culture and Tourism (www.turizm.gov.tr) Government information on tourism, culture, archaeology and history.

Ministry of Foreign Affairs (www.mfa.gov.tr) Up-to-date visa and security information.

My Merhaba (www.mymerhaba.com) Aimed at expats, but has lots of general information that's of use to visitors too, including entertainment listings.

The New Anatolian (www.thenewanatolian.com) Website of the English-language daily newspaper.

Time Out İstanbul (www.timeout.com.tr) The online site of this excellent monthly magazine has a good listings section.

Today's Zaman (www.todayszaman.com) Website of the English-language daily newspaper.

Turism Turkey (www.tourismturkey.org) Government website with a grab-bag of articles and information.

Turkey Travel Planner (www.turkeytravelplanner.com) An ever-growing site about travel in Turkey put together by well-known writer and Turkey expert, Tom Brosnahan.

Turkish Daily News (www.turkishdailynews.com.tr) Website of the long-standing English language daily newspaper.

BACKGROUND

HISTORY

Earliest Times

Semistra, the earliest-known settlement on the site of İstanbul, was probably founded around 1000 BC, a few hundred years after the Trojan War and in the same period that kings David and Solomon ruled in Jerusalem. Semistra was followed by a fishing village named Lygos, which occupied Seraglio Point (Seray Burnu) where Topkapı Palace stands today.

Around 700 BC, colonists from Megara (near Corinth) in Greece founded the city of Chalcedon (now Kadıköy) on the Asian shore of the Bosphorus. Chalcedon became one of a dozen Greek fishing colonies along the shores of the Propontis (the ancient name for the Sea of Marmara). The historian Theopompus of Chios, cited in John Freely's *Istanbul: The Imperial City,* wrote in the latter half of the 4th century that its inhabitants 'devoted themselves unceasingly to the better pursuits of life'. Their way of life was apparently in stark contrast to that of the dissolute Byzantines, who founded their settlement across the Bosphorus at Seraglio Point in 657 BC.

First Incarnation: Byzantium

Legend tells us that Byzantium was founded by a Megarian colonist named Byzas, the son of the god Poseidon and the nymph Keroessa, daughter of Zeus and Io. Before leaving Greece, Byzas had asked the oracle at Delphi where he should establish his new colony. The enigmatic answer was 'Opposite the blind'. All this made sense when Byzas and his fellow colonists sailed up the Bosphorus and noticed the colony on the Asian shore at Chalcedon. Looking west, they saw the small fishing village of Lygos, built on a magnificent and easily fortified natural harbour of the Golden Horn (known to the Greeks as Chrysokeras) on the European shore. Thinking, as legend has it, that the settlers of Chalcedon must have been blind to disregard such a superb position, Byzas and his mates settled here and their new town came to be called Byzantium after its founder.

The new colony quickly prospered, largely due to its ability to levy tolls and harbour fees on ships passing through the Bosphorus, then as now an important waterway. A thriving marketplace was established and the inhabitants lived on traded goods and the abundant fish stocks in the surrounding waters. In all, the early Byzantines were a fortunate lot. They walled their city to ensure its invincibility from attack, enslaved the local Thracian population to do most of the hard work and worshipped the Greek Olympian gods. Theopompus of Chios might have thought that the Chalcedons lived a good clean life when they first established their city on the opposite shore, but he had no such compliment for the Byzantines, writing that they 'accustomed themselves to amours and drinking in the taverns'.

In 512 BC Darius, emperor of Persia, captured the city during his campaign against the Scythians. Following the retreat of the Persians in 478 BC, the town came under the influence and protection of Athens and joined the Athenian League. It was a turbulent relationship, with Byzantium

TIMELINE

1000 BC	657 BC	335 BC
The settlements of Lygos and Semistra are founded by Thracian tribes; Plinius mentions the founding of Semistra in his historical accounts and a few traces of Lygos remain near Seraglio Point	The god Poseidon and the nymph Keroessa, daughter of Zeus and Io, have a son, Byzas, who travels up the Bosphorus and founds Byzantium on the site of Lygos	Byzantium is granted independence but stays under the Athenian umbrella, withstanding with Athenian help a siege by Philip, father of Alexander the Great, in 340 BC

İSTANBUL'S HISTORIAN

This book is littered with mentions of the writings of John Freely (born 1926), an American academic who has been living, working and writing in the İstanbul on and off since 1960. Put simply, what Freely doesn't know about the architectural and cultural history of İstanbul probably isn't worth knowing. His eminently readable books include the following:

- *The Byzantine Monuments of Istanbul* (with Ahmet Çakmak; 2004)
- *Inside the Seraglio: Private Lives of the Sultans in Istanbul* (1999)
- *Istanbul: The Imperial City* (1996)
- *Sinan: Architect of Süleyman the Magnificent* (photographs by Ara Guler; 1992)
- *Strolling through Istanbul* (with Hilary Sumner-Boyd) (1972)

revolting a number of times, only to be defeated by the Athenians. During one of the revolts, the Athenian navy mounted an expedition against Byzantium and Chalcedon and sailed up the Bosphorus to establish a settlement at Chrysopolis ('the City of Gold'), site of the present-day suburb of Üsküdar. From this base they successfully besieged Byzantium.

The Spartans took the city after the end of the Peloponnesian War (404 BC) but were ousted in 390 BC, when Byzantium once again joined the League of Athens. It was granted independence in 355 BC but stayed under the Athenian umbrella, withstanding with Athenian help a siege by Philip, father of Alexander the Great, in 340 BC.

By the end of the Hellenistic period, Byzantium had formed an alliance with the Roman Empire. It retained its status as a free state, which it even kept after being officially incorporated into the Roman Empire in AD 79 by Vespasian, but it paid significant taxes for the privilege. Life was relatively uneventful until the city's leaders made a big mistake: they picked the wrong side in a Roman war of succession following the death of the Emperor Pertinax in AD 193. When Septimius Severus emerged victorious over his rival Pescennius Niger, he mounted a three-year siege of the city, eventually massacring Byzantium's citizens, razing its walls and burning it to the ground. Ancient Byzantium was no more.

The new emperor was aware of the city's important strategic position, and he soon set about rebuilding it. He pardoned the remaining citizens and built a circuit of walls that stretched roughly from where the Yeni Camii is today (Map p63) to the Bucoleon Palace (Map p50), enclosing a city twice the size of its predecessor. The Hippodrome (p56) was built by Severus, as was a colonnaded way that followed the present path of Divan Yolu. He also erected a gateway known as the Miliarium Aureum or, more simply, the Milion. A marble stellae from this gate can still be seen today (Map p50). Severus named his new city Augusta Antonina and it was subsequently ruled by a succession of emperors, including the great Diocletian (r 284–303).

Decline of Rome & the Rise of Constantinople

Diocletian had decreed that after his retirement, the government of the Roman Empire should be overseen by co-emperors Galerius in the east (Augusta Antonina) and Constantine in the west (Rome). This resulted in a civil war, which was won by Constantine in AD 324 when he defeated Licinius, Galerius' successor, at Chrysopolis.

With his victory, Constantine became sole emperor (r 324–37) of a reunited empire. He also became the first Christian emperor, though he didn't formally convert until on his deathbed. To solidify his power he summoned the First Ecumenical Council at Nicaea (İznik) in 325, which established the precedent of the emperor's supremacy in church affairs.

AD 79	330	379
Byzantium is officially incorporated into the Roman Empire by the soldier-emperor Vespasian, who was described by the Roman senator and historian Tacitus as 'infamous and odious'	Constantine the Great declares Byzantium the capital of the Roman Empire, names it New Rome and commences an ambitious building program; the city soon becomes known as Constantinople in his honour	The emperor Theodosius I (the Great) makes Christianity the official religion of the Roman Empire; he erects the Obelisk of Theodosius, pilfered from Karnak in Egypt, at the Hippodrome in 390

Constantine also decided to move the capital of the empire to the shores of the Bosphorus. He built a new, wider circle of walls around the site of Byzantium and laid out a magnificent city within. The Hippodrome was extended and a forum was built on the crest of the second hill, near today's Nuruosmaniye Camii (Map p63). The city was dedicated on 11 May 330 as New Rome, but soon came to be called Constantinople. First settled as a fishing village over 1000 years earlier, the settlement on Seraglio Point was now the capital of the Eurasian world and would remain so for almost another 1000 years.

Constantine died in 337, just seven years after the dedication of his new capital. His empire was divided up between his three sons: Constantius, Constantine and Constans. Constantinople was part of Constantius' share. His power base was greatly increased in 353 when he overthrew both of his brothers and brought the empire under his sole control.

Constantius died in 361 and was succeeded by his cousin Julian. Emperor Jovian was next, succeeded by Valens (of aqueduct fame, p82).

The city continued to grow under the rule of the emperors. Theodosius I ('the Great') had a forum built on the present site of Beyazıt Square and a massive triumphal gate built in the city walls, the Porta Aurea (Golden Gate; p128). He also erected the Obelisk of Theodosius (p56) at the Hippodrome. His grandson Emperor Theodosius II (r 408–50) came to the throne as a boy, heavily influenced by his sister Pulcheria, who acted as regent until her brother was old enough to rule in his own right. Threatened by the forces of Attila the Hun, he ordered that an even wider, more formidable circle of walls be built around the city. Encircling all seven hills of the city, the walls were completed in 413, only to be brought down by a series of earthquakes in 447. They were hastily rebuilt in a mere two months – the rapid approach of Attila and the Huns acting as a powerful stimulus. The Theodosian walls successfully held out invaders for the next 757 years and still stand today, though they are in an increasingly dilapidated state of repair.

Theodosius II's other achievements were the compilation of the *Codex Theodosianus*, a collection of all of the laws that had been enacted since the reign of Constantine the Great, and the erection of a new cathedral, the Sancta Sophia (Aya Sofya; p49), which replaced an earlier church of the same name that had been burned down during a riot in 404.

Justinian & Theodora

Theodosius died in 450 and was succeeded by a string of emperors, including the most famous of all Byzantine emperors, Justinian.

During the 5th and 6th centuries, as the barbarians of Europe captured and sacked Rome, the new eastern capital grew in wealth, strength and reputation. Justinian (r 527–65) had much to do with this. A former soldier, he and his great general Belisarius reconquered Anatolia, the Balkans, Egypt, Italy and North Africa. They also successfully put down the Nika riots of 532, killing 30,000 of the rioters in the Hippodrome in the process.

Three years before taking the throne, Justinian had married Theodora, a strong-willed former courtesan who is credited with having great influence over her husband. Together, they further embellished Constantinople with great buildings, including SS Sergius and Bacchus, now known as Küçük Aya Sofya (p57), Hagia Eirene (Aya İrini; p65) and the Basilica Cistern (p58). Justinian's personal triumph was the new Sancta Sophia (Aya Sofya, p49), which was completed in 537.

Justinian's ambitious building projects and constant wars of reconquest exhausted his treasury and his empire. Following his reign, the Byzantine Empire would never again be as large, powerful or rich.

408	524	527
Theodosius' grandson Theodosius II inherits the throne as a child; his sister Pulcheria, a devout Christian, takes a vow of virginity to avoid being forced into marriage and acts as her brother's regent	Justinian, who will become the most famous of all of the Byzantine emperors, marries a courtesan called Theodora, the daughter of a bear-keeper at the Hippodrome	Justinian takes the throne and makes Theodora joint ruler; the Imperial Council counsels the Emperor to flee the city during the Nika riots in 532, but Theodora persuades him to stay and fight

Under Siege & In Decline

From 565 to 1025, a succession of warrior emperors kept invaders such as the Persians and the Avars at bay. Though the foreign armies often managed to get as far as Chalcedon, none were able to breach Theodosius' great walls. The Arab armies of the nascent Islamic empire tried in 669, 674, 678 and 717–18, each time in vain. Inside the walls the city was undergoing a different type of threat: the Iconoclastic Crisis. This began in 726 when Emperor Leo III launched his quest to rid the empire of all forms of idolatry. Those who worshipped idols, including the followers of many saints, revolted and a number of uprisings ensued. The emperor was ultimately triumphant and his policy was adopted by his successors. It was first overturned in 780, when the Empress Eirene, mother of the child emperor Constantine VI, set out to restore icons. The issue was finally put to rest by the Empress Theodora, mother of Michael III, another child emperor, in 845.

The powerful emperors of the Bulgarian empire besieged the city in 814, 913 and 924, never conquering it. Under Emperor Basil II (r 976–1025), the Byzantine armies drove the Arab armies out of Anatolia and completely annihilated the Bulgarian forces. For this feat he was dubbed Bulgaroctonus, the 'Bulgar-slayer'.

In 1071 Emperor Romanus IV Diogenes (r 1068–1071) led his army to eastern Anatolia to do battle with the Seljuk Turks, who had been forced out of Central Asia by the encroaching Mongols. However, at Manzikert (Malazgirt) the Byzantines were disastrously defeated, the emperor captured and imprisoned, and the former Byzantine heartland of Anatolia thus thrown open to Turkish invasion and settlement. Soon the Seljuks had built a thriving empire of their own in central Anatolia, with their capital first at Nicaea and later at Konya.

As Turkish power was consolidated in Anatolia to the east of Constantinople, the power of Venice – always a maritime and commercial rival to Constantinople – grew in the west. This coincided with the launch of the First Crusade and the arrival in Constantinople of the first of the Crusaders in 1096.

The Crusaders: Interlopers from the West

Soldiers of the Second Crusade passed through the city in 1146 during the reign of Manuel I, son of John Comnenus II 'The Good' and his empress, Eirene, both of whose mosaic portraits can be seen in the gallery at Aya Sofya (p49). In 1171 Manuel evicted Venetian merchants from their neighbourhood in Galata. The Venetians retaliated by sending a fleet to attack Byzantine ports in Greece.

The convoluted, treacherous imperial court politics of Constantinople have given us the word 'Byzantine'. Rarely blessed with a simple, peaceful succession, Byzantine rulers were always under threat from members of their own families as well as would-be tyrants and foreign powers. This internecine plotting was eventually to lead to the defeat of the city by the Crusaders.

In 1195 Alexius III deposed and blinded his brother, Emperor Isaac II, claiming the throne for himself. Fleeing to the West, Isaac's oldest son, Prince Alexius, pleaded to the Pope and other Western rulers for help in restoring his father to the Byzantine throne. At the time, the Fourth Crusade was assembling in Venice to sail to Egypt and attack the infidel. Knowing this, Prince Alexius sent a message to the Crusaders offering to agree to a union of the Greek and Roman churches under the papacy if the Crusaders could put his father back on the throne. He also promised to pay richly for their assistance. The Crusader leaders agreed, and Enrico Dandolo, Doge of Venice, led the crusaders to Constantinople, arriving in 1203.

548	565	717
Theodora dies; during her reign she was known for establishing homes for ex-prostitutes, granting women more rights in divorce cases, allowing women to own and inherit property, and enacting the death penalty for rape	Justinian dies; his lasting memorial is the church of Hagia Sophia (Aya Sofya), which was to be the centre of Eastern Orthodox Christianity for many centuries	Leo III, a Syrian, becomes emperor after deposing Theodosius III; he introduces a series of edicts against the worship of images, ushering in the age of iconoclasm

Rather than facing the Crusaders, Alexius III fled with the imperial treasury. The Byzantines swiftly restored Isaac II to the throne and made Prince Alexius his co-emperor. Unfortunately, the new co-emperors had no money to pay their allies. They were also deeply unpopular with their subjects, being seen as Latin toadies. Isaac fell ill (he died in 1204), and the Byzantines swiftly deposed Alexius and crowned a new emperor, Alexius V. The new emperor foolishly ordered the Crusaders to leave his territory, conveniently ignoring the fact that they believed themselves to be owed a considerable amount of money by the Byzantines. Their patience exhausted, the Crusaders attacked. On 13 April 1204 they broke through the walls, and sacked and pillaged the rich capital of their Christian ally.

When the smoke cleared, Dandolo took control of three-eighths of the city, including Aya Sofya, leaving the rest to his co-conspirator Count Baldwin of Flanders. The Byzantine nobility fled to what was left of their estates and fought among themselves in best Byzantine fashion for control of the shreds of the empire.

After Dandolo's death, Count Baldwin had himself crowned emperor of Romania ('Kingdom of the Romans'), his name for his new kingdom. Never a strong or effective state, Baldwin's so-called empire steadily declined until, just over half a century later in 1261, it was easily re-captured by the soldiers of Michael VIII Palaeologus, formerly the emperor of Nicaea, where the Byzantine Empire in exile sat. The Byzantine Empire was restored.

The Ottomans: Upstarts from the East

Two decades after Michael reclaimed Constantinople, a Turkish warlord named Ertuğrul died in the village of Söğüt near Nicaea. He left his son Osman, who was known as Gazi (Warrior for the Faith), a small territory. Osman's followers became known in the Empire as Osmanlıs and in the West as the Ottomans.

Osman died in 1324 and was succeeded by his son Orhan. In 1326 Orhan captured Bursa, made it his capital and took the title of sultan. A victory at Nicaea followed, after which he sent his forces further afield, conquering Ankara to the east and Thrace to the west. His son Murat I (r 1362–89) took Adrianople (Edirne) in 1371 and extended his conquests to Kosovo, where he defeated the Serbs and Bosnians.

Murat's son Beyazıt (r 1389–1402) unsuccessfully laid siege to Constantinople in 1394, then defeated a Crusader army 100,000 strong on the Danube in 1396. Though temporarily checked by the armies of Tamerlane and a nasty war of succession between Beyazıt's four sons that was eventually won by Mehmet I (r 1413–21), the Ottomans continued to grow in power and size. By 1440 the Ottoman armies under Murat II (r 1421–51) had taken Thessalonica, unsuccessfully laid siege to Constantinople and Belgrade, and battled Christian armies for Transylvania. It was at this point in history that Mehmet II 'The Conqueror' (r 1451–81) came to power and vowed to attain the ultimate prize – Constantinople.

The Conquest

By 1450, the Byzantine emperor had control over little more than Constantinople itself.

The first step in Mehmet's plan to take the city was construction of the great fortress of Rumeli Hisarı (see p217), which was completed in 1452. He also repaired Anadolu Hisarı, the fortress on the Asian shore that had been built by his great-grandfather. Between them, the two great fortresses then closed the Bosphorus at its narrowest point, blockading the imperial capital from the north.

1203	1261	1451
Enrico Dandolo, Doge of Venice, leads the crusaders of the Fourth Crusade in a defeat of Constantinople; after his burial in Aya Sofya his bones are disinterred by locals and thrown to the dogs	Constantinople is recaptured by the soldiers of Michael VIII Palaeologus, formerly the emperor of Nicaea, where the Byzantine Empire in exile sat; the Byzantine Empire is restored	Mehmet's army defeats that of the Byzantine emperor and he takes power in İstanbul, becoming known as El-Fatih, 'The Conqueror'; he commissions the Italian painter Gentile Bellini to paint his portrait in 1479 and dies in 1481

The Byzantines had closed the mouth of the Golden Horn with a heavy chain (on view in İstanbul's Askeri Müzesi, p114) to prevent Ottoman ships from sailing in and attacking the city walls on the north side. Mehmet outsmarted them by marshalling his boats at a cove where Dolmabahçe Palace (p116) now stands, and having them transported overland during the night on rollers and slides up the valley (where the İstanbul Hilton now stands) and down the other side into the Golden Horn at Kasımpaşa. As dawn broke his fleet attacked the city, catching the Byzantine defenders by surprise. Soon the Golden Horn was under Ottoman control.

As for the mighty Theodosian land walls to the west, a Hungarian cannon founder named Urban had offered his services to the Byzantine emperor for the defence of Christendom. Finding that the emperor had no money, he conveniently forgot about defending Christianity and went instead to Mehmet, who paid him richly to cast an enormous cannon capable of firing a huge ball right through the city walls.

Despite the inevitability of the conquest (Mehmet had 80,000 men compared with Byzantium's 7000), Emperor Constantine XI (r 1449–53) refused the surrender terms offered by Mehmet on 23 May 1453, preferring to wait in hope that Christendom would come to his rescue. On 28 May the final attack commenced: the mighty walls were breached between the gates now called Topkapı and Edirnekapı, the sultan's troops flooded in and by the evening of the 29th they were in control of every quarter. Constantine, the last emperor of Byzantium, died fighting on the city walls.

The City Ascendant

The 21-year-old conqueror saw himself as the successor to the imperial throne of Byzantium by right of conquest, and he began to rebuild and repopulate the city. Aya Sofya was converted to a mosque; a new mosque, the Fatih (Conqueror) Camii (p95), was built on the fourth hill; and the Eski Saray (Old Palace) was constructed on the third hill, followed by a new palace at Topkapı (p62) a few years later. The city walls were repaired and a new fortress, Yedikule (p128), was built. İstanbul, as it was often called, became the new administrative, commercial and cultural centre of the ever-growing Ottoman Empire. Mehmet encouraged Greeks who had fled the city to return and issued an imperial decree calling for resettlement; Muslims, Jews and Christians all took up his offer and were promised the right to worship as they pleased. The Genoese, who had fought with the Byzantines, were pardoned and allowed to stay in Galata, though the fortifications that surrounded their settlement were torn down. Only Galata Tower (p104) was allowed to stand.

Mehmet died in 1481 and was succeeded by Beyazıt II (r 1481–1512), who was ousted by his son, the ruthless Selim the Grim (r 1512–20), famed for executing seven grand viziers and numerous relatives during his relatively short reign.

The building boom that Mehmet kicked off was continued by his successors, with Selim's son Süleyman the Magnificent (r 1520–66) being responsible for more construction than any other sultan. Blessed with the services of Mimar Sinan (1497–1588), Islam's greatest architect, the sultan and his family, court and grand viziers crowded the city with great buildings. Under Süleyman's 46-year reign, the longest of any sultan, the empire expanded its territories and refined its artistic pursuits at its court. None of the empires of Europe or Asia were as powerful.

Rule of the Women

Süleyman's son Selim II ('the Sot', r 1566–74) and his successors lost themselves in the pleasures of the harem and the bottle, and cared little for the administration of the empire their forebears

1520	1550–57	1556
Selim's son Süleyman, who would come to be known as 'The Magnificent', ascends to the throne; his first acts as sultan are a series of military conquests in Syria, Hungary and Rhodes	Süleyman's chief architect, Mimar Koca Sinan, designs and oversees construction of the great Süleymaniye mosque complex for his patron; he is buried in a tomb just outside its walls	Süleyman dies while on a military campaign in Hungary; his death is kept secret for days while word is sent to his son Selim so that he can take control in İstanbul before word arrives

had built. While they were carousing, a succession of exceptionally able grand viziers dealt with external and military affairs.

Before the drunken Selim drowned in his bath, his chief concubine Nurubanu called the shots in the palace and ushered in the so-called 'Rule of the Women', whereby a series of chief concubines and mothers (*valide sultans*) of a series of dissolute sultans ruled the roost at court. Among the most fascinating of these women was Kösem Sultan, the favourite of Sultan Ahmet I (r 1603–17). She influenced the course of the empire through Ahmet, then through her sons Murat IV (r 1623–40) and İbrahim, ('the Mad', r 1640–48) and finally through her grandson Mehmet IV (r 1648–87). Her influence over Mehmet lasted only a few years and she was strangled in 1651 at the command of the *valide sultan* Turhan Hatice, Mehmet's mother.

For the next century the sultans continued in Selim's footsteps. Their dissolute and often unbalanced behaviour led to dissatisfaction among the people and the army, which would eventually prove to be the empire's undoing.

Decline, then Attempts at Reform

The motor that drove the Ottoman Empire was military conquest, and when the sultan's armies reached their geographical and technological limits, decline set in for good. In 1683 the Ottomans laid siege for the second time to Vienna, but failed again to take the city. With the Treaty of Karlowitz in 1699, the Austrian and Ottoman emperors divided up the Balkans, and the Ottoman Empire went on the defensive.

By this time Europe was well ahead of Turkey in politics, technology, science, banking, commerce and military development. Sultan Selim III (r 1789–1807) initiated efforts to catch up to Europe, but was overthrown in a revolt by janissaries (the sultan's personal bodyguards). The modernisation efforts were continued under Mahmut II (r 1808–39). He founded a new army along European lines, provoking a riot among the janissaries, so that in 1826 he had to send his new force in to crush them, which it did. The bodies of janissaries filled the Hippodrome and the ancient corps, once the glory of the empire, was no more.

Sultan Abdül Mecit (r 1839–61) continued the catch-up, continuing the Tanzimat (Reorganisation) political and social reforms that had been initiated by his father Mahmut II. But these efforts were too little, too late. During the 19th century, ethnic nationalism, a force more powerful even than Western armies, penetrated the empire's domain and proved its undoing.

Ethnic Nationalism

For centuries, the non-Turkish ethnic and non-Muslim religious minorities in the sultan's domains had lived side by side with their Turkish neighbours, governed by their own religious and traditional laws. The head of each community – chief rabbi, Orthodox patriarch etc – was responsible to the sultan for the community's wellbeing and behaviour.

Ottoman decline and misrule provided fertile ground for the growth of ethnic nationalism among these communities. The subject peoples of the Ottoman Empire rose in revolt, one after another, often with the direct encouragement and assistance of the European powers, who coveted parts of the sultan's vast domains. After bitter fighting in 1831 the Kingdom of Greece was formed; the Serbs, Bulgarians, Romanians, Albanians, Armenians and Arabs would all seek their independence soon after.

1574	1826	1839
Selim II – known as 'The Sot' – drowns after falling in his bath while drunk and is succeeded by his son Murat III, who orders the murder of his five younger brothers to ensure his accession	The Vakayı Hayriye, or 'Auspicious Event' is decreed under which the corrupt and powerful imperial bodyguard known as the Janissary Corps is abolished	Mahmut II implements the Tanzimat reforms, which aim to stop the rise of nationalist movements by integrating non-Muslims and non-Turks into Ottoman society through civil liberties and regulations

As the sultan's empire broke up, the European powers (Britain, France, Italy, Germany and Russia) hovered in readiness to colonise or annex the pieces. They used religion as a reason for pressure or control, saying that it was their duty to protect the sultan's Catholic, Protestant or Orthodox subjects from misrule and anarchy.

The Russian emperors put pressure on the Turks to grant them powers over all Ottoman Orthodox Christian subjects, whom the Russian emperor would thus 'protect'. The result was the Crimean War (1853–56), with Britain and France fighting on the side of the Ottomans against the growth of Russian power. During the war, wounded British, French and Ottoman soldiers were brought to İstanbul for treatment at the Selimiye Army Barracks, now home to the Florence Nightingale Museum (p124), and the foundations of modern nursing practice were laid.

Even during the war, the sultan continued the imperial building tradition. Vast Dolmabahçe Palace (p116) and its mosque were finished in 1856, and the palaces at Beylerbeyi (p215), Çırağan (p119) and Yıldız (p119) would be built before the end of the century. Though it had lost the fabulous wealth of the days of Süleyman the Magnificent, the city was still regarded as the Paris of the East. It was also the terminus of the *Orient Express*, which connected İstanbul and Paris – the world's first great international luxury express train.

Abdül Hamit II & the Young Turks

Amid the empire's internal turmoil, Abdül Hamit II (r 1876–1909) assumed the throne. Mithat Paşa, a successful general and powerful grand vizier, managed to introduce a constitution at the same time, but soon the new sultan did away both with Mithat Paşa and the constitution, and established his own absolute rule.

Abdül Hamit modernised without democratising, building thousands of kilometres of railways and telegraph lines and encouraging modern industry. However, the empire continued to disintegrate, and there were nationalist insurrections in Armenia, Bulgaria, Crete and Macedonia.

The younger generation of the Turkish elite – particularly the military – watched bitterly as their country fell apart, then organised secret societies bent on toppling the sultan. The Young Turk movement for Western-style reforms gained enough power by 1908 to force the restoration of the constitution. In 1909 the Young Turk-led Ottoman parliament deposed Abdül Hamit and put his hopelessly indecisive brother Mehmet V on the throne.

When WWI broke out, the Ottoman parliament and sultan made the fatal error of siding with Germany and the Central Powers. With their defeat, the Ottoman Empire collapsed, İstanbul was occupied by the British and the sultan became a pawn in the hands of the victors.

Republican İstanbul

The situation looked very bleak for the Turks as their armies were being disbanded and their country was taken under the control of the Allies, but what first seemed a catastrophe provided the impetus for rebirth.

Since gaining independence in 1831, the Greeks had entertained the Megali Idea (Great Plan) of a new Greek empire encompassing all the lands that had once had Greek influence – in effect, the refounding of the Byzantine Empire, with Constantinople as its capital. On 15 May 1919, with Western backing, Greek armies invaded Anatolia in order to make the dream a reality.

1854–56	1915	1920–22
The Crimean War is fought between Imperial Russia and an alliance that includes the Ottoman Empire; Florence Nightingale arrives at the Selimiye Army Barracks near Üsküdar to nurse the war-wounded	Armenian populations are rounded up and marched into the Syrian desert; Armenians allege that Ottoman authorities were intent on eradicating the Armenian population from İstanbul and Anatolia	Turkish Nationalist forces led by Atatürk fight off Greek, French and Italian invasion forces in the War of Independence

Even before the Greek invasion an Ottoman general named Mustafa Kemal, the hero of the WWI battle at Gallipoli, had decided that a new government must take over the destiny of the Turks from the ineffectual sultan. He began organising resistance to the sultan's captive government on 19 May 1919.

The Turkish War of Independence, in which the Turkish Nationalist forces led by Mustafa Kemal fought off Greek, French and Italian invasion forces, lasted from 1920 to 1922. Victory in the bitter war put Mustafa Kemal (1881–1938) in command of the fate of the Turks. The sultanate was abolished in 1922, as was the Ottoman Empire soon after. The republic was born on 29 October 1923.

Downgraded: No Longer the Capital

The nation's saviour, proclaimed Atatürk (Father Turk) by the Turkish parliament, decided to move away, both metaphorically and physically, from the imperial memories of İstanbul. He established the seat of the new republican government in a city (Ankara) that could not be threatened by foreign gunboats. Robbed of its importance as the capital of a vast empire, İstanbul lost much of its wealth and glitter in succeeding decades.

Atatürk had always been ill at ease with Islamic traditions and he set about making the Republic of Turkey a secular state. The fez (Turkish brimless cap) was abolished, as was polygamy; Friday was replaced by Sunday as the day of rest; surnames were introduced; the Arabic alphabet was replaced by a Latin script; and civil (not religious) marriage became mandatory. The country's modernisation was accompanied by a great surge of nationalistic pride, and though it was no longer the political capital, İstanbul continued to be the centre of the nation's cultural and economic life.

Atatürk died in İstanbul in 1938, just before WWII broke out, and was succeeded as president by Ismet İnönü. Still scarred from the calamity of its involvement in the Great War, Turkey managed to successfully stay out of the new conflict until 1945, when it entered on the Allied side.

The Coup Years

The Allies made it clear that they believed that Turkey should introduce democracy. The government agreed and called parliamentary elections. The first opposition party in Turkey's history – the Democratic Party led by Adnan Menderes – won the first of these elections in 1950.

Though he started as a democrat, Menderes became increasingly autocratic. In 1960 the military staged a coup against his government and convicted him and two of his ministers of treason. All three were hanged in 1961. New elections were held and a government was formed, but it and ensuing administrations were dogged by corruption charges, and constitutional violations and amendments. In 1971 the military staged another coup, only to repeat the process in 1980 and install a military junta, which ruled for three years before new elections were called. It seemed to many observers that the far left and extreme right factions in the country would never be able to reconcile, and that military coups would be a constant feature of the modern political landscape. However, voters in the 1983 election refused to see this as a *fait accompli* and, rather than voting in the military's preferred candidates, elected the reforming Motherland party of economist Turgut Özal. A new era had begun.

1922–23	1934	2005
The Grand National Assembly, led by Atatürk, abolishes the Ottoman sultanate and proclaims the Turkish Republic; Atatürk becomes its first president	Women are given the vote; by 1935 4.6% of the national parliament's representatives are female, a percentage that sadly hasn't increased much to this day	Europe commences accession talks with Turkey regarding its candidacy bid for the EU; the French aren't keen but the UK is a staunch supporter

THE RECENT PAST

Under the presidency of economist Turgut Özal, the 1980s saw a free market-led economic and tourism boom in Turkey and its major city. Özal's government also presided over a great increase in urbanisation, with trainloads of peasants from eastern Anatolia making their way to the cities – particularly İstanbul – in search of jobs in the booming industry sector. The city's infrastructure couldn't cope back then and is still catching up, despite nearly three decades of large-scale municipal works being undertaken.

The municipal elections of March 1994 were a shock to the political establishment, with the upstart religious-right Refah Partisi (Welfare Party) winning elections across the country. Its victory was seen in part as a protest vote against the corruption, ineffective policies and tedious political wrangles of the traditional parties. In İstanbul Refah was led by Recep Tayyip Erdoğan, a proudly Islamist candidate. He vowed to modernise infrastructure and restore the city to its former glory.

In the national elections of December 1996, Refah polled more votes than any other party (23%), and eventually formed a government vowing moderation and honesty. Emboldened by political power, Prime Minister Necmettin Erbakan and other Refah politicians tested the boundaries of Turkey's traditional secularism, alarming the powerful National Security Council, the most visible symbol of the centrist military establishment's role as the caretaker of secularism and democracy.

In 1997 the council announced that Refah had flouted the constitutional ban on religion in politics and warned that the government should resign or face a military coup. Bowing to the inevitable, Erbakan did as the council wished. In İstanbul, Mayor Erdoğan was ousted by the secularist forces in the national government in late 1998.

National elections in April 1999 brought in a coalition government led by Bülent Ecevit's left-wing Democratic Left Party. After years under the conservative right of the Refah Partisi, the election result heralded a shift towards European-style social democracy, something highlighted by the country's successful bid to be accepted as a candidate for membership of the European Union. Unfortunately for the new government there was a spectacular collapse of the Turkish economy in 2001, leading to an electoral defeat in 2002. The victorious party was the moderate Islamic Justice and Development Party, led by Phoenix-like Recep Tayyip Erdoğan who – despite continuing tensions with military hardliners (see p38) – has run an increasingly stable and prosperous Turkey ever since.

ARTS

Turks have a unique attitude towards the arts, being as likely to read, view and listen to works created a century or a decade ago as they are to buy a newly released novel or album. This merging of the old and the new can be initially disconcerting for the foreign observer used to gravitating towards the fresh and new, but it makes for a rich cultural landscape and gives contemporary artists a solid base on which to build their practices. Traditional art forms such as carpet weaving are pretty well bound by tradition and have remained unchanged over the centuries, but there's no lack of innovative contemporary art in İstanbul, particularly within the disciplines of music, literature and cinema.

CARPETS

Turkish women have been weaving carpets for a very long time. These beautiful and durable floor coverings were a nomadic family's most valuable and practical 'furniture', warming and brightening the clan's oft-moved homes. The oldest-known carpet woven in the double-knotted Gördes style (Gördes is a town in the mountains of northwest Turkey) dates from between the 4th and 1st centuries BC.

It is thought that hand-woven carpet techniques were introduced to Anatolia by the Seljuks in the 12th century, so it's not surprising that Konya, the Seljuk capital, was mentioned by Marco Polo as a centre of carpet production in the 13th century.

The general pattern and colour scheme of old carpets was influenced by local traditions and the availability of certain types of wool and colours of dyes. Patterns were memorised and women usually worked with no more than 45cm of the carpet visible. Each artist imbued her work with her own personality, choosing a motif or a colour based on her own artistic preferences, and even events and emotions in her daily life.

In the 19th century, the European rage for Turkish carpets spurred the development of carpet companies. The companies, run by men, would deal with customers, take orders, purchase and dye the wool according to the customers' preferences, and contract local women to produce the finished product. The designs were sometimes left to the women, but more often were provided by the company based on the customers' tastes. Though well made, these carpets lost some of the originality and spirit of the older work.

NAMING RIGHTS

Even when it was ruled by the Byzantines, Constantinople was informally known as 'the city' (*polis*). The name İstanbul probably derives from this (the Greek for 'to the city' is *'eis ten polin'*). Though the Turks kept the name Constantinople, they also used other names, including İstanbul and Dersaadet (City of Peace and/or Happiness).

The city's name was officially changed to İstanbul by Atatürk in the early republican years and the use of the name Constantinople was banned for having, it was thought, unfortunate imperial connotations.

Carpets made today often use traditional patterns such as the commonly used eye and tree patterns, and incorporate all sorts of symbols that can be 'read' by those in the know. At a glance, two carpets might look identical, but closer examination reveals the subtle differences that give each Turkish carpet its individuality and charm.

Traditionally, village women wove carpets for their own family's use, or for their dowry. Knowing they would be judged on their efforts, the women took great care over their handiwork – hand-spinning and dyeing the wool, and choosing what they judged to be the most interesting and beautiful patterns. These days the picture is more complicated. Many carpets are made to the dictates of the market rather than according to local traditions. Weavers in eastern Turkey might make carpets in popular styles native to western Turkey. Long-settled villagers might duplicate the wilder, hairier and more naive *yörük* (nomad) carpets.

Village women still weave carpets, but most of them work to fixed contracts for specific shops. Usually they work to a pattern and are paid for their final effort rather than for each hour of work. A carpet made to a fixed contract may still be of great value to its purchaser. However, the selling price should be lower than for a one-off piece.

Other carpets are the product of division of labour, with different individuals responsible for dyeing and weaving. What such pieces lose in individuality and rarity is often more than made up for in quality control. Most silk Hereke carpets (Hereke is a small town near İzmit, about 100km southeast of İstanbul) are mass-produced, but to standards that make them some of the most sought-after of all Turkish carpets.

Fearing that old carpet-making methods would be lost, the Ministry of Culture now sponsors a number of projects to revive traditional weaving and dyeing methods in western Turkey. Some carpet shops will have stocks of these 'project carpets', which are usually of high quality with prices reflecting that fact. Some of these carpets are also direct copies of antique pieces in museums.

Most carpet shops have a range of pieces made by a variety of techniques. Besides the traditional pile carpets, they usually offer double-sided flat-woven mats, such as kilims. Some traditional kilim motifs are similar to patterns found at the prehistoric mound of Çatal Höyük, testifying to the very ancient traditions of flat-woven floor coverings in Anatolia. Older, larger kilims may actually be two narrower pieces of similar, but not always identical, design stitched together. As this is now rarely done, any such piece is likely to be fairly old.

Other flat-weave techniques include *sumak,* a style originally from Azerbaijan, in which intricate details are woven with coloured thread by wrapping them around the warp. The loose weft ends are left hanging at the back of the rug. *Cicims* are kilims with small and lively patterns embroidered on the top.

As well as Turkish carpets, many carpet shops in İstanbul sell pieces from other countries, especially from Iran, Afghanistan and from the ex-Soviet Republics of Azerbaijan, Turkmenistan and Uzbekistan. The major difference is that Turkey favours the double-knot technique and Iran favours the single knot. Turkish carpets also tend to have a higher pile, more dramatic designs and more varied colours than their Iranian cousins.

If you're keen to read more about Turkish carpets and rugs, it's worth getting hold of *The Classical Tradition in Anatolian Carpets* by Walter B Debby, *Kilims: The Complete Guide* by

Alastair Hull or *Oriental Carpets: A Buyer's Guide* by Eessie Sakhai. Most serious collectors eagerly await their bimonthly copy of the excellent magazine *Hali,* published in the UK.

For information on buying a carpet when in İstanbul, see p136.

LITERATURE

Turkey has a rich but relatively young literary tradition. Its brightest stars are greatly revered throughout the country and bookshop shelves groan under the weight of new local releases, a growing number of which are being translated into English. From its refined Ottoman roots through the flowering of politically driven literary movements in the 19th and 20th centuries, it has progressed to being predominantly concerned with investigating what it means to be a Turk in the modern age, particularly if one is displaced (either by the physical move from country to city or by virtue of one's ethnic background).

Ottoman Literature

Under the sultans, literature was really a form of religious devotion. Ottoman poets, borrowing from the great Arabic and Persian traditions, wrote sensual love poems of attraction, longing, fulfilment and ecstasy in the search for union with God. Occasionally they wrote about more worldly pleasures and triumphs, as Nabi Yousouf Efendi's 16th century *Eulogy of Constantinople* (republished in Chronicle Books' *Chronicles Abroad: Istanbul*) attests.

Early 20th Century & Nationalist Literature

By the late 19th century the influence of Western literature began to be felt. This was the time of the Tanzimat political and social reforms initiated by Sultan Abdül Mecit, and in İstanbul a literary movement was established that became known as 'Tanzimat Literature'. Its major figures were Sinasi, Ziya Paşa, Namık Kemal and Ahmet Mithat Efendi, all of whom sought to broaden the appeal of literature and bring it into line with developments in the West.

The Tanzimat movement was responsible for the first serious attacks on the ponderous cadences of Ottoman courtly prose and poetry, but it wasn't until the foundation of the republic that the death knell of this form of literature finally rang. Atatürk decreed that the Turkish language should be purified of Arabic and Persian borrowings, and that in future the nation's literature should be created using the new Latin-based Turkish alphabet. Major figures in the new literary movement (dubbed 'National Literature') included poets Yahya Kemal Beyatli and Mehmet Akıf Ersoy, and novelists Halide Edib Adıvar, Ziya Gokalp, Ömer Seyfettin and Aka Gündüz.

Of these figures, İstanbullu Halide Edib Adıvar (1884–1964) is particularly interesting. A writer and vocal leader of the emerging women's emancipation movement in Turkey, she was an ally of Atatürk and a leading figure in the War of Independence. Her 1926 autobiographical work *Memoir of Halide Edib* recounts her privileged upbringing in Beşiktaş and Üsküdar, progressive education at the American College for Girls in Arnavutköy and subsequent marriage to a noted mathematician, who humiliated her by taking a second wife. After leaving him, she joined the Nationalists, remarried, worked closely with Atatürk and wrote a popular history of the War of Independence called *The Turkish Ordeal* (1928). In later years she worked as a university lecturer, wrote over 20 novels – the most famous of which was probably the 1938 work, *Thewn and his Daughter* – and had a brief stint as a member of parliament. A fictionalised account of the early part of this fascinating woman's life can be found in *Halide's Gift*, an enjoyable novel by American writer Frances Kazan.

Though not part of the National Literature movement, İrfan Orga (1908–70) is probably the most famous Turkish literary figure of the 20th century. His 1950 masterpiece *Portrait of a Turkish Family* is his memoir of growing up in İstanbul at the start of the century and is probably the best writing about the city ever published. Exiled from the country of his birth, he also wrote a swathe of nonfiction titles, including the fascinating *The Caravan Moves On: Three Weeks among Turkish Nomads.* English translations of both works are available internationally.

Late 20th Century Writers

The second half of the 20th century saw a raft of local writers gain popularity in Turkey. Many were socialists, communists or outspoken critics of the government, and spent long and repeated periods in jail. The most famous of these writers was poet and novelist Nâzım Hikmet (1902–63). Internationally acclaimed for his poetry, Hikmet was in and out of Turkish jails for 30 years due to his alleged communist activity. Released in 1950 after a concerted lobbying effort by the Turkish and international intelligentsia, he left the country and died in exile. His masterwork is the five-volume collection of lyric and epic poetry entitled *Human Landscapes from My Country*. The most readily available English-language translation of his poems is *Beyond the Walls: Selected Poems*.

Yaşar Kemal (born 1923) is another major literary figure whose work has a strong political flavour. A former agricultural labourer and factory worker, he writes highly regarded epic novels dealing with the human condition. Kurdish by birth, his best-known work is probably 1955's *Mehmed, My Hawk*, which deals with the lives of Kurds in Turkey. Two of his novels – *The Birds are Also Gone* and *The Sea-Crossed Fisherman* – are set in İstanbul. Kemal was shortlisted for the Nobel Prize for Literature in 1999.

Aziz Nesin (1915–95) was perhaps the most prolific of all the Turkish political writers of the 20th century. A satirist, he published over 100 books and was jailed several times for his colourful indictments of the country's overly bureaucratic system and social inequalities. *Out of the Way! Socialism's Coming!* is one of the few of Nesin's works to be translated into English.

Since Halide Edib Adıvar blazed the trail, there have been a number of prominent female writers in Turkey, chief among them Sevgi Soysal, Erendiz Atasü, Buket Uzuner, Latife Tekin and Elif Şafak.

During her short life, Sevgi Soysal (1936–76) was known as the author of strong works promoting women's rights in Turkey. Her 1975 novel *Noontime in Yenişehir* won the most prestigious local literary prize, the Orhan Kemal Novel Award.

Another writer who focuses on the experiences of women in Turkey is Erendiz Atasü (born 1947), a retired professor of pharmacology. Her highly acclaimed 1995 novel *The Other Side*

ORHAN PAMUK

When the much-fêted Orhan Pamuk (born 1952) was awarded the 2006 Nobel Prize for Literature, the international cultural sector was largely unsurprised. The writing of the İstanbul-born, now US based, novelist had already attracted its fair share of critical accolades, including the €100,000 IMPAC Dublin Literary Award, *The Independent* newspaper's Foreign Fiction Award of the Month and every local literary prize on offer. The only prize Pamuk hadn't accepted was the prestigious title of State Artist, which was offered to him in 1999 by the Turkish Government but which he knocked back as, he stated, his protest against the government's incarceration of writers, 'narrow-minded nationalism' and an inability to address the Kurdish problem with anything but force.

In their citation, the Nobel judges said that in his 'quest for the melancholic soul of his native city' (ie İstanbul), Pamuk had 'discovered new symbols for the clash and interlacing of culture'. The only voices heard to criticise their judgment hailed from Turkey. Like Elif Şafak, Pamuk had been charged with 'Insulting Turkishness' under Article 301 of the Turkish Criminal Code (the charges were dropped in early 2006), and some local commentators alleged that in his case the Nobel Prize was awarded for political (ie freedom of speech) reasons rather than purely on the merit of his literary oeuvre. Whatever the reason, most Turks were thrilled to hear of the country's very first Nobel Prize win, and rushed to local bookstores to buy copies of his backlist titles.

Most critics describe Pamuk's novels as post-modernist, citing similarities to the work of Umberto Eco and Italo Calvino. He often uses a 'point of view' technique whereby he presents the internal monologues of interdependent characters, splicing them together so as to construct a meticulous overall narrative, often around a murder-mystery theme. Though not the easiest books to read (some critics have called them difficult and self-absorbed), they're meticulously researched and extraordinarily evocative of place. Most are set in his home town, İstanbul.

Pamuk has written seven novels to date. His first, *Cevdet Bey & His Sons* (1982), is a dynastic saga of the İstanbul bourgeoisie. *The Silent House* (1983) and *The White Castle* (1985) both won local literary awards and cemented his reputation, but were nowhere near as successful as his bizarre Beyoğlu detective novel *The Black Book* (1990), which was made into a film (*Gizli Yüz*) by director Omer Kavur in 1992. After this came *The New Life* (1995), followed by his most lauded book to date, *My Name is Red* (1998). A murder mystery set among the calligraphers of the sultan's court in the 16th century, *My Name is Red* took six years to write and was described by the IMPAC judges as 'A rare *tour de force* of literary imagination and philosophical speculation'. Pamuk's most recent novel is *Snow* (2002), which explores issues around the conflict of Western and Islamic ideologies in modern Turkey and is his most accessible work to date. In 2005, he published a memoir, *İstanbul: Memories of a City*, and in 2007 he published *Other Colours: Essays and Stories*. Of these titles, only *Cevdet Bey & His Sons* and *the Silent House* are not available in English translation.

BACKGROUND ARTS

of the Mountain looks at three generations of a family from the end of the Ottoman Empire to the 1990s, focussing on a central female character. It was published in English through a grant from the Arts Council of England. Atasü has also written *That Scorching Season of Youth* (1999) and three volumes of short stories.

Buket Uzuner (born 1955) writes short stories and novels, the best-known being *Sound of Fish Steps* (1992), which was greatly admired by the local literary set when it was first released.

Latife Tekin (born 1957) has built a reputation as Turkey's major magic-realist novelist. Her first novel, *Dear Shameless Death* (1983), which told the story of a family's difficult migration to a big city, had a strongly political subtext and was well received by local readers. Tekin's subsequent novels have included 1984's *Berji Kristin: Tales from the Garbage Hills,* another look at the displaced members of society, *Night Lessons* (1986), *Swords of Ice* (1989) and *Signs of Love* (1995).

High-profile writer Elif Şafak was born in Paris in 1971 and has lived and worked in France, Spain, Ankara, İstanbul and the US. She is currently based in Tucson, Arizona, where she works in the Near Eastern Studies Department at the University of Arizona. Şafak's first novel, *Pinhan (The Sufi)* was awarded the Mevlana Prize for the best work in mystical literature in Turkey in 1998. Since then she has released five novels that have either been written in, or translated into, English: *Mirrors of the City* (1999), which won the Union of Turkish Writers Prize in 2000, *The Gaze* (2000), *The Flea Palace* (2002), *The Saint of Incipient Insanities* (2004) and the controversial *The Bastard of Istanbul* (2006). In 2006, Şafak and her Turkish translator and publisher were charged with 'insulting Turkishness' under the notorious Article 301 of the Turkish Criminal Code for raising the issue of the alleged genocide of the Armenians in *The Bastard of Istanbul* (the Turkish translation of which is 'The Father and the Bastard'). The case was eventually dismissed for lack of evidence. In the novel, Şafak tells the story of two families – one based in Istanbul, the other an exiled Armenian family living in San Francisco – who share a family secret connected with Turkey's turbulent past.

Turkish-born (but American-based) writer Alev Lytle Croutier, internationally known for her bestselling *Harem: The World Behind the Veil,* has also written a children's book set in İstanbul called *Leyla: The Black Tulip.*

MUSIC

Turks love music and listen to it in many forms, the most popular of which are the overwrought vocal style called *arabesk* and the slick Western-influenced pop styles performed by artists such as Tarkan. Though many foreigners immediately conjure up the trance-like sounds of Sufi Mevlevi music when they try to categorise Turkey's musical heritage, the reality is worlds away, sitting squarely within the cheerful modern-day vulgarity of Eurovision-style musical romps. These forays into the international scene stem from a solidly populist tradition of *arabesk* and folk, and are packaged with a thickly applied veneer of Western pop. Some local product can't be easily pigeonholed – the fusion sounds of Baba Zulu, for instance – but overall there are four dominant genres today: folk, *arabesk,* fasıl and pop.

Ottoman, Classical & Sufi Music

The Ottoman court liked to listen to traditional classical music, which utilised a system of *makams* (modalities), an exotic-sounding series of notes similar in function to the familiar Western scales of whole and half-tone intervals. The result was a lugubrious sound that owed a lot to Persian and Arabic classical influences. Usually improvised, it was performed by chamber groups. Though out of favour for over a century, this form has recently undergone a slight revival, largely due to the work of İstanbul-based ensembles such as Al-Kindi. Its *Parfums Ottomans* double album makes great listening.

While the court was being serenaded by such music at its soirees, another classical genre, the music of the Sufi Mevlevi, was inspiring followers of the religious sect. Its complex and refined sound was often accompanied by vocal pieces featuring the words of Celaleddin Rumi (Mevlâna), the 13th-century founder of the sect.

After the founding of the republic, the performance of traditional classical music was actively discouraged by Atatürk and his government. The great man considered it to be too redolent of contaminating Arabic influences, and he encouraged musicians and the public to instead turn their attention to Western classical music. The fate of Sufi music under the republic was even more extreme. With the forced closure of the Sufi *tekkes* (lodges) in 1923, the music of the order was in effect banned, only re-emerging when Prime Minister Turgut Özal overturned the ban on Sufi worship after he came to power in 1983. Today there's a healthy recording tradition among Sufi musicians and a whole new genre of Sufi-inspired electronic-techno sounds by musicians such as Mercan Dede, whose albums *Nar, Seyahatname, Su* and *Nefes* have built huge international fan bases over recent years.

Anatolian Folk Music

As well as encouraging Western classical music, the republican government began a programme of classifying, archiving and promoting *halk müziği* (Anatolian folk music). Spanning 30 years and involving 10,000 songs, the programme had its positives and negatives. On the plus side, parts of a rich musical heritage were documented and promoted. Less positively, any music that was deemed 'un-Turkish' (usually due to its roots in the music of ethnic minorities) was struck from the record or forced to conform with the dominant sub-genre.

Until the 1960s and 1970s it was still possible to hear Turkish troubadours (*aşik*) in action around the countryside, playing their particular variety of *halk müziği*. These *aşik* were members of the Alevî sect of central Anatolia and had a set repertoire of mystical songs always featuring the *saz* (Turkish long-necked, stringed instrument) and vocals. Fortunately their music has been revived in studio form, with artists such as Ruhi Su, Arif Sağ, Yavuz Top and Musa Eroğlu reinterpreting the music of the wandering *aşik* for modern audiences.

Folk Revival: Türkü, Arabesk & Fasıl

In the 1980s traditional *halk müziği* underwent a revival, popularised by musicians such as the soulful Belkis Akkale, who fused it with pop to form a new sub-genre known as *Türkü*. The extremely popular İbrahim Can and Nuray Hafiftaş followed Akkale's lead.

Even before Belkis et al were experimenting with *Türkü*, rock musicians such as Cem Karaca were using folk influences to develop a distinctive form of Anadolu rock featuring politically charged lyrics. Since his death in 2004, Karaca's *Hayvan Terli* album has gained a whole new audience for this type of music. The music of Zülfü Livaneli, a popular singer and *saz* player who incorporates Western instrumentation into his protest songs, clearly shows the influence of Karaca and is best known internationally for his music for Yılmaz Güney's film *Yol* (The Road).

The popularity of some musical genres defied the government's early attempts to promote a national music based solely on *halk müziği*. Two examples were fasıl and *arabesk,* and they're still going strong today.

A mix of folk, classical and fasıl traditions, *arabesk*'s name attests to its Arabic influences, specifically Egyptian dance music. First popularised by a local lad, Kaydar Tatliyay, in the 1940s, it was frowned upon by the nationalist government because of its Arabic influences and mournful tone. The government went so far as to first restrict and then ban Arabic musical films and recordings from Egypt and Lebanon to stop further 'contamination' of local musical tastes. Turkish devotees ignored the ban and tuned in to Radio Cairo for regular fixes of their favourite sounds.

Arabesk songs have traditionally been geared towards a working-class audience from central and eastern Anatolia and are inevitably about the oppressed – sometimes the singer is oppressed by love, sometimes by his lot in life. Though artists such as Müslüm Gürses have their devoted followers, two singers are the undisputed kings of the genre: İbrahim Tatlıses and Orhan Gencebey. A Turk of Kurdish descent, Tatlıses is from the southeastern town of Urfa and sells truckloads of CDs; Gencebey, who is also an actor, is possibly even more popular – have a listen to his *Akma Gözlerimden* and you'll see why.

As the soulful laments of *arabesk* were building the genre's national following, fasıl (sometimes referred to as Gypsy) music was taking the taverns and nightclubs of İstanbul by storm. Usually performed by Turks of Armenian, Jewish, Greek or Gypsy origin who had no religious scruples preventing them performing in places where alcohol was served, this lively music usually featured the *klarnet* (clarinet) and *darbuka* (drum played with the hands). Solo improvisations from the stars of the orchestra were commonplace, as were boisterous renditions of emotionally charged songs by vocalists. Today this is the most popular form of music played in the city's many meyhanes (see p148).

Turkish Pop & Rock

On the streets you may hear the plaintive strains of *arabesk,* but they're likely to be overlaid by the powerful sounds of Turkish pop, which is pumped out of shopfronts and cars across the city. Dominated by solo artists rather than bands, pop's pantheon of performers have built their success on a long and rich tradition of popular solo vocal artists trained in *sanat,* or art music. Many have also been influenced by *arabesk.*

The first of these vocal stars to build a popular following was the fabulously camp Zeki Müren, Turkey's very own Liberace. Müren released his first album in 1951 and went on to record in classical and *arabesk* styles. Like Liberace, he liked nothing better than frocking up (his stage performances saw him appear in everything from gladiator costumes to sequin-and-feather confections) and was particularly beloved by middle-aged women. He died on stage at a comeback concert in İzmir in 1996 but recordings such as *Kahir Mektubu* still sell like hotcakes.

Following in Müren's cross-dressing footsteps is talented vocalist Bülent Ersoy, whose restrained classical idiom is best heard in her reinterpretation of late-19th-century repertoire, *Alaturka 1995.* Born in 1952, Ersoy is known by her many fans as Abla (Big Sister) as a show of support for her gender change (male to female). Before her operation she was banned from performing because of her 'effeminate ways'; afterwards she managed to successfully lobby Prime Minister Turgut Özal (a big fan) for her right to perform and also for the general civil rights of transsexuals in Turkey.

Though Bülent has attained diva status, her profile comes nowhere near to attaining the royal status given to Sezen Aksu. Aksu's influence on Turkey's popular music industry has been enormous. She's done everything from overseeing the Turkish contributions to the annual Eurovision contest to recording innumerable blockbuster albums of her own, along the way grooming up-and-coming stars such as Tarkan and Sertab Erener. In among her musical accomplishments she's managed to be an outspoken and controversial commentator on feminism and politics. Her most popular album is probably *Deliveren* (2001), though everything she's done since hitting the music scene in the 1970s has been pretty impressive.

Relative newcomer Sertab Erener has a lot to live up to if she's to take over the throne from Aksu one day. The İstanbul-born winner of the 2003 Eurovision contest hit the big time with her album *No Boundaries,* which sold over four million copies. Her winning track 'Every Way That I Can' was performed and recorded in English (the first time that a Turkish Eurovision entry wasn't performed in Turkish) and has built her a loyal international following.

Popular rock outfits such as Duman, Replikas, 110 (electronica) and Yakup regularly play gigs in İstanbul and are worth catching if you get the chance.

Finally, no discussion of contemporary Turkish music would be complete without a mention of the two very different pin-up boys: Tarkan and Ceza.

Tarkan's albums regularly sell millions of copies and his catchy brand of music is the stuff of which recording empires are made. Pretty-boy looks and a trace of attitude are all part of the Tarkan package, and have landed him a mega-lucrative Pepsi contract among other endorsements. His most successful album to date, 1998's *Ölürüm Sana* (I'd Die For You), featured tracks written by former collaborator Sezen Aksu and sold 3.5 million copies in Turkey alone. His *A-acıypsin* (1994) sold over two million copies in Turkey and one million in Europe, making him Turkey's most successful recording artists ever. He even released a self-titled perfume a few years ago (we kid you not).

Ceza is the king of the local rap/hip-hop scene; his fan base is so devoted that he is regularly mobbed in the street. Have a listen to his *Rapstar Ceza* and you'll get an idea about what gets them so excited.

CINEMA
Birth of an Industry

Just a year after the Lumière brothers presented their first cinematic show in 1895, cinema first appeared in Turkey. At first it was only foreigners and non-Muslims who watched movies, but by 1914 there were cinemas run by and for Muslims as well, and the Turks' great love for the artform was up and running.

The War of Independence inspired actor Muhsin Ertuğrul, Turkey's cinema pioneer, to establish a film company in 1922 and make patriotic films. The company's first release was *The Ordeal,* based on a novel about the War of Independence by eminent writer and republican Halide Edib Adıvar. Within a decade Turkish films were winning awards in international competitions, even though a mere 23 films had been made.

After WWII the industry expanded rapidly, with new companies and young directors. Lütfi Akad's *In the Name of the Law* (1952), Turkey's first colour film, brought realism to the screen in the place of melodrama, which had been the main fodder for audiences throughout the 1940s.

Cinema as Social Commentary

By the 1960s, Turkish cinema was delving deeply into social and political issues. Metin Erksan's *Dry Summer* (1964) won a gold medal at the Berlin Film Festival and another award in Venice. Yılmaz Güney, the fiery actor-director, directed his first film *Horse, Woman, Gun* in 1966 and scripted Lütfi Akad's *The Law of the Borders,* which he also starred in. His 1970 film *Hope* was a turning point for national cinema, kick-starting a trend towards simple neorealist treatments of contemporary social issues that continues today. In this and similar films the commentary about life in modern Turkey was bleak indeed, and the exploration of issues such as the poverty-driven drift from rural areas to congested urban environments introduced a theme that would return again and again. The titles of Güney's subsequent films were representative of the industry's lack of optimism about the future of the country and their industry: after *Hope,* he released *Lament* in 1971, followed by *Sorrow.* It's not surprising that the government imprisoned him for three years after the 1971 coup.

The 1970s brought the challenge of TV, dwindling audiences, political pressures and unionisation of the industry. This was highlighted at the inaugural İstanbul International Film Festival in 1976, when the jury determined that no film was worthy of the award for best film. Despite the depressed start to the decade, the quality of films improved, and social issues such as the plight of Turkish workers in Europe were treated with honesty, naturalism and dry humour. By the early 1980s, several Turkish directors were well recognised in Europe and the USA, though they were having trouble getting their films shown at home. Despite winning the Palme D'Or at the Cannes Film Festival, Yılmaz Güney's bleak *The Road,* which explores the dilemmas faced by a group of men on temporary release from prison, was banned for 15 years in Turkey before finally being released in 2000. Güney had worked on the film while in jail (his second jail term), passing directions on to co-director Şerif Gören. His last film, *Duvar* (1983), made before his untimely death aged only 46, was a wrist-slashing prison drama.

Though the industry wasn't yet booming, things were looking up by the 1980s, with some excellent films having redemptive themes symbolic of the more optimistic political climate. The most successful film of the decade was probably 1983's *A Season in Hakkâri,* directed by Erdan Kıral, which addressed some of the issues surrounding the plight of Turkey's oppressed Kurdish population.

Critical Acclaim

The 1990s were an exciting decade for the national cinema, with films being critically and popularly received both in Turkey and internationally. Notable among the many releases were Zeki Demirkubuz's *Innocence* (1997), which followed the story of an ex-con trying to survive in a society that had changed radically since his incarceration a decade before; and Omer Kavur's *Journey on the Hour Hand* (1997), a very different type of film, which can best be described as an existential mystery.

Many of the most highly regarded films of the 1990s were set in İstanbul. These included *Journey to the Sun* by Yeşim Ustaoğlu, which won the top prize at the İstanbul International Film Festival in 1999; the wonderful 1995 *İstanbul Beneath My Wings*; 1998's *Cholera Street* by Mustafa Altıoklar; and *The Bandit* (1996) by Yavuz Turgul. Many of these films explore important social and political themes. *Journey to the Sun,* for instance, is about a boy from the provinces who comes to the big city and is frequently mistaken for a Kurd due to his dark skin. Needless to say, he's treated appallingly as a result.

Cinema Today

Turks have taken to cinema-going with alacrity over the past decade, and the industry has gone from strength to strength. Some local releases are accruing box-office receipts from audiences numbering over four million, which is sure to encourage the industry to grow and prosper. Recent local tours de force in both box-office and critical terms have included the controversial *Valley of the Wolves IRAQ* (Serdar Akar, 2004), the dramatic *My Father and My Son* (Çağarn Irmak, 2006), *Ice Cream* (Yüksel Aksu, 2006) and the laugh-one-minute-cry-the-next *The Magician* (Cem Yılmaz, 2006).

İSTANBUL THROUGH FOREIGN EYES

Writers and film-makers have long tried to capture the magic and mystery of İstanbul in their work. For a taste of the city, try the following:

- **Aziyadé** Few artists have been as deeply enamoured of the city as the French novelist Pierre Loti (1850–1923). His romantic novel introduced Europe to both Loti's almond-eyed Turkish lover and the mysterious and all-pervasive attractions of the city itself.
- **James Bond** The sultan of all secret agents pops up twice in İstanbul, first in 1974's *From Russia with Love* and then in 1999's *The World is Not Enough*. The city provides a great backdrop for his suave manoeuvres and sophisticated seductions.
- **L'Immortelle** Alain Robbe-Grillet directed this 1963 film before going on to collaborate with Alain Resnais on *Last Year at Marienbad,* and both films score high on the Esoteric-O-Meter. Here, a man is obsessed with a woman who is being followed around İstanbul (gloriously shot) by a sinister man and his two dogs. Go figure.
- **Midnight Express** Alan Parker's 1978 film has three major claims to fame: Giorgio Moroder's insufferable score, Brad Davis' homosexual sex scene and the Turkish tourism industry's virtual demise on the film's release. Mention it to a Turk at your peril.
- **Murder on the Orient Express** Hercule Poirot puts ze leetle grey cells to good use on the famous train in this 1934 novel by Agatha Christie. It was made into a film by Sidney Lumet in 1974 and features a few opening shots of İstanbul.
- **The Inspector Ikmen Novels** Barbara Nadel investigates İstanbul's underbelly in a suitably gripping style. Whether they're set in Balat or Beyoğlu, her books are always evocative and well researched (see boxed text, p95).
- **The Turkish Embassy Letters** This 18th-century memoir was written by Lady Mary Wortley Montagu, the observant wife of the British Ambassador to the Sublime Porte. Based on letters she sent during the posting, it's a fascinating account of life in and around the Ottoman court and city.
- **The Mask of Dimitrios** This 1944 spy thriller directed by James Negulesco is based on an Eric Ambler novel. A ripping yarn, it opens with a body being fished out of the Bosphorus. Sydney Greenstreet and Peter Lorre give great performances.
- **Tintin** You'll see the T-shirts everywhere in the Grand Bazaar, but true devotees should check out this 1961 film by Jacques Vierne, which has the Belgian boy detective accompanying Captain Haddock to İstanbul.
- **Topkapi** Melina Mercouri's funky outfits, Peter Ustinov's hilarious performance and great shots of İstanbul make Jules Dassin's 1964 comedy spoof worth a view.
- **Constantinople** Orhan Pamuk says that this travelogue, written by Italian Edmondo De Amicis in 1878, is the best book ever written about İstanbul.
- **The Janissary Tree** Author Jason Goodwin also wrote the highly regarded *Lords of the Horizon: A History of the Ottoman Empire*. In this crime novel, he has Yashim Togalu, court eunuch, unravelling intrigue and murder in 1836 İstanbul. The courtly detective reappears in a 2007 sequel, *The Snake Stone*.
- **The Sultan's Seal** Another historical crime novel set in the city. Jenny White's hero is Kamil Pasha, a magistrate in one of the new Ottoman secular courts who is asked to investigate the murder of an English governess working for Sultan Abdülaziz's granddaughter.
- **Innocents Abroad** Mark Twain's account of his 'grand tour' includes sharp observations of İstanbul.
- **Sweet Waters** Before he became Mr Vita Sackville-West, Harold Nicolson wrote this extremely moving love story cum political thriller set in İstanbul during the Balkan Wars.
- **Enlightenment** Though best known as Orhan Pamuk's English translator and John Freely's daughter, Maureen Freely is also a well-regarded novelist. In her latest novel, which is set in İstanbul and has the ostensible structure of a thriller, she writes about truth, repression and the personal and political risks of becoming enmeshed in a foreign culture.

Contemporary directors of note include Ferzan Özpetek, whose 1996 film *Hamam*, set in İstanbul, was a big hit on the international festival circuit and is particularly noteworthy for addressing the hitherto hidden issue of homosexuality in Turkish society. His most recent release, *Saturno Contro* (2007), was an enormous success in Italy, where the filmmaker lives and makes most of his films. Though Özpetek hasn't shot a film in Turkey for a number of years, he recently chaired the jury for the national competition at the İstanbul International Film Festival.

Nuri Bilge Ceylan's 2003 film *Distant* received a rapturous response from critics and audiences alike when it was released, winning the Jury Prize at Cannes among other accolades. The story of two cousins – played by Muzaffer Özdemir and Mehmet Emin Toprak – who are both alienated from society, is in the bleak but visually beautiful tradition of Güney's films. His most recent film, *Climates* (2006), was also in official competition at the Cannes Film Festival.

Contrary to what film festival catalogues would encourage the international filmgoer to believe, the local industry does venture into territory outside political commentary and lamentations on the emptiness of the human condition. Reasonably recent examples have included the blockbuster action/revenge flick *Wildheart – Boomerang Hell* (2002), directed by Osman Sınav; and the hilarious outer-space spoof *G.O.R.A.* (2004) directed by Faruk Sorak.

VISUAL ARTS

The visual-arts scene has played second fiddle to that of music, cinema and theatre for years, but all of this is changing with the opening of a swathe of top-notch privately funded contemporary art galleries in the city. See The Arts chapter (p185) for more details.

ENVIRONMENT & PLANNING

İstanbul has been plagued by hyper-growth during the last few decades as villagers move to the city by the tens of thousands in search of a better life. This has placed great pressure on infrastructure and services. On some issues the government is making real progress (see p39), on others it still faces significant challenges.

Many of the green areas in and around the city have been developed for housing, making open space a rare commodity. Although there are a few protected areas around the city – the Princes' Islands (Kızıl Adalar) and the Beykoz Nature Forests near Polonezköy, for example – a low average of just over 1 sq metre of forest reserve is put aside per person; conservationists say the average in Europe is about 40 sq metres per person.

Air pollution in the city is a big problem. Though clean-burning Russian natural gas has replaced dirty lignite (soft coal) as the preferred winter heating fuel, air pollution is still significant, largely due to the ever-increasing number of cars jamming city roads. The national Ministry of Environment, established in 1991, is trying to implement programs to reduce smog across the country's large cities, but the International Energy Agency has criticised its efforts, saying that current measures don't go far enough.

The major environmental threat to the city is pollution of its waterways. Increased oil exports from the Caspian Sea region to Russian and Georgian ports and across the Black Sea has led to increased oil-tanker traffic (and risk of accident) through the narrow and winding Turkish Straits, which comprise the Dardanelles, the Sea of Marmara and the Bosphorus. With 50,000 vessels per year using this route, and one in 10 of these carrying oil or liquefied natural gas, the threat of a major spill is very real. Accidents are increasing in frequency, with the worst probably being the March 1994 collision of the Greek tanker *Nassia* with another ship. Thirty seamen were killed in this incident and 20,000 tons of oil were spilled into the Straits a few kilometres north of İstanbul, triggering an inferno that raged for five days. The possibility of this happening closer to the city is very real, as was illustrated in November 2003 when a Georgian-flagged ship ran aground and broke in two – fortunately it was carrying dry goods rather than oil.

Ships using these waters also cause major water pollution by releasing contaminated water as they ballast their holds. Though government has made genuine efforts to flush water through the Bosphorus and Golden Horn (the relocation of the current-blocking 19th-century Galata Bridge and municipal rubbish-removal programs being perfect examples), the waters are still

WAITING FOR THE QUAKE

İstanbul lies over the North Anatolian Fault, which runs for about 1500km between the Anatolian and Eurasian tectonic plates. As the Arabian and African plates to the south push northward, the Anatolian plate is shoved into the Eurasian plate, and squeezed west towards Greece. This movement creates stress along the North Anatolian Fault, which accumulates, and then releases pressure as earthquakes. Thirteen major quakes in Turkey have been recorded since 1939, with the latest in August 1999 devastating İzmit and Adapazarı, about 90km east of İstanbul, leaving nearly 20,000 dead and 100,000 homeless. İstanbul remained relatively unscathed, although the suburb of Avcılar to the west of the city suffered hundreds of deaths when jerry-built dwellings collapsed.

This pattern of earthquakes leaves İstanbul in an unenviable position. Locals are half-panicked, half-fatalistic about the next one, but no-one doubts that it's coming. The city has been hit four times by major earthquakes in the last 500 years and experts predict that the strain placed by İzmit's earthquake on nearby stress segments along the fault could lead to another major quake within the next few decades.

As the destruction at Avcılar illustrated, much of the city's urban development in the last few decades has been poorly built and is unlikely to make it through a major quake. Sadly, the government doesn't seem to be forcing developers to raise their game when it comes to building quality, and when the big one comes the consequences are likely to be catastrophic. Then again, Aya Sofya has made it through more than its fair share of quakes and still crowns the first of the city's hills. Many locals look at it and take heart.

highly polluted and have contributed to a major decline in local fish stocks. Overfishing has also been a contributing factor.

GOVERNMENT & POLITICS

Though the Turks are firm believers in democracy, the tradition of popular rule is relatively short. Real multiparty democracy came into being only after WWII, and has been interrupted several times by military coups, though government has always eventually been returned to civilians.

The historical power of the military is embodied in the make-up of the National Security Council (NSC), which comprises high-level government and military leaders and meets monthly to 'advise' the government. Its relationship with the ruling Justice and Development Party (AKP) national government is extremely uneasy, largely due to the AKP's soft Islamist ideology and the military's firm allegiance to the ideal of the Turkish secular state. In 2007, the AKP insisted on elevating former foreign minister Abdullah Gül to the position of president, replacing the strongly secular Ahmet Necdet Sezer. The army went into a frenzy, arguing that the fact that Mr Gül's wife wore the headscarf (see p40) meant that the country's secularist status would be irrevocably compromised on the international stage. The situation was so serious that some Turks feared another military coup. Prime Minister Recep Tayyıp Erdoğan called a general election to sort the issue for once and all, and the election campaign that followed was fought pretty well solely on the Islamist vs secular-state issue, with Mrs Gül's right to wear a headscarf being heatedly debated. The result, when it came, was an enormous shock to the NSC and a ringing endorsement of the government. Over 47% of the electorate was clearly happy with the way in which the prime minister and his government were running the economy and the EU accession process, and had no problem with the AKP's Islamist bias (nor, it can be inferred, were they fussed about whether the first lady wore a headscarf or not). Retreating to lick its wounds, the army was forced to come to terms with the fact that it is no longer the main player on the national political stage and that a pious and increasingly prosperous Anatolian middle class has become the nation's new major power bloc. The jury is out as to whether the generals will take this lying down or not; the overwhelming yes vote in an October 2007 referendum proposing that Turks directly elect the president was the political equivalent of rubbing salt into the army's wounds, and will probably only feed its resentment of the AKP.

Another interesting outcome from the election was the successful candidacies of 19 members of the pro-Kurdish Democratic Socialist party. It was the first time since the early 1990s that overtly nationalistic Kurds had taken seats in the 550-member legislature, something that infuriated the far-right Nationalist Action Party, which won 71 seats and has called for the execution of PKK (Kurdistan Workers' Party) leader Abdullah Öcalan, who has been incarcerated in a Turkish jail since being found guilty of treason in 1999. Nationalist Action Party supporters became even more infuriated, and gained extra recruits, after a spate of incidents in which Turkish soldiers were killed by PKK fighters on or near the Iraq border. This led the Turkish government to pass unprecedented legislation authorising cross-border raids allowing the Turkish army to pursue and apprehend PKK fighters on Iraqi territory, something that the Iraqi government strongly protests.

LOCAL GOVERNMENT

İstanbul itself is actually two political entities: the city and the province. The city is organised as a *büyükşehir belediyesi,* or metropolitan municipality, with several large sub-municipalities under the overall authority of a metropolitan city government.

The current metropolitan city government is perceived to be doing a pretty good job of coping with the demands on city infrastructure that the continuing influx of migrants from the provinces is making. It's also considered by most to be doing an excellent job with the provision of municipal services such as transport, and with the introduction of environmental programs such as the clean-up of the city's waterways. Accusations of corruption and crony-ism are of course made from time to time (particularly about the sub-municipality governing Sultanahmet), but overall, voter approval is quite high.

It's true to say that this positive view of İstanbul's municipal government kicked off during the office of Recep Tayyıp Erdoğan, the current prime minister, who was elected the Refah Mayor of İstanbul in 1994. Before being ousted by secularist forces in the national government in late 1998, he made many changes and improvements, not least being to the population's overall confidence and pride in its home town. The current city mayor, Kadir Topbaş, worked as an adviser to Erdoğan (he's also a member of the AKP) before going on to become the mayor of Beyoğlu, one of the largest sub-municipalities. An architect by profession, he concentrated on the suburb's urban fabric while in office and did much to improve the safety, amenity and appearance of its streets and public buildings. The fact that he was elected mayor of the city in March 2004 with a huge majority is testament to the fact that İstanbullus approved of what he did in Beyoğlu and wanted to see the same types of programs occur over the city as a whole. And this does indeed seem to be happening, with huge and visionary public works projects such as the Marmaray project (p234) now underway in the city.

MEDIA

Turkey is going to have to lift its game when it comes to the promotion of a free and diverse media if it is to have its bid to join the EU taken seriously. At present 70% of the Turkish media is under the control of only two companies: the Doğan and Bilgin groups. Doğan owns eight newspapers, including *Hürriyet, Milliyet* and *Radikal,* as well as the CNN Türk and Kanal D TV channels. It controls between 40% and 60% of national advertising revenue and 80% of distribution channels, and also has interests in banking, tourism, electricity and fuel distribu-tion. Bilgin owns *Sabah* newspaper, ATV TV and dozens of periodicals. Like Doğan, it has interests in many other industries.

In 2002, local and international media analysts were outraged when the Ankara government passed legislation smoothing the way for media groups to enter into public tenders and trade on the stock exchange. Seen by many as a move tailor-made for Aydın Doğan, the head of the Doğan Group, the legislation made it possible for Turkish media barons to bid for govern-ment contracts and acquire stakes in the many state-owned companies being earmarked for privatisation. Critics feared (and still do) that the media channels owned by these barons would be pressured to present government-friendly media analysis as a way of staying sweet with Ankara and promoting the financial interests of their parent companies. The jury's still out as to whether the demands of the EU for the sanctity and importance of a free press will prevail over the behind-the-scenes machinations of powerful tycoons.

FASHION

Fashion in İstanbul is best described as eclectic. Every season the latest trends spotted on the catwalks in Paris, Rome or New York are reworked for and by the local market, hitting the shelves in a remarkably short period of time. Though international chains such as Zara do

THE HEADSCARF DEBATE

No issue is as hotly debated in Turkey as the Constitutional Court's imposition of a national ban on the headscarf (*eşarp* or *türban*) being worn in the public domain. The fact that girls and women are kept out of schools, universities and professions as a result of the ban is considered by many to be a national disgrace. Others argue that the headscarf is a challenge to the national identity that cannot be countenanced; allow the headscarf, they argue, and the secular state fought for by Atatürk's generation is totally undermined. National newspapers, such as the pro-Islamic daily *Zaman*, point out that any argument that defines secularism as totally against every kind of social and public manifestation of religion is both naive and misguided, but they haven't yet managed to prompt the ruling Justice and Development Party (AKP) to force a constitutional amendment overturning the ban. Such an amendment looks as if it's on the horizon, though, particularly since the AKP's emphatic win in the 2007 national election, in which the right to wear the headscarf was a major issue.

Passions within the AKP run at fever pitch on this issue. The wives and daughters of a majority of cabinet members (including the Prime Minister and President) wear the headscarf, and they and many Turks have been outraged when their choice of head covering has led to them being excluded from important ceremonial events. Equally contentious was the expulsion from the national parliament of a deputy from İstanbul, Merve Kavakçı, who insisted on taking her oath of office while wearing a headscarf. Ms Kavakçı was subsequently stripped of her parliamentary immunity and prosecuted. Democracy in action? We think not.

this supremely well, local store Yargıcı (p143) is the most popular outlet for main street fashion, and can always be relied upon for a fetching summer frock in the latest colours and style or an accessory *de jour*. Glam areas such as Nişantaşı and Teşvikiye (p114) or swish shopping malls such as Kanyon (p143) are the places to go to access real European designer items, which are snapped up by the blond-tipped, tanned and immaculately groomed wives of the city's bankers, industrialists and politicians.

At the other extreme are the young suburban women sporting the latest in Islamic chic, invariably a long denim skirt instead of jeans, a fitted (but not too revealing) top and a colour-coordinated headscarf. Cleverly applied makeup to feature the eyes is all part of the demure but modern package. The most popular fashion trend of all is a perennial one: young Turks love their jeans, and currently wear them tight and slung low. Local chain Mavi (p141) is where both male and female aficionados choose to shop for their latest pair.

The local designer fashion scene is thriving and does an inspired line in Ottoman-influenced styles created using rich fabrics and embroidery. Gönül Paksoy (described as the 'new Hussein Chalayan') is probably the queen of this trend, but there are plenty of aspirants dotted throughout Nişantaşı and Çukurcuma just waiting to hit the pages of *Wallpaper* or *French Vogue*.

The uncompromising Chalayan (known in Turkey as Hüseyin Çağlayan) is, of course, the king of the scene, albeit from a distance. Despite the fact that his clothes are difficult to find in İstanbul – we've seen them at Harvey Nichols at Kanyon (p143) but nowhere else – his influence is felt everywhere. After all, he's a local boy who's made it to the big time (well, nearly local – he is in fact a Turkish Cypriot who trained in London), and he's proud of his heritage. More of a conceptual artist than a fashion designer, he undertakes intense historical research as part of his creative process, and has referenced Byzantine, Ottoman, Georgian, Armenian and Greek historical styles in a number of his collections. He freely admits that he likes taking ideas from the past and putting them into contemporary garments, and this appropriation has characterised most of his collections.

LANGUAGE

Writing of Constantinople in 1857, Herman Melville said 'You feel you are among the nations', and when it comes to language, the city hasn't changed much. Melville saw this Babel-like reality as a curse, and after taking the reins of government half a century later, Atatürk and his republican colleagues agreed, establishing the modern Turkish language to take over from its 'contaminated' Ottoman predecessor, which was full of Arabic and Persian influences. All Turks were encouraged to learn and speak the new language (and its Latin alphabet) rather than Ottoman Turkish, regional dialects or foreign languages.

FREEDOM TO SPEAK

Although Turkey has been implementing a wide range of reforms for its EU membership bid, the country's new penal code still retains the infamous Article 301, which prohibits people from 'insulting Turkishness'. This article has been the basis for a series of recent high-profile prosecutions of journalists, writers and artists, exposing Turkey's freedom of expression credentials (or lack thereof) to the world.

The most famous case to hit the headlines was that of Turkey's Nobel Prize–winning novelist, Orhan Pamuk, who was tried after publication of an interview he gave to a Swiss newspaper in which he referred to the ongoing Armenian controversy and the government's heavyhanded response to the Kurdish issue during the 1990s. Charges were dropped in early 2006, but Pamuk had become a reluctant political symbol and a target for nationalists, and the damage to Turkey's international reputation had been done.

Lesser-known but just as important cases have followed. Journalist and author Perihan Mağden was tried for 'turning people against military service' after she wrote an article in the *Yeni Aktuel* titled 'Conscientious objection is a human right'. Her case, heard in the Sultanahmet law courts in mid-2006, was a debacle because ultranationalists were allowed to demonstrate loudly outside the courtroom throughout the hearing. Critics claim that the fact that security forces did little to quell the protestors makes them complicit. A similar situation occurred at the trial of Elif Şafak, author of the *Bastard of Istanbul* (see p30), who, along with her publisher and Turkish translator, was prosecuted for comments made by Armenian characters in her book. Charges against her were also eventually dropped.

Most disturbing of all was the assassination of Turkish-Armenian journalist and editor Hrant Dink in İstanbul in January 2007. Editor-in-chief of the bilingual Turkish-Armenian newspaper *Agos* and a controversial figure for his outspoken views on what he described as the genocide of Armenians at the hands of Ottoman Turks in 1915, Dink was shot to death by a 17-year-old Turkish nationalist, who had no doubt been motivated by the fact that the outspoken journalist had been charged on three occasions under Article 301.

Verity Campbell & Virginia Maxwell

Fortunately, contemporary Turkey is reclaiming its polyglot heritage as well as taking pride in its own national language and you'll have no trouble at all communicating in English and, to a lesser extent, French, German or Russian when you're here. Snippets of many foreign languages can be heard throughout Old İstanbul (particularly in the Grand Bazaar) and you'll also notice that the city has particular quarters in which dialects are spoken. Two examples are Ladino, a medieval Spanish dialect that is still used by some descendants of the Sephardic community that migrated here during the Spanish Inquisition; and Aramaic, which is still spoken by many members of the city's Assyrian Church (see boxed text, p138).

By learning a few Turkish phrases you'll do your bit to charm the locals; see the Language chapter (p245) for tips.

NEIGHBOURHOODS

top picks

- **Aya Sofya** (p49)
  Justinian's most magnificent achievement never ceases to amaze.
- **Basilica Cistern** (p58)
  The Old City's watery underworld has bucketloads of atmosphere.
- **Topkapı Palace** (p62)
  This seat of the sultans deserves its spot as the city's number-one tourist attraction.
- **İstanbul Archaeology Museums** (p70)
  Home to one of the world's great museum collections.
- **Süleymaniye Camii** (p80)
  Sinan's design for Süleyman the Magnificent lives up to its patron's nickname.
- **Chora Church** (p93)
  Exquisite is the only word to use when describing these Byzantine mosaics and frescoes.
- **İstanbul Modern** (p102)
  There's more to this new art gallery than hype.
- **Dolmabahçe Palace** (p116)
  The best place to overdose on Ottoman ostentation.

NEIGHBOURHOODS

The French writer Pierre Loti said in 1890 that of all the names that could still enchant him, Stamboul remained the most magical. We know exactly how he felt. Ever since 657 BC, when Byzas first sailed up to where the Golden Horn, the Bosphorus and the Sea of Marmara meet, this place has bewitched, bothered and bewildered travellers, leaving an indelible stamp on their memories.

Each of today's older neighbourhoods hold remnants of ancient Byzantium, Roman Constantinople and Ottoman İstanbul, but have also developed their own modern signatures, often influenced by the ethnic or religious groups within their boundaries. By exploring them you'll certainly develop an understanding of the city and its people. You may even, like Loti and so many visitors since, develop a life-long infatuation with their charms.

The most important area for tourists, particularly those who are visiting the city for the first time, is Sultanahmet. This is where the largest concentration of historic sights is, and where the vast majority of the city's mid-range and budget accommodation options is located. Standing in Sultanahmet Meydanı (Sultanahmet Square) and looking one way towards Aya Sofya (p49) and the other towards the Blue Mosque (p54) is an experience that stays with many people for a lifetime.

North of Sultanahmet is Topkapı Palace (p62), for centuries the seat of the Ottoman sultans. This runs down the hill to the transport hub of Eminönü, picturesquely situated at the mouth of the Golden Horn.

West of Sultanahmet is the beguiling Bazaar District, home to the famous Grand Bazaar (p76) and Spice Bazaar (p82), as well as a clutch of the city's most significant Ottoman mosques. Unlike Sultanahmet and the area around Topkapı Palace, this is a neighbourhood that's geared towards the needs of locals rather than tourists – İstanbullus have been shopping, studying and praying in these streets for centuries and show no sign of decamping anywhere in the future.

West of the Bazaar District, over the major artery of Atatürk Bulvarı, are the conservative Western Districts, once home to large Jewish and Greek populations and also the location of a number of historically important mosques. Running from Adnan Menderes Caddesi, which punches through Justinian's historic walls at Topkapı Gate, this neighbourhood runs down to the Golden Horn.

Writing about the Galata Bridge (p74) in the 1870s, Edmondo de Amicis said that though a hundred thousand people crossed it every day, 'not a single idea passes in 10 years'. The difference between the neighbourhoods of the Old City and the European-flavoured neighbourhoods of Beyoğlu, on the other side of the bridge, isn't as stark these days as it was in De Amicis' time, but there is still a decidedly different atmosphere and physical appearance. The bustling but still slightly down-at-heel suburbs of Galata, Karaköy and Tophane are growing more fashionable by the day, and the famous boulevard of İstiklal Caddesi and symbolic heart of Taksim Square are *the* places to come to eat, drink and indulge in the arts.

Down the hill from Taksim Square are the Bosphorus suburbs of Beşiktaş and Ortaköy, full of Ottoman palaces and oh-so-glam restaurants and nightclubs. The sultans' buildings here are reminiscent of Coleridge's 'stately pleasure-domes' and are well worth a visit.

These excesses along the Bosphorus stand in stark contrast to the fascinating neighbourhoods of Üsküdar and Kadıköy across the strait on the Asian side of town. Full of residents shopping in street markets, worshipping in mosques and gossiping on street corners, this is where you'll get a true feel for what it's like to live in this extraordinary megalopolis.

BEŞİKTAŞ & ORTAKÖY (p116)

TAKSİM, HARBİYE & NİŞANTAŞI (p114)

İSTİKLAL & AROUND (p106)

GALATA & TOPHANE (p102)

WESTERN DISTRICTS (p93)

BAZAAR DISTRICT (p76)

TOPKAPI PALACE & AROUND (p62)

SULTANAHMET (p49)

ÜSKÜDAR (p121)

KADIKÖY (p126)

Bosphorus (Boğaziçi)

Golden Horn (Haliç)

SEA OF MARMARA (MARMARA DENİZİ)

0   1 km
0   0.5 miles

Rumi Mehmet Paşa
Ayazma
Salıcak
Gülfem Hatun
İhsaniye
Selman
Hacı Hesna Hatun
Solak Sinan
T Hacı Mehmet
Toygar Hamza
Tabaklar
Hayrettin Cavuş
Selman Ağa
Kefçe Dede
Arakiyeci Hacı Cafer
Aşcıbaşı
Harem
Selimiye
Haydarpaşa
Kadıköy

Gümüşsuyu
Nişantaşı
Elmadağ
Dolapdere
Taksim
Harbiye
Piyalepaşa
Kurtuluş
Halıcıoğlu
Hasköy
Kulaksız
Kasımpaşa
Vişnezade
Beşiktaş
Ortaköy
Kabataş
Fındıklı
Cihangir
Tünel
Tophane
Karaköy
Galatasaray
Tepebaşı
Asmalimescit
Şişhane
Galata
Eminönü

Sütlüce
Eyüp
Nişanca
Topçular
Ayvansaray
Balıkhane
Balat
Fener
Fatih
Zeyrek
Vefa
Unkapanı
Küçükpazar
Süleymaniye
Sururi
Cambaziye
Demirtaş
Sarachane
Aksaray
Nişanca
Kumkapı
Yenikapı
Cankurtaran
Topkapı
Ahırkapı
Sirkeci
Avcı Bey
Draman
Kasım Gösim
Karagümrük
Beyceğiz
Çarşamba
Hızır Cavuş
Edirnekapı
Derviş Ali
Hatice Sultan
Şehremini
Mevlanakapı
Çapa
Fındıkzade
Haseki
Taşkasap
Altımermer
Cerrahpaşa
Samatya
Kocamustafapaşa
Silivrikapı
Belgratkapı

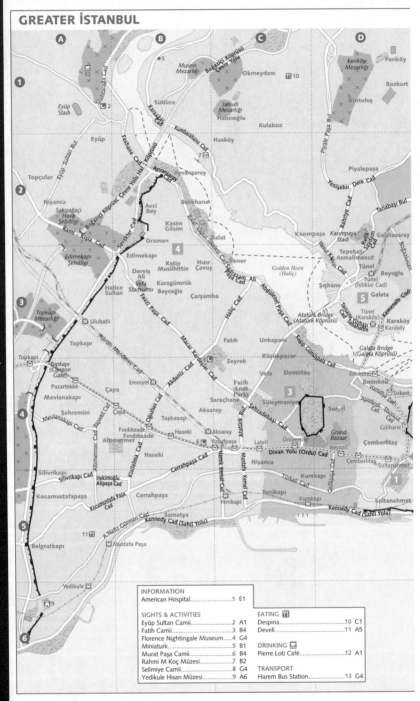

INFORMATION
American Hospital......................1 E1

SIGHTS & ACTIVITIES
Eyüp Sultan Camii......................2 A1
Fatih Camii..............................3 B4
Florence Nightingale Museum.....4 G4
Miniaturk................................5 B1
Murat Paşa Camii......................6 B4
Rahmi M Koç Müzesi..................7 B2
Selimiye Camii..........................8 G4
Yedikule Hisarı Müzesi................9 A6

EATING
Despina..................................10 C1
Develi.....................................11 A5

DRINKING
Pierre Loti Café.........................12 A1

TRANSPORT
Harem Bus Station.....................13 G4

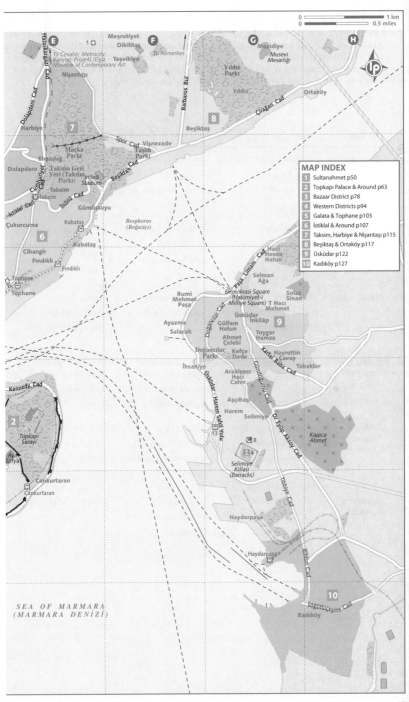

0   1 km
0   0.5 miles

MAP INDEX
1 Sultanahmet p50
2 Topkapı Palace & Around p63
3 Bazaar District p78
4 Western Districts p94
5 Galata & Tophane p103
6 İstiklal & Around p107
7 Taksim, Harbiye & Nişantaşı p115
8 Beşiktaş & Ortaköy p117
9 Üsküdar p122
10 Kadıköy p127

GREATER İSTANBUL

ITINERARY BUILDER

The table below allows you to plan a day's worth of activities in any area of the city. Simply select which area you wish to explore, and then mix and match from the corresponding listings to build your day. The first item in each cell represents a well-known highlight of the area, while the other items are more off-the-beaten-track gems.

Areas	Sightseeing	Eating & Drinking	Shopping
Sultanahmet	Aya Sofya (opposite) Blue Mosque (p54) Basilica Cistern (p58)	Teras Restaurant (p158) Mozaik (p159) Hotel Nomade Terrace Bar (p172)	İznık Classics and Tiles (p135) Cocoon (p135) Mehmet Çetinkaya Gallery (p135)
Topkapı Palace & Around	Topkapı Palace (p62) İstanbul Archaeology Museums (p70) Gülhane Parkı (p72)	Set Üstü Çay Bahçesi (p173) Konyalı (p160) Hafız Mustafa Şekerlemeleri (p137)	Vakko İndirim (p136) Ali Muhiddin Hacı Bekir (p136) Sofa (p136)
Bazaar District	Grand Bazaar (p76) Süleymaniye Camii (p80) Spice Bazaar (p82)	Hamdi et Lokantası (p161) Zinhan Kebap House at Storks (p161) Lale Bahçesi (p174)	Derviş (p138) Şişko Osman (p139) Muhliş Günbattı (p139)
Galata & Tophane	İstanbul Modern (p102) Galata Tower (p104)	Tarıhı Karaköy Balık Lokantası (p164) İstanbul Modern Cafe (p163) Anemon Galata Bar (p175)	İstanbul Modern Gift Shop (p140) Karaköy Güllüglu (p165)
İstiklal & Around	Pera Museum (p110) Galata Mevlevihanesi (p106) Çiçek Pasajı (p110)	Mikla (p165) Hacı Abdullah (p167) Leb-i Derya Richmond (p176) Nu Teras (p176)	art.i.choke (p141) Sedef Çalarkan (p141) Lale Plak (p142)
Üsküdar & Kadıköy	Atik Valide Camii (p121) Çinili Camii (p121) Şemsi Paşa Camii (p123)	Karga Bar (p177) Kanaat Lokantası (p169) Çiya Sofrası (p170)	Greenhouse Bookshop Cafe (p144) Salı Pazarı (p143)

SULTANAHMET

Drinking p172; Eating p158; Shopping p134; Sleeping p198

Many visitors to İstanbul never make it out of Sultanahmet. And while this is a shame, it's hardly surprising. After all, not many cities have such a concentration of major sights, shopping precincts, hotels and eateries within easy walking distance. The heart of both Byzantium and the Ottoman Empire, it's the area where emperors and sultans built grand places of worship and major public buildings; where court officials lived, schemed and planned advantageous marriages; and where conquering armies declared their victories with obligatory rite of drunken pillage and plunder in the Hippodrome. Today, armies of tourists congregate around this ancient arena, their only battles being with overenthusiastic carpet touts and postcard sellers.

Occupying a large slab of the promontory that runs from the eastern side of Eminönü on the Golden Horn (Haliç) to Küçük Aya Sofya on the Sea of Marmara, this neighbourhood is where most of İstanbul's major sights and hotels are located. It incorporates a number of small suburbs, including Binbirdirek, which takes its name from the Byzantine cistern and is home to shops and offices; Cankurtaran, where a good percentage of the city's hotels and hostels are located; Çemberlitaş (the eastern half), a shopping district around busy Divan Yolu; Küçük Aya Sofya, a quiet residential area with some significant historical buildings and a few hotels; and Sultanahmet proper, the area around Aya Sofya and the mosque that gives the neighbourhood its name.

This is historical İstanbul, and not the hip East-meets-West city beloved of the current crop of international fashion and travel magazines. Morals and dress are conservative around here and while there's lots of money being thrown around by tourists, there's no trace of the conspicuous local consumption that is the signature over the Golden Horn and along the Bosphorus. Here, people rise early, go to work, have a home-cooked dinner and then go to bed. If you're looking for nightclubs, bars and theatres, don't look here – cross the Galata Bridge instead. On weekends, the tenor of the neighbourhood changes slightly, with residents of other city suburbs visiting to soak up some culture, eat *köfte* at Tarihi Sultanahmet Köftecisi Selim Usta (p160), wander around the Hippodrome and drink coffee in one of the new chain outlets along Divan Yolu.

The neighbourhood's major thoroughfares are Divan Yolu Caddesi, which runs from Aya Sofya up towards the Grand Bazaar; and Hüdavendigar Caddesi, which runs north from Divan Yolu down towards Eminönü. There is an excellent tram service that starts at Zeytinburnu in the city's west, runs along these two boulevards, makes its way down to Eminönü, crosses the Golden Horn and terminates at Kabataş where it transfers passengers to a funicular travelling up the hill to Taksim Square in Beyoğlu.

AYA SOFYA Map p52

Hagia Sofia; ☎ 212-522 0989; Aya Sofya Square; adult/child under 6 YTL10/free, official guide (45 mins) €25 one person, €30 two people; ⏰ 9am-7.30pm Tue-Sun, upper gallery closes 7pm; ⑨ Sultanahmet

Called Hagia Sofia in Greek, Sancta Sophia in Latin and the Church of the Divine Wisdom in English, İstanbul's most famous monument has a history as long as it is fascinating. Built by Emperor Justinian (r AD 527–65), it was constructed on the site of Byzantium's acropolis, which had also been the site of two earlier Aya Sofyas – the first a basilica with a timber roof completed in 360 by Constantine's son and successor, Constantinius, and burned down in a riot in 404; and the second a building commissioned by Theodosius II in 415 and destroyed in the Nika riots of 532.

Justinian's church, which dwarfed all other buildings in the city, was completed in 537 and reigned as the greatest church in Christendom until the Conquest of Constantinople in 1453, when Mehmet the Conqueror took possession of it for Islam and immediately converted it into a mosque. As significant to Muslims as it is to Christians, it was proclaimed a museum by Atatürk in 1934. Ongoing restoration work (partly Unesco funded) means that the interior is filled with scaffolding, but not even this can detract from the experience of visiting one of the world's truly great buildings.

On entering his great creation for the first time, Justinian exclaimed, 'Glory to God that I have been judged worthy of such a work. Oh Solomon! I have outdone you!' Entering the building today, it is easy to excuse his self-congratulatory tone. The

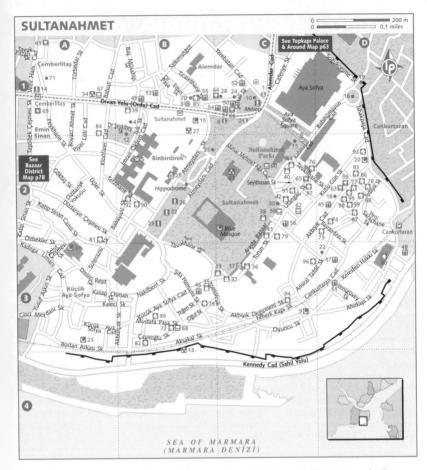

exterior may be somewhat squat and unattractive but the interior, with its magnificent domed ceiling soaring heavenward, is so sublimely beautiful that many seeing it for the first time are quite literally stunned into silence.

The original achievement of Aya Sofya's architects Anthemeus of Tralles and Isidorus of Miletus, who worked without the benefits of today's technology and materials, remains unequalled. The Byzantines gasped in amazement at the sense of air and space in the nave and the 30 million gold mosaic tiles (tesserae) that covered the dome's interior. Most of all, they marvelled at the apparent lack of support for the enormous dome. How was it possible, they asked? In fact, the original dome lasted only two decades before an earthquake

brought it down in 559. It was rebuilt to a slightly less ambitious design, with a smaller base and steeper sides, and the basilica was reopened in 563. Over subsequent centuries it was necessary for succeeding Byzantine emperors and Ottoman sultans to rebuild the dome several times, to add buttresses and other supports and to steady the foundations.

The dome, which is 30m in diameter, is supported by 40 massive ribs constructed of special hollow bricks made in Rhodes from a unique light and porous clay, resting on four huge pillars concealed in the interior walls. The great Ottoman architect Sinan, who spent his entire professional life trying to design a mosque to match the magnificence and beauty of Aya Sofya, used the same trick of concealing pillars

SULTANAHMET

INFORMATION
ATM..............................1 C1
ATMs.............................2 C1
Café Turka Internet Café...........3 A1
PopUp Laundry.....................4 B1
PTT...............................5 B2
PTT Booth.........................6 C2
Tourism Police....................7 C1
Tourist Information Office.........8 C1

SIGHTS & ACTIVITIES   (pp49–61)
Akbıyık Camii.....................9 C3
Basilica Cistern.................10 C1
Baths of Lady Hürrem.............11 C2
Binbirdirek Cistern..............12 B1
Bucoleon Palace..................13 B3
Çemberlitaş......................14 A1
Firuz Ağa Camii..................15 B1
Fountain of Sultan Ahmet III.....16 D1
Great Palace Mosaics Museum..17 C3
Hassle Free Travel Agency........18 D2
Imperial Gate, Topkapı Palace...19 D1
İshak Paşa Camii.................20 D2
Kaiser Wilhelm's Fountain........21 B2
Kirkit Voyage....................22 D3
Küçük Aya Sofya Camii............23 A3
Les Arts Turcs...................24 C1
Museum of Turkish & Islamic
    Arts.........................25 B2
Obelisk of Theodosius............26 B2
Palace of Antiochus..............27 B1
Pride Travel Agency..............28 C1
Rough-Stone Obelisk..............29 B2
Senkron Travel Agency............30 C2
Sokollu Mehmet Paşa Camii........31 A3
Spiral Column....................32 B2
Tomb of Sultan Ahmet I..........33 C2
Tombs............................34 A1

SHOPPING 🛍   (pp131–44)
Cocoon (1&2).....................35 C3
Cocoon 3.........................36 C3

Er & Ne & Met....................37 C3
Galeri Cengiz....................38 C2
Galeri Kayseri...................39 B1
İstanbul Handicrafts
    Market.......................40 C2
İznik Classics & Tiles 1.........41 C2
İznik Classics & Tiles 2.........42 C2
Mehmet Çetinkaya Gallery.........43 B3
Yeşil Ev.........................44 C2

EATING 🍴   (pp145–8, 157–70)
Albura Café & Restaurant.........45 D2
Ayasofya Kebap House.............46 B3
Balıkçı Sabahattin...............47 D3
Cankurtaran Sosyal Tesisleri.....48 D3
Çiğdem Pastenesi.................49 B1
Dubb.............................50 C1
Giritli..........................51 D3
House of Medusa..................52 C1
Karadeniz Aile Pide ve Kebap
    Salonu.......................53 B1
Lale Restaurant
    (Pudding Shop)...............54 C1
Mozaik Restaurant................55 B1
Rami.............................56 C2
Tarihi Sultanahmet Köftecisi Selim
    Usta.........................57 C1
Teras Restaurant.............(see 80)

DRINKING 🍺 🍷   (pp172–3)
Café Meşale......................58 C2
Cheers Bar.......................59 D2
Derviş Aile Çay Bahçesi..........60 C2
Fes Cafe.........................61 A1
Hotel Nomade Terrace Bar......(see 85)
Java Studio......................62 C2
Just Bar.........................63 D2
Şah Pub & Bar....................64 C1
Seven Hills Terrace Bar..........65 C2
Sultan Pub.......................66 C1
Türk Ocağı Kültür Sanat Merkezı
İktisadi İşletmesi Çay Bahçesi..67 A1

Yeni Marmara.....................68 B3
Yeşil Ev Garden Bar/Café.....(see 44)

NIGHTLIFE ⭐   (pp179–84)
Şafak Sinemaları.................69 A1

SPORTS & ACTIVITIES   (pp191–6)
Ambassador Hotel Spa
    Center.......................70 B1
Çemberlitaş Hamamı...............71 A1

SLEEPING 🛏   (pp197–209)
Artefes Hotel....................72 B3
Bahaus Guesthouse................73 D2
Big Apple Hostel.................74 D2
Dersaadet Oteli..................75 B3
Four Seasons Hotel
    İstanbul.....................76 C2
Hanedan Hotel....................77 D2
Hotel Alp Guesthouse.............78 D2
Hotel Ararat.....................79 C2
Hotel Armada.....................80 D3
Hotel Daphne.....................81 A2
Hotel Deniz Konak................82 B3
Hotel Empress Zoe................83 D2
Hotel Halı.......................84 A1
Hotel Nomade.....................85 B1
Hotel Peninsula..................86 D2
Hotel Poem.......................87 D2
Hotel Şebnem.....................88 D2
Hotel Sultan's Inn...............89 B3
Hotel Turkoman...................90 B2
Hotel Uyan İstanbul..............91 C2
İbrahim Paşa Oteli...............92 B2
Mavi Guesthouse..................93 D2
Naz Wooden House.................94 C3
Orient International
    Hostel.......................95 D2
Sarı Konak Oteli.................96 C3
Side Hotel & Pension.............97 C2
Sultan Hostel....................98 D2
Tria Hotel İstanbul..............99 D2

when designing the Süleymaniye Camii (p80) almost 1000 years later. To truly appreciate what a difference the concealment makes, we suggest that you compare Aya Sofya's pillar-free central space with that of the nearby Blue Mosque (p54), which features four huge freestanding pillars. You'll find that Aya Sofya shines in comparison.

In Justinian's time, a street led uphill from the west straight to the main door. Today the ticket kiosk is at the southwest side. Past the security check you'll see the sunken ruins of a Theodosian church (404–15) and the low original steps. Entering through the main entrance, all visitors are immediately struck by the ethereal beauty of the interior – this is in part due to the innumerable windows with their jewel-like stained glass. It is these windows, with the many arcades, that give the building its famous 'transparency'. Making your

way through the outer narthex, you'll walk through the inner narthex and then into the main space. Far ahead of you, in the apse at the other side of the building, is a semidome glowing with a gold mosaic portrait of the Madonna and Child. Above this is another semidome, and above that is the famous, gigantic main dome of the church, which seems to be held up by nothing.

During its almost 1000 years as a church, only imperial processions were permitted to enter through the central, imperial door. You can still notice the depressions in the stone by each door just inside the threshold where imperial guards stood. Also note the matched marble panels in the walls and the breccia (a type of rock made up of angular fragments) columns.

The chandeliers hanging low above the floor are Ottoman additions. Previously, rows of glass oil lamps lined the balustrades

GROUND FLOOR

of the gallery and the walkway at the base of the dome. Imagine them all lit to celebrate some great state occasion, with the smell of incense and the chants of the Orthodox (and later the Latin) liturgy reverberating through the huge interior space.

The Byzantine emperor was crowned while seated in a throne placed within the omphalion, the square of inlaid marble in the main floor. The nearby raised platform was added by Sultan Murat III (r 1574–95), as were the large alabaster urns so that worshippers could perform their ritual ablutions before prayer. During the Ottoman period the *mimber* (pulpit) and the mihrab (prayer niche indicating the direction of Mecca) were also added.

The large 19th-century medallions inscribed with gilt Arabic letters are the work of master calligrapher Mustafa İzzet Efendi, and give the names of God (Allah), Mohammed and the early caliphs Ali and Abu Bakr. Though impressive works of art in their own right, they seem out of place here and unfortunately detract from the purity of the building's interior form.

The curious elevated kiosk screened from public view is the imperial loge *(hünkar*

mahfili). Sultan Abdül Mecit (r 1839–61) had it built in 1848 so he could come, pray and go unseen, preserving the imperial mystique. The ornate library behind the omphalion was built by Sultan Mahmut I in 1739.

In the side aisle to the northeast of the imperial door is the weeping column, with a worn copper facing pierced by a hole. Legend has it that the pillar is that of St Gregory the Miracle Worker and that putting one's finger in the hole can lead to ailments being healed if the finger emerges moist.

Upstairs in the floor of the south gallery, near the Deesis Mosaic, you will see the tomb of Enrico Dandolo (c 1108–1205). Dandolo, who became doge of Venice in 1192, came from the prominent Venetian family that supplied Venice with four doges, numerous admirals and a colonial empire. During the Fourth Crusade (1203–04), he diverted the Crusader armies from their goal of an assault on the infidels to an assault on the friendly but rival Christian city of Constantinople. Aya Sofya was ransacked during the assault, with the altar being destroyed. Venice got the better part of the rich spoils from the sacking of the city, as well as numerous Byzantine territories. Dandolo ruled three-eighths of conquered Constantinople, including Sancta Sophia, until his death in 1205, when he was buried here. Tradition tells us that Dandolo's tomb was broken open after the Conquest of the city in 1453, and his bones thrown to the dogs. Also upstairs (this time in the western gallery) is a large circle of green marble marking the spot where the throne of the empress once stood.

As you exit the building, the fountain (şadırvan) to the right was for ablutions. To your left is the church's baptistry, converted after the Conquest to a tomb for sultans Mustafa and İbrahim (the Crazy). These are not open to the public. Other tombs are clustered behind it, including those of Murat III, Selim 'the Sot' II (designed by Sinan and featuring gorgeous İznik tiles) and Mehmet III. Selim's tomb is particularly poignant as it houses the graves of five of his sons, murdered on the same night in December 1574 to ensure the peaceful succession of the oldest, Murat III. It also houses the graves of 19 of Murat's sons, murdered in January 1595 to ensure Mehmet III's succession. They were the last of the royal princes to be murdered – after this, the younger brothers of succeeding sultans were confined to the kafes (cage) in Topkapı instead. To the southeast of the building a wall hides excavations on a section of the Great Byzantine Palace (p56). To the left of the entrance is a small Ottoman primary school built by Mahmut I in 1740.

The first of Aya Sofya's minarets was added by Mehmet the Conqueror (r 1451–81). Sinan designed the others for sultans Beyazıt II (r 1481–1512) and Selim II (r 1566–74).

BATHS OF LADY HÜRREM Map p50
Haseki Hürrem Hamamı; ☎ 212-638 0035; Aya Sofya Square 4; admission free; ☾ 8.30am-6.30pm Tue-Sun summer, 8.30am-5.30pm Tue-Sun winter; 🚇 Sultanahmet

Traditionally, every mosque had a hamam included in or around its complex of buildings. Aya Sofya was no exception and this elegant symmetrical building, designed by Sinan between 1556 and 1557, was built just across the road from the great mosque by Süleyman in the name of his wife Hürrem Sultan, known to history as Roxelana. The hamam was one of 32 Sinan designed and is widely thought be his best. It operated until 1910 and now functions as a carpet shop (p135) run by the Ministry of Culture rather than a bath. Fortunately, the management of the carpet shop doesn't seem to mind if visitors wander through the building to admire the interior spaces rather than the rugs. At the time of research there were rumours around town that the lease on the building had been sold to a local entrepreneur and that he was planning to re-open the place as a tourist hamam.

Designed as a 'double hamam' with identical baths for men and women, the centre wall dividing the two has now been

SAVING THE SOUL OF SULTANAHMET
Nurdoğan Şengüler is a member of a loose collective of Sultanahmet-based artists, academics, journalists, professional guides and businessmen who are working behind the scenes to preserve the traditional character of this historic suburb. He established a Sultanahmet-based company called Les Arts Turcs (p241) in 1997 that aims to, in his words, 'explore little-travelled routes of communication between cultures' through tours, workshops and other cultural events. Asked if Sultanahmet has changed much over the 10 years that Les Arts Turcs has been operating, Nurdoğan laughs and says 'yes, a lot!'. The challenge, he says, is to ensure that the area isn't totally overrun by tourism-related industries and operators. He believes that retaining the Sultanahmet tradition of being the city's home to artisans is important, and takes heart from the fact that there are still many artists working in the areas around Aya Sofya and Topkapı Palace, including those at Caferağa Medresesi (p73) and Celik Gulersoy's İstanbul Handicrafts Market (p135). Another positive initiative is the establishment of the independent Sultanahmet newspaper, which is published monthly in both Turkish and English and distributed free in shops, hotels and businesses around the suburb. The news isn't all good, though. As Nurdoğan says: 'The danger of the Old City losing its character is getting bigger every day. Individual businesses are being kicked out of the Sultanahmet, Grand Bazaar and Spice Market areas to make way for big tourism outfits and this will cause the area to become one big touristic ghetto.' Asked if local government is doing anything to prevent this, he says that the Eminönü municipality isn't very effective, but that the İstanbul Tourism Studio Workshop established by the mayor of İstanbul, Kadir Topbaş, is making an effort to visit local artists and small businesses and canvas their ideas about the suburb's future.

MOSAICS

Justinian was understandably proud of Aya Sofya's great dome, but he was just as proud of its magnificent mosaic work. Originally, the great dome, the semidomes, the north and south tympana (semicircles) and the vaults of narthex, aisles and galleries were all covered in gold mosaics. Remnants exist and are a highlight of any visit, but one can only imagine what the place must have looked like when the entire interior glittered and gleamed with *tesserae*. Unsurprisingly, when the Turks took Constantinople and converted Hagia Sofya to a mosque, they decided that the mosaics had to go: fortunately they were covered with plaster rather than destroyed, and some were successfully uncovered and restored by Swiss architects Gaspere and Guiseppe Fossati, working for the sultan, from 1847 to 1849. Though once again covered (this time by paint), they were left in good condition for a final unveiling when the mosque was deconsecrated and the museum opened.

From the floor of Aya Sofya, 9th-century mosaic portraits of St Ignatius the Younger (c 800), St John Chrysostom (c 400) and St Ignatius Theodorus of Antioch are visible high up at the base of the northern tympanum (semicircle) beneath the dome. Next to these three, and seen only from the upstairs east gallery, is a portrait of Alexandros. In the apse is a wonderful mosaic of the Madonna and Child; nearby mosaics depict the archangels Gabriel and Michael, though only fragments of Michael remain. Above the imperial door in the inner narthex there is a striking depiction of Christ as Pantocrator (Ruler of All). He holds a book that carries the inscription 'Peace be with you. I am the Light of the World' and to his right an emperor (probably Leo VI) prostrates himself. As you exit the inner narthex and enter the passage to leave the building, make sure you turn and look up above the door to see one of the church's finest late 10th-century mosaics. This shows Constantine the Great, on the right, offering Mary, who holds the Christ Child, the city of Constantinople; Emperor Justinian, on the left is offering her Aya Sofya.

The upstairs galleries house the most impressive of Aya Sofya's mosaics and mustn't be missed. They can be reached via a switchback ramp at the northern end of the inner narthex. The magnificent Deesis Mosaic (The Last Judgement) in the south gallery dates from the early 14th century. Christ is at the centre, with the Virgin Mary on the left, and John the Baptist on the right.

At the eastern (apse) end of the south gallery is the famous mosaic portrait of Empress Zoe (r 1028–50). When this portrait was done she was 50 years old and newly married to the aged Romanus III Argyrus. Upon Romanus' death in 1034, she had his face excised from the mosaic and that of her virile new husband, Michael IV, put in its place. Eight years later, with Michael dead from an illness contracted on campaign, Zoe and her sister Theodora ruled as empresses in their own right, but did it so badly that it was clear she had to marry again. At the age of 64, Zoe wed an eminent senator, Constantine IX Monomachus, whose portrait remains only because he outlived the empress. The inscription reads 'Constantine, by the Divine Christ, Faithful King of the Romans'.

To the right of Zoe and Constantine is another mosaic depicting characters with less saucy histories: in this scene Mary holds the Christ Child, centre, with Emperor John Comnenus II (Johannes the Good) to the left and Empress Eirene, known for her charitable works, to the right. Their son Alexius, who died soon after this portrait was made, is depicted next to Eirene.

breached by a small doorway. Both sides have separate entrances and the three traditional rooms: first the square *camekan* for disrobing (on the men's side, this has a pretty marble fountain and stained-glass windows); then the long *soğukluk* for washing; and finally the octagonal *hararet* for sweating and massage. The most impressive features are the domes, with their star-like apertures. Also of note are the four *eyvan* (niches) and the four semi-private washing rooms in the *hararet*, as well as the *göbektaşı* (hot platform) in the men's bath, which is inlaid with coloured marble. In all, the place gives a good idea of how hamams are set up – perfect for those not convinced that they want to bare all in one of the city's still-functioning establishments.

BLUE MOSQUE Map p50

Sultan Ahmet Camii; ☎ 212-518 1319; Hippodrome; donation requested; ⏰ closed during prayer times; 🚇 Sultanahmet

With this mosque, Sultan Ahmet I (r 1603–17) set out to build a monument that would rival and even surpass the nearby Aya Sofya (p49) in grandeur and beauty. So enthusiastic was the sultan about his grand project that he is said to have worked with the labourers and craftsmen on site, pushing them along and rewarding extra effort. Ahmet did in fact come close to his goal of rivalling Aya Sofya, and in so doing achieved the added benefit of making future generations of hotel owners in Sultanahmet happy – a 'Blue Mosque view' from the roof terrace being the number-one selling point of the fleet of hotels in the area.

The mosque's architect, Mehmet Ağa, who had trained with Sinan, managed to orchestrate the sort of visual wham-bam effect with the mosque's exterior that Aya Sofya achieved with its interior. Its curves are voluptuous, it has more minarets than any other İstanbul mosque (in fact, there was consternation at the time of its construction that the sultan was being irreverent in specifying six minarets – the only equivalent being in Mecca) and the courtyard is the biggest of all the Ottoman mosques. The interior is conceived on a similarly grand scale: the blue tiles that give the building its unofficial name number in the tens of thousands, there are 260 windows and the central prayer space is huge. No wonder its picture graces a million postcards!

In order to fully appreciate the mosque's design you should approach it via the middle of the Hippodrome rather than walking straight from Sultanahmet Park through the crowds. When inside the courtyard, which is the same size as the mosque's interior, you'll be able to appreciate the perfect proportions of the building. Walk towards the mosque through the gate in the peripheral wall, noting on the way the small dome atop the gate: this is the motif Mehmet Ağa uses to lift your eyes to heaven. As you walk through the gate, your eyes follow a flight of stairs up to another gate topped by another dome; through this gate is yet another dome, that of the ablutions fountain in the centre of the mosque courtyard. As you ascend the stairs, semidomes come into view: first the one over the mosque's main door, then the one above it, and another, and another. Finally the main dome crowns the whole, and your attention is drawn to the sides, where forests of smaller domes reinforce the effect, completed by the minarets, which lift your eyes heavenward.

The mosque is such a popular tourist sight that admission is controlled so as to preserve its sacred atmosphere. In the tourist season (May to September), only worshippers are admitted through the main door; tourists must use the north door. Shoes must be taken off and women who haven't brought their own headscarf or are too scantily dressed will be loaned a headscarf and/or robe. There's no charge for this, but donations for the mosque are requested.

Inside, the stained-glass windows and İznik tiles immediately attract attention. Though the windows are replacements, they still create the luminous effects of the originals, which came from Venice. The tiles line the walls, particularly in the gallery (which is not open to the public). There are so many of these tiles that the İznik workshops producing the finest examples could not keep up with demand, and alternative, less skilled, workshops were called in to fill the gap. The mosque's tiles are thus of varying quality.

You can see immediately why the mosque, which was constructed between 1606 and 1616, over 1000 years after Aya Sofya, is not as daring as its predecessor. Four massive 'elephant's feet' pillars hold up the less ambitious dome, a sturdier solution lacking the innovation and grace of the dome in Justinian's cathedral.

The semidomes and the dome are painted in graceful arabesques. Of note in the main space are the imperial loge, covered with marble latticework, which is to the left of the mihrab; the mihrab itself, which features a piece of the sacred Black Stone from the Kaaba in Mecca; and the high, elaborate mahfil (chair) from which the imam gives the sermon on Friday. The beautifully carved white marble mimber with its curtained doorway at floor level features a flight of steps and a small kiosk topped by a spire.

Mosques built by the great and powerful usually included numerous public-service institutions. Clustered around the Blue Mosque were a medrese (theological college); an imaret (soup kitchen) serving the poor; a hamam so that the faithful could bathe on Friday, the holy day; and shops (the Arasta Bazaar), the rent from which supported the upkeep of the mosque.

The türbe (tomb) of the Blue Mosque's great patron, the Tomb of Sultan Ahmet I (donation expected; ☾ 9.30am-4.30pm), is on the north side facing Sultanahmet Park. Ahmet, who had ascended to the imperial throne aged 13, died one year after the mosque was constructed, aged only 27. Buried with Ahmet are his wife, Kösem, who was strangled to death in the Harem, and his sons, Sultan Osman II, Sultan Murat IV and Prince Beyazıt (murdered by Murat). Like the mosque, the türbe features fine İznik tiles.

GREAT PALACE MOSAICS MUSEUM
Map p50

Büyüksaray Mozaik Müzesi; ☎ 212-518 1205; Torun Sokak; admission YTL5; ☾ 9am-4.30pm Tue-Sun; ⊛ Sultanahmet

When archaeologists from the University of Ankara and the University of St Andrews (Scotland) dug at the back of the Blue Mosque in the mid 1950s, they uncovered a stunning mosaic pavement dating from early Byzantine times. Restored from 1983 to 1997, it is now preserved in this museum.

Thought to have been added by Justinian (r 527–565) to the Great Byzantine Palace (below), the pavement is estimated to have measured from 3500 to 4000 sq metres in its original form. The 250 sq metres that is preserved here is the largest discovered remnant – the rest has been destroyed or remains buried underneath the Blue Mosque and surrounding shops and hotels.

The pavement is filled with bucolic imagery as well as intricate hunting and mythological scenes. Note the gorgeous ribbon border with heart-shaped leaves surrounding the mosaic. In the westernmost room is the most colourful and dramatic picture, that of two men in leggings carrying spears and holding off a raging tiger. Also here is an amusing depiction of a donkey kicking its load and rider off its back.

The museum has informative panels documenting the floor's rescue and renovation.

HIPPODROME Map p50
🎦 Sultanahmet

The Hippodrome (Atmeydanı) was the centre of Byzantium's life for 1000 years and of Ottoman life for another 400 years. It was the scene of countless political dramas during the long life of the city. In Byzantine times, the rival chariot teams of 'Greens' and 'Blues' had separate sectarian connections. Support for a team was akin to membership of a political party and a team victory had important effects on

GREAT BYZANTINE PALACE

Constantine the Great built the Great Byzantine Palace soon after he founded Constantinople in AD 324. It was renovated and added to by successive Byzantine leaders. The opulent palace was a series of buildings set in parklands and terraces, stretching from the Hippodrome over to Aya Sofya and down the slope, ending at the sea walls and the Bucoleon Palace (Map p50). The palace was abandoned in the 13th century and its ruins were covered in earth and built upon after the Conquest.

policy. A Byzantine emperor might lose his throne as the result of a post-match riot.

Ottoman sultans also kept an eye on activities in the Hippodrome. If things were going badly in the empire, a surly crowd gathering here could signal the start of a disturbance, then a riot, then a revolution. In 1826, the slaughter of the corrupt janissary corps (the sultan's personal bodyguards) was carried out here by the reformer Sultan Mahmut II. And in 1909 there were riots that caused the downfall of Abdül Hamit II and the repromulgation of the Ottoman constitution.

Though the Hippodrome might be the scene of their downfall, Byzantine emperors and Ottoman sultans outdid one another in beautifying it. Unfortunately, many priceless statues carved by ancient masters have disappeared from their original homes here. Chief among the villains responsible for such thefts were the soldiers of the Fourth Crusade, who invaded Constantinople, a Christian ally city, in 1204. After sacking Aya Sofya, they tore all the bronze plates from the stone obelisk at the Hippodrome's southern end in the mistaken belief that they were gold. The crusaders also stole the famous *quadriga*, or team of four horses cast in bronze, a copy of which now sits atop the main door of the Basilica di San Marco in Venice (the original is inside the basilica).

The level of the Hippodrome rose over the centuries, as successive civilisations piled up their dust and refuse here. A number of its monuments were cleaned out and tidied up by the British troops who occupied the city after the Ottoman defeat in WWI.

Near the northern end of the Hippodrome, the little gazebo in beautiful stonework is actually Kaiser Wilhelm's Fountain. The German emperor paid a state visit to Abdül Hamit II in 1901 and presented this fountain to the sultan and his people as a token of friendship. According to the Ottoman inscription, the fountain was built in the Hejira (Muslim lunar calendar) year of 1316 (AD 1898–99). The monograms in the stonework are those of Abdül Hamit II and Wilhelm II, and represent their political union.

The impressive granite Obelisk of Theodosius was carved in Egypt around 1450 BC. According to the hieroglyphs, it was erected in Heliopolis (now a Cairo suburb) to commemorate the victories of Thut-

The Hippodrome may have been the centre of the city's life in Byzantine and Ottoman times, but this certainly isn't the case these days – that honour is proudly claimed by Taksim Square in Beyoğlu (p111). However, for four weeks of every year the Hippodrome regains its symbolic supremacy in the minds of İstanbullus as the host of the city's most popular Ramazan (aka Ramadan) carnival. Every evening after İftar (the breaking of the fast at sunset) the arena is lined with temporary stalls selling fast foods, toys, dried fruits, CDs and sweets to thousands of revellers. Popular snacks include popcorn, roasted corn, gözleme (Turkish crepes cooked on a griddle with cheese, spinach or potato) or döner kebaps. Children beg their indulgent parents for lokma (a type of fried doughnut in syrup), macun (luridly coloured twisted candy on a stick) or fairy floss (cotton candy), and queues form at temporary cafés brewing delicious közde kahve (slow-cooked Turkish coffee) on charcoal braziers. Coloured lights and decorations are everywhere, music by the latest darlings of the Turkish airwaves blares from speakers, the stall-owners shout buyurun! (an expression meaning welcome) and the crowd is smiling and laughing, relieved to have finally eaten and drunk after a long day of fasting. If you're in town over Ramazan (see p239), don't miss it.

mose III (r 1504–1450 BC). The Byzantine emperor, Theodosius, had it brought from Egypt to Constantinople in AD 390. He then had it erected on a marble pedestal engraved with scenes of himself in the midst of various imperial pastimes. Though Theodosius' self-promoting marble billboards have weathered badly over the centuries, the magnificent obelisk, spaced above the pedestal by four bronze blocks, is as crisply cut and shiny as when it was carved in Upper Egypt some 3500 years ago.

South of the obelisk is a strange column coming up out of a hole in the ground. Known as the Spiral Column, it was once much taller and was topped by three serpents' heads. Originally cast to commemorate a victory of the Hellenic confederation over the Persians, it stood in front of the temple of Apollo at Delphi from 478 BC until Constantine the Great had it brought to his new capital city around AD 330. Though badly bashed up in the Byzantine struggle over the role of images in the church, the serpents' heads survived until the early 18th century. Now all that remains of them is one upper jaw, housed in the İstanbul Archaeology Museums (p70).

All that is known about the Rough-Stone Obelisk at the southern end of the Hippodrome is that it was repaired by Constantine VII Porphyrogenitus (r 913–59), and that its bronze plates were ripped off during the Fourth Crusade.

KÜÇÜK AYA SOFYA CAMİİ Map p50
Little Aya Sofya, SS Sergius & Bacchus Church; ☎ 212-458 0776; Küçük Aya Sofya Caddesi; donation requested; ⬛ Sultanahmet

Justinian and Theodora built this little church sometime between 527 and 536 (just before Justinian built Aya Sofya) and you can still see their monogram worked into some of the frilly white capitals. It was named after the two patron saints of Christians in the Roman army. The building, which has recently been restored, is one of the most beautiful in the city. Its dome is architecturally noteworthy and its plan – an irregular octagon – is quite unusual. Like Aya Sofya (p49), its interior was originally decorated with gold mosaics and featured columns made from fine green and red marble. The mosaics are long gone, but the impressive columns remain. The church was converted into a mosque by the chief white eunuch Hüseyin Ağa around 1500; his tomb is to the north of the building.

The medrese cells, arranged around the mosque's forecourt, are now used by second-hand booksellers and bookbinders. In the leafy forecourt there is a tranquil çay bahçesi (tea garden) where you can relax over a glass of tea.

MUSEUM OF TURKISH & ISLAMIC ARTS Map p50
Türk ve İslam Eserleri Müzesi; ☎ 212-518 1805; Hippodrome 46, Atmeydanı Sokak; admission YTL5; ⏰ 9.30am-4.30pm Tue-Sun; ⬛ Sultanahmet

This impressive museum is housed in the Palace of İbrahim Paşa, built in 1524 on the western side of the Hippodrome.

İbrahim Paşa was Süleyman the Magnificent's close friend and brother-in-law. Captured by Turks as a child in Greece, he had been sold as a slave into the imperial household in İstanbul and worked as a page in Topkapı, where he became friendly with Süleyman, who was the same age. When his friend became sultan, İbrahim was made in turn chief falconer, chief of the royal bedchamber and grand vizier. This palace was bestowed on him by Süleyman the year before he was given the hand of Süleyman's sister, Hadice, in marriage. Alas, the fairy tale was not to last for poor İbrahim. His wealth, power and influence on the monarch became so great that others wishing to influence the sultan became envious, chief among them Süleyman's powerful wife, Haseki Hürrem Sultan (Roxelana). After a rival accused İbrahim of disloyalty, Roxelana convinced her husband that İbrahim was a threat and Süleyman had him strangled in 1536.

The museum's exhibits date from the 8th and 9th centuries up to the 19th century. Highlights include the superb calligraphy exhibits, including writing sets, imperial edicts (fermans) with monograms (tuğras) and illuminated manuscripts. In the largest room (and last room on the 1st floor) have a look at the wooden inlaid Quran stands and chests from the 16th century, as well as the colourful Turkish miniatures. This room also has an extraordinary collection of enormous antique carpets – whatever you do, don't miss them.

The lower floor of the museum houses ethnographic exhibits.

Labels are in Turkish and English. The coffee shop in the courtyard of the museum, which also has tables on the terrace overlooking the Hippodrome, is a welcome refuge from the press of crowds and touts in the area.

SOKOLLU MEHMET PAŞA CAMİİ
Map p50

Şehit Çeşmesi Sokak 20-22, Küçük Aya Sofya; donation requested; ☒ Sultanahmet
Sinan designed this mosque in 1571, at the height of his architectural career. Though named after the grand vizier of the time, it was really sponsored by his wife Esmahan, daughter of Sultan Selim II. Besides its architectural harmony, typical of Sinan's greatest works, the mosque is unusual because the medrese is not a separate building but actually part of the mosque structure, built around the forecourt. If the mosque isn't open, wait for the guardian to appear; he may offer photos for sale and will certainly appreciate a tip.

When you enter, notice the harmonious form, the coloured marble and the spectacular İznik tiles – some of the best ever made. The stained glass is also particularly fine. The mosque contains four fragments from the sacred Black Stone in the Kaaba at Mecca: one above the entrance framed in gold, two in the mimber and one in the mihrab. Interestingly, the marble pillars by the mihrab revolve if the foundations have been disturbed by an earthquake – an ingenious early warning device – though apparently they didn't move during the earthquake of 1999 as one was 'out of order'!

BASILICA CISTERN Map p50
Sunken Cistern, Yerebatan Sarnıçı; ☎ 212-522 1259; www.yerebatansarnici.com; Yerebatan Caddesi 13; admission YTL10; ☒ 9am-6.30pm summer, 9am-5.30pm winter; ☒ Sultanahmet
When those Byzantine emperors built something, they certainly did it properly! This extraordinary subterranean structure, built by Justinian in 532 (perhaps on the site of an earlier cistern), is the largest surviving Byzantine cistern in İstanbul. Now one of the city's most popular tourist attractions, it's a great place to while away 30 minutes or so, especially during summer when its cavernous depths stay wonderfully cool.

The cistern's roof is 65m wide and 143m long, and is supported by 336 columns arranged in 12 rows. It once held 80,000 cubic metres of water, delivered via 20km of aqueducts from a reservoir near the Black Sea.

Constructed using columns, capitals and plinths from ruined buildings, the cistern's symmetry and sheer grandeur of conception are quite extraordinary. Don't miss the two columns in the northwestern corner supported by blocks carved into Medusa

top picks

FOR CHILDREN

- Basilica Cistern (above)
- Gülhane Parkı (p72)
- Askeri Müzesi (p114)
- İstanbul Modern (p102)
- Rahmi M Koç Müzesi (p128)

heads or the column towards the centre featuring a teardrop design – we don't know where these columns originally came from but it's great to speculate.

Walking on the raised wooden platforms, you'll feel the water dripping from the vaulted ceiling and see schools of ghostly carp patrolling the water. Lighting is atmospheric and the small café near the exit is certainly an unusual spot to enjoy a cup of tea.

Like most of the sites in İstanbul, the cistern has an unusual history. Known in Byzantium as the Basilica Cistern because it lay underneath the Stoa Basilica, one of the great squares on the first hill, it was used to store water for the Great Palace and surrounding buildings. Eventually closed, the cistern seems to have been forgotten by the city authorities some time before the Conquest. Enter scholar Petrus Gyllius, who in 1545 was researching Byzantine antiquities in the city and was told by locals that they were able to miraculously obtain water by lowering buckets in their basement floors. Some were even catching fish this way. Intrigued, Gyllius explored the neighbourhood and finally discovered a house through whose basement he accessed the cistern. Even after his discovery, the Ottomans (who referred to the cistern as Yerebatan Saray) didn't treat the underground palace with the respect it deserved – it became a dumping ground for all sorts of junk, as well as corpses. Fortunately, later restorations, most notably in the 18th century and between 1955 and 1960, saw it properly maintained. It was cleaned and renovated in 1985 by the İstanbul Metropolitan Municipality and opened to the public in 1987.

BİNBİRDİREK CISTERN Map p50
Cistern of 1001 Columns, Binbirdirek Sarnıcı; ☎ 212-517 8725; İmran Öktem Sokak 4, Binbirdirek; admission YTL10; 🕙 9am-7pm summer, 9am-6pm winter; 🚊 Sultanahmet
Constantine built Binbirdirek in AD 330. During Ottoman times it was converted into a *khan* for silk manufacturers. Closed for decades, it was restored a few years ago and functions as a café and venue for exhibitions and concerts. Not as impressive as the Basilica Cistern (largely because it has been emptied of its water reserves and has a false floor), the only time this place is really worth a visit is when it hosts concerts –

check the board at its exit for details. The admission price includes one drink.

ÇEMBERLİTAŞ Map p50
🚊 Çemberlitaş
Close to the Çemberlitaş tram stop, in a plaza packed with pigeons, you'll find one of the city's most ancient and revered monuments: a derelict column known as Çemberlitaş (also known as the Hooped, Banded Stone or Burnt Column). Erected by Constantine the Great (r 324–37) to celebrate the dedication of Constantinople as capital of the Roman Empire in 330, the column was placed in what was the grand Forum of Constantine and was topped by a statue of the great emperor himself. The column lost its crowning statue of Constantine in 1106 and was damaged in the 1779 fire that ravaged the nearby Grand Bazaar. At the time of research it in the process of being restored and so was covered in hoardings.

Also in this vicinity is the historic Çemberlitaş Hamam (p193).

SULTANAHMET WALK
Walking Tour
1 Aya Sofya This is the most famous building (p49) in Turkey, and for good reason. Built over a millennium ago by the Emperor Justinian, its design has inspired the world's architects ever since. The soaring dome, gleaming gold mosaics and innumerable stained-glass windows give it an extraordinary sense of space, mystery and majesty.

2 Baths of Lady Hürrem Süleyman the Magnificent built this double hamam (p53) in 1557 and named it for his beloved wife Roxelana. Designed by the Ottoman Empire's most famous architect, Mimar Koca Sinan, it hasn't functioned as bathhouse for a century but its interior spaces are remarkably intact.

3 Arasta Bazaar It's worth strolling along this historic arcade to get a feel for the mercantile history of the neighbourhood. And if you're in the mood for a spot of shopping, there are plenty of possibilities here.

4 Blue Mosque The funkiest mosque (p54) in town, with more minarets and visual pizzazz than any mosque should rightly lay claim to. It takes its name from the tens of thousands of blue tiles adorning its exterior walls, but a visit makes it clear that for Sultan Ahmet, it was all about outward appearances. Still, it makes a nice spot to take a moment's contemplation.

5 Great Palace Mosaics Museum Accessed on the east side of the Arasta Bazaar, the huge mosaic on show at this museum (p55) once graced the floor of Justinian's Great Byzantine Palace. Mosaic images of donkeys, tigers, hunters and landscapes were miraculously preserved under the soil of centuries and are now on show after excavation and restoration work.

6 Küçük Aya Sofya Camii After being listed on the World Monument Fund's register of the 100 most endangered buildings, Little Aya Sofya (p57) has been recently restored and is looking terrific. Justinian and Theodora, who built it between 527–536 BC, would be chuffed if they saw it today.

7 Hippodrome Rival chariot teams raced on this course (p56) in Byzantine times and Emperor Theodosius erected the Egyptian Obelisk of Theodosius that is still here 1600 years later. Fortunately, it's in better con-

WALK FACTS

Start Aya Sofya
End Basilica Cistern
Distance 2.5km
Duration Six hours
Fuel stops Everywhere you look

SULTANAHMET WALK

dition than Constantine the Great's sad-looking Spiral Column, which lost its crown of serpents' heads in the eighteenth century. Check out the German contribution, while you are there.

8 Museum of Turkish & Islamic Arts Once the palace of Süleyman the Magnificent's best friend and grand vizier, this handsome museum (p57) now houses an impressive collection of carpets and calligraphy.

9 Basilica Cistern Investigate the watery depths of this huge Byzantine cistern (p58), which once stored water for the Great Palace. It's got atmosphere in buckets (and water, too), and two Medusa heads.

10 Tea and Nargileh Footsore? You have earned a shady rest-stop, so relax for a bit at Türk Ocağı Kültür ve Sanat Merkezi İktisadi İşletmesi Çay Bahçesi (p173). And if you can say that five times quickly, you'll blend right in…

TOPKAPI PALACE & AROUND

Drinking p173; Eating p160; Shopping p136; Sleeping p203

This is the neighbourhood of the Seraglio, dominated by a huge palace park stretching from Aya Sofya all the way down to Seraglio Point. It's where Mehmet the Conqueror set up house after he barged into Constantinople, and where generations of his descendants lived highly privileged but strangely cloistered lives until they decamped over the water to the European-style Dolmabahçe Palace (p116).

Centred on the magnificent Topkapı Palace, this part of the Old City is the most Ottoman in flavour and character. Here there are rows of Ottoman timber houses built into the palace walls, a Sinan-designed *medrese* (p73) built for a chief black eunuch of the court, an archaeological museum filled with plunder from the countries of the Ottoman Empire and a huge park that was once the private garden of the sultans.

And then there's the pavilioned palace itself. Like the Forbidden City in Beijing or the Alhambra in Granada, this place was a world of its own, with intrigue and excess its major pastimes. As you walk through the First Court of the Palace, you can see grand Byzantine structures such as Aya Sofya and Aya İrini, but as soon as you pass through the Middle Gate and enter the Second Court all traces of that earlier age is gone. Now you're in the sultans' personal domain, with its huge Treasury, magnificent Imperial Council Chamber and exquisite Harem.

After the magnificence of the palace, it can come as a relief to visit a relatively modest, albeit beautiful, structure such as the Caferağa Medresesi (p73) or walk around the tree-filled Gülhane Parkı (p72) and claim a table at its spectacularly sited *çay bahçesi* for a restorative glass of tea. Then its back to Ottoman overkill, passing by the rococo doorway known as the Sublime Porte en route to one of Turkey's best museums, the İstanbul Archaeology Museums (p70).

This hasn't been a residential area since the sultans moved out. There's a small enclave of hotels and offices across Alemdar Caddesi, and a busy commercial precinct around Sirkeci Railway Station (p73) down on the shores of the Golden Horn. The tram between Zeytinburnu and Kabataş stops at Gülhane, which is convenient for all of the sights here.

Midway between Topkapı Palace and the Grand Bazaar is the suburb of Cağaloğlu. The major street here, Nuruosmaniye Caddesi, is home to upmarket jewellery shops and an ever-increasing number of Western coffee chain franchises. The tables at these cafés are invariably claimed by the new breed of Old City merchant, businessmen and women with laptops and mobile phone at the ready, who come here to swap news, do deals and drink horrible concoctions such as caramel latte.

The city's major transport hub is at Eminönü, at the mouth of the Golden Horn. Bosphorus and Marmara ferries dock here, Galata Bridge traffic from Beyoğlu passes through, buses leave Rüstempaşa Bus Station next to the water for all parts of the city, and the tram passes through on its way between Zeytinburnu and Kabataş. If you want to observe the city's population in all of its glorious diversity, this is the place to do it.

TOPKAPI PALACE Map p64

Topkapı Sarayı; ☎ 212-512 0480; Soğukçeşme Sokak, Topkapı; admission YTL10; ⏰ 9am-7pm Wed-Mon; ⓖ Gülhane

Home to Selim the Sot, who drowned in the bath after drinking too much champagne; İbrahim the Mad, who lost his reason after being locked up for four years in the infamous palace *kafes* (cages); and Roxelana, beautiful and malevolent consort of Süleyman the Magnificent, Topkapı would have to be the subject of more colourful stories than most of the world's museums put together. No wonder it's been the subject of an award-winning feature film, an opera (Mozart's *The Abduction*

from the Seraglio) and a blockbuster social history (John Freely's wonderful *Inside the Seraglio*). Make sure you dedicate at least half a day to exploring, because tourist attractions rarely come any better than this.

Mehmet the Conqueror built the first stage of the palace shortly after the Conquest in 1453, and lived here until his death in 1481. Subsequent sultans lived in this rarefied environment until the 19th century, when they moved to ostentatious European-style palaces such as Dolmabahçe (p116), Çırağan (p119) and Yıldız (p119) that they built on the shores of the Bosphorus. Mahmut II (r 1808–39) was the last sultan to live in Topkapı.

TOPKAPI PALACE & AROUND

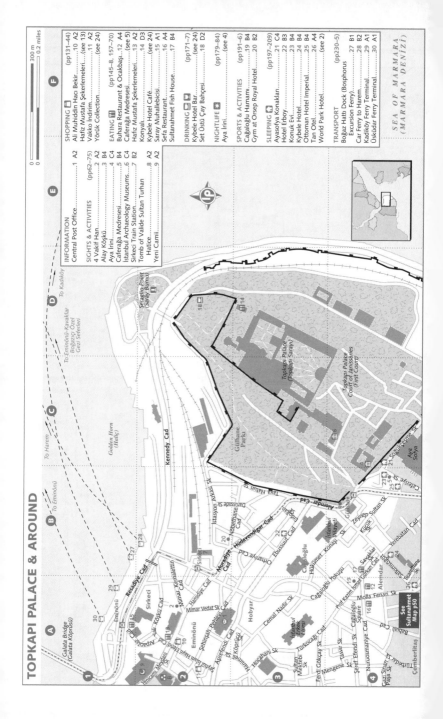

INFORMATION
Central Post Office.................................1 A2

SIGHTS & ACTIVITIES   (pp62–75)
4 Vakıf Han..2 A2
Alay Köşkü...3 B4
Aya İrini...4 C4
Caferağa Medresesi.................................5 B4
İstanbul Archaeology Museum...............6 C4
Sirkeci Train Station................................7 B2
Tomb of Valide Sultan Turhan
Hatice...8 A2
Yeni Camii...9 A2

SHOPPING   (pp131–44)
Ali Muhiddin Hacı Bekir........................10 A2
Hafız Mustafa Şekerlemeleri..............(see 13)
Vakko Indirim..11 A2
Yörük Collection...............................(see 24)

EATING   (pp145–8, 157–70)
Buhara Restaurant & Ocakbaşı...........12 A4
Caferağa Medresesi...........................(see 5)
Hafız Mustafa Şekerlemeleri.................13 A2
Konyalı..14 D3
Kybele Hotel Café.............................(see 24)
Saray Muhallebicisi..............................15 A1
Sefa Restaurant....................................16 A4
Sultanahmet Fish House........................17 B4

DRINKING   (pp171–7)
Kybele Hotel Bar..............................(see 24)
Set Üstü Çay Bahçesi............................18 D2

NIGHTLIFE   (pp179–84)
Aya İrini...(see 4)

SPORTS & ACTIVITIES   (pp191–6)
Çağaloğlu Hamamı.................................19 B4
Gym at Orsep Royal Hotel....................20 B2

SLEEPING   (pp197–209)
Ayasofya Konakları................................21 C4
Hotel Erboy...22 B3
Konuk Evi..23 B4
Kybele Hotel..24 B4
Ottoman Hotel Imperial.........................25 B4
Tan Otel..26 A4
World Park Hotel...............................(see 2)

TRANSPORT   (pp230–5)
Boğaz Hatlı Dock (Bosphorus
Excursion Ferry).....................................27 B1
Car Ferry to Harem................................28 B2
Kadıköy Ferry Terminal..........................29 A1
Üsküdar Ferry Terminal.........................30 A1

SEA OF MARMARA
(MARMARA DENİZİ)

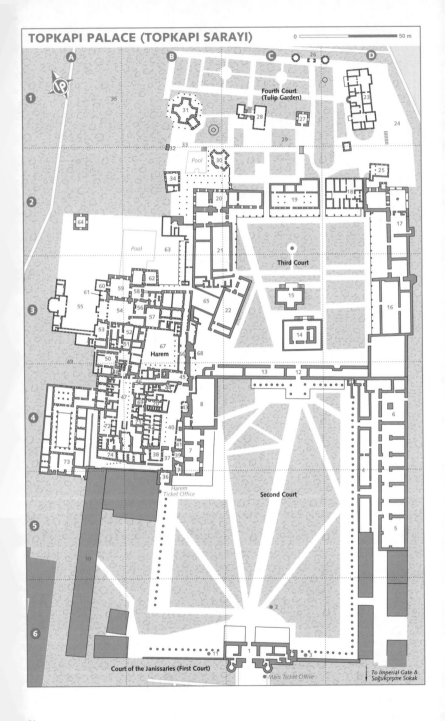

TOPKAPI PALACE (TOPKAPI SARAYI)

0 _____ 50 m

Fourth Court
(Tulip Garden)

Pool

Third Court

Pool

Harem

Second Court

Harem
Ticket Office

Court of the Janissaries (First Court)

Main Ticket Office

To Imperial Gate &
Soğukçeşme Sokak

SECOND COURT		
Middle Gate	1	C6
Audio Tour Booth	2	C6
Imperial Carriages	3	C6
Palace Kitchens	4	D5
Chinese & Japanese		
Porcelain	5	D5
Helvahane	6	D4
Imperial Council Chamber	7	B4
Inner Treasury	8	B4
Kiosk	9	B4
Imperial Stables	10	A5
Book & Gift Shop	11	B6

THIRD COURT		
Gate of Felicity	12	C4
White Eunuchs' Quarters	13	C4
Audience Chamber	14	C3
Library of Ahmet III	15	C3
Dormitory of the Expeditionary Force		
(Costumes)	16	D3
Imperial Treasury	17	D2
Museum Directorate	18	D2
Treasury Dormitory	19	C2
Sacred Safekeeping Rooms	20	B2
Quarters of Pages in Charge of the		
Sacred Safekeeping Rooms		
(Paintings & Calligraphy)	21	B2
Mosque of the Eunuchs &		
Library	22	C3

FOURTH COURT		
Mecidiye Köşkü	23	D1
Konyalı Restaurant	(see 23)	
Cafe Terraces	24	D1
Sofa or Terrace Mosque	25	D2
Gate of the Privy Gardens	26	C1
Chief Physician's Room	27	C1
Kiosk of Mustafa Pasha	28	C1
Tulip Garden	29	C1
Revan Kiosk	30	B2
Baghdad Kiosk	31	B1
İftariye Baldachin	32	B2
Marble Terrace & Pool	33	B1
Circumcision Room	34	B2
Lower Gardens of the Imperial Terrace	35	A1

HAREM		
Carriage Gate	36	B5
Dome with Cupboards	(see 36)	
Hall with Şadırvan	37	B4
Black Eunuchs' Mosque	38	B4
Tower of Justice	39	B4
Courtyard of the Black Eunuchs	40	B4
Harem Eunuchs' Mosque	41	B4
Black Eunuchs' Dormitories	42	B4
Harem Chamberlain's Room	43	B4
Chief Black Eunuch's Room	44	B4
Main Gate	45	B4
Second Guard Room	(see 45)	
Concubines' Corridor	46	B4

Concubines' & Consorts'		
Courtyard	47	A4
Sultan Ahmet's Kiosk	48	A4
Harem Garden	49	A3
Valide Sultan's Quarters	50	A3
Sultan's Hamam	51	B3
Valide Sultan's Hamam	52	B3
Chamber of Abdül Hamit I	53	A3
Imperial Hall	54	A3
Terrace of Osman III	55	A3
Room with Hearth	56	B3
Room with Fountain	(see 56)	
Consultation Place of the Genies	57	B3
Beautifully Tiled Antechamber	58	B3
Privy Chamber of Murat III	59	A3
Library of Ahmet I	60	A3
Dining Room of Ahmet III	61	A3
Twin Kiosk	62	B3
Courtyard of the Favourites	63	B2
Private Prison	64	A2
Harem Mosque	65	B3
Golden Road	66	B3
Courtyard of the Valide Sultan	67	B3
Birdcage Gate	68	B3
Harem Kitchen	69	B4
Imperial Princes' School	70	B4
Women's Hamam	71	B4
Women's Dormitory	72	A4
Harem Hospital	73	A4
Laundry Room	74	A4

Buy your tickets to the Palace at the main ticket office just outside the gate to the Second Court. Tickets to the Harem (see p68) are available at the ticket box outside the Harem itself. Guides to the palace congregate next to the main ticket office. A one-hour tour cost €10 per person for large-ish groups, you need to negotiate if you're in a small group or by yourself. Alternatively, an audio guide in English, French, Italian, Spanish or German will cost you YTL5. These are available at the audio booth just inside the turnstile entrance to the Second Court. Note that the palace is undergoing a prolonged program of conservation works and its buildings are being closed to the public in turn while they are being restored. A board listing which buildings are currently closed to the public is to the left of the ticket office.

Before you enter the Imperial Gate (Bab-ı Hümayun; Map p50) of Topkapı, take a look at the ornate structure in the cobbled square near the gate. This is the Fountain of Sultan Ahmet III, built in 1728 by the sultan who so favoured tulips. It replaced a Byzantine fountain at the same spring. Typical of architecture during the Tulip Period, it features delicate Turkish rococo decorations (note the floral carvings).

As you pass through the Imperial Gate, you enter the First Court, known as the Court of the Janissaries, also known as the Parade Court. On your left is Aya İrini, also known as Hagia Eirene or the Church of the Divine Peace. There was a Christian church here from earliest times and, before that, a pagan temple. The early church was replaced by the present one, commissioned by Justinian in the 540s. It is almost exactly as old as its close neighbour, Aya Sofya. When Mehmet the Conqueror began building his palace, the church was within the grounds and was most fortunately retained. It was used as an arsenal for centuries, then as an artillery museum and now occasionally as a concert hall (especially during the International İstanbul Music Festival, see p16). Its serenely beautiful interior and superb acoustics mean that tickets to concerts here are usually the most sought-after in town. If you're fortunate enough to be here during the festival, think about visiting the temporary box office, located outside Aya İrini, to see if any tickets are available.

Janissaries, merchants and tradespeople could circulate as they wished in the Court of the Janissaries, but the Second Court was restricted. The same is true today, as you must have a ticket to the palace to enter the Second Court. Just past the ticket windows is a little fountain where the imperial executioner used to wash the tools of his trade after decapitating a noble or rebel who had displeased the sultan. The head of the unfortunate victim was put on a pike and exhibited above the gate you are about to enter.

The Middle Gate (Ortakapı or Bab-üs Selâm) led to the palace's Second Court, used for the business of running the empire. Only the sultan and the valide sultan (queen mother) were allowed through the Middle Gate on horseback. Everyone else, including the grand vizier, had to dismount. The gate was constructed by Süleyman the Magnificent in 1524, utilising architects and workers he had brought back from his conquest of Hungary.

To the right after you enter are models and a map of the palace. Beyond them, in a nearby building, you'll find imperial carriages made in Paris, Turin and Vienna for the sultan and his family.

The Second Court has a beautiful, park-like setting. Topkapı is not based on a typical European palace plan – one large building with outlying gardens – but is a series of pavilions, kitchens, barracks, audience chambers, kiosks and sleeping quarters built around a central enclosure.

The great Palace Kitchens, on your right, hold a small portion of Topkapı's vast collection of Chinese celadon porcelain, valued by the sultans for its beauty but also because it was reputed to change colour if touched by poisoned food. In a building close by are the collections of European, Russian and Ottoman porcelain, silverware and glassware. Some of the huge pots and pans that were used in the palace's heyday are exhibited in the last of the kitchens, the Helvahane, in which all the palace sweets were made.

On the left (west) side of the Second Court is the ornate Imperial Council Chamber, also called the Divan Salonu. It's beneath the squarish Tower of Justice, the palace's highest point. The Imperial Divan (council) met in the Imperial Council Chamber to discuss matters of state while the sultan eavesdropped through a grille high on the wall. During the great days of the empire, foreign ambassadors were received on days when the janissaries were to get their pay. Huge sacks of silver coins were brought to the Imperial Council Chamber. High-court officers would dispense the coins to long lines of the tough, impeccably costumed and faultlessly disciplined troops as the ambassadors looked on in admiration.

North of the Imperial Council Chamber is the Inner Treasury, which today exhibits Ottoman and European armour.

The entrance to the palace's most famous sight, the Harem (p68), is beneath the Tower of Justice (Adalet Kulesi) on the left-hand side of the Second Court. The tower is not open to the public.

If you enter the Third Court after visiting the Harem (and thus by the back door), you should head for the main gate into the court and enter again to truly appreciate the grandeur of the approach to the heart of the palace. This main gate, known as the Gate of Felicity or Gate of the White Eunuchs, was the entrance into the sultan's private domain. As is common with oriental potentates, the sultan preserved the imperial mystique by appearing in public very seldom. The Third Court was staffed and guarded by white eunuchs, who allowed only a few very important people in. As you enter the Third Court, imagine it alive with the movements of imperial pages and white eunuchs scurrying here and there in their palace costumes. Every now and then the chief white eunuch or the chief black eunuch would appear, and all would bow. If the sultan walked across the courtyard, all activity stopped until the event was over.

An exception to the imperial seclusion was the ceremony celebrating a new sultan's accession to the throne. After girding the Sword of Osman, which symbolised imperial power, the new monarch would sit enthroned before the Gate of Felicity and receive the obeisance, allegiance and congratulations of the empire's high and mighty.

Before the annual military campaigns in summertime, the sultan would also appear before this gate bearing the standard of the Prophet Mohammed to inspire his generals to go out and conquer all for Islam.

Inside the Gate of Felicity is the Audience Chamber, constructed in the 16th century but refurbished in the 18th century. Important officials and foreign ambassadors were brought to this little kiosk to conduct the high business of state. An ambassador, frisked for weapons and held on each arm by a white eunuch, would approach the sultan. At the proper moment, he knelt and kowtowed; if he didn't, the eunuchs would urge him ever so forcefully to do so.

The sultan, seated on the divans whose cushions are embroidered with over 15,000 seed pearls, inspected the ambassador's gifts and offerings as they were passed through the small doorway on the left. Even if the sultan and the ambassador could converse in the same language (sultans in the later years knew French and ambassadors often learned Turkish), all conversation was with the grand vizier. The sultan would not deign to speak to a foreigner and only the very highest Ottoman officers were allowed to address the monarch directly.

Right behind the Audience Chamber is the pretty Library of Ahmet III, built in 1719 by Sultan Ahmet III. Light-filled, it has comfortable reading areas and stunning inlaid woodwork.

To the right of the Audience Chamber (ie on the opposite side of the Harem exit) are the rooms of the Dormitory of the Expeditionary Force, which now house the rich collections of imperial robes, kaftans and uniforms worked in silver and gold thread. Also here is a fascinating collection of talismanic shirts, which were believed to protect the wearer from enemies and misfortunes of all kinds. Textile design reached its highest point during the reign of Süleyman the Magnificent, when the imperial workshops produced cloth of exquisite design and work. Check out the absolutely gorgeous silk kaftan of Sultan Süleyman II with its appliquéd tulip design.

Next to the Dormitory of the Expeditionary Force is the Imperial Treasury, which features an incredible collection of precious objects made from or decorated with gold, silver, rubies, emeralds, jade, pearls and diamonds. The building itself was constructed by Mehmet the Conqueror in 1460 and has always been used to store works of art and treasure. In the first room, look for the jewel-encrusted sword of Süleyman the Magnificent and the Throne of Ahmed I, inlaid with mother-of-pearl and designed by Mehmet Ağa, architect of the Blue Mosque. In the second room, the tiny Indian figures, mainly made from seed pearls, are well worth seeking out, as are the bizarre and vaguely sinister relics of the Arm and Skull of St John the Baptist, which are cased in jewels. Both had originally been in the possession of the Byzantines and fell into Ottoman hands after the Conquest.

After passing through the third room and having a gawk at the enormous gold and diamond candlesticks, each weighing 48kg, you come to a fourth room and the Treasury's most famous exhibit: the Topkapı Dagger. The object of the criminal quest in the 1964 movie Topkapi, it features three enormous emeralds on the hilt and a watch set into the pommel. Also here is the Kaşıkćı (Spoonmaker's) Diamond, a teardrop-shaped

86-carat rock surrounded by dozens of smaller stones. First worn by Mehmet IV at his accession to the throne in 1648, it's the world's fifth-largest diamond. It's called the Spoonmaker's Diamond because it was originally found at a rubbish dump in Eğrıkapı and purchased by a street peddler for three spoons.

Opposite the Treasury on the other side of the Third Court, there's another set of wonders, the holy relics in the Suite of the Felicitous Cloak, nowadays called the Sacred Safekeeping Rooms. These rooms, sumptuously decorated with İznik faïence, constitute a holy of holies within the palace. Only the chosen could enter the Third Court, but entry into these special rooms was for the chosen of the chosen, and even then only on ceremonial occasions. During the empire, this suite of rooms was opened only once a year so that the imperial family could pay homage to the memory of the Prophet on the 15th day of the holy month of Ramazan. Even though anyone, prince or commoner, faithful or infidel, can enter the rooms now, you should respect the sacred atmosphere by observing decorous behaviour, as this is still a place of pilgrimage for Muslims.

In the east entry room, notice the carved door from the Kaaba in Mecca and, hanging from the ceiling, gilded rain gutters from the same place.

To the right (north), a room contains a hair of Prophet Mohammed's beard, his footprint in clay, his sword, tooth and more. There is a glass booth here from which a seated imam chants passages from the Quran. The felicitous cloak itself resides in a golden casket in a small adjoining room along with the battle standard.

Also in the Third Court are the Quarters of Pages in Charge of the Sacred Safekeeping Rooms, where the palace school for pages and janissaries was located. These days the building features exhibits of Turkish miniature paintings, calligraphy and portraits of the sultans. Notice the graceful, elaborate tuğra (monogram) of the sultans. The tuğra, placed at the top of any imperial proclamation, contains elaborate calligraphic rendering of the names of the sultan and his father, eg 'Abdül Hamit Khan, son of Abdül Mecit Khan, Ever Victorious'.

Other buildings in the Third Court include the Mosque of the Eunuchs and a small library.

Pleasure pavilions occupy the northeastern corner of the palace, sometimes called the Tulip Gardens or Fourth Court. A late addition to Topkapı, the Mecidiye Köşkü, was built by Abdül Mecit (r 1839–61) according to 19th-century European models. Beneath this is the Konyalı restaurant (p160).

West of the Mecidiye Köşkü is the sultan's Chief Physician's Room. Interestingly, the chief physician was always one of the sultan's Jewish subjects. Nearby, you'll see the Kiosk of Mustafa Pasha, sometimes called the Sofa Köşkü. Outside the kiosk, during the reign of Ahmet III, the Tulip Garden was filled with the latest varieties of the flower. Little lamps would be set out among the tulips at night.

Up the stairs at the end of the Tulip Garden are two of the most enchanting buildings in the palace, joined by a marble terrace with a beautiful pool. Murat IV (r 1623–40) built the Revan Kiosk in 1636 after reclaiming the city of Yerevan (now in Armenia) from Persia. In 1639 he constructed the Baghdad Kiosk, one of the last examples of classical palace architecture, to commemorate his victory over that city. Notice the superb İznik tiles, the mother-of-pearl and tortoiseshell inlay, and the woodwork.

Jutting out from the terrace is the golden roof of the İftariye Baldachin, the most popular happy-snap spot in the palace grounds. İbrahim the Mad built this small structure in 1640 as a picturesque place to break the fast of Ramazan.

On the west end of the terrace is the Circumcision Room (Sünnet Odası), used for the ritual that admits Muslim boys to manhood. Built by İbrahim in 1641, the outer walls of the chamber are graced by particularly beautiful tile panels.

TOPKAPI HAREM Map p64
Topkapı Palace; admission YTL10; ✆ 10.15am-7pm Wed-Mon

If you decide to tour the Harem at Topkapı Palace (p62) – and we highly recommend you do – you'll need to buy a dedicated ticket from the ticket office outside the Harem's entrance. The fact that there is an extra entry charge means that many stingy tour companies neglect to bring their customers through here – dreadful for people on tours but great for the rest of us, because as a result it has become one of the least crowded areas of the palace. It's a welcome relief after the experience

of shuffling through the horrendously crowded Treasury, for instance.

As popular belief would have it, the Harem was a place where the sultan could engage in debauchery at will (and Murat III did, after all, have 112 children!). In more prosaic reality, these were the imperial family quarters, and every detail of Harem life was governed by tradition, obligation and ceremony. The word harem literally means 'private'.

Every traditional Muslim household had two distinct parts: the *selamlık* (greeting room) where the master greeted friends, business associates and tradespeople; and the harem (private apartments), reserved for himself and his family. The Harem, then, was something akin to the private apartments in Buckingham Palace or the White House.

The women of the Harem had to be foreigners, as Islam forbade enslaving Muslims. Girls were bought as slaves (often having been sold by their parents at a good price) or were received as gifts from nobles and potentates. A favourite source of girls was Cssia, north of the Caucasus Mountains in Russia, as Cssian women were noted for their beauty.

Upon entering the Harem, the girls would be schooled in Islam and Turkish culture and language, as well as the arts of make-up, dress, comportment, music, reading, writing, embroidery and dancing. They then entered a meritocracy, first as ladies-in-waiting to the sultan's concubines and children, then to the sultan's mother and finally, if they were the best, to the sultan himself.

Ruling the Harem was the *valide sultan*, the mother of the reigning sultan. She often owned large landed estates in her own name and controlled them through black eunuch servants. Able to give orders directly to the grand vizier, her influence on the sultan, on the selection of his wives and concubines, and on matters of state was often profound.

The sultan was allowed by Islamic law to have four legitimate wives, who received the title of *kadın* (wife). If a wife bore him a son she was called *haseki sultan; haseki kadın* if it was a daughter. The Ottoman dynasty did not observe primogeniture (the right of the first-born son to the throne), so in principle the throne was available to any imperial son. Each lady of the Harem contrived mightily to have her son proclaimed heir to the throne, to thus assure her own role as the new *valide sultan*.

As for concubines, Islam permits as many as a man can support in proper style. The Ottoman sultans had the means to support many, sometimes up to 300, though they were not all in the Harem at the same time. The domestic thrills of the sultans were usually less spectacular, however. Mehmet the Conqueror, builder of Topkapı, was the last sultan to have four official wives. After him, sultans did not officially marry, but instead kept four chosen concubines without the associated legal encumbrances, thereby saving themselves the embarrassments and inconveniences suffered by another famous Renaissance monarch, King Henry VIII. The exception to this rule was Süleyman the Magnificent (r 1520–66), who famously married his favourite concubine, Roxelana.

The Harem was much like a village with all the necessary services. About 400 or 500 people lived in this section of the palace at any one time. Not many of the ladies stayed in the Harem all their lives. The sultan might grant them their freedom, after which they would often marry powerful men who wanted the company of these well-educated women, not to mention their connections with the palace. And the relationship was twofold: the sultan was also happy to have the women, educated to be loyal, spread throughout the empire to help keep tabs on political affairs via their husbands.

The chief black eunuch, the sultan's personal representative in administration of the Harem and other important affairs of state, was the third-most powerful official in the empire, after the grand vizier and the supreme Islamic judge.

The earliest of the 300-odd rooms in the Harem were constructed during the reign of Murat III (r 1574–95). In 1665 a disastrous fire destroyed much of the complex, which was rebuilt by Mehmet IV and later sultans.

Although the Harem is built into a hillside and has six levels, you'll only be able to visit one of these. Fortunately, the most important rooms in the complex are here. Interpretive panels in Turkish and English have been placed throughout the building.

You enter the Harem by the Carriage Gate, through which Harem ladies would enter in their carriages. Inside the gate is the Dome with Cupboards. Beyond it is the Hall with Fountain (Hall with Şadırvan), a room decorated with fine Kütahya tiles from the 17th century. This is where the Harem's eunuch guards were stationed; the fountain that gave it its name is now in the Pool of the Privy Chamber of Murad III. To the left is a doorway to the Black Eunuchs' Mosque; on the right is the doorway to the Tower of Justice, which rises above the Imperial Council Chamber. Neither is open to the public.

Beyond the Hall with Fountain is the narrow Courtyard of the Black Eunuchs (Harem Ağaları Taşlığı), also decorated in Kütahya tiles. Behind the marble colonnade on the left are the Black Eunuchs' Dormitories. In the early days white eunuchs were used, but black eunuchs sent as presents by the Ottoman governor of Egypt later took control. As many as 200 lived here, guarding the doors and waiting on the women of the Harem.

Near the far end of the courtyard on the left, a staircase leads up to the rooms in which imperial princes were given their primary schooling. These are not open to the public. On the right is the Chief Black Eunuch's Room.

At the far end of the courtyard, safely protected by the eunuchs, is the Main Gate (Cümle Kapısı) into the Harem proper, as well as a guard room featuring two gigantic gilded mirrors dating from the 18th century. From this, the Passage of Concubines (Cariye Koridoru) on the left leads to the Court of the Concubines and the Sultan's Consorts Courtyard (Cariyeler ve Kadınefendiler Taşlığı). This is surrounded by baths, a laundry fountain, a laundry, dormitories and the apartments of the Sultan's chief consorts.

Next you'll go through the pretty Sultan Ahmet's Kiosk, with its tiled chimney, and into the Apartments of the Valide Sultan (Valide Sultan Dairesi), the centre of power in the Harem. These rooms include a large salon, a small bedroom, a room for prayer and other small chambers. From these ornate rooms the *valide sultan* oversaw and controlled her huge 'family'. After his accession to the throne, a new sultan came here to receive the allegiance and congratulations of the people of the Harem. The later rococo mezzanine was added by the mother of Murat III in the 1580s. Of particular note in these quarters are the charming small hamam designed by Sinan and the lovely 19th-century murals featuring panoramic views of İstanbul.

LIFE IN THE CAGE

As children, imperial princes were brought up in the Harem, where they were taught and cared for by its women and servants.

In the early centuries of the empire, Ottoman princes were schooled as youths in combat and statecraft by direct experience. They practised soldiering, fought in battles and were given provinces to administer. But as the Ottoman dynasty did not observe primogeniture (succession of the firstborn), the death of the sultan regularly resulted in a fratricidal bloodbath as his sons battled it out among themselves for the throne. In the case of Beyazıt II (r 1481–1512), his sons began the battles even before the sultan's death, realising that to lose the battle for succession meant their own death. The victorious son, Selim I (r 1512–20), not only murdered his brothers but even forced Sultan Beyazıt to abdicate and may even have had him murdered as he went into retirement.

Fratricide was not practised by Ahmet I (r 1603–17), who could not bring himself to murder his mad brother Mustafa. Instead, he kept him imprisoned in the Harem, beginning the tradition of cage life (kafes hayatı). This house arrest, adopted in place of fratricide by later sultans, meant that princes were prey to the intrigues of the women and eunuchs, kept ignorant of war and statecraft, and thus usually rendered unfit to rule if and when the occasion arose. Luckily for the empire in this latter period, there were able grand viziers.

In later centuries the dynasty adopted the practice of having the eldest male in the direct line assume the throne.

As he walked these corridors, the sultan wore slippers with silver soles. As no woman was allowed to show herself to the sultan without specific orders, the clatter of the silver soles warned residents of the sultan's approach, allowing them to disappear from his sight. This rule no doubt solidified the *valide sultan*'s control, as *she* got to choose the most beautiful, talented and intelligent of the Harem girls for her son.

The tour passes through the private hamams and toilets of the *valide sultan* to the Imperial Hall (Hünkar Fofrası), decorated in Delft tiles. This grand room is the largest in the Harem and was where the sultan and his ladies gathered for entertainment, often with musicians in the balcony. Designed perhaps by Sinan during the reign of Murat III (r 1574–95), it was redecorated in baroque style by Osman III (r 1754–57).

The tour then enters the Privy Chamber of Murat III (1579), one of the most sumptuous rooms in the palace. Dating from 1578, virtually all of the decoration is original. It is thought to be the work of Sinan. Besides the gorgeous İznik tiles and a copper fireplace, there is a three-tiered marble fountain to give the sound of cascading water and, perhaps not coincidentally, to make it difficult to eavesdrop on the sultan's conversations. The gilded canopied seating areas are later 18th-century additions.

Northeast (to the right) of the Privy Chamber of Murat III are two of the most beautiful rooms in the Harem – the Twin Kiosk/Apartments of the Crown Prince (Çifte Kasırlar/Veliahd Dairesi). These two rooms date from around 1600; note the painted canvas dome in the first room and the fine İznik tile panels above the fireplace in the second. The fabulous stained glass is also noteworthy.

North and east of the Twin Kiosk is the Courtyard of the Favourites (Gözdeler/Mabeyn Taşlığı Ve Dairesi). The Turkish word for 'favourite', *gözde*, literally means 'in the eye' (of the sultan). Over the edge of the courtyard (really a terrace) you'll see a large pool. Just past the courtyard (but on the floor above) are the many small dark rooms that comprised the Private Prison (kafes) where the unwanted brothers or sons of the sultan were kept (see boxed text, above).

A corridor leads east to the Golden Road (Altinyol), a passage leading south. A servant of the sultan's would toss gold coins to the women of the Harem here, hence the name. It is among the oldest parts of the palace, having been built by Mehmet the Conqueror.

The Harem tour then re-enters the guardroom with the huge gilded mirrors, then exits through the Birdcage Gate into the palace's Third Court.

İSTANBUL ARCHAEOLOGY MUSEUMS Map p63

Arkeoloji Müzeleri; ☎ 212-520 7740; Osman Hamdi Bey Yokuşu, Gülhane; admission YTL5; ⌚ 9am-4pm Tue-Sun (last exit 5pm); ⓖ Gülhane

It may not pull the number of visitors that flock to nearby Topkapı, but this is a stunner of a museum complex that shouldn't be missed. It can be easily reached by walking down the slope from Topkapı's Court of the Janissaries First Court, or by walking up the hill from the main gate of Gülhane Parkı, just near the tram stop.

The complex is divided into three buildings: the Archaeology Museum (Arkeoloji Müzesi), the Museum of the Ancient Orient (Eski Şark Eserler Müzesi) and the Tiled Pavilion (Çinili Köşk). These museums house the palace collections, formed during the late 19th century by museum director, artist and archaeologist Osman Hamdi Bey and added to greatly since the republic. While not immediately as dazzling as Topkapı, they contain a wealth of artefacts from the 50 centuries of Anatolia's history. Excellent interpretive panels are in both Turkish and English. A board at the entrance lists which of the exhibits are open and which are closed on the day.

The first building on your left as you enter the museum complex is the Museum of the Ancient Orient. Overlooking the park, it was designed by Alexander Vallaury and built in 1883 to house the Academy of Fine Arts. It displays Anatolian pieces (from Hittite empires) as well as pre-Islamic items collected from the expanse of the Ottoman Empire. You can't miss the series of large glazed-brick panels depicting various animals such as lions and bulls. These beautiful blue-and-yellow panels lined the processional street and the Ishtar gate of ancient Babylon from the time of Nebuchadnezzar II (605–562 BC). Other treats here are the amazing 1st century BC alabaster statue heads from Yemen and the oldest surviving political treaty: a copy of the Kadesh Treaty drawn up in the 13th century BC between the Egyptians and Hittites. There are also clay tablets bearing Hammurabi's famous law code (in cuneiform, of course), ancient Egyptian scarabs and Assyrian reliefs.

On the opposite side of the courtyard is the Archaeology Museum, housed in an imposing neoclassical building. The major building in the complex, it features an extensive collection of Hellenic, Hellenistic and Roman statuary and sarcophagi.

A Roman statue of Bes, an impish half-god of inexhaustible power and strength who was thought to protect against evil, greets you as you enter the main entrance of the museum. Turn left into Room 1, and walk to the dimly lit rooms beyond, where the museum's major treasures – sarcophagi from the Royal Necropolis of Sidon – are displayed. These sarcophagi were unearthed in 1887 by Osman Hamdi Bey in Sidon (Side in modern-day Lebanon). As soon as they were discovered the sarcophagi were swiftly whisked out of the country in a complex operation that involved them being carried on rails laid to the coast and then rafted out to sea, where they were hoisted onto ships and brought to İstanbul. In Room 2 you will see a sarcophagus that is Egyptian in origin; it was later reused by King Tabnit of Sidon. Also here is a beautifully preserved Lycian sarcophagus made from Paros marble dating from the end of the 5th century. It depicts horses, centaurs and human figures with beautifully rendered expressions on their faces. Next to this is the Satrap sarcophagus with its everyday scenes featuring the provincial governor. After admiring these, pass into Room 3 to see one of the most accomplished of all classical artworks, the famous marble Alexander sarcophagus – so named not because it belonged to the Macedonian general, but because it depicts him among his army battling the Persians (long pants, material headwear), who were led by King Abdalonymos and whose sarcophagus it was. Truly exquisite, it is carved out of Pentelic marble and dates from the last quarter of the 4th century BC. Alexander, on horseback, has a lion's head as a headdress. Remarkably, the sculpture has remnants of its original red-and-yellow paintwork. At the end of this room the Mourning Women sarcophagus also bears traces of its original paintwork. Its depiction of the women is stark and very moving.

In the next room you'll find an impressive collection of ancient grave cult sarcophagi from Syria, Lebanon, Thessalonica and Ephesus. Beyond that is a room called 'The Columned Sarcophagi of Anatolia', filled with amazingly detailed sarcophagi dating from between 140–270 AD. Many of these look like tiny temples or residential buildings; don't miss the Sidamara Sarcophagus from Konya.

Further rooms contain examples of Anatolian architecture from antiquity and Lycian monuments.

Turn back and retrace your steps towards the statue of Bes. The underwhelming 'Anatolia and Troy Through the Ages' exhibition is accessed via a staircase between the rooms hosing the Alexander and Satrap sarcophagi; there are also toilets here.

Returning to Bes, you should then move into Room 4, the first of the museum's statuary galleries. It and Rooms 5 and 6 exhibit a selection of fine works, including a delicate Attic horse's head in Room 6. Alexander makes another appearance (Room 7) – you'll see his bust and statue from the Hellenistic period. In Room 8 don't miss the Ephebos of Tralles, a statue of a young boy wrapped in a cape and leaning against a pillar. And in Room 9, which is crowded with busts, note both the stunning head of the poetess Sappho, a copy of an original from the Hellenistic period, and the exquisite head of a child from Pergamum.

Artisans at Anatolia's three main sculpture centres – Aphrodisias, Ephesus and Miletus – turned out thousands of beautiful works, some of which have been collected in Room 10. There's a beautiful relief from Aphrodisias showing the struggle of Athena and the Giants, and a statue from Miletus showing Apollo wearing ornate sandals and playing a lyre. The last room has examples of sculpture from throughout the Roman Empire. Check out the delicately carved draperies on the Roman statue of Cornelia Antonia, which dates from the second half of the 2nd century AD.

In the annex behind the main ground floor gallery there is an unimpressive mock-up of the facade of the Temple of Athena at Assos (Behramkale). On the mezzanine level above the Temple of Athena is an exhibition called İstanbul Through the Ages, tracing the city's history through its neighbourhoods during different periods: Archaic, Hellenistic, Roman, Byzantine and Ottoman. This is well worth a visit, particularly for its new exhibit on the excavation of the Byzantine harbour and boats at Yenikapı, uncovered in 2004 during excavation works for İstanbul's huge Marmaray transport project.

While children will be bored stiff with the naff dioramas of early Anatolian life in the Children's Museum found off Room 1, they will no doubt be impressed by the large-scale model of the Trojan Horse, which they can climb into.

The last of the complex's museum buildings is the Tiled Pavilion of Sultan Mehmet the Conqueror. Thought to be the oldest surviving nonreligious Turkish building in İstanbul, it was built in 1472 as an outer pavilion of Topkapı Palace and was used for watching sporting events. The recessed doorway area is covered with tiles – some with white calligraphy (*sülüus*) on blue. The

geometric patterns and colour of the tiles – turquoise, white, black – on the facade show obvious Seljuk influence. The portico, with its 14 marble columns, was constructed during the reign of Abdülhamid I (1774–89) after the original one burned down in 1737.

Much of the interior of the kiosk is covered with triangular and hexagonal tiles of brown, green, yellow and blue. On display is the best collection of Seljuk, Anatolian and Ottoman tiles and ceramics in the country; these date from the end of the 12th century to the beginning of the 20th century. The collection includes İznik tiles from the period in the 17th and 18th centuries when that city produced the finest coloured tiles in the world. When you enter the first room you can't miss the stunning mihrab from the İbrahim Bey Mosque, built in 1432. Also of note is the pretty peacock-adorned fountain recessed into the wall in the room to the left at the back of the kiosk; this dates from 1590.

GÜLHANE PARKI Map p63
Gülhane Park; Gülhane

Gülhane Parkı was once the palace park of Topkapı. Now, crowds of locals come here at weekends to enjoy its shade, street food and the occasional live concert. The trees here are lovely and the views over the water impressive, but many of the fountains and other features added in recent times are blots on the landscape – the horrible concrete water feature near the main gate being the major offender.

At the far (north) end of the park, up the hill, there is a series of terraces with a tea garden, the Set Üstü Çay Bahçesi (p173) offering superb views of the Bosphorus and Sea of Marmara.

To the right of the south exit is a bulbous little kiosk built into the park wall. Known as the Alay Köşkü (Parade Kiosk), this is where the sultan would sit and watch the periodic parades of troops and trade guilds that commemorated great holidays and military victories.

Across the street and 100m northwest of Gülhane gate is an outrageously curvaceous rococo gate leading into the precincts of what was once the grand vizierate, or Ottoman prime ministry, known in the West as the Sublime Porte. Today the buildings beyond the gate hold various offices of the İstanbul provincial government (the Vilayeti).

SOĞUKÇEŞME SOKAK Map p63

🚋 Gülhane

Soğukçeşme Sokak, or Street of the Cold Fountain, runs between the Topkapı Palace walls and Aya Sofya. In the 1980s, the Turkish Touring & Automobile Association (Turing) acquired a row of buildings on the street and decided to demolish most of them to build nine re-creations of the prim Ottoman-style houses that had occupied the site in the previous two centuries. A vitriolic battle played out on the pages of İstanbul's newspapers ensued, with some experts arguing that the city would be left with a Disney-style architectural theme park rather than a legitimate exercise in conservation architecture. Turing eventually got the go-ahead (after the intervention of the Turkish president, no less) and in time opened all of the re-created buildings as Ayasofya Konakları (p204), one of the first boutique heritage hotels in the city. Conservation theory aside, the colourful buildings and cobbled street are particularly picturesque and worth wandering past.

CAFERAĞA MEDRESESİ Map p63

☎ 212-513 3601; Caferiye Sokak; admission free; ⏰ 8.30am-7pm; 🚋 Sultanahmet

This lovely little building, which is tucked away in the shadows of Aya Sofya, was designed by Sinan on the orders of Cafer Ağa, Süleyman the Magnificent's chief black eunuch. Built in 1560 as a school for Islamic and secular education, today it is home to the Turkish Cultural Services Foundation (p237), which runs workshops in traditional Ottoman arts such as calligraphy, ebru (traditional Turkish marbling) and miniature painting. Some of the arts and crafts produced here are for sale and there's a pleasant lokanta (see p161) in the courtyard.

SİRKECİ RAILWAY STATION Map p63

Sirkeci İstasyonu; Ankara Caddesi, Sirkeci; 🚋 Sirkeci

The romance of the Orient Express and other locomotives of the era was reflected in the design for this train station, built as the terminus of European routes in 1881. Designed by a German architect, it is an excellent example of Islamic Eclecticism, an architectural movement introduced into İstanbul by European architects at the end of the 19th century. The structure replaced one of the Topkapı Palace pavilions and it

reflects this Ottoman heritage, though its clock tower, arches and large rose windows clearly mirror the neoclassicism popular in Europe at the time. At the time of research the station was still functioning as the city's terminus for European routes, though its future was uncertain.

Though the Marmaray project (see p234) may disrupt things, at the time of writing Dervishes had been conducting a sema (whirling ceremony; ☎ information & bookings 212-458 8834; adult/student under 24 YTL30/25) in the exhibition hall on platform 1 at 7.30pm every Sunday, Wednesday and Friday.

YENİ CAMİİ Map p63

New Mosque; ☎ 212-527 8505; Yenicami Meydanı Sokak, Eminönü; donation requested; 🚋 Eminönü

Only in İstanbul would a 400-year-old mosque be called 'New'. The Yeni Camii was begun in 1597, commissioned by Valide Sultan Safiye, mother of Sultan Mehmet III (r 1595–1603). The site was earlier occupied by a community of Karaite Jews, radical dissenters from Orthodox Judaism. When the valide sultan decided to build her grand mosque here, the Karaites were moved to Hasköy, a district further up the Golden Horn that still bears traces of their presence.

Safiye lost her august position when her son the sultan died and the mosque was completed six sultans later in 1663 by Valide Sultan Turhan Hadice, mother of Sultan Mehmet IV (r 1648–87).

In plan, the Yeni Camii is much like the Blue Mosque (p54) and the Süleymaniye Camii (p80), with a large forecourt and a square sanctuary surmounted by a series of semidomes crowned by a grand dome. The interior is richly decorated with gold, coloured İznik tiles and carved marble. It also has an impressive mihrab.

The mosque was created after Ottoman architecture had reached its peak. Consequently, even its tiles are slightly inferior products, the late 17th century having seen a diminution in the quality of the products coming out of the İznik workshops. You will see this if you compare these tiles with the exquisite examples found in the nearby Rüstem Paşa Camii (p82), which are from the high period of İznik tilework. Nonetheless, it is a popular working mosque and a much-loved adornment to the city skyline.

Across the road from the mosque is the tomb of Valide Sultan Turhan Hadice, the woman who completed construction of the Yeni Camii. Buried with her are no fewer than six sultans, including her son Mehmet IV, plus dozens of imperial princes and princesses. Further east, on Hamidiye Caddesi, are two of the best places in town to buy fresh Turkish delight, Hafiz Mustafa Şekerlemeleri (p137) and Ali Muhiddin Hacı Bekir (p136).

GALATA BRIDGE Map p63

Galata Köprüsü; 🚊 **Eminönü or Karaköy**

Nothing is quite as evocative as walking across the Galata Bridge. At sunset, when the Galata Tower (p104) is surrounded by shrieking seagulls and the mosques atop the seven hills of the city are thrown into relief against a soft red-pink sky, the view from the bridge is spectacularly beautiful. During the day, it carries a constant flow of

İstanbullus crossing to and from Beyoğlu and Eminönü, a handful or two of hopeful anglers trailing their lines into the waters below, and a constantly changing procession of street vendors hawking everything from fresh-baked *simit* (bread-rings) to Rolex rip-offs. This is İstanbul at its most magical.

Underneath the bridge, touristy restaurants and cafés serve drinks and food all day and night. Come here to inhale the evocative scent of apple tobacco wafting out of the nargileh cafés and to watch the passing parade of ferries zooming past. There's even a shop selling fishing equipment for those who aspire to emulate the anglers up on the bridge.

The present, quite ugly, bridge was built in 1992 to replace an iron structure dating

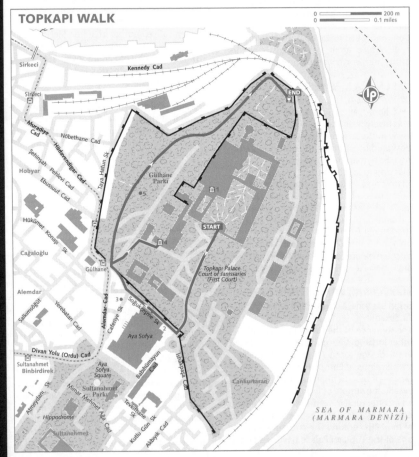

TOPKAPI WALK

from 1909 to 1912, which in turn had replaced two earlier structures. The iron bridge was famous for the ramshackle fish restaurants, teahouses and nargileh joints that occupied the dark recesses beneath its roadway, but it had a major flaw: it floated on pontoons that blocked the natural flow of water and kept the Golden Horn from flushing itself free of pollution. In the late 1980s the municipality started to draw up plans to replace it with a new bridge that would allow the water to flow. A fire expedited these plans in the early 1990s and the new bridge was built a short time afterwards. (The remains of the old, much-loved bridge were moved further up the Golden Horn near Hasköy.)

TOPKAPI WALK
Walking Tour

1 Topkapı Palace This palace (p62) is where the sultans and their womenfolk set up households from the time of Mehmet the Conqueror until his descendant Abdül Mescit defected to the European side of town. The sheer number of lavishly decorated buildings and treasures in them mean that you'll need at least a few hours here.

2 Soğukçeşme Sokak This cobbled street (p73) hugging the palace's walls is a popular thoroughfare for locals and tourists alike. Its Ottoman housing might not be original, but

WALK FACTS
Start Topkapı Palace
End Gülhane Parkı
Distance 2km
Time Six hours
Fuel stop Set Üstü Çay Bahçesi (p173), Gülhane Parkı

it's certainly pretty as a picture, and well worth a wander with camera in hand.

3 Caferağa Medresesi Cafer Ağa, who built and endowed this charming theological college (p73) in 1560, wasn't himself endowed – he was Süleyman the Magnificent's chief black eunuch. Designed by Sinan, the building is beautifully proportioned and now houses artists workshops and a small lokanta.

4 İstanbul Archaeology Museums This museum (p70) is one of the best in the city. Don't miss the exquisitely carved sarcophagi from the Royal Necropolis at Sidon, the huge collection of classical sculpture and the charming Tiled Pavilion of Sultan Mehmet the Conqueror.

5 Gülhane Parkı Once the Topkapı Palace park, this oasis (p72) of tall trees and grassed terraces is a favourite picnic spot for families and courting couples. Enjoy a glass of tea at Set Üstü Çay Bahçesi (p173) while marvelling at the view over the Golden Horn and up the Bosphorus.

BAZAAR DISTRICT

Drinking p174; Eating p161; Shopping p137; Sleeping p205

As well as being home to two world-famous bazaars – one grand and one full of spices – this district is also where you'll find the frantically busy shopping precinct of Tahtakale, located behind and to the west of the Spice Bazaar. Here, vendors with carts full of everything from *simit* (bread-rings) to strawberries make their way through narrow streets full of shoppers, delivery vans and tourists valiantly fighting their way through the chaos.

At the top of a hill mounting from the Golden Horn is the city's first and most evocative shopping mall – the venerable Grand Bazaar (Kapalı Çarşı, below), established during the rule of Mehmet the Conqueror (r 1451–81) and still going strong. Getting lost in its maze of laneways is obligatory for all first-time visitors; those who have visited previously are quick to gravitate towards their favourite shops, coffee houses and restaurants.

Near the bazaar are three great Ottoman mosques: the splendid Süleymaniye Camii (p80), the dignified Beyazıt Camii (p80), and the charming Şehzade Mehmet Camii (p81). All three provide wonderfully contemplative spaces to escape from the mercantile madness of the surrounding streets. The Süleymaniye gives its name to the suburb surrounding it and although the official name for the square on which Beyazıt Camii is located is Hürriyet Meydanı, everyone in town knows it as Beyazıt Square.

On the square is İstanbul University, one of the city's premier institutions of learning. This brings lots of students into this neighbourhood and they enliven it considerably, outnumbering the bazaar crowds in the many local *çay bahçesis* (tea gardens) and fast-food joints. If you want to sample the delights of a nargileh (the local equivalent of a drink after work), places such as Lale Bahçesi (p174) and Erenler Çay Bahçesi (p174) are where you should head.

The neighbourhood is sliced into north and south halves by Ordu Caddesi, the western continuation of Divan Yolu Caddesi. The tramline between Zeytinburnu and Kabataş runs along this major road, and there are three tram stops: Laleli, Üniversite and Beyazıt. On the southern side of Ordu Caddesi are the residential suburbs leading down to the Sea of Marmara. These include Kumkapı – famous for its fish market and fish restaurants – Gedik Paşa and Kadırga. Though not as conservative as some parts of Sultanahmet, these suburbs are resolutely working class and not at all affluent.

GRAND BAZAAR Map p77

Kapalı Çarşı, Covered Market; ☺ 9am-7pm Mon-Sat; ▨ Beyazıt

Before you visit this, the most famous *souq* in the world, make sure you prepare yourself properly. First, make sure you're in a good mood and ready to swap friendly banter with the hundreds of shopkeepers who will attempt to lure you into their establishments. There's no use getting tetchy with the touts here – this is their turf and it would be delusional of you to think that you're anything more than putty in their hands (and liras in their cash registers). Second, allow enough time to look into every nook and cranny, drink innumerable cups of tea, compare price after price and try your hand at the art of bargaining. Shoppers have been doing this here for centuries and, frankly, it would be unbecoming for you to do any less. (For tips on bargaining, see p132.) And third: never, ever forget your baggage allowance. There's nothing worse than that sinking feeling when you

airport check-in counter when you realise that your Grand Bazaar–induced shopping frenzy means that the dreaded term 'excess baggage' is about to become a reality and test your already sorely abused credit card to its limits.

The bazaar is the heart of the city in much more than a geographical sense and has been so for centuries. With over 4000 shops and several kilometres of lanes, as well as mosques, banks, police stations, restaurants and workshops, it's a covered city all of its own. Though there's no doubt that it's a tourist trap *par excellence,* it's also a place where business deals are done between locals, and where import/export businesses flourish. And it also functions as the nucleus of a large commercial neighbourhood, with most of the surrounding streets (Mahmutpaşa Yokuşu is a good example) catering to every conceivable local shopping need.

Starting from a small masonry *bedesten* (warehouse) built in the time of Mehmet

GRAND BAZAAR (KAPALI ÇARŞI)

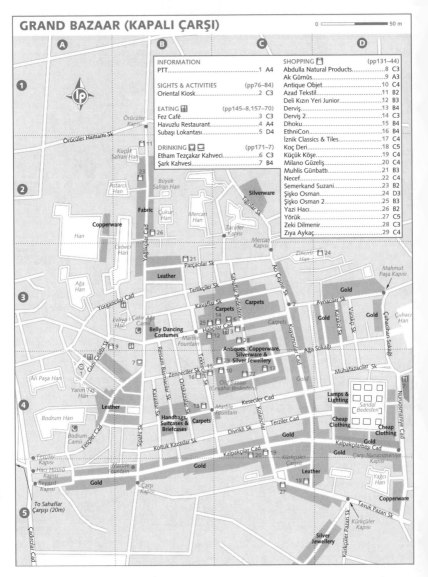

INFORMATION	
PTT	1 A4

SIGHTS & ACTIVITIES	(pp76–84)
Oriental Kiosk	2 C3

EATING	(pp145–8,157–70)
Fez Café	3 C3
Havuzlu Restaurant	4 A4
Subaşı Lokantası	5 D4

DRINKING	(pp171–7)
Etham Tezçakar Kahveci	6 C3
Şark Kahvesi	7 B4

SHOPPING	(pp131–44)
Abdulla Natural Products	8 C3
Ak Gümüs	9 A3
Antique Objet	10 C4
Azad Tekstil	11 B2
Deli Kızın Yeri Junior	12 B3
Derviş	13 B4
Derviş 2	14 C3
Dhoku	15 B4
EthniCon	16 B4
İznik Classics & Tiles	17 C4
Koç Deri	18 C5
Küçük Köşe	19 C4
Milano Güzeliş	20 C4
Muhlis Günbattı	21 B3
Necef	22 C4
Semerkand Suzani	23 B2
Şişko Osman	24 D3
Şişko Osman 2	25 B3
Yazi Hacı	26 B2
Yörük	27 C5
Zeki Dilmenir	28 C3
Ziya Aykaç	29 C4

the Conqueror, the bazaar grew to cover a vast area as neighbouring shopkeepers decided to put up roofs and porches so that commerce could be conducted comfortably in all weather. Finally, a system of locked gates and doors was provided so that the entire mini-city could be closed up tight at the end of the business day. Street names refer to trades and crafts: Kuyumcular Caddesi (Jewellers St) and İnciciler

Sokağı (Pearl Merchants' St) are two that you're bound to walk down. Large sections of the bazaar have been destroyed by fire and earthquake a number of times in its history (most recently in 1954), but have always been rebuilt.

Just inside the Nuruosmaniye Kapısı (doorway), on the southeast corner of the market, you'll find a glittering street filled with the stores of gold merchants. This is

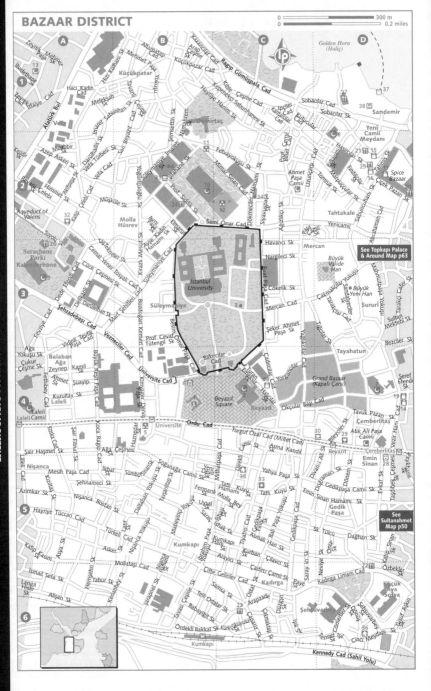

BAZAAR DISTRICT

BAZAAR DISTRICT

INFORMATION		Ekincioğlu Toys & Gifts	...........15 D2	DRINKING 🍺 🍷	(pp171–7)
Tourist Information Office	.............1 B4	Kurukahveci Mehmet Efendi		Balkan Türkleri Dayanışma ve Kültür	
		Mahdumları	.......................16 D2	Derneği	.....................29 D4
SIGHTS & ACTIVITIES	(pp76–84)	Mehmet Kalmaz Baharatçı	.....17 D2	Erenler Çay Bahçesi	................30 D4
Beyazıt Camii	.................2 C4	Sahaflar Çarşısı	......................18 C4	Lale Bahçesi	..........................31 B2
Beyazıt Tower	.................3 C3	Sofa	......................................19 D4	Vefa Bozacisi	.........................32 A2
Dârüzziyafe (Former Soup Kitchen)	.4 B2				
Forum of Theodosius Columns	.......5 B4	EATING 🍴	(pp145–8, 157–70)	NIGHTLIFE 🎭	(pp179–84)
Museum of Turkish Calligraphic		Bab-i Hayat	...........................20 D2	Orient House	.........................33 C5
Art	....6 B4	Dârüzziyafe Restaurant	...........(see 4)		
Nuruosmaniye Camii	...................7 D4	Hamdi Et Lokantası	................21 D2	SPORTS & ACTIVITIES	(pp191–6)
Rüstem Paşa Camii	.................8 D2	Imren Lokantası	.....................22 D6	Süleymaniye Hamamı	............34 C2
Şehzade Mehmet Camii	.............9 A3	Kör Agop Restaurant	.............23 C6		
Süleymaniye Camii	.................10 D2	Meshur Kuru Fasülyeci	..........24 B2	SLEEPING 🛏	(pp197–209)
Tomb of Mimar Sinan	..................11 B2	Nimla Pastırmacı	....................25 D2	Hotel Niles	...........................35 C5
Tombs of Süleyman the Magnificent &		Şehzade Mehmed Sofrası	........26 A3	Hotel Türkuaz	.......................36 D6
Roxelana	.................................12 C2	Zinhan Kebap House at			
Zeyrek Camii	...............................13 A1	Storks	...................................27 D1	TRANSPORT	(pp230–5)
				Golden Horn (Haliç) Ferries	.....37 D1
SHOPPING 🛍	(pp131–44)	ARTS 🎨	(pp185–90)	Rüstempaşa/Eminönü Bus	
Design Zone	.............................14 D4	Dance of Colours	...................28 D5	Stand	..................................38 D1

called Kalpakçılarbaşı Caddesi and it's the closest thing the bazaar has to a main street. Most of the bazaar is on your right (north) in the crazy maze of tiny streets and alleys. You'll inevitably get lost when exploring them, but hey, that's part of the fun!

Make sure you pop into the Sandal Bedesten off Kalpakçılarbaşı Caddesi. This rectangular hall with a domed roof supported by 12 large pillars is also called the Yeni Bedesten (New Warehouse), as it was built after Mehmet's central *bedesten*, some time in the 17th century.

The Old Bazaar, also known as Cevahir Bedesteni (Jewellery Warehouse), is at the centre of the market. Thought to be the first building Mehmet the Conqueror built, its structure is similar to the Sandal Bedesten. Inside, you'll find innumerable small shops selling quality jewellery, silver, ceramics and antiques.

When wandering, seek out north–south Sipahi Caddesi and its famous Şark Kahvesi (p174), a worn-out but charming relic of Old İstanbul whose walls feature quirky images of dervishes on flying carpets. This is a great place to linger over a game of backgammon and a few glasses of tea. Other places that make good coffee and tea stops in the bazaar are the pricey Fez Café and the cheaper Etham Tezçakar Kahvesi (p174), both on atmospheric Halıcılar Caddesi near the Old Bazaar.

In the bazaar itself, the best place for a meal is Havuzlu Restaurant (p162), located in a *han* near the PTT in Gani Çelebi Sokak; two nearby lokantas – Subaşı Lokantası (p162) and Sefa Restaurant (p161) – are also popular with the bazaar's shopkeepers.

Near the junction of Halıcılar Caddesi and Kuyumcular Caddesi you'll find the crooked Oriental Kiosk, which was built as a coffee house and now functions as a jewellery shop. North from here, up Acı Çeşme Sokak, is the gorgeous pink Zincirli Han, home to one of the bazaar's most famous carpet dealers, Şişko Osman (p139).

Bibliophiles will want to head towards Sahaflar Çarşısı (Old Book Bazaar; Map p78), which is found in a shady little courtyard west of the bazaar at the end of Kalpakçılarbaşı Caddesi. The book bazaar dates from Byzantine times. Today, many of the booksellers are members of a dervish order called the Halveti after its founder, Hazreti Mehmet Nureddin-i Cerrahi-i Halveti. They sell wares both new and old, and though it's unlikely you'll uncover any underpriced antique treasures, you'll certainly be able to find old engravings, a curiosity or two, phrasebooks and books on İstanbul and Turkish culture in several languages.

To check out what to buy in the bazaar and where to buy it, refer to p133. One of the most intriguing aspects of a visit to the bazaar is noticing its juxtaposition of tourist tat and precious objects, proving the point that the place really does cater to every possible shopping desire!

NURUOSMANİYE CAMİİ Map p78

Light of Osman Mosque; Vezir Hanı Caddesi;
🚇 **Beyazıt**

Facing Nuruosmaniye Kapısı, one of several doorways into the Grand Bazaar, this mosque was built in Ottoman baroque style between 1748 and 1755. Construction was started by Mahmut I and finished by his successor Osman III. Though meant to exhibit the sultans' 'modern' taste, the baroque building has very strong echoes of Aya Sofya, specifically the broad, lofty dome, colonnaded mezzanine galleries, windows topped with Roman arches and the broad band of calligraphy around the interior. Despite its prominent position on the busy pedestrian route from Cağaloğlu Square and Nuruosmaniye Caddesi to the bazaar, it is surprisingly peaceful and contemplative inside.

BEYAZIT SQUARE & İSTANBUL UNIVERSITY Map p78

Beyazıt

Beyazıt Square is officially called Hürriyet Meydanı (Freedom Square), though everyone knows it simply as Beyazıt. Under the rule of the Byzantines it was called the Forum of Theodosius. Sections of the forum's columns decorated with stylised oak-knot designs were dug up from the square during the 1950s and can be seen on the other side of Yeniçeriler Caddesi. Today the square is home to street vendors, students from İstanbul University and plenty of pigeons, as well as a few policemen who like to keep an eye on student activities.

The square is backed by the impressive portal of the University. After the Conquest, Mehmet the Conqueror built his first palace here, a wooden structure called the Eski Sarayı (Old Seraglio). After Topkapı was built the Eski Sarayı became home to women when they were pensioned out of the main palace – this is where *valide sultans* came when their sultan sons died and they lost their powerful position as head of the harem. The original building was demolished in the 19th century to make way

top picks

IT'S FREE

- Grand Bazaar (p76)
- Spice Bazaar (p82)
- Hippodrome (p56)
- Galata Bridge (p74)
- Florence Nightingale Museum (p124)
- All mosques

for a grandiose Ministry of War complex designed by Auguste Bourgeois; this now houses the university. The stone tower, visible from most of Old İstanbul, was built as a lookout for fires. Both the university and tower are off limits to travellers.

BEYAZIT CAMİİ Map p78

Mosque of Sultan Beyazıt II; ☎ 212-519 3644; Yeniçeriler Caddesi; Beyazıt

Dating from 1501 to 1506, this was the second imperial mosque to be built in the city after Mehmet the Conqueror's Fatih Camii (p95), and was the prototype for other imperial mosques. In effect, it is the link between Aya Sofya (p49), which obviously inspired its design, and the great mosques such as Süleymaniye (below), which are realisations of Aya Sofya's design fully adapted to Muslim worship.

Of particular note is the mosque's exceptional use of fine stone: marble, porphyry, verd antique and rare granite. The mihrab is simple, except for the rich stone columns framing it, and the courtyard, with its 24 small domes and central fountain, is particularly pretty.

Some of the other buildings of Beyazıt's *külliye* (mosque complex) have been well utilised. The soup kitchen has been turned into a library, while the *medrese* is now the Museum of Turkish Calligraphic Art (below). Unfortunately the once-splendid hamam is still waiting to be restored. Beyazıt's *türbe* is behind the mosque.

MUSEUM OF TURKISH CALLIGRAPHIC ART Map p78

Türk Vakıf Hat Sanatları Müzesi; ☎ 212-527 5851; Hürriyet Meydanı, Beyazıt; admission YTL3; 9am-4pm Tue-Sat; Beyazıt

Housed in a small building at the western side of Beyazıt Square, this museum contains wall hangings and manuscripts illustrating mainly cursive calligraphic styles, many dating from the 13th century. There are also some examples of calligraphy on stone, tile and glass. The building, once the *medrese* of Beyazıt Camii, is a series of rooms surrounding a leafy courtyard.

SÜLEYMANİYE CAMİİ Map p78

Mosque of Sultan Süleyman the Magnificent; ☎ 212-514 0139; Prof Sıddık Sami Onar Caddesi; donation requested; tombs 9.30am-5.30pm; Beyazıt

The Süleymaniye crowns one of the seven hills, and dominates the Golden Horn, providing a landmark for the entire city. It was commissioned by the greatest, richest and most powerful of Ottoman sultans, Süleyman I (r 1520–66), known as 'The Magnificent', and was the fourth imperial mosque built in İstanbul, following the Fatih, Beyazıt and Selim I complexes.

Though it's not the largest of the Ottoman mosques, the Süleymaniye is certainly the grandest. It was designed by Mimar Sinan, the most famous and talented of all imperial architects. Though Sinan described the smaller Selimiye Camii in Edirne as his best work, he chose to be buried here in the Süleymaniye complex, probably knowing that this would be the building that he would be best remembered for. His tomb is just outside the mosque's walled garden, next to the *medrese* building.

The mosque was built between 1550 and 1557; records show that 3523 craftspeople worked on its construction. Though it's seen some hard times, being damaged by fire in 1660 and having its wonderful columns covered by cement and oil paint at some point after this, a restoration in 1956 and decades of subsequent care mean that it's in great shape these days. It's also one of the most popular mosques in the city, with worshippers rivalling the Blue Mosque in number.

The mosque's setting and plan are particularly pleasing, with well-tended gardens and a three-sided forecourt surrounded by a wall with grilled windows and featuring a central domed ablutions fountain. Its four minarets with their beautiful balconies are said to represent the fact that Süleyman was the fourth of the Osmani sultans to rule the city.

Inside, the mosque is breathtaking in its size and pleasing in its simplicity. It is also remarkably light. Sinan's design is particularly ingenious due to the fact that the buttresses used to support the four columns are incorporated into the walls of the building, masked by galleries with arcades of columns running between the buttresses. Put simply, the architect, ever challenged by the technical accomplishments of Aya Sofya, took the floor plan of that church and here perfected its adaptation to the requirements of Muslim worship.

There is little interior decoration other than some very fine İznik tiles in the mihrab, gorgeous stained-glass windows done by one İbrahim the Drunkard, and four massive columns – one from Baalbek in modern-day Lebanon, one from Alexandria and two from Byzantine palaces in İstanbul. The painted arabesques on the dome are 19th-century additions, recently renewed. If you visit when the stairs to the gallery on the northeast side (ie facing the Golden Horn) are open, make sure you go upstairs and out to the balcony. The views from this vantage point are among the best in the city.

The *külliye* of the Süleymaniye, which is outside the walled garden, is particularly elaborate, with the full complement of public services: soup kitchen, hostel, hospital etc. Today the soup kitchen, with its charming garden courtyard, houses the Dârüzziyafe Restaurant, which is a lovely place to enjoy a *çay* (tea). Lale Bahçesi (p174), located in a sunken courtyard next to Dârüzziyafe, is an atmospheric venue for *çay* and nargileh. Both it and the nearby Meşhur Kuru Fasülyeci (p162), are extremely popular with students and locals. Those in need of an energy boost could make the short trip to Vefa Bozacısı (p174), the most famous place in the city to sample *boza*, the İstanbullu tonic drink made with fermented grain.

The mosque's hamam (p193) still functions.

Near the southeast wall of the mosque is the cemetery, with the tombs of Süleyman and his wife Haseki Hürrem Sultan (Roxelana). The tilework in both is superb. In Süleyman's tomb, little jewel-like lights in the dome are surrogate stars. In Hürrem's tomb, the many tile panels of flowers and the delicate stained glass produce a serene effect.

ŞEHZADE MEHMET CAMİİ Map p78
Mosque of the Prince; Şehzadebaşı Caddesi; Ⓜ Laleli

Süleyman the Magnificent built this mosque between 1543 and 1548 as a memorial to his son, Mehmet, who died of smallpox in 1543 at the age of 22. It was the first important mosque to be designed by Mimar Sinan. Although not one of his best works, it has two beautiful minarets and attractive exterior decoration. Among the many important people buried in tile-encrusted tombs here are Prince Mehmet, his brothers and sisters, and Süleyman's grand viziers, Rüstem Paşa and İbrahim Paşa. After you've visited the mosque, make sure you stop for a tea or lunch at Şehzade Mehmed Sofrası (p162), housed in one of the *külliye* buildings behind the mosque.

ZEYREK CAMİİ Map p78
Church of the Pantocrator; İbadethane Sokak; 🚇 Laleli

Zeyrek Camii was originally part of an important Byzantine sanctuary comprising two churches, a chapel and a monastery. The monastery is long gone and the northernmost church is derelict, but the southern church still has some features intact, including a magnificent marble floor. Empress Eirene had the church built before her death in 1124 (she features in a mosaic at Aya Sofya with Emperor John II Comnenus). The church and the attached chapel, built by John II, now function as a mosque. Outside prayer times a caretaker is usually available to show visitors around and will gratefully accept a donation in return. Ask him to pull back the carpet to reveal part of the splendid mosaic floor.

RÜSTEM PAŞA CAMİİ Map p78
Mosque of Rüstem Pasha; ☎ 212-526 7350; Hasırcılar Caddesi; 🚇 Eminönü

Plonked in the middle of the busy Tahtakale district, this little-visited mosque is a gem. Built in 1560 by Sinan for Rüstem Paşa, son-in-law and grand vizier of Süleyman the Magnificent, it is a showpiece of the best Ottoman architecture and tilework, albeit on a small scale. It is thought to have been the prototype for Sinan's greatest work, the Selimiye in Edirne.

At the top of the entry steps there's a terrace and the mosque's colonnaded porch. You'll notice at once the panels of İznik faïence set into the mosque's facade. The interior is covered in similarly gorgeous tiles and features a lovely dome, supported by four tiled pillars.

The preponderance of tiles was Rüstem Paşa's way of signalling his wealth and influence – İznik tiles being particularly expensive and desirable. It may not have assisted his passage into the higher realm, though, because by all accounts he was a loathsome character. His contemporaries dubbed him Kehle-i-Ikbal (the Louse of Fortune) because even though he was found to be infected with lice before his marriage to Mihrimah, Süleyman's favourite daughter, this did not prevent the marriage

or his subsequent rise to great fame and fortune. He is best remembered for plotting with Roxelana to turn Süleyman against his favourite son, Mustafa. They were successful and Mustafa was strangled in 1553 on his father's orders.

The mosque is easy to miss because it's not at street level. There's a set of access stairs on Hasırcılar Caddesi and another on the small street that runs right (north) off Hasırcılar Caddesi to the Golden Horn.

SPICE BAZAAR Map p78
Mısır Çarşısı, Egyptian Market; ⏱ 8.30am-6.30pm Mon-Sat; 🚇 Eminönü

Need a herbal love potion or natural Turkish Viagra? This is the place to find them, although we wouldn't vouch for the efficacy of either! As well as *baharat* (spices), nuts, honey in the comb and olive oil soaps, the bustling spice bazaar sells truckloads of *incir* (figs), *lokum* (Turkish delight) and *pestil* (fruit pressed into sheets and dried). The number of shops selling tourist trinkets increases annually, yet this remains a great place to stock up on edible souvenirs, share a few jokes with the vendors and marvel at the well-preserved building. It's also home to one of the city's oldest restaurants, Pandeli, and to its attractive new competitor Bab-i Hayat (p162).

The market was constructed in the 1660s as part of the Yeni Camii complex (p73); the rent from the shops supports the upkeep of the mosque and its charitable activities, which include a school, baths, hospital and public fountains. It was called the Egyptian Market because it is thought that it was initially endowed with taxes levied on goods imported from Egypt.

Between the market and the Yeni Camii is the city's major outdoor market for flowers, plants, seeds and songbirds. There's a toilet *(tuvalet)* down a flight of stairs, subject to a small fee.

On the west side of the market there are outdoor produce stalls selling fresh foodstuff from all over Anatolia. Also here is the most famous coffee supplier in İstanbul, Kurukahveci Mehmet Efendi Mahdumları (p137), established over 100 years ago.

AQUEDUCT OF VALENS Map p78
Bozdoğan Kemeri; 🚇 Aksaray

Rising majestically over the traffic on busy Atatürk Bulvarı, this limestone structure is one of the city's most distinctive landmarks. Visitors often gasp in amazement on seeing it for the first time (amazement often turns into consternation when they notice excited fans from the nearby Vefa football stadium doing perilous victory dances waving their team's colours from its dizzy heights).

We don't know for sure that that the aqueduct was constructed by the Emperor Valens (r 364–78), but we do know that it has been repaired a number of times, the first in 1019 and the last in the late 1980s. It's thought that the aqueduct carried water over this valley to a cistern at Beyazıt Square before finally ending up at the Great Byzantine Palace. After the Conquest it supplied the Eski (Old) and Topkapı Palaces with water.

BAZAAR DISTRICT WALK
Walking Tour

1 Nuruosmaniye Camii This Ottoman baroque mosque (p79) stands at the Nuruosmaniye Gate, one of the main entrances to the Grand Bazaar. It's always busy at prayer time, but is wonderfully peaceful at other times. The gold emblem above the gateway into the bazaar is the Ottoman armorial emblem with the sultan's monogram.

2 Grand Bazaar When Mehmet the Conqueror laid the foundation stone for this bazaar (p76), he set off a craze for shopping malls that İstanbullus have cultivated ever since. His original *bedesten* (covered market), now an antiques and curios hall, spread and engulfed surrounding *han*s (caravansaries), creating the chaotic shopping crush you see today.

3 Sahaflar Çarşısı This rather picturesque book bazaar (p76) dates from Byzantine times. Today, many of the booksellers are members of a dervish order called the Halveti

WALK FACTS

Start Nuruosmaniye Camii
End Yeni Camii
Distance 4km
Duration Five hours
Fuel stop Şehzade Mehmed Sofrası (p162), in the grounds of Şehzade Mehmet Mosque

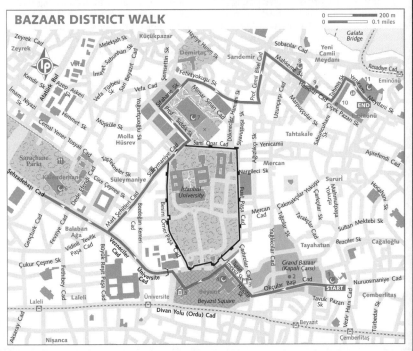

BAZAAR DISTRICT WALK

83

after its founder, Hazreti Mehmet Nureddin-i Cerrahi-i Halveti.

4 Beyazıt Camii The city's second imperial mosque (p80), this prominent landmark has recently had a spit-n-polish job, and is looking mighty handsome as a result. Make sure you wander around its interior courtyard, with its 24 small domes and central fountain.

5 Museum of Turkish Calligraphic Art
You will have seen reproductions of Ottoman calligraphy plastered over T-shirts, postcards and ceramics in the city's souvenir shops, but this is the place (p80) to admire the real thing, executed on manuscripts, wall hangings, glass, stone and tile and dating from as early as the 13th century.

6 Şehzade Mehmet Camii This quiet and attractive mosque (p81) has minarets whose pointed perfection are unrivalled in the city. Set in beautifully maintained gardens featuring a beautiful restaurant/çay bahçesi (p162), it was built by Süleyman the Magnificent as a memorial for his son Mehmet, who died young.

7 Süleymaniye Camii The Süleymaniye (p80) was the crowing glory of Sinan's prodigious architectural output and is widely acknowledged to be the most important Ottoman building in İstanbul. Its sprawling *külliye* (outbuildings) include a soup kitchen, hos-

tel, hospital, hamam and *medrese*. Simply spectacular.

8 Rüstem Paşa Camii This diminutive mosque (p82) is the most charming in the city. Nestled amongst the confusion and chaos of the Tahtakale shopping district, its walls are encrusted with exquisite turquoise-coloured İznik tiles and its graceful colonnaded terrace provides a true urban haven.

9 Hasircilar Caddesi If you're after freshly ground coffee, aromatic spices, dried figs, nuts or tea, this is where you should come. The tourists visit the Spice Bazaar, but this street is one where you'll find the locals buying up big.

10 Spice Bazaar The vividly coloured pyramids of spices and ornate displays of jewel-like *lokum* provide eye candy for the thousands of tourists who tramp through this Ottoman marketplace (p82) every day. And though the sultan's head chef no longer shops here, there's still an undeniably Ottoman air about the place.

11 Yeni Camii It's over 400 years old, but that doesn't stop the locals referring to this building as the 'New Mosque' (p73). A commanding location overlooking the Eminönü docks means that this is one of the most loved and familiar sights of the city.

ARCHITECTURE

Inside the Blue Mosque (p54)

Every garden needs a Süleymaniye Camii (p80)

top picks

İSTANBUL'S ARCHITECTURAL MUST-SEES

Choosing 10 İstanbul buildings of note out of a field of thousands is a tough job, but here's our best attempt:

- Süleymaniye Camii (p80)
- Küçük Aya Sofya Camii (p57)
- Blue Mosque (p54)
- Aya Sofya (p49)
- Basilica Cistern (p58)
- Topkapı Palace (p62)
- Baths of Lady Hürrem (p53)
- Rumeli Hisarı (p217)
- Kanyon (p143)
- Beylerbeyi Palace (p215)

Urban designers wanting to study the world's best practice when it comes to putting together a city skyline need go no further than İstanbul. Forget Chicago and New York with their overwhelming skyscraper canyons, or London with its gimmicky Eye and squat clock tower – İstanbul is the real thing. Here you'll find delicate minarets reaching towards the heavens, distinctive domes crowning hills, and austere and elegant medieval towers commanding views across the waters.

This imperial city is the architectural equivalent of a chocolate box with the best possible mixed assortment of treats – Byzantine churches sit beside Ottoman mosques, *medreses* (theological schools) and hamams (steam baths); 19th-century timber *yalıs* (seaside villas) adorn the Bosphorus shore; and neoclassical embassies are dotted along Beyoğlu's boulevards. There's little of note from the second half of the 20th century, so the city is consolidating its time-capsule status, undergoing a continuous program of restoration and attempting to legislate to protect its revered skyline. Time capsule doesn't mean Disney-like, though: İstanbullus still worship in historic mosques and churches, live in the timber houses, run restaurants in *medreses*, sweat out their anxieties in hamams and attend cocktail parties in the embassies. Today's İstanbul is a living testimonial to the architects and patrons who have contributed to its contemporary form. It's also proof that back in the old days, they sure knew how to build great buildings.

The Fountain of Sultan Ahmet III (p65) whets the appetite for the grandeur of Topkapı Palace

Try and decipher the Arabic calligraphy inside Ortaköy Camii (p120) before resting at one of the nearby cafés

The oldest surviving buildings are in Old İstanbul, with a number of Byzantine structures including churches, cisterns, fortresses and fortified walls remaining. Urban spaces such as the Hippodrome and ceremonial boulevards such as Divan Yolu also date from this era. In Beyoğlu, traces of the Genoese presence dating back to the final years of the Byzantine Empire can be found, as can buildings from every stage of Ottoman rule. Early essays in the development of a national architectural movement in the early 20th century are found on both sides of the Golden Horn (Haliç). These areas are where most visitors spend their time, but there are discoveries galore through every part of the city. In fact, that's what makes the place so fascinating – the layers of history have a physical manifestation here. There might be stellae from a Roman ceremonial way on one corner and an Ottoman *han* (caravanserai) on another... you'll end up acting like an archaeologist, looking to make new discoveries each time you leave your hotel room.

Decorate your place like Topkapı Palace (p62)

top picks

TOP BOOKS ON İSTANBUL'S ARCHITECTURE

Check the following for the low-down on the architecture and urban design of İstanbul:

- *Strolling Through Istanbul* by Hilary Sumner-Boyd and John Freely. The walking tours in this guide offer a fascinating overview of the city's buildings and urban design.
- *Istanbul: An Architectural Guide* by Christa Beck and Christiane Forsting. This pocket-sized book is one of few English-language books to discuss the city's 20th-century buildings.
- *Sinan Diaryz: A Walking Tour of Mimar Sinan's Monuments* by Ann Pierpont. Once you've seen one of Sinan's buildings you'll to want to see more – this book will help you in your quest.
- *A Guide to the Works of Sinan the Architect in Istanbul* by Reha Günay. More for the Sinan devotee.
- *Architectural Guide to İstanbul* by the Chamber of Architects of the Turkey İstanbul Metropolitan Branch This book is another good one of the few English-language references to discuss the city's 20th-century building stock.

BYZANTINE ARCHITECTURE

The city spent 1123 years as a Christian metropolis and there are a surprising number of structures surviving from this era. The big-ticket items are churches, but there are also examples of Byzantine walls, cisterns and aqueducts.

When Mehmet the Conqueror descended on İstanbul in 1453 many churches were converted into mosques; despite the minarets, you can usually tell a church-cum-mosque by the distinctive red bricks, characteristic of all İstanbul's Byzantine churches.

During Justinian's reign, architects were encouraged to surpass each other's achievements when it came to utilising the domed, Roman-influenced basilica form. Aya Sofya (p49), built in 537 and with a dome diameter of over 30m, is the supreme example of this.

From the outside, Byzantine churches lacked ornamentation and were often dull, with the dome being the only striking external feature. For example, both Aya Sofya and the Chora Church (Church of the Holy Saviour, Kariye Müzesi; p93) display relatively drab exteriors, giving no hint of the interior mosaics, which glint and gleam and make the soul soar.

Early Byzantine basilica design used a centralised polygonal plan with supporting walls and a dome set on top, inside rectangular external walls. The lovely Küçük Aya Sofya Camii (p57), built around 530, is an example. Later, a mixed basilica and centralised polygonal plan developed. This was the foundation for church design from the 11th century until the Conquest (1453) and many Ottoman mosques were inspired by it. The Zeyrek Camii (Church of the Pantocrator; p82) is a good example of this.

The Byzantines also had a yen for building fortifications. The greatest of these is the still-standing land wall. Twenty kilometres long, it protected the city during multiple sieges until it was finally breached in 1453. Constructed in the 5th century, the wall remained relatively intact

Despite its terrible state of repair, Zeyrek Camii (p82) still offers some beautiful sights

Just a taste of the wonders at Aya Sofya (p49)

Piece together the glorious mosaics at Chora Church (p93)

until the 1950s, when parts were removed. Consisting of a moat, an outer wall and towers, it has a monumental appearance befitting its purpose.

Constantine named his city 'New Rome'. Chief among its great public works was the stone aqueduct (p82) built by Emperor Valens between 368 and 373. The aqueduct fed a series of huge cisterns built across the city, including the Basilica Cistern (p58) and Binbirdirek (Cistern of 1001 Columns; p59).

Like Rome, the city was built on seven hills and to a grid pattern that included ceremonial thoroughfares such as Divan Yolu. Every emperor wanted a major public space carrying his name. These punctuated the ceremonial ways and acted as sites for celebrations and great public gatherings. The greatest of all the Byzantine public spaces is the Hippodrome (p56).

SAVING THE AYA SOFYAS

Every two years, the World Monuments Fund (WMF) releases its high-profile list of the 100 most endangered cultural heritage sites in the world. In recent years, a number of İstanbul's buildings and structures have featured, including Aya Sofya (1996 and 1998), Zeyrek Camii (2000) and Küçük Aya Sofya Camii (2002, 2004, 2006). The enormous international attention that a listing elicits has helped to preserve both Aya Sofya and Küçük Aya Sofya Camii, with the big church receiving funding for a painstaking and seemingly interminable restoration and the little church recently being unveiled after similarly meticulous but faster conservation works. Unfortunately, the Zeyrek Camii remains in a dreadful state of repair.

The 2008 list features another of the city's heritage treasures, and this time the fund's citation for its inclusion is blunt. Justinian's city walls are, according to the WMF, in extreme danger due to exposure to the elements and urban environment, as well as lack of an effective conservation management plan.

The 15th-century fortress Rumeli Hisarı (p217) has been a barracks, a prison, a tollbooth and a theatre

OTTOMAN ARCHITECTURE

After the conquest of Constantinople in 1453, the sultans wasted no time in putting their architectural stamp on the city. Mehmet didn't even wait until he had the city under his control, building the monumental Rumeli Hisarı (Fortress of Europe; p217) on the Bosphorus. The fortress was the first of many Ottoman structures built in elevated positions commanding extraordinary views and contributing to the skyline.

Once in the city, Mehmet kicked off a centuries-long Ottoman building spree, constructing a number of buildings including a mosque on the fourth hill. After these he started work on the building that attracts more visitors to Istanbul visit than any other: Topkapı Palace (p62).

Mehmet had a penchant for palaces, but his great-grandson, Süleyman the Magnificent, was more of a mosque man. With his court architect, Mimar Sinan (see opposite), he built the greatest of the city's

Does the Blue Mosque (p54) look blue to you? Have a look inside

THE GREAT SINAN

None of today's star architects come close to having the influence over a city that Mimar Koca Sinan had over Constantinople during his 50-year career.

Born in 1497, Sinan was a recruit to the *devşirme,* the annual intake of Christian youths into the janissaries, becoming a Muslim (as all such recruits did) and eventually taking up a post as a military engineer in the corps. Süleyman the Magnificent appointed him the chief of the imperial architects in 1538.

Sinan designed a total of 321 buildings, 85 of which are still standing in İstanbul. He died in 1588 and is buried in a self-built *türbe* located in one of the corners of the Süleymaniye Camii (p80), the building that many believe to be his greatest work.

Prepare to be dazzled at the opulent Dolmabahçe Palace (p116)

Ottoman imperial mosques. Sinan was inspired by the Aya Sofya. His prototype mosque form has a forecourt with a *şadırvan* (fountain) and domed arcades on three sides. On the fourth side is the mosque, with a two-storey porch. The main prayer hall is covered by a central dome surrounded by smaller domes and semidomes. There was usually one minaret, though imperial mosques had either two or four; and one imperial mosque, the later Blue Mosque (p54), has six.

Each imperial mosque had a *külliye* (mosque complex) clustered around it. This was a philanthropic complex including a hospital, asylum, orphanage, *imaret* (soup kitchen), hospices for travellers, *medrese,* library, hamam and cemetery. Over time, many of these buildings were demolished; fortunately, many of the buildings in the magnificent Süleymaniye Camii complex (p80) are intact.

Later sultans continued Mehmet's palace-building craze. No palace would rival Topkapı, but Sultan Abdül Mecit I tried his best with the grandiose Dolmabahçe Palace (p116). Abdül Aziz I built the extravagant Çırağan Palace (p119) and Beylerbeyi Palace (p215). These and other buildings of the era have been collectively dubbed 'Turkish baroque'.

These mosques and palaces dominate the landscape and skyline of the city, but there are other quintessentially Ottoman buildings: the hamam and the Ottoman timber house. Hamams were usually built as part of a *külliye,* and provided an important point of social contact as well as facilities for ablutions. Architecturally significant hamams include Sinan's exquisite Baths of Lady Hürrem (p53), and the still-functioning hamams of Çemberlitaş and Cağaloğlu (p193).

The Ottomans built many timber houses, called *yalıs,* along the shores of the Bosphorus (p212) for the Ottoman nobility and foreign ambassadors; city equivalents were sometimes set in a garden but were usually part of a crowded, urban streetscape. Unfortunately, not too many of these houses survive, a result of the fires that regularly raced through the Ottoman city.

ISLAMIC ECLECTICISM & MODERNISM

In the late 19th and early 20th centuries, architects created a blend of European architecture alongside Turkish baroque, with some concessions to classic Ottoman style. This style has been dubbed 'Islamic Eclecticism'. Examples include the 1889 Sirkeci Railway Station (p73), the Central Post Office in Eminönü (1909), and a bank building called 4 Vakıf Han, also in Eminönü, which now houses the World Park Hotel.

During the same period, Art Nouveau hit the city. Raimondo D'Aronco, an Italian architect, designed a number of elegant buildings, including the Egyptian consulate (p216) and the gorgeous but sadly dilapidated Botter House (p113).

When Atatürk proclaimed Ankara the capital of the republic, İstanbul lost much of its glamour and investment capital. Modernism was played out on the new canvas of Ankara, while İstanbul's dalliances went little further than the İstanbul City Hall, built in 1953; the İstanbul Hilton Hotel; and the much-maligned Atatürk Cultural Centre (p188) by Hayati Tabanlıoğlu, built in 1956 and now threatened with demolition.

Recent architecture in the city can hardly be called inspiring. One building of note is Kanyon (p143), a mixed residential, office and shopping development designed by the LA-based Jerde Partnership with local architects Tabanlıoğlu Partnership. Also noteworthy are new art museums, some of which feature impressive new wings or inspired architectural conversions of industrial spaces. The best are İstanbul Modern (p102), by Tabanlıoğlu Partnership; the Sakıp Sabancı Müzesi (p218) and santralistanbul (p186). Exciting projects on the drawing board include a vast new city waterfront extension near the Grand Prix track at Kartal-Pendik, which will be designed by the darling of the international architectural scene, Zaha Hadid.

Maybe you will see the Orient Express at Sirkeci Railway Station (p73)

WESTERN DISTRICTS

Eating p163

This part of the city is one of the least visited by visitors and that's a shame, because it's one of the most interesting. Those travellers interested in veering off the tourist track and exploring will find that spending a day here is extremely rewarding.

As İstanbul grew over the centuries, its boundaries moved westward and a series of successive city walls were put up to protect the city. In these western suburbs, populations of two major ethnic groups settled – the Jews in Balat and the Greeks in Fener. Today, their synagogues and churches are among the most interesting sights to visit in the neighbourhood – along with one of the most splendid examples of Byzantinian religious art in the world, the Chora Church (Kariye Müzesi; below).

Though remnants of the Western Districts' diverse populations still live around here, most of the current inhabitants are from the east of Turkey and are more conservative than the rest of the city's population. You'll notice, for instance, that headscarves are *de rigueur* here, with some women even wearing chadors. These areas are also conspicuously less affluent than the suburbs around Beyoğlu, the Bosphorus or even Sultanahmet.

The neighbourhood is bounded by the Golden Horn to the east and follows this waterway as far north as Edirnekapı. The major through-roads are Mürsel Paşa Caddesi (at various points also called Abdülezel Paşa Caddesi and Sadrazam Ali Paşa Caddesi), which follows the shore of the Golden Horn, and Fevzi Paşa Caddesi (the continuation of Macar Kardeşler and Şehzadebaşı Caddesis), which runs from Beyazıt and punches through the walls at Edirnekapı. Major transport is provided by bus along Fevzi Paşa Caddesi and by the Eminönü–Eyüp ferry along the Golden Horn.

CHORA CHURCH Map p96

Kariye Müzesi; ☎ 212-631 9241; Kariye Camii Sokak, Edirnekapı; admission YTL10; ⏱ 9am-6.30pm Thu-Tue; 🚌 Edirnekapı

Chora literally means 'country', and when it was built Chora Church, or the Church of the Holy Saviour Outside the Walls, was indeed outside the city walls built by Constantine the Great. However, within a century it was engulfed by Byzantine urban sprawl and enclosed within a new set of walls built by Emperor Theodosius II.

It was not only the environs of the church that changed over the years. For four centuries the building served as a mosque, Kariye Camii, but it's now a museum. And what you see today is not the original church-outside-the-walls. Rather, this one was built in the late 11th century, with reworking in the succeeding centuries. Virtually all of the interior decoration – the famous mosaics and the less-renowned but equally striking frescoes – dates from 1312 and was funded by Theodore Metochites, a man of letters who was auditor of the Treasury under Andronikos II (between 1282 and 1328). One of the museum's most wonderful mosaics (map item 48), found above the door to the nave in the inner narthex, depicts Theodore offering church to Christ.

The mosaics, which depict the lives of Christ and Mary, are stunning. See the plan on p96. Look out for the Khalke Jesus (map item 33), which shows Christ and Mary with two donors – Prince Isaac Komnenos and Melane, daughter of Mikhael Palaiologos VIII. This is under the right dome in the inner narthex. On the dome itself is a stunning depiction of Jesus and his ancestors (the Genealogy of Christ; map item 27). On the narthex's left dome is a serenely beautiful mosaic of Mary and the Child Jesus surrounded by her ancestors (map item 34).

In the nave are three mosaics: of Christ (map item 50c), of Mary and the child Jesus (map item 50b) and of the Dormition (Assumption; map item 50a) of the Blessed Virgin – turn around to see this, it's over the main door you just entered. The 'infant' being held by Jesus is actually Mary's soul.

To the right of the nave is the parecclesion, a side chapel built to hold the tombs of the church's founder and his relatives, close friends and associates. It is decorated with frescoes that deal with the themes of death and resurrection, depicting scenes taken from the Old Testament. The striking painting in the apse known as the Anastasis (map item 51) shows a powerful Christ raising Adam and Eve out of their sarcophagi, with saints and kings in attendance. The gates of

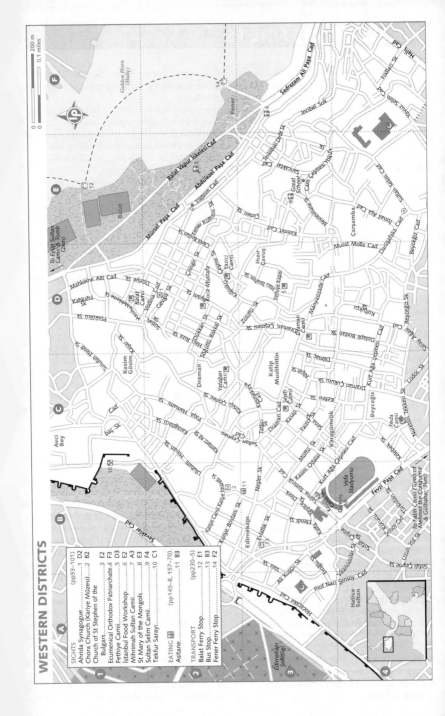

WESTERN DISTRICTS

SIGHTS (pp93–101)
Ahrida Synagogue........................1 D2
Chora Church (Kariye Müzesi)........2 B2
Church of St Stephen of the
  Bulgars....................................3 E2
Ecumenical Orthodox Patriarchate...4 F3
Fethiye Camii............................5 D3
Istanbul Food Workshop................6 E2
Mihrimah Sultan Camii.................7 A3
St Mary of the Mongols................8 E3
Sultan Selim Camii.......................9 F4
Tekfur Saray..............................10 C1

EATING (pp145–8, 157–70)
Astane.....................................11 B3

TRANSPORT (pp230–5)
Balat Ferry Stop.........................12 E1
Bus Stop..................................13 B3
Fener Ferry Stop........................14 F2

94

BARBARA NADEL'S İSTANBUL

Çetin İkmen is a typical Turkish male. He smokes like a chimney, is unfailingly courteous to strangers and dotes on his children. Unlike the rest of his compatriots he also happens to be an Inspector in the İstanbul Police Department, a devotee of the brandy bottle and the possessor of special powers of divination passed down from his Albanian mother, who was known in her local neighbourhood of Scutari as being a witch. His sexy sidekick, Mehmet Süleyman, comes from a privileged Ottoman background, is as sensitive and intelligent as he is attractive, but is strangely unhappy despite possessing these palpable assets. Together, they form a successful but unorthodox crime-solving team gracing the pages of Barbara Nadel's wonderful series of İkmen crime novels.

Nadel is a British writer who knows İstanbul well and loves it with a passion. Her 10 İkman novels to date are all set in the city and conjure up its neighbourhoods with extraordinary colour and detail. In *Belshazzar's Daughter,* the first of the series, most of the action is in Balat and Beyoğlu; in *A Chemical Prison* (Nadel's favourite of all of the books) it's in the area around Topkapı Palace; and in *Pretty Dead Things,* her most recent novel, part of the action is in Karaköy. The other titles in the series – *Arabesk, Deep Waters, Harem, Dance With Death* and *A Passion for Killing* – all lovingly evoke different areas of the city. The only time Nadel has allowed İkman to stray from İstanbul was in 2005's *Deadly Web,* where he investigates a cold case in Cappadocia.

There is one part of the city that Nadel finds particularly fascinating – the old Jewish quarter of Balat. It features in both *Belshazzar's Daughter* and *Petrified,* and the denouement in *Pretty Dead Things* occurs here also. In the books, İkman's much-loved daughter and ever-present character, Hulya, marries a Jewish friend of the family and moves to Balat, so the suburb is bound to stay centre stage in the future, too. When walking around the suburb, scenes from *Petrified* are immediately called to mind. The Church of St Stephen of the Bulgars (p98), where Russian villain Valery Rostov stages a fake drug drop to humiliate the police; the residential quarter around the Church of St Mary of the Mongols (p97), where artist Melih Akdeniz and his family live; the junkyard near the rear of the Hotel Daphnis where Eren Akdeniz gives the police the slip – all of these sites are easy to identify and testify to Nadel's extensive on-the-ground research in the neighbourhood.

hell are shown under Christ's feet. Less majestic but no less beautiful are the frescoes (map item 65) adorning the dome, which show Mary and 12 attendant angels.

Though no one knows for certain, it is thought that the frescoes were painted by the same masters who created the mosaics. Theirs is an extraordinary accomplishment, as the paintings, with their sophisticated use of perspective and exquisitely portrayed facial expressions, rival those painted by the Italian master Giotto, the painter who more than any other ushered in the Italian Renaissance.

Between 1948 and 1959 the decoration was carefully restored under the auspices of the Byzantine Society of America. Plaster and whitewash covering the mosaics and frescoes was removed and the works were cleaned. Unfortunately, the mosaics seem to be in need of further work today, with damp appearing under the Perspex covers on some of the outer narthex's examples.

This is one of the city's best museums and deserves an extended visit. On leaving, we highly recommend sampling the delectable Ottoman menu at the Asitane restaurant (p163), which is under the next-door Kariye Oteli.

Finally, a plea: despite signs clearly prohibiting the use of flashes in the museum, many visitors wilfully ignore this rule. Please don't be one of them.

FATİH CAMİİ off Map p94

Mosque of the Conqueror; Fevzi Paşa Caddesi; ⏱ tombs 9.30am-4.30pm; 🚌 Fatih

The Fatih was the first great imperial mosque built in İstanbul following the Conquest. For its location Mehmet the Conqueror chose the hilltop site of the ruined Church of the Apostles, burial place of Constantine and other Byzantine emperors. The mosque complex, finished in 1470, was enormous; set in extensive grounds, it included in its *külliye* 15 charitable establishments such as religious schools, a hospice for travellers and a caravanserai. Unfortunately, the mosque you see today is not the one Mehmet built. The original stood for nearly 300 years before toppling in an earthquake in 1766. Though rebuilt, it was destroyed by fire in 1782. The present mosque dates from the reign of Abdül Hamit I and is on a completely different plan. Though traces of Mehmet's mosque remain – the courtyard and its main entrance portal – the interior of the Fatih, with its ugly drinking fountain, is relatively unimpressive.

CHORA CHURCH (KARİYE MÜZESİ)

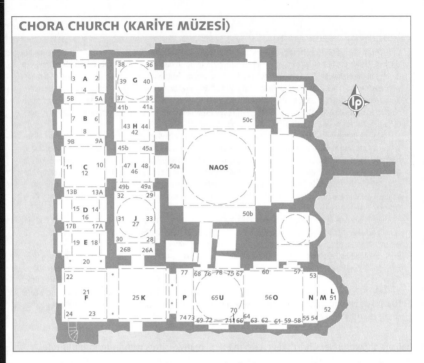

Directly behind the mosque are the tombs of Mehmet the Conqueror and his wife Gülbahar. Confusingly, Mehmet isn't buried here, but rather under the *mimber* in the mosque. Muslims consider Mehmet's tomb a very holy site. It's inevitably filled with worshippers.

The grassed outer courtyard of the mosque is a favourite place for locals to congregate and for families to picnic, especially on Sunday. On Wednesday both the courtyard and the surrounding streets host the Fatih Pazarı, a weekly market selling fresh produce and clothing.

MİHRİMAH SULTAN CAMİİ Map p94
Ali Kuşçu Sokak, Edirnekapı; 🚇 Edirnekapı
The great Sinan put his stamp on the entire city and this mosque, constructed in the 1560s next to the Edirnekapı section of Theodosius' great wall, is one of his best works. Commissioned by Süleyman the Magnificent's favourite daughter, Mihrimah, it has recently been restored. The mosque is noted for its delicate stained-glass windows and its large interior space, made particularly light by its 19 windows in each arched tympanum. The mosque occupies

the highest point in the city and its dome and one slender minaret are major adornments to the city skyline; they are particularly prominent on the road from Edirne.

TEKFUR SARAYI Map p94
Palace of the Sovereign, Palace of Constantine Porphyrogenitus; Hocaçakır Caddesi; 🚇 Edirnekapı
Sacred buildings often endure because they continue to be used, even though they may be converted for use in another religion. Put simply, there's something a bit iffy about razing a place of worship, and not too many people want to do it. No such squeamishness surrounds secular buildings such as palaces, though, and history shows that these are often torn down and rebuilt to cater to the tastes and needs of different generations. İstanbul is no different – the Byzantine palaces that once crowded Sultanahmet Square are all gone, so is the great Palace of Blachernae, which was also in this neighbourhood. Only the Tekfur Sarayı remains.

Though the building is only a shell these days, it is remarkably preserved considering its great age. Built in the late 13th or early 14th century and located close to the end of Theodosius' wall, it was a large three-

MOSAICS

The voyage of the Virgin to Bethlehem
and the dream of Joseph.............................1
The census held for the enrolment for
taxation and registration of Mary and
Joseph in the presence of Cyrenius,
Governor of Syria..2
Jesus going with Mary and Joseph to
Jerusalem..3
Remains of mosaics – Jesus amongst
the doctors in the temple...........................4
St Trachos..5a
St Andronikus...5b
The birth of Jesus...6
The return of the Virgin Mary with Jesus......7
The attempts of Satan to deceive Jesus........8
St Georgios...9a
St Demetrius...9b
Jesus and the inscription 'the
dwelling-place of the living'...................10
The prayer of the Virgin and the
attendant angels......................................11
The wedding at Cana and the miracles......12
Depiction of the saints...........................13a
Depiction of the saints...........................13b
The Magi on their way to Jerusalem
riding on horseback and the three
Magi in audience with King Herod.........14
Elizabeth and John the Baptist running
away from a pursuing soldier..................15
Remains of mosaics.....................................16
Depiction of the saints...........................17a
Depiction of the saints...........................17b
The scene of King Herod's
investigation and a guard standing.........18
The mourning mothers................................19
No mosaics left..20
A decorative medallion...............................21
The meeting of Jesus with the Samaritan
woman at the well.................................. 22
The healing of a paralysed person by Jesus..23
King Herod giving the order for the
massacre of the innocents and the
execution thereof.....................................24
Remains of mosaics.....................................25
The healing by Jesus of a young man
with an injured arm..............................26a

The healing by Jesus of leprous man........26b
Twenty-four of the early ancestors of
Jesus (Genealogy of Christ)..................... 27
The healing by Jesus of a woman asking
for the restoration of her health..............28
The healing by Jesus of the mother-in-law
of St Peter..29
The healing by Jesus of a deaf person........30
Dispersion of good health by Jesus to
the people...31
The healing by Jesus of two blind men.......32
The Khalke Jesus and the praying Virgin....33
The Virgin and the child Jesus.................... 34
Joachim in the mountains praying to
have a child.. 35
No mosaics left..36
The breaking of the good news of the birth
of Jesus to Mary – The Annunciation......37
The chief priest Zacchariah judging
the Virgin...38
Mary and Joseph bidding each other
farewell..39
The breaking of the good news of the
birth of Mary to Anne.............................40
The meeting of Anne and Joachim..........41a
Joseph bringing the Virgin into his
house..41b
Mary in the arms of Anne and Joachim,
and the blessing by the priests................42
Giving of the stick with young shoots,
indicating Joseph as Mary's fiancé.........43
The birth of the Virgin Mary........................44
The first seven steps of the Virgin,
and below, St Peter................................45a
The prayer of the chief priest Zacchariah
in front of the twelve idols....................45b
The presentation of Mary (age three) to
the temple by her parents.......................46
The Virgin taking the skeins of wool to
weave the veil for the temple.................47
Theodore Metochites presenting a small
model of the church to Jesus...................48
The feeding of the Virgin by an angel,
and below, St Peter...............................49a
Remains of mosaics – Directives given to
the Virgin at the temple.......................49b
The death of the Virgin..........................50a

Mary and the child Jesus...........................50b
Jesus in a standing posture, holding the
bible in his hand....................................50c

FRESCOES

The Anastasis...51
The church fathers.......................................52
The raising (resurrection of the
widow's son...53
The healing of the daughter of Jairus........54
The Virgin Elousa...55
The Last Judgment.......................................56
Abraham and the beggar Lazzarus on
his lap...57
St. George..58
Rich man burning in Hell's fire...................59
Those entering Heaven and the Angel
Seraphim with the semi-nude good thief.60
Depiction of Andronikus II and his family,
and the inscription and depiction above
of Makarios Tornikes and his
wife Eugenia..61
The Bearing of the Ark of the Covenant.....62
St. Demetrius...63
St. Theodore Tiro...64
Mary and child Jesus with the twelve
attending angels.......................................65
Four Gospel Writers (Hymnographers):
St. Cosmos..66
Four Gospel Writers (Hymnographers):
St. John of Damascene.............................67
Four Gospel Writers (Hymnographers):
St. Theophanes...68
Four Gospel Writers (Hymnographers):
St. Joseph...69
St. Theodore Stratelates..............................70
King Solomon and the Israelites.................71
Placement into the temple of The Ark
of the Covenant.......................................72
The combat of an angel with the Asurians
in the outskirts of Jerusalem...................73
St. Procopios, St. Sabas Stratelates............74
Moses in the bushes....................................75
Jacob's ladder and the angels.....................76
Aaron and his sons carrying votive
offerings, in front of the altar..................77
St. Samonas and Guiras...............................78

storeyed palace that may have been an annex of the Palace of Blachernae. Later uses were not so regal: after the Conquest it functioned in turn as a menagerie for exotic wild animals, a brothel and a poorhouse for destitute Jews.

To see it, wander into the sportsground next door. The site itself is fenced.

FETHİYE CAMİİ Map p94

Mosque of Victory; Fethiye Kapısı; 🔊 Fener or 🚇 Fener

The Fethiye Camii was built in the 12th century as the Church of the Theotokos Pammakaristos or Church of the Joyous Mother of God. It is usually closed so if you want to enter you'll need to organise a time with the caretaker at Aya Sofya (☎ 212-522 0989).

The original monastery church was added to several over the centuries before being converted to a mosque in 1573 to commemorate Sultan Murat III's victories in Georgia and Azerbaijan. Before its conversion it served as the headquarters of the Ecumenical Orthodox Patriarch (1456–1568); not long

after the Conquest Mehmet the Conqueror visited to discuss theological questions with Patriarch Gennadios. They talked in the side chapel known as the parecclesion, which has been restored to its former Byzantine splendour and functions as a museum; the rest of the building remains a mosque. Though not as splendid as those in the nearby Kariye Müzesi, the building's Byzantine mosaics have been beautifully restored and are well worth seeing, particularly the Pantocrator and 12 Prophets adorning the dome, and the Christ Hyperagathos with the Virgin and St John the Baptist in the apse.

CHURCH OF ST MARY OF THE MONGOLS Map p94

Church of Panaghia Mouchliotissa, Kanlı Kilise; Tevkii Cafer Mektebi Sokak, Fener; 🔊 Fener or 🚇 Fener

History buffs will find a visit here more satisfying than those specifically interested in architecture, as this squat red-brick church is quite unprepossessing from the outside and an unfortunate exercise in ecclesiastical decorative overkill inside. Historically, though, it is extremely significant, being the only Byzantine church in İstanbul which has not, at some stage or another, been in Ottoman hands. It was consecrated in the 13th century and saved from conversion into a mosque by the personal decree of Mehmet the Conqueror. If you ring the bell on the outside gate you may attract the attention of the caretaker, who is usually happy to show visitors the church in exchange for a tip.

AHRIDA SYNAGOGUE Map p94
Ahrida Sinagogu; Kürkçüçeşme Sokak 9, Balat; 🚇 Balat or 🚋 Balat
Balat once housed a large portion of the city's Jewish population. Sephardic Jews, driven from Spain by the judges of the Inquisition, found refuge in the Ottoman Empire in the late 15th and early 16th centuries and settled in this quarter of the city. Many of their descendants still live here and speak the native Spanish dialect of Ladino. Like all other religious 'nations' within the empire, the Jewish community was governed by its supreme religious leader, the Chief Rabbi, who oversaw its adherence to religious law and who was responsible to the sultan for the community's good conduct. Today, you'll need to contact the current Chief Rabbinate of Turkey (🕿 212-243 5166; fax 212-244 1980; info@musevicemaati.com) if you wish to visit this or the neighbouring Yanbol synagogue. Ahrida is the oldest and most beautiful of the two, having been built before the Conquest.

To visit, you must contact the rabbinate at least 24 hours before your visit. You'll need to fax a copy of your passport identification papers. Call between 9.30am and 5pm Monday to Thursday, 9.30am and 1pm Friday.

CHURCH OF ST STEPHEN OF THE BULGARS Map p94
🕿 212-521 1121; Mürsel Paşa Caddesi 85, Fener; 🚇 Fener or 🚋 Fener
These days we're accustomed to kit homes and assemble-yourself furniture from Ikea, but back in 1871, when this Gothic Revival cast-iron church was constructed from pieces shipped down the Danube and across the Black Sea from Vienna on 100 barges, the idea was novel to say the least.

It's hard to say which is the more unusual: the building and its interior fittings –

all made completely of cast iron – or the history of its congregation.

During the 19th century, ethnic nationalism swept through the Ottoman Empire. Each of the empire's many ethnic groups wanted to rule its own affairs. Groups identified themselves on the basis of language, religion and racial heritage. This sometimes led to problems, as with the Bulgars.

Originally a Turkic-speaking people, the Bulgars came from the Volga in about AD 680 and overwhelmed the Slavic peoples living in what is today Bulgaria. They adopted the Slavic language and customs, and founded an empire that threatened the power of Byzantium. In the 9th century they were converted to Christianity.

The Orthodox Patriarch, head of the Eastern church in the Ottoman Empire, was an ethnic Greek; in order to retain as much power as possible, the patriarch was opposed to any ethnic divisions within the Orthodox church. He put pressure on the sultan not to allow the Bulgarians, Macedonians and Romanians to establish their own religious groups.

The pressures of nationalism became too great, however, and the sultan was finally forced to recognise some sort of religious autonomy for the Bulgars. He established not a Bulgarian patriarchate, but an 'exarchate', with a leader supposedly of lesser rank, yet independent of the Greek Orthodox patriarch. In this way the Bulgarians would achieve their desired ethnic recognition and would get out from under the dominance of the Greeks, but the Greek Patriarch would allegedly suffer no diminution of his glory or power. St Stephen's functioned as the main church of the Bulgarian exarch.

Architectural historians believe that the cast-iron building, based on a design by the Ottoman architect Housep Aznavour (1853–1935), replaced an earlier timber church on the site. Its interior, which features screens, a balcony and columns all cast from iron, is extremely beautiful, with the gilded iron glinting in the hazy light that filters in through stained-glass windows.

If the church isn't open, see if you can find the caretaker who lives on the grounds – he's usually happy to open the gate in exchange for a tip.

ECUMENICAL ORTHODOX PATRIARCHATE Map p94

Patrikhane; ☎ 212-531 9670; www.ec-patr.org; Sadrazam Ali Paşa Caddesi, Fener; donation requested; ⏰ 9am-5pm; 🚊 Fener or 🚋 Fener

The Ecumenical patriarch is a ceremonial head of the Orthodox Church, though most of the churches in Greece, Cyprus, Russia and other countries have their own patriarchs or archbishops who are independent of İstanbul. Nevertheless, the symbolic importance of the patriarchate, here in the city that saw the great era of Byzantine and Orthodox influence, is considerable. The patriarchate has been located in this district since 1601.

To the Turkish government, the patriarch is a Turkish citizen of Greek descent nominated by the church and appointed by the government as an official in the Directorate of Religious Affairs. In this capacity he is the religious leader of the country's Orthodox citizens and is known officially as the Greek Patriarch of Fener (Fener Rum Patriği). The relationship of the patriarchate and the wider Turkish community has been strained in the past, no more so than when Patriarch Gregory V was hanged for treason after inciting Greeks to overthrow Ottoman rule at the start of the Greek War of Independence (1821–32). The lingering antagonism over this and the Greek occupation of parts of Turkey in the 1920s no doubt explains the elaborate security around the patriarchate, including a security checkpoint at the main entrance.

The Church of St George within the patriarchate compound is a modest structure built in 1720. Its main glory is the ornate patriarchal throne that is thought to date from the last years of Byzantium. In 1941 a disastrous fire destroyed many of the buildings but spared the church.

SULTAN SELİM CAMİİ Map p94

Mosque of Yavuz Selim; Yavuz Selim Caddesi; ⏰ tomb 9.30am-4.30pm Tue-Sun; ferry from Eminönü, 🚊 Fener or 🚋 Fener

By all accounts the sultan to whom this mosque was dedicated (Süleyman the Magnificent's father, Selim I, known as 'the Grim') was a nasty piece of work. He is famous for having his father poisoned and for killing two of his brothers, six of his nephews and three of his own sons. Odd, then, that his mosque is one of the most loved in the city. The reason becomes clear when a visit reveals the mosque's position on a lawned terrace with spectacular views of the Golden Horn – picnic spots don't come much better than this. The building itself, constructed in 1522, is a bit run-down, but is well used by local worshippers. Inside, its tilework and painted woodwork provide its most distinctive features.

EYÜP SULTAN CAMİİ & TOMB off Map p94

Mosque of the Great Eyüp; Camii Kebir Sokak, Eyüp; ⏰ tomb 9.30am-4.30pm; 🚊 Eyüp or 🚋 Eyüp

This mosque complex occupies what is reputedly the burial place of Ayoub al-Ansari (Eyüp Ensari in Turkish), a friend of the Prophet's and a revered member of Islam's early leadership. Eyüp fell in battle outside the walls of Constantinople while carrying the banner of Islam during the Arab assault and siege of the city from 674 to 678. He was buried outside the walls and, ironically, his tomb later came to be venerated by the Byzantine inhabitants of the city.

When Mehmet the Conqueror besieged Constantinople in 1453, he built a grander and more fitting tomb. The mosque that he built on the site became the place where the Ottoman princes came for the Turkish equivalent of coronation: to gird the Sword of Osman, signifying their power and their title as *padişah* (king of kings), or sultan. In 1766 Mehmet's building was levelled by an earthquake; a new mosque was built on the site by Sultan Selim III in 1800.

If you arrive by ferry (the best way), cross the road from the ferry stop and walk up İskele Caddesi, the main shopping street, until you reach the mosque complex. From the plaza outside the complex, enter the great doorway to a courtyard shaded by a huge plane tree; the mosque is to your right and the tomb, rich with silver, gold, crystal chandeliers and coloured İznik tiles, is to your left. Even though women pray in a separate room to the right of the mosque, females can usually enter the mosque itself and stand at the rear if they are properly covered.

Be careful to observe the Islamic proprieties when visiting, as this is an extremely sacred place for Muslims, ranking fourth after the big three: Mecca, Medina and Jerusalem.

During your visit you may see boys dressed up in white satin suits with spangled caps and red sashes emblazoned with the word 'Maşallah'. These lads are on the way to their circumcision and have made a stop beforehand at this holy place. See boxed text, p99.

After visiting the mosque, many visitors head north up the hill to Pierre Loti Café (8pm-midnight), where the famous French novelist is said to have come for inspiration. Loti loved İstanbul, its decadent grandeur and the late-medieval customs of a society in decline. When he sat in this café, under a shady grapevine sipping tea, he saw a Golden Horn busy with caïques (long, thin rowboats), schooners and a few steam vessels. The water in the Golden Horn was still clean enough to swim in and the vicinity of the café was given over to pasture. The café that today bears his name has no connection to Loti, but it occupies a similar spot and offers views similar to the ones he must have enjoyed. It's in a warren of streets on a promontory surrounded by the Eyüp Sultan Mezarlığı (Cemetery of the Great Eyüp). Many important people, including lots of grand viziers, are buried here.

The surest way to find the café is to walk out of the mosque complex to the plaza, turn right, and walk around the mosque complex (keeping it on your right) until you see a set of stairs and a steep cobbled path going uphill into the cemetery. Hike up the steep hill for 10 to 15 minutes to reach the café. Alternatively, a cable car (YTL1.30 each way, Akbil accepted) joins the waterfront with the top of the hill. The café serves çay (YTL1.60), *Türk kahvesi* (YTL2.70) and nargilehs (YTL8). Be sure to check the bill before paying. There's also a souvenir store here that sells postcards featuring historical views of the city.

WESTERN DISTRICT WALK
Walking Tour
1 Mihrimah Sultan Camii This mosque (p96) was designed by Sinan on the orders of Mihrimah, Süleyman's favourite daughter. Sited by the gate of Theodosius' great wall it's always been hard to overlook. Make sure you admire its delicate stained-glass windows.

2 Chora Church We're going to go out on a limb here, and say that this is the best museum (Kariye Müzesi; p93) in the city. The exquisite Byzantine mosaics and frescoes were funded by Theodore Metochites, the auditor of the imperial treasury, and he certainly got lots of bang for his buck. It can be tricky to find, but is worth the effort. Refuel near here at Asitane (p163).

3 Sultan Selim Camii Süleyman the Magnificent built this mosque (p99) to honour his father, Selim the Grim. He didn't go overboard, and history indicates why – dad was famous for killing his own father, two of his brothers, six of his nephews and three of his own sons.

4 Ecumenical Orthodox Patriarchate After the Conquest, the patriarchate was kicked out of the building it used in Aya Sofya. It eventually found a home here in Fener and has happily existed in this location (p99) ever since. More interesting historically than architecturally, the compound is still worth a visit.

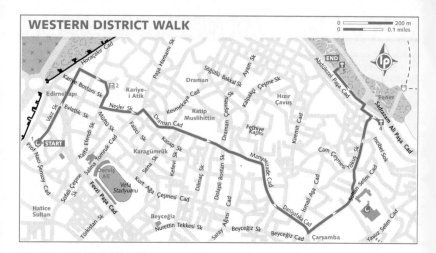

WESTERN DISTRICT WALK

0 ——— 200 m
0 ——— 0.1 miles

WALK FACTS

Start Mihrimah Sultan Camii
End Church of St Stephen of the Bulgars
Distance 2km
Time Five hours
Fuel stops Enjoy an Ottoman lunch fit for a sultan at Asitane (p163)

5 Church of St Stephen of the Bulgars

Is this the city's most unusual building (p98)? It and all of its fittings are made of cast iron – it's a sort of kit-home prototype. Allow some time to admire the stained-glass windows. You'll find the church on the shore of the Golden Horn, close to the Fener ferry terminal, from where you can catch a boat back to Eminönü or continue up to Eyüp.

GALATA & TOPHANE

Drinking p174; Eating p163; Sleeping p205

Beyoğlu (bey-oh-loo), the 'new' or 'European' section of İstanbul on the northern side of the Golden Horn, isn't really new. In the 19th century, new ideas brought from Europe by traders and diplomats walked into Ottoman daily life down its streets and boulevards. The Europeans who lived here in Pera, as the neighbourhood was formerly known, imported new fashions, machines, arts and manners to the city. This part of town had telephones, an underground train, a tramway, electric light and modern municipal government. There were even European-style patisseries and shopping arcades. In contrast, Old İstanbul (Stamboul), on the south bank of the Golden Horn, kept its oriental bazaars, great mosques, draughty palaces, narrow streets and traditional values – it seemed almost to be living in the Middle Ages when compared with its sophisticated neighbour.

There was a settlement in Galata/Karaköy before the birth of Christ. By the time of Theodosius II (r 408–50), it was large enough to become an official suburb of Constantinople. Theodosius built a fortress here to complete the defence system of his great land walls, and he called it Galata, as the suburb was then the home of many Galatians (Celtic people from Asia Minor). The neighbouring suburb of Tophane, which stretches along the banks of the Bosphorus, dates from a slightly later period and has historically been known as a maritime suburb where boats docked and offloaded cargo to huge warehouses. These days some of these are being converted into public spaces such as the exciting İstanbul Modern (below). The suburb took its name from a cannon foundry (*tophane*) that was built there during the reign of Mehmet the Conqueror.

Galata was home to traders from Genoa and Venice during both Byzantine and Ottoman times, and functioned almost like a separate colony, with distinct architecture, a preponderance of taverns and a decidedly European flavour. From the 16th century onwards, it had a largely Jewish population, hence the number of synagogues in the neighbourhood. In the 19th century, European émigrés arrived and built grandiose churches, schools and bank buildings – all reminders of the time when most of the empire's bankers and businesspeople were non-Muslims.

By the end of the last century, the once grand suburb was looking worse for wear. The city's largest municipal brothel was here, as well as drinking dens, vagrants and street prostitution. Visiting the city in the 1870s, Edmondo de Amicis wrote that it was '…full of shady characters of every description'. Fortunately times have changed, and these days the inexorable process of gentrification is under way, with tatty but grand apartment buildings being restored, and the city's artistic and student communities working and living here. Some commercial offices and banks, as well as small traders, remain, but it's largely residential and retains its European flavour.

The tramline between Zeytinburnu and Kabataş passes through Galata/Karaköy and Tophane, and there's a ferry terminal with some services to Kadıköy dock. The world's shortest and oldest (and probably most ornate) underground railway, the Tünel, runs up the hill from Karaköy Meydanı (Karaköy Square) to Tünel Square, at the southwestern end of İstiklal Caddesi. At the time of research, the railway was closed for renovation.

İSTANBUL MODERN Map p103

☎ 212-334 7300; www.istanbulmodern.org; Meclis-I Mebusan Caddesi, Tophane; adult/child under 12yr YTL7/free; ⏰ 10am-6pm Tue-Wed & Fri-Sun, 10am-8pm Thu; 🚊 Tophane

In recent years İstanbul's contemporary-art scene has boomed. Facilitated by the active cultural philanthropy of the country's industrial dynasties – many of which have built extraordinary arts collections – museum buildings are opening nearly as often as art exhibitions. İstanbul Modern, funded by the Eczacıbaşı family, is the big daddy of them all. Opened with great fanfare in 2005, this huge converted shipping terminal has a stunning location right on the shores of the Bosphorus at Tophane and is easily accessed by tram from Sultanahmet.

The museum's curatorial program is twofold: the first floor highlights the Eczacıbaşı family's collection of Turkish 20th century and contemporary art using a thematic approach; and the downstairs spaces host temporary exhibitions from local and international artists. While the first floor exhibits are interesting – look for works by Şekere Ahmet Ali Paşa (1841–1907), Orhan Peker (1927–78), İsmet Doğan (1957–), Omer

GALATA & TOPHANE

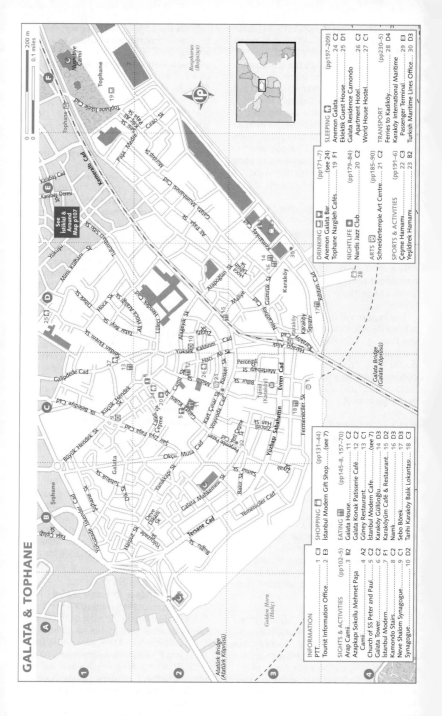

INFORMATION	
PTT................................	1 C3
Tourist Information Office......	2 E3

SIGHTS & ACTIVITIES	(pp102–5)
Arap Camii......................	3 B2
Azapkapı Sokollu Mehmet Paşa	
Camii...........................	4 A2
Church of SS Peter and Paul..	5 C2
Galata Tower...................	6 C2
İstanbul Modern...............	7 F1
Kamondo Stairs................	8 C2
Neve Shalom Synagogue......	9 C1
Synagogue.....................	10 D2

SHOPPING	
İstanbul Modern Gift Shop....	(see 7)

EATING	(pp145–8, 157–70)
Galata House..................	11 C2
Galata Konak Patisserie Café..	12 C2
Güney Restaurant..............	13 C1
İstanbul Modern Cafe..........	(see 7)
Karaköy Güllüoğlu.............	14 D3
Karaköyüm Café & Restaurant.	15 D2
Namli..........................	16 D3
Sebo Börek....................	17 D3
Tarihi Karaköy Balık Lokantası.	18 C3

DRINKING	(pp171–7)
Anemon Galata Bar............	(see 24)
Tophane Nargileh Cafes.......	19 F1

NIGHTLIFE	(pp179–84)
Nardis Jazz Club...............	20 C2

ARTS	(pp185–90)
Schneidertemple Art Centre....	21 C2

SPORTS & ACTIVITIES	(pp191–6)
Çeşme Hamamı................	22 C3
Yeşildirek Hamamı............	23 B2

SLEEPING	(pp197–209)
Anemon Galata................	24 C2
Eklektik Guest House...........	25 D1
Galata Residence Camondo	
Apartment Hotel..............	26 C2
World House Hostel............	27 C1

TRANSPORT	(pp230–5)
Ferries to Kadıköy.............	28 D4
Karaköy International Maritime	
Passenger Terminal...........	29 E3
Turkish Maritime Lines Office..	30 D3

103

Kaleşi (1932–), Cihat Burak (1915–94), İhsan Cemal Karaburçak (1897–1970), Avni Arbaş (1919–2003), Sema Gürbüz (1960–) and Adnan Çoker (1927–) – it's the temporary exhibitions and permanent installations in the downstairs spaces that really stand out. Unfortunately, plans by Museum Director David Elliott to replace the less interesting works in the upstairs exhibit with international acquisitions and to give even greater emphasis to travelling exhibitions were scuttled in 2007 after a disagreement about the museum's future direction with the gallery's main donor, Oya Eczcıbaşı, led to his resignation.

Downstairs, don't miss Richard Wentworth's *False Ceiling* (1995–2005), an installation of Turkish and Western books floating overhead that hints at important issues around the negotiation of cultural difference. The knockout piece in the permanent collection is probably Adnan Çoker's huge abstract canvas, *Retrospective* (1997).

The museum also has a dedicated interactive exhibition space for children called Genç (Young). Conceived and designed in association with the Centre Georges Pompidou in Paris, it runs education programs for children aged between six and 12. This is hands-on fun that also bolsters arts awareness – great stuff.

GALATA TOWER Map p103

Galata Kulesi; Galata Meydanı, Galata; admission YTL10; ⏱ 9am-8pm; ⓐ Karaköy

The cylindrical Galata Tower stands sentry over the approach to 'new' İstanbul. For centuries the tallest structure in Beyoğlu, it dominates the skyline north of the Golden Horn.

Originally constructed in 1348, the tower was the high point (at 67m, literally and figuratively) in the Genoese fortifications of Galata, and has been rebuilt many times. It has survived a number of earthquakes, as well as the demolition of the rest of the Genoese walls in the mid-19th century.

The paved public square surrounding the tower was created by the municipality as part of the ongoing Beyoğlu Beautification Project and it's been a big hit with locals of all ages, who gather each day to play football and backgammon, drink tea, buy food from the street vendors and swap local news.

There is a cafeteria (tea YTL3.50, beer YTL7) on the 8th floor of the tower where you can enjoy a drink, and a vertiginous panorama balcony offering spectacular 360-degree views of the city. To be frank, we don't think the view (as spectacular as it is) justifies the steep admission cost.

AZAPKAPI SOKOLLU MEHMET PAŞA CAMİİ Map p103

Tersane Caddesi, Galata; ⓐ Karaköy or ⓔ Tersane Caddesi

This pretty mosque, designed by Sinan and built in 1577, is unusual in that it and the minaret are raised on a platform. Like Sinan's Rüstem Paşa Camii over the Golden Horn (also on a raised platform), it was commissioned by Sokollu Mehmet Paşa, a grand vizier of Süleyman the Magnificent. Today it's overshadowed by the approach to Atatürk Bridge and seems to almost shrink back from the traffic mayhem of Tersane Caddesi. Still, it's well worth a visit, particularly for its fine marble mihrab and *mimber*. Look for the attendant if the mosque is locked; a tip is expected. Don't miss the nearby rococo fountain *(sebil)* built by Saliha Valide Hatun, mother of Mahmut I.

ARAP CAMİİ Map p103

Arab Mosque; Galata Mahkemesi Sokak, Galata; ⓐ Karaköy or ⓔ Tersane Caddesi

This mosque is the only surviving place of worship built by the Genoese; it was the largest of the Latin churches in the city. Dating from 1337, it was converted to a mosque by Spanish Moors in the 16th century. It has a simple plan – long hall, tall square belfry-cum-minaret – with ornate flourishes such as the galleries added in the 20th century. Look for an attendant if the mosque is locked; he may be willing to show you the interior in exchange for a tip.

KAMONDO STAIRS Map p103

Galata; ⓐ Karaköy or ⓔ Tersane Caddesi

The curvaceous 18th-century Kamondo Stairs, one of Beyoğlu's most distinctive pieces of urban design, run south from Kart Çınar Sokak. Around the corner from the stairs you'll find the Schneidertempel Art Centre (p187). This art gallery, which is housed in a modest former synagogue, hosts shows of Jewish art, usually contemporary and local in origin.

CHURCH OF SS PETER & PAUL
Map p103

SS Pierre et Paul; ☎ 212-249 2385; Galata Kulesi Sokak 44, Galata; ⏰ mass 7.30am daily & 11am Sun (in Italian); Ⓜ Karaköy

Tucked away in one of the steep streets below Galata Tower you'll find the small grey-and-white doorway to the courtyard of the Church of SS Peter and Paul. A Dominican church originally stood on this site, but the building you see today dates from the mid-19th century. It's the work of the Fossati brothers who also designed the Dutch and Russian consulate buildings (both in Beyoğlu). Like many other Latin churches in the city, its courtyard design reflects the Ottoman ruling that Latin churches could not be built directly fronting onto a road or on top of a hill (the Church of St Mary Draperis on İstiklal Caddesi is another example of this). The church backs onto a section of the Genoese fortifications. It's not open very often – ring the bell and try your luck.

NEVE SHALOM SYNAGOGUE
Map p103

☎ 212-293 7566; Büyük Hendek Caddesi 61, Galata; Ⓜ Karaköy

During the 19th century, Galata had a large Sephardic Jewish population and a number of synagogues. Most of this community has now moved to other residential areas in the city, but the synagogues remain. Tragically, this building in particular seems to have become a target for anti-Jewish extremists and it has suffered two attacks in recent decades – a brutal massacre by Arab gunmen during the summer of 1986 and a 2003 car bomb attack carried out by a motley group of Turkish Muslims inspired by Osama bin Laden.

GALATA WALK
Walking Tour

1 İstanbul Modern It's hip, it's hot and it's undeniably the centre of a happening scene. One of a number of impressive new art galleries to have opened in İstanbul in the past few years, İstanbul Modern (p102) has a great location, an interesting permanent collection and a program of knockout temporary exhibitions.

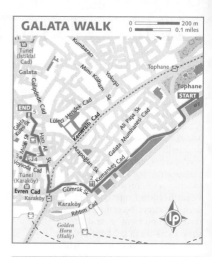

WALK FACTS

Start İstanbul Modern
End Galata Tower
Distance 1.5km
Time Two hours
Fuel stops Karaköy Güllüğlu (p165), Galata Konak Patisserie Café (p164)

2 Sugar hit Snaffle an assortment of the best baklava in the city at Karaköy Güllüğlu (p165).

3 Kamondo Stairs Built in the 18th century by the Jewish banking family after whom they are named, the Kamondo Stairs (opposite) are one of Beyoğlu's most distinctive pieces of urban design. They also featured in a famous photograph by Henri Cartier-Bresson.

4 Schneidertempel Art Center The modest synagogue in which this art gallery (p187) is housed attests to this area's Jewish heritage. Nearby Voyvoda Caddesi was once full of banks run by Jewish and Armenian businessmen, and a number of synagogues remain in the area.

5 Galata Tower The most notable structure on the Beyoğlu skyline, this tower (opposite) was built by the Genoese in 1348. Originally named the Tower of Christ, it has been a prison, observatory and lookout but now is strictly for tourists. The view from the top is quite spectacular.

Drinking p175; Eating p165; Shopping p140; Sleeping p206

İstiklal Caddesi (Independence Ave) is the backbone of Beyoğlu. Formerly known as the Grande Rue de Pera, it has historically been home to the city's smartest shops, European embassies and churches, many impressive residential buildings and a scattering of fashionable teashops and restaurants. To be in the groove last century, İstanbullus needed to work, sleep and shop within its orbit.

All this changed after independence when the capital moved to Ankara; the glamorous shops and restaurants closed, the grand buildings became dilapidated and the surrounds took on a decidedly sleazy air. Fortunately, the new millennium has brought about a rebirth, and the boulevard is once again crowded with throngs of locals who come to eat in the atmosphere-laden restaurants, drink in the bars and clubs that line the side streets and browse in the hundreds of shops crammed along its length. This *zeitgeist* can be attributed to the inspired Beyoğlu Beautification Project, an initiative that has been steered by the municipality and which has seen the street becoming a pedestrian thoroughfare, security being a focus, buildings being restored, and awnings and street signage conforming to rigid urban design specifications (all shop signs are in gold, for instance).

Known to locals simply as İstiklal, the street stretches between Tünel and Taksim Squares. An historic tram rattles along its length every 30 minutes or so – you'll need to buy a ticket from the Tünel station or a vendor in Taksim Square or have an Akbil (see p233) to get on. To the northwest of Tünel is the area known as Asmalımescit, filled with meyhanes, stylish Western-style brasseries and art galleries. Tepebaşı, the pocket that is home to the famous Pera Palas Oteli (Pera Palace Hotel; p110) and the newly opened Pera Museum (p110), is behind Asmalımescit.

Midway along the boulevard is Galatasaray Square, occupied since 1868 by its namesake, the Galatasaray Lycée. This school was established by Sultan Abdül Aziz, who wanted a place where students could listen to lectures in both Turkish and French. Today it's a prestigious public school. On the opposite side of the street are the Çiçek Pasajı (Flower Passage; p110), the busy Balık Pazar (Fish Market) and Nevizade Sokak, the most famous restaurant strip in the city.

To the east and south of the lycée are the areas known as Çukurcuma and Cihangir. Çukurcuma is where you'll find many of the city's best antique shops and Cihangir is an upmarket residential area where trendy bars and cafés are found and where much of the city's Western expat community lives.

Beyoğlu is one of the city's major transport hubs. Buses to every part of the city leave from the bus station at Taksim Square and a modern metro system travels between Taksim and the ritzy residential and shopping suburbs to its north, terminating in Levent. A recently opened funicular between the square and the terminus of the Zeytinburnu–Kabataş tramline has delighted commuters and made accessing this most fascinating suburb from the Old City extemely easy.

GALATA MEVLEVİHANESİ Map p107

Museum of Court Literature, Divan Edebiyatı Müzesi; ☎ 212-245 4141; Galipdede Caddesi 15, Tünel; admission YTL2; ☯ 9.30am-5pm Tue-Sun; ⓧ Karaköy, then funicular to Tünel

If you thought the Hare Krishnas or the Harlem congregations were the only religious orders to celebrate their faith through music and movement, think again. Those sultans of spiritual spin known as the 'whirling dervishes' have been twirling their way to a higher plane ever since the 13th century and show no sign of slowing down soon.

The Mevlevi *tarika* (order), founded in Konya during the 13th century, flourished throughout the Ottoman Empire. Like several other orders, the Mevlevis stressed the unity of humankind before God regardless of creed.

The whirling dervishes took their name from the great Sufi mystic and poet, Celaleddin Rumi (1207–73), called Mevlana (Our Leader) by his disciples. Sufis seek mystical communion with God through various means. For Mevlana, it was through a *sema* (ceremony) involving chants, prayers, music and a whirling dance. The whirling induced a trancelike state that made it easier for the mystic to seek spiritual union with God.

Dervish orders were banned in the early days of the Turkish republic because of their ultraconservative religious politics.

İSTİKLAL & AROUND

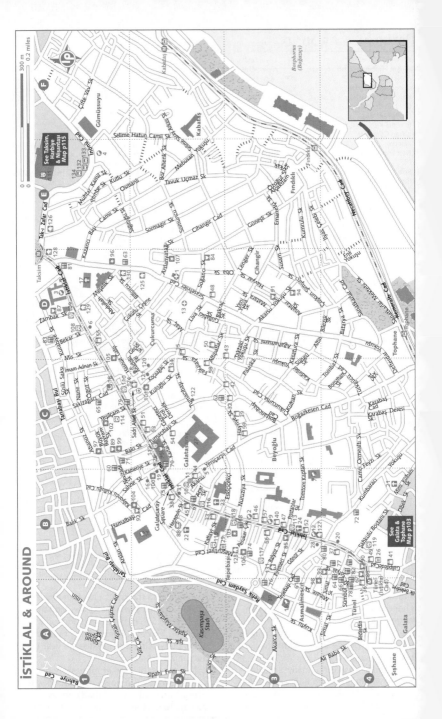

İSTİKLAL & AROUND

INFORMATION
Alman Hastanesi (German
  Hospital)..................................1 D2
Canadian Consulate...................2 B3
French Consulate........................3 D1
German Consulate.....................4 E1
Goethe Institut..........................5 B2
İstanbul Kitabevi (Biletix)..........6 D1
Italian Consulate........................7 B3
Lambda......................................8 C2
Netherlands Consulate...............9 B3
PTT...10 B2
Robin Hood Internet Café.........11 B2
Russian Consulate.....................12 B3
Taksim Hastanesi...................... 13 D2
UK Consulate.............................14 B2
US Consulate..............................15 A3

SIGHTS & ACTIVITIES   (pp106–13)
Avrupa & Aslihan Pasajis...........16 B2
Aya Triyada Kilisesi....................17 D1
Ağa Camii..................................18 C1
Balık Pazar.................................19 C2
Botter House..............................20 B4
Christ Church.............................21 B4
Church of Panaya Isodyon........22 B4
Church of San Antonio di
  Padua......................................23 B2
Church of St Mary Draperis......24 B3
Çiçek Pasajı................................25 C2
Galata Mevlevihanesi................26 B4
Galatasaray Lycée......................27 C2
Patisserie Markiz........................28 B3
Pera Museum.............................29 B2
Pera Palas Oteli.........................30 A3
Yapı Kredi Bankası Gallery.........31 B2

SHOPPING   (pp131–44)
A la Turca..................................32 C3
Ambar.......................................33 B2
Anadol Antik.............................34 C2
art.i.choke.................................35 D2
Artrium......................................36 A4
Beyoğlu Hali Evi........................37 B4
Bis..38 B2
Bis 2..39 C3
Denizler Kitabevi.......................40 B3
Elvis...41 B4
Galeri Alfa.................................42 C3
Hikmet & Pinar..........................43 D3
Homer Kitabevi.........................44 B2
İpek...45 B2
İstanbul Kitapçısı.......................46 B3
İyigün Oyuncak.........................47 B3
La Cave Wine Shop...................48 D2
Lale Plak....................................49 B4

Leyla Seyhanlı..........................50 D2
Mavi Jeans................................51 C2
Mavi Jeans 2.............................52 B3
Mephisto...................................53 C2
Mor Taki....................................54 C2
Mudo Pera.............................(see 47)
Pandora.....................................55 D1
Paşabahçe..................................56 B3
Robinson Crusoe.......................57 B3
Sedef Çalarkan..........................59 C3

EATING   (pp145–8, 157–70)
360..(see 116)
Boncuk Restaurant....................60 C1
Canım Ciğerim İlhan Usta..........61 A3
Cezayir.......................................62 C2
Changa......................................63 D1
Flamm..64 B4
Hacı Abdullah............................65 C1
Helvetica Lokanta......................66 A4
House Café.................................67 A4
İnci Pastanesi............................ 68 B3
Kafe Ara.....................................69 B2
Konak..70 C2
Krependeki İmroz Restaurant....71 C1
Leb-i Derya................................72 B4
Lokal..73 B4
Lokanta......................................74 B3
Mado...75 B2
Mikla..76 A3
Nu Teras.................................(see 74)
Refik...77 B4
Saf' Organic Bistro.....................78 A4
Saray Muhallebicisi....................79 C1
Şimdi...80 B4
Simit Sarayı................................81 D1
Sofyalı 9.....................................82 B4
Zencefil......................................83 D1

DRINKING   (pp171–7)
5 Kat..84 D2
Ada...85 B3
Badehane...................................86 B4
Büyük Londra Oteli Bar.........(see 123)
Club 17......................................87 D1
Haco Pulo..................................88 B2
James Joyce Irish Pub................89 C1
Kaffeehaus.................................90 B4
Keve.......................................(see 36)
Leb-i Derya...........................(see 72)
Leb-i Derya Richmond.........(see 127)
Leyla..91 D3
Nu Teras.................................(see 74)
Pano...92 B2
Pasific House..............................93 B4

Smyrna.......................................94 D3
Urban...95 C2

NIGHTLIFE   (pp179–84)
Andon...96 D1
Araf..97 C1
Babylon......................................98 A3
Balans Music Hall......................99 C1
Cumhuriyet..............................100 B2
Degustasyon........................(see 19)
Déjà Vu....................................101 C2
Gabile......................................102 C1
Garibaldi..................................103 B3
Ghetto......................................104 B2
Jazz Cafe..................................105 D1
Kokosh by Asmali.....................106 B3
Roxy...107 D2
Tonique.................................(see 99)

ARTS   (pp185–90)
AFM Fitaş.................................108 D1
Akbank Culture & Arts Centre..109 D1
Alkazar Sinema Merkezi...........110 C1
Atatürk Cultural Centre............111 E1
Atlas Sinemaları.......................112 C2
Borusan Arts & Culture Centre.113 B3
Emek..114 C1
Galeri Nev................................115 B2
Galerist....................................116 B2
Italian Cultural Centre.............117 B3
Platform Garanti Contemporary
  Art Centre.............................118 B3
Tarık Zafer Tunaya Kültür
  Merkezi.................................119 B3

SPORTS & ACTIVITIES   (pp191–6)
Aquarius..................................120 C2
Ağa Hamamı............................121 C2
Tarhihi Galatasaray Hamamı...122 C2

SLEEPING   (pp197–209)
Büyük Londra Oteli..................123 B3
Hotel Residence.......................124 C2
Lush Hip Hotel.........................125 D2
Marmara Pera......................(see 76)
Marmara İstanbul....................126 E1
Richmond Hotel.......................127 B3
Taksim Square Hotel................128 D1
Triada Residence......................129 D1
Vardar Palace Hotel.................130 D1
Yenişehir Palas.........................131 B3

TRANSPORT   (pp230–5)
Kamil Koç Bus Ticket Office.....132 E1
Ulusoy Bus Ticket Office..........133 E1
Varan Bus Ticket Office...........134 E1

Although the ban has been lifted, only a handful of functioning *tekkes* (dervish lodges) remain in İstanbul, including this one. Konya remains the heart of the Mevlevi order. For more information check www.emav.org.

The museum was originally a Mevlevihanesi (whirling-dervish hall) and a meeting place for Mevlevi (whirling) dervishes. The first building here was erected by a

high officer in the court of Sultan Beyazıt II in 1491. Its first *şeyh* (sheik) was Mohammed Şemai Sultan Divani, a grandson of the great Mevlana. The building burned in 1766, but was repaired that same year by Sultan Mustafa III.

Nowadays this former monastery has become a slightly run-down compound with overgrown gardens and shady nooks. As you approach the Mevlevihanesi, notice the graveyard on the left and its stones with graceful Ottoman inscriptions. The shapes atop the stones reflect the headgear of the deceased, each hat denoting a different religious rank. The tomb of Galip Dede, the 17th-century Sufi poet who the street was named after, is here. Note also the tomb of the sheik by the entrance passage and the ablutions fountain.

Inside the Mevlevihanesi the central area is where the dervishes whirl. The galleries above were traditionally for visitors and separate areas were set aside for the orchestra and for female visitors (who were concealed behind the lattices). These days the upstairs area is only for the musicians who play during the ceremony. There are also exhibits of Mevlevi calligraphy, writing and musical instruments in the display cases surrounding the central area. The monastery was slated for a restoration as this book went to print.

CHRIST CHURCH Map p107

☎ 212-241 5616; Serdarı Ekrem Sokak 82-84, Tünel; ☾ prayer times 9-10am & 6-7pm daily, 10am Sun for communion; 🚈 Karaköy, then funicular to Tünel

Designed by CE Street (who also did London's Law Courts), the cornerstone of this Anglican church was laid in 1858 by Lord Stratford de Redcliffe, known as 'The Great Elchi' (elçi, meaning ambassador) because of his paramount influence in mid-

19th-century Ottoman affairs. The church, dedicated in 1868 as the Crimean Memorial Church, is the largest of the city's Protestant churches. It was restored and renamed in the mid-1990s.

PATISSERIE MARKIZ Map p107

İstiklal Caddesi 360-2; 🚈 Karaköy, then funicular to Tünel

In Pera's heyday, there was no more glamorous spot to be seen than Patisserie Lebon in the Grand Rue de Pera (now İstiklal Caddesi). The place to enjoy gateaux and gossip, it was favoured by the city's European elite, who dressed to kill when they popped in for afternoon tea. Noting this, tailors, furriers and milliners opened shops in the adjoining Passage Orientale and did a brisk trade, making it the city's most exclusive retail precinct.

Part of the patisserie's attraction was its gorgeous Art Nouveau interior. Four large tiled wall panels had been designed around the theme of the four seasons by Alexandre Vallaury, the architect of the Pera Palas Oteli, and were created in France. Unfortunately, only two (Autumn and Spring) survived the trip from France – they have adorned the walls ever since. With chandeliers, fragile china, gleaming wooden furniture and decorative tiled floor, the place was as stylish as its clientele.

In 1940 the Lebon was taken over by Avedis Çakır, who renamed it Patisserie

SEEING THE DERVISHES WHIRL

Even in Ottoman times, Galata's Mevlevihanesi was open to all who wished to witness the *sema* (ceremony), including foreign, non-Muslim visitors. Though banned for a short period in the 1920s by Atatürk, the tradition remained strong and continues today. It is a highlight for many visitors to the city.

When this book went to print, the dervishes whirled at 5pm every second and last Sunday from May to September, and at 3pm from October to April. The performance (adult/student under 24yr YTL30/25) lasted for 90 minutes, starting with a live performance of Sufi music. Though no official announcements had been made, it was thought that the ceremony would potentially be moved permanently to another *tekke* (dervish lodge) in Mevlanakapı in 2008.

There is a performance (☎ information & bookings 212-458 8834; adult/student under 24 YTL30/25) by the same group of dervishes in the exhibition hall on platform 1 at Sirkeci Railway Station near Sultanahmet at 7.30pm every Sunday, Wednesday and Friday. Works on the station building in 2008 could well mean that these performances relocate – ask your hotel for an update.

The most authentic ceremony can be seen most Monday nights at the Fatih *tekke* in the Western Districts of the Old City. This is the real deal, not a performance put on for tourists, and is highly recommended. The easiest way to attend is to go with Les Arts Turcs (☎ 212-520 7743; www.lesartsturcs.com; İncili Çavuş Sokak 37, Kat 3, Sultanahmet), an arts organisation cum tour company that charges YTL50 per person to give you a briefing about the meaning of the ceremony, take you to the *tekke* from its office near Aya Sofya and bring you back after the ceremony.

Remember that the ceremony is a religious one – by whirling, the adherents believe that they are attaining a higher union with God – so don't talk, leave your seat or take flash photographs while the dervishes are spinning.

Markiz. It continued to trade until the 1960s, when Pera's decline and a lack of customers led to its closure. Fortunately, closure didn't mean destruction – the building was boarded up and left just as it had been, fittings and all. In the 1970s, local artists and writers lobbied the authorities to have the patisserie and passage added to the country's register of historical buildings; this occurred in 1977, ensuring the entire building's preservation.

In late 2003 the magnificently restored patisserie re-opened to great acclaim. It is now is run by Roberts Coffee: the coffee and cake are disappointing, but the glorious interior means that a stop here is worthwhile regardless.

PERA PALAS OTELİ Map p107

Pera Palace Hotel; Meşrutiyet Caddesi 98-100, Tepebaşı; 🚇 **Karaköy, then funicular to Tünel**
The Pera Palas was built by Georges Nagelmackers, the Belgian entrepreneur who founded the *Compagnie Internationale des Wagons-Lits et Grands Express Européens* in 1868. Nagelmackers, who had succeeded in linking Paris and Constantinople by luxury train with his famed *Orient Express,* found that once he had transported his esteemed passengers to the Ottoman imperial capital there was no suitable place for them to stay. What was Nagelmackers to do? Why, build a new luxury hotel of course!

The hotel opened in 1892 and advertised itself as having 'a thoroughly healthy situation, being high up and isolated on all four sides', and 'overlooking the Golden Horn and the whole panorama of Stamboul'. Numbered among its guests were Agatha Christie, who supposedly wrote *Murder on the Orient Express* in Room 411; Mata Hari, who no doubt frequented the elegant bar with its lovely stained-glass windows and excellent eavesdropping opportunities; and Greta Garbo, who probably enjoyed her own company in one of the spacious suites.

As this book went to print the hotel was undergoing a total renovation and was covered in hoardings. Some consternation was being aired around town as to how sympathetic the renovation will be to the building's rich cultural and architectural history.

PERA MUSEUM Map p107

☎ 212-3349900; www.peramuzesi.org.tr; Meşrutiyet Caddesi 65, Tepebaşı; adult/students & child over 12yr/child under 12yr YTL7/3/2;

🕐 10am-7pm Tue-Sat, noon-6pm Sun; 🚇 Karaköy, then funicular to Tünel
The most beloved painting in the Turkish canon – Osman Hamdı Bey's *The Tortoise Trainer* – sold at auction in late 2005 for a massive US$3.5 million, making it the most expensive art purchase of recent times. Turks were worried that the painting might be lost to the nation, so there was rejoicing when this new, privately funded museum announced that it had been the successful bidder and that the painting would be the focal point of its wonderful Orientalist painting collection. Acquired by Suna and İnan Kıraç over decades, this collection consists of more than 300 paintings with Turkish Orientalist themes. Its canvasses by Turkish and European artists provide fascinating glimpses into the Ottoman world from the 17th to the early 20th century. Sometimes these treatments are realistic, at other times they are highly romanticised – what's consistent is their focus on the rich costumes, fascinating domestic settings and varied individuals of the period.

The museum has conceived a program of long-term thematic exhibitions to showcase these Orientalist paintings, and has been loaned important Orientalist works from the Sevgi and Erdoğan Gönül Collection to supplement its holdings. At the time of research a show titled 'Portraits of the Empire' had been hung on the third floor and it was a total joy to visit – we're hoping that future shows will be just as good.

The museum also has two permanent exhibits: a top-notch collection of Kütahya tiles and ceramics, and a somewhat esoteric collection of Anatolian weights and measures. Three further floors are devoted to temporary exhibitions, mostly of local contemporary works in mixed media.

ÇİÇEK PASAJI Map p107

İstiklal Caddesi; 🚇 **Kabataş, then funicular to Taksim**
Back in the days when the *Orient Express* was rolling into Old Stamboul and promenading down İstiklal Caddesi was the fashionable thing to do (how little things change…), the Cité de Pera building was the most glamorous address in town. Built in 1876 and decorated in Second Empire style, it housed a shopping arcade as well as apartments. As Pera declined, so too did the building, its stylish shops giving way to cheap restaurant-taverns where in good weather beer barrels were rolled out onto

the pavement, marble slabs were balanced on top, wooden stools were arranged and enthusiastic revellers caroused the night away. Renamed Çiçek Pasajı (Flower Passage), it continued in this vein until the late 1970s, when parts of the building collapsed. When it was reconstructed, the passage was 'beautified'. That is, its makeshift barrel heads and stools were replaced with comfortable and solid wooden tables and benches, and its broken pavement was covered with smooth tiles. The passage also acquired a glass canopy to protect pedestrians from foul weather. These days its raffish charm is nearly gone and locals in the know bypass the touts and the mediocre food on offer here and instead make their way behind the passage to Nevizade Sokak if they are seeking a great night on the town.

Next to the Çiçek Pasajı you'll find the Balık Pazar (Fish Market), where small stands sell *midye* (skewered mussels) fried in hot oil (get a skewer that's been freshly cooked). You'll also find stalls selling fruit, vegetables, pickles and other produce here.

At 24A Sahne Sokak, look for the gigantic black doors to the courtyard of the Üç Horan Ermeni Kilisesi (Armenian Church of Three Altars). Visitors can enter the church providing the doors are open. Opposite the church are the neoclassical Avrupa Pasajı (European Passage; aka Aynalı Pasajı or Arcade of Mirrors), a small gallery with marble paving and shops selling tourist wares and some antique goods, and Aslıhan Pasajı, an arcade jampacked with second-hand book and record stalls.

TAKSİM SQUARE Map p107
🚊 Kabataş, then funicular to Taksim

The symbolic heart of modern İstanbul, this busy square is named after the stone reservoir on its western side, once part of the city's old water-conduit system. The main water line from the Belgrade Forest, north of the city, was laid to this point in 1732 by Sultan Mahmut I (r 1730–54). Branch lines then led from the *taksim* to other parts of the city.

Hardly a triumph of urban design, the square has a chaotic bus terminus on one side, a slightly pathetic garden laid out in its centre and the tracks of the İstiklal Caddesi tram circumnavigating this garden. Nonetheless, this doesn't prevent locals nominating it as a favoured meeting point and making the terraces of the nearby

Burger King and Simit Sarayı, which afford views over it, two of the most popular fast-food stops in the city. The government and municipality often organise for official events – usually related to the police or military – to be held here. During such events it's not unusual to see tanks and riot police surrounding the square and police sharpshooters atop nearby buildings.

The prominent modern building at the eastern end of the plaza is the Atatürk Cultural Centre (Atatürk Kültür Merkezi, sometimes called the Opera House; p188). In the summertime, during the International İstanbul Music Festival, tickets for the various concerts are on sale in the ticket office here, and numerous performances are staged in the centre's halls.

At the western end of the square is the Cumhuriyet Anıtı (Republic Monument), created by Canonica, an Italian sculptor, in 1928. It features Atatürk, his assistant and successor, İsmet İnönü, and other revolutionary leaders. The monument's purpose was not only to commemorate revolutionary heroes, but also to break down the Ottoman-Islamic prohibition against the making of 'graven images'.

İSTİKLAL CADDESİ WALK
Walking Tour
1 Taksim Square Start this afternoon walk at Beyoğlu's busy nerve centre, Taksim Square (left). This is where locals meet before setting off to promenade down İstiklal Caddesi. Named after the stone water reservoir on its western side, it's home to the city's major performing arts centre, the modernist Atatürk Cultural Centre.

2 Çiçek Pasajı The picturesque Flower Passage (opposite) has been hosting raucous crowds of drinkers since the late 1800s, and shows no sign of changing its ways any time soon. The Balık Pazar (Fish Market) on its western side is a great place to grab a fishy street snack.

3 Avrupa Pasajı One of many covered arcades in the Beyoğlu area, the European Passage (off Çiçek Pasajı, see opposite) is the most attractive, and though its shops are touristy it's worth a visit for its architecture alone.

4 British Consulate General This *palazzo*-style hulk was built in 1845 to plans by Sir Charles Barry, architect of London's

İSTIKLAL CADDESI WALK

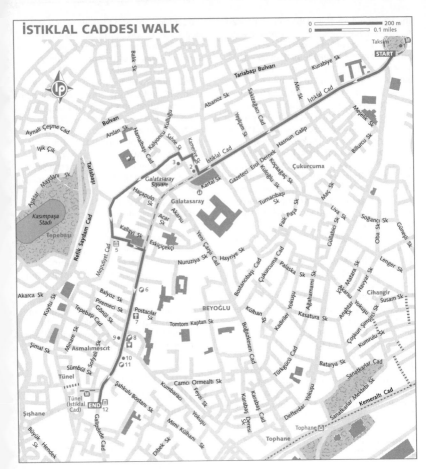

WALK FACTS

Start Taksim Square
End Galata Mevlevihanesi
Distance 2km
Duration Three hours
Fuel stop Leb i-Derya Richmond (p176)

Houses of Parliament. Home to the British Consul General ever since, it has recently been restored after a dreadful bomb attack in 2003.

5 Pera Museum If, like many travellers, you have seen reproductions of the famous Osman Hamdi Bey painting *The Tortoise Trainer* and fallen in love with it, this is the place to view the painting itself. It's part of the museum's (p110) wonderful collection of Orientalist paintings.

6 Netherlands Consulate General This handsome building dating from 1855 was designed by the Swiss-born Fossati brothers, who had been architects to the Russian tsar before they arrived in İstanbul to take the town by architectural storm and design many of its foreign embassies.

7 Church of St Mary Draperis Built in 1904, this church is behind an iron fence and down a flight of steps. It occupies the site of its previous building, destroyed by fire in 1870. During the Ottoman period, there was a law that prevented non-Muslim spires from appearing on the city skyline – no doubt the reason for this 'sunken' location.

8 Russian Consulate Another grand embassy designed by the Fossati brothers, this building dates from 1837. It replaced an earlier Russian embassy (now known as the Narmanlı Han) which is a bit further down İstiklal Caddesi on the opposite side of the road.

9 Patisserie Markiz The coffee and cake at this café (p109) are nothing to get excited about, but the Art Nouveau interior certainly is. It features gorgeous tiled wall panels designed around the theme of the four seasons by Alexandre Vallaury, the architect of the nearby Pera Palas Oteli.

10 Botter House Designed by Raimondo D'Aronco for the chief tailor to the imperial court of Sultan Abdül Hamit II, this was the first Art Nouveau building in Pera. Unfortunately, it's currently in a deplorable state of repair and has been scaffolded for safety reasons.

11 Royal Swedish Consulate Yep, it's another grand embassy building. This one was built by the Swedes when they were one of Europe's major powers and is suitably grandiose.

12 Galata Mevlevihanesi As part of Atatürk's reforms in the 1920s, all the *tekke* (dervish lodges) in İstanbul were closed. While most are now in ruins, this Mevlevihanesi (whirling-dervish hall; p106), the most important of them all, remains open as a small museum.

TAKSİM, HARBİYE & NİŞANTAŞI

Shopping p142; Sleeping p208

If you're a dab hand at air-kissing and striking a pose over a café latte, these leafy and exclusive suburbs are for you.

ASKERİ MÜZESİ Map p115

Military Museum; ☎ 212-233 2720; Vali Konağı Caddesi, Harbiye; admission YTL4; ⏱ 9am-5pm Wed-Sun; ⏹ Kabataş, then funicular to Taksim

For a rousing museum experience, present yourself at this splendid museum, located 1km north of Taksim. Try to visit in the afternoon so that you can enjoy the concert given by the Mehter, the medieval Ottoman Military Band, which occurs between 3pm and 4pm daily (see below).

The large museum is spread over two floors. On the ground floor are displays of weapons, a 'martyrs' gallery (şehit galerisi) with artefacts from fallen Turkish soldiers of many wars, displays of Turkish military uniforms through the ages, and glass cases holding battle standards, both Turkish and captured. These include Byzantine, Greek, British, Austro-Hungarian, Italian and Imperial Russian standards. Perhaps the most interesting of the exhibits are the imperial pavilions (sayebanlar). These luxurious cloth shelters, heavily worked with fine silver and gold thread, jewels, precious silks and elegant tracery, were the battle headquarters for sultans during the summer campaign season.

Also on show are a portion of the great chain that the Byzantines stretched across the mouth of the Golden Horn to keep out the sultan's ships during the battle for Constantinople in 1453; and a tapestry woven by Ottoman sailors (who must have had lots of time on their hands) showing the flags of all of the world's important maritime nations.

The upper floor has more imperial pavilions and a room devoted to Atatürk, who was, of course, a famous Ottoman general before he became founder and commander-in-chief of the republican army and first president of the Turkish Republic. This floor is where you really feel the spirit of the Ottoman Empire. It has exhibits of armour (including cavalry), uniforms, field furniture made out of weapons (eg chairs with rifles for legs), and a Türk-Alman Dostluk Köşesi (Turco-German Friendship Corner) with mementos of Turkish and German military collaboration before and during WWI.

Outside the museum, to the east of the building, you'll find cannons, including Gatling guns cast in Vienna, bearing the sultan's monogram. More of the Golden Horn's great chain is here as well.

Perhaps the best reason to visit this museum is to view the short concert by the Mehter. According to historians, the Mehter was the world's first true military band. Its purpose was not to make pretty music for dancing, but to precede the conquering Ottoman paşas (governor) into vanquished towns, impressing upon the defeated populace their new, subordinate status. Children in particular will love watching them march with their steady, measured pace, then turning all together to face the left side of the line of march, then the right side.

The easiest way to get to the museum is to walk up Cumhuriyet Caddesi from Taksim Square. This will take around 15 minutes.

TAKSİM, HARBİYE & NİŞANTAŞI

0 |————————————| 200 m
0 |————————————| 0.1 miles

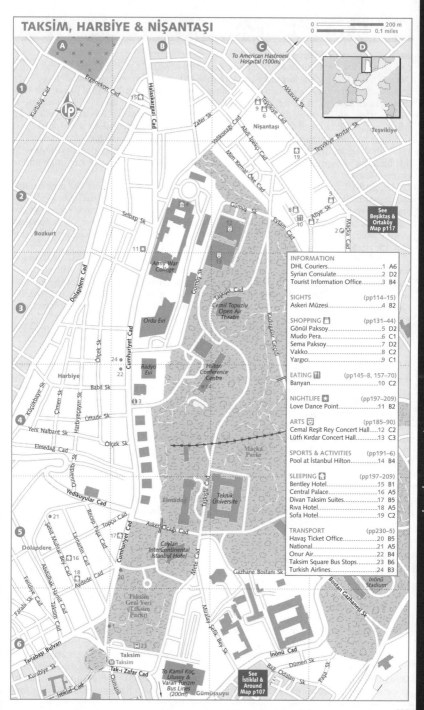

To American Hastenesi
Hospital (100m)

Nişantaşı

Teşvikiye

See
Beşiktaş &
Ortaköy
Map p117

Bozkurt

Army War
College

Cemil Topuzlu
Open Air
Theatre

Ordu Evi

Radyo
Evi

Harbiye

Hilton
Conference
Centre

Maçka
Parkı

Elmadağ

Teknik
Üniversite

Dolapdere

Ceylan
InterContinental
Istanbul Hotel

İnönü
Stadium

Taksim
Gezi Yeri
(Taksim
Parkı)

Taksim

Taksim

To Kamil Koç,
Ulusoy &
Varan Turizm
Bus Lines
(200m)

Gümüşsuyu

See
İstiklal &
Around
Map p107

INFORMATION		
DHL Couriers	1	A6
Syrian Consulate	2	D2
Tourist Information Office	3	B4

SIGHTS	(pp114–15)	
Askeri Müzesi	4	B2

SHOPPING 🛍	(pp131–44)	
Gönül Paksoy	5	D2
Mudo Pera	6	C1
Sema Paksoy	7	D2
Vakko	8	C2
Yargıcı	9	C1

EATING 🍴	(pp145–8, 157–70)	
Banyan	10	C2

NIGHTLIFE ★	(pp197–209)	
Love Dance Point	11	B2

ARTS 🎭	(pp185–90)	
Cemal Reşit Rey Concert Hall	12	C2
Lütfi Kırdar Concert Hall	13	C3

SPORTS & ACTIVITIES	(pp191–6)	
Pool at Istanbul Hilton	14	B4

SLEEPING 🛏	(pp197–209)	
Bentley Hotel	15	B1
Central Palace	16	A5
Divan Taksim Suites	17	B5
Rıva Hotel	18	A5
Sofa Hotel	19	C2

TRANSPORT	(pp230–5)	
Havaş Ticket Office	20	B5
National	21	A5
Onur Air	22	B4
Taksim Square Bus Stops	23	B6
Turkish Airlines	24	B3

BEŞİKTAŞ & ORTAKÖY

Drinking p177; Eating p169; Sleeping p209

As well as being a major transport hub and the home of one of the 'Big Three' football teams (see p196), Beşiktaş has the largest concentration of Ottoman pleasure palaces and pavilions in İstanbul. French writer Pierre Loti described the shoreline here as a '…line of palaces white as snow, placed at the edge of the sea on marble docks' and the description is still as accurate as it is evocative. This is where the unrepentantly over-the-top Dolmabahçe Palace (below) and the ritzy Çirağan Palace Hotel Kempinski (p177), a former Ottoman royal palace, are located.

A slightly more restrained tone is evident at Yıldız Şale, a palace set in the Yıldız Parkı (p119). While its designer didn't go as far as eschewing the ornate and ostentatious (heaven forbid!), this building has a more human scale than its waterside equivalents and scores high on the charm-o-meter.

The nearby suburb of Ortaköy is nowhere near as grand as Beşiktaş, but has considerable charm, particularly on warm summer nights, when its main square is crowded with locals dining at its trendy waterside restaurants or enjoying an after-dinner coffee and ice cream by the water. Later in the evening, the clubbing set hits the nearby super-venues on the Bosphorus, most of which are located on or near Muallim Naci Caddesi. Known as the 'Golden Mile', this sybaritic stretch finishes at the next-door suburb of Kureçeşme.

It can be difficult to access Yıldız and Ortaköy, as narrow Çirağan/Muallim Naci Caddesi provides the only vehicular access and is inevitably jammed bumper-to-bumper with commuters making their way to or from the Bosphorus suburbs. This means that taxi rides here can be slow and expensive. Buses also get caught in the traffic jam and can be unpleasantly crowded. As a result, many people choose to catch a ferry or bus to Beşiktaş and walk the kilometre or so to Ortaköy rather than driving, bussing or catching a taxi.

If you're visiting Dolmabahçe only, this is easily accessed by foot (15 minutes) from the Kabataş tram stop and the lower stop of the Taksim Square–Kabataş funicular.

DOLMABAHÇE PALACE Map p117

Dolmabahçe Sarayı; ☎ 212-236 9000; Dolmabahçe Caddesi, Beşiktaş; admission Selamlık & Harem-Cariyeler YTL20, Selamlık only YTL15, Harem-Cariyeler only YTL10, camera YTL6, video camera YTL15; ☯ 9am-4pm Tue, Wed & Fri-Sun summer, 9am-3pm winter; 🚌 or 🚋 to Kabataş & then walk These days it's fashionable for architects and critics influenced by the less-is-more aesthetic of the Bauhaus masters to sneer at buildings such as Dolmabahçe. The crowds that throng to this imperial pleasure palace with its neoclassical exterior and over-the-top interior fit out clearly don't share their disdain, though.

More rather than less was was certainly the philosophy of Sultan Abdül Mecit, who, deciding that it was time to give the lie to talk of Ottoman military and financial decline, decided to move from Topkapı to a lavish new palace on the shores of the Bosphorus. For a site he chose the *dolma bahçe* (filled-in garden) where his predecessor Sultan Ahmet I (1607–17) had filled in a little cove in order to build an imperial pleasure kiosk surrounded by gardens. Other wooden buildings succeeded the original kiosk, but all burned to the ground

in 1814. In 1843 Abdül Mecit commissioned imperial architects Nikoğos and Garabed Balyan to construct an Ottoman-European palace that would impress everyone who set eyes on it. Traditional Ottoman palace architecture was eschewed – there are no pavilions here and the palace turns its back to the splendid view rather than celebrating it. The designer of the Paris Opera was brought in to do the interiors, which perhaps explains their exaggerated theatricality. Construction was finally completed in 1856. Though it had the wow factor in spades, Abdül Mecit's project also did more to precipitate the empire's bankruptcy than to dispel rumours of it, and signalled the beginning of the end for the Osmani dynasty. During the early years of the republic, Atatürk used the palace as his İstanbul base. He died here in 1938.

The palace, which is set in well-tended gardens and entered via its ornate imperial gate, is divided into two sections, the Selamlık (Ceremonial Suites; p118) and the Harem-Cariyeler (Harem and Concubines' Quarters; p118). You must take a guided tour (around 35 people per group) to see either section – if you have only enough time for

BEŞİKTAŞ & ORTAKÖY

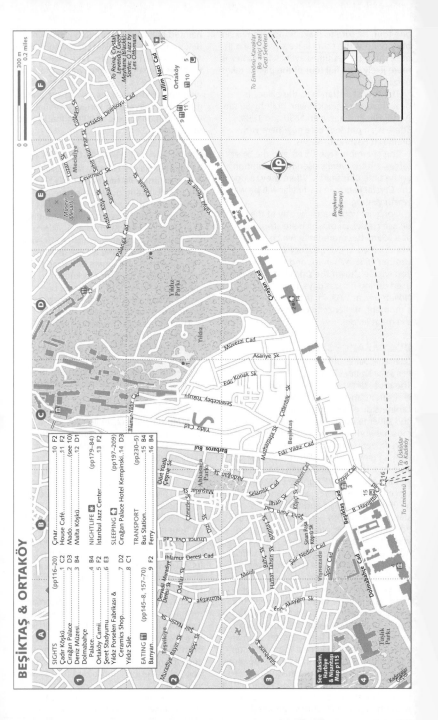

SIGHTS   (pp116–20)
Çadır Köşkü....................................1 C2
Çırağan Palace...............................2 D3
Deniz Müzesi..................................3 B4
Dolmabahçe
   Palace......................................4 B4
Ortaköy Camii................................5 F2
Şeref Stadyumu..............................6 E3
Yıldız Porselen Fabrikası &
   Ceramics Shop...........................7 D2
Yıldız Şale.....................................8 C1

Çınar..10 F2
House Café...................................11 F2
Mado...(see 10)
Malta Köşkü................................12 D1

NIGHTLIFE   (pp179–84)
İstanbul Jazz Center......................13 F2

SLEEPING   (pp197–209)
Çırağan Palace Hotel Kempinski...14 D3

TRANSPORT   (pp230–5)
Bus Station..................................15 B4
Ferry...16 B4

EATING   (pp145–8, 157–70)
Banyan...9 F2

Bosphorus (Boğaziçi)

To Reina, Crystal,
Lucca (Levent),
Meyhane (Black K),
Sortie, Q Jazz by
Les Ottomans

To Eminönü–Kavaklar
Bo azıçı Özel
Gezi Seferı

To Üsküdar
& Kadıköy

To Eminönü

See Taksim,
Harbiye
& Nişantaşı
Map p115

one tour, be sure to make it the Selamlık. In busy periods the tours leave every five minutes; during quiet times every 25 minutes is more likely. The full tour of the palace takes two hours.

The tourist entrance to the palace is near the ornate clock tower, built by Sultan Abdül Hamit II between 1890 and 1894. There is an outdoor café near here with premium Bosphorus views.

The charming Crystal Palace and the Dolmabahçe Art Gallery were closed for restoration at the time of research. When they re-open, the Crystal Palace in particular will be well worth visiting.

Don't set your watch by any of the palace clocks, all of which are stopped at 9.05am, the moment at which Kemal Atatürk died in Dolmabahçe on 10 November 1938. When touring the harem you will be shown the small bedroom he used during his last days. Each year on 10 November, at 9.05am, the country observes a moment of silence in commemoration of the great leader.

DOLMABAHÇE SELAMLIK

Ceremonial Suites; at Dolmabahçe Palace; admission Selamlık only YTL15

The tour starts by passing through opulent salons and halls to a room with glass cabinets displaying gaudy crystal, gold and silver tea sets. After visiting the palace mosque and ablutions room, things really start to get extravagant at the staircase, with a French crystal balustrade made by Baccarat. Here the Bohemian chandelier weighs close to 1000kg. The hallway at the top of the stairs has two Russian bearskins, a 2000kg chandelier and candelabras standing about 3m tall. Off this is a reception hall featuring ornate gilt ceiling and walls. These and the enormous carpet from Iran must have impressed the official visitors who came here to be received by the sultan.

If your eyes are popping out of your head, you haven't seen anything yet; the tour continues past exquisite parquetry floors, Sèvres vases and Czechoslovakian meringue-like tiled fireplaces, through an exquisite hamam and past more monster candelabras. But even these extravagances are a mere prelude to the magnificent Imperial Ceremonial Hall, or Throne Room. Used in 1877 for the first meeting of the Ottoman Chamber of Deputies, this lavishly

painted hall comes complete with a chandelier made of Irish glass that weighs over 4000kg – the tour guides here maintain that it is the largest in the world. There are grated windows, from which the resident women could watch the goings-on, and gilt on every available surface. The hall was designed to hold 2500 dignitaries and other guests.

DOLMABAHÇE HAREM-CARIYELER

Harem & Concubines' Quarters; at Dolmabahçe Palace; admission Harem-Cariyeler only YTL10

This pink building houses the harem and concubines' quarters, which are not as lavish as the Selamlık but still worth touring. Though relatively cramped and plain by Dolmabahçe standards (which isn't saying much), they have some bizarre features, including the huge ornate bed used by Sultan Abdül Aziz, who was known by his subjects as Güresçi (the Wrestler) due to his great size, considerable strength and predilection for the sport.

The tour passes through a post-circumcision resting hall, a couple of hamams and the Blue Hall, the sultan's reception hall in the harem. Note the hand-painted ceilings throughout and the amazing wallpaper in Atatürk's bedroom.

DENIZ MÜZESI Map p117

Naval Museum; ☎ 212-261 0040; cnr Cezayir & Beşiktaş Caddesis, Beşiktaş; admission YTL4; ⏰ 9am-12.30pm & 1.30-5pm Wed-Sun; 🚌 or � to Kabataş & then walk

Though this museum is picturesquely situated on the Bosphorus shore, most landlubbers (including us) find it just a tad dull. Still, those of the naval persuasion will no doubt feel like dropping an anchor here for an hour or so.

Though the Ottoman Empire is most remembered for its conquests on land, its maritime power was equally impressive. During the reign of Süleyman the Magnificent (r 1520–66), the eastern Mediterranean was virtually an Ottoman recreational lake. The sultan's navies cut a swathe in the Indian Ocean as well. Sea power was instrumental in the conquests of the Aegean coasts and islands, Egypt and North Africa. Discipline, logistics and good ship design contributed to Ottoman victories.

The museum's prize exhibits are the sleek and swift imperial caïques in which the sultan would speed up and down the Bosphorus from palace to palace. These boats are over 30m in length but only 2m wide. With 13 banks of oars, the caïques were the speed boats of their day. Those with latticework screens were for the imperial women.

You may also be curious to see a replica of the *Map of Piri Reis,* an early Ottoman map (1513), which purports to show the coasts and continents of the New World. It's assumed that Piri Reis (Captain Piri) got hold of the work of Columbus for his map. The original map is now kept in Topkapı Palace (p62).

There's an outdoor display of cannons (including Selim the Grim's 21-tonne monster) and a statue of Barbaros Hayrettin Paşa (1483–1546), the famous Turkish admiral known also as Barbarossa who conquered North Africa for Süleyman the Magnificent. The admiral's tomb, designed by Sinan, is in the square opposite the museum.

ÇIRAĞAN PALACE Map p117

Çırağan Sarayı; Çırağan Caddesi 84, Beşiktaş; 🚌 Yıldız

Not satisfied with the architectural exertions of his predecessor at Dolmabahçe, Sultan Abdül Aziz (r 1861–76) built his own grand residence at Çırağan, on the Bosphorus shore only 1.5km away from Dolmabahçe. The architect was Nikoğos Balyan, one of the designers of Dolmabahçe, and here he created an interesting building melding European neoclassical with Ottoman and Moorish styles.

Abdül Aziz's extravagance may have been one of the reasons why he was deposed in 1876, to be replaced by his mentally unstable and alcoholic nephew, Murat. Abdül Aziz later died in Çırağan under mysterious circumstances, probably suicide. Murat was in turn swiftly deposed by Abdül Hamit II, who kept his predecessor and brother a virtual prisoner in Çırağan. Murat died in the palace in 1904. In 1909 it became the seat of the Ottoman Chamber of Deputies and Senate, but in 1910 it was badly damaged by fire under suspicious circumstances.

The palace, which is now part of the Çırağan Palace Hotel Kempinski (p209), has recently undergone a full restoration under the supervision of Ottoman art specialist, Professor Nurhan Atasoy.

YILDIZ PARKI Map p117

Yıldız Park; ☎ 212-261 8460; Çırağan Caddesi; admission free; ⏰ 10am-9pm summer, 9am-5.30pm winter; 🚌 Yıldız

Sultan Abdül Hamit II (r 1876–1909) didn't allow himself to be upstaged by his predecessors. He built his own fancy palace by adding considerably to the structures built by earlier sultans in Yıldız Parkı, continuing the Ottoman tradition of palace pavilions that had been employed so wonderfully at Topkapı. It was to be the last sultan's palace built in İstanbul.

The park began life as the imperial reserve for the Çırağan Sarayı, but when Abdül Hamit built Yıldız Şale, largest of the park's surviving structures, the park then served that palace and was planted with rare and exotic trees, shrubs and flowers. It also gained carefully tended paths and superior electric lighting and drainage systems. The landscape designer, G Le Roi, was French.

The park, with its kiosks, had become derelict, but was restored by the Turkish Touring & Automobile Association (Turing) in the 1980s, under lease from the city government. In 1994 the newly elected city government declined to renew the lease and took over operation of the park. Today it's a pretty, leafy retreat alive with birds, picnickers and couples enjoying a bit of hanky-panky in the bushes.

Near the top of the hill (to the left of the road if you enter by the Çırağan Caddesi entrance), you'll see the Çadır Köşkü. Built between 1865 and 1870, the ornate kiosk is nestled beside a small lake and now functions as a café.

At the top of the hill, enclosed by a lofty wall, is the Yıldız Şale (Yıldız Chalet Museum; Map p117; ☎ 212-259 4570; admission YTL4, camera YTL6, video camera YTL15; ⏰ 9.30am-5pm Tue-Wed & Fri-Sun, until 4pm winter), a 'guesthouse' built in 1875 and expanded in 1889 and 1898 by Abdül Hamit – both times for the use of Kaiser Wilhelm II of Germany during state visits. As you enter the palace, a Turkish-speaking guide will take you on a half-hour tour through the building. The chalet isn't as plush as Dolmabahçe, but it's far less crowded (in fact, it's often empty), so you get more time to feast your eyes on the exhibits.

It would seem the Kaiser had enough space to move in, as the chalet has 64 rooms. After his imperial guest departed, the sultan became quite attached to his 'rustic' creation and decided to live here himself, forsaking the palaces on the Bosphorus shore.

Abdül Hamit was paranoid, and for good reason. When eventually deposed, he left this wooden palace in April 1909 and boarded a train that took him to house arrest in Ottoman Salonika (today Thessaloniki, Greece). He was later allowed by the Young Turks' government to return to İstanbul and live out his years in Beylerbeyi Sarayı, on the Asian shore of the Bosphorus.

Yıldız Şale was to be associated with more dolorous history. The last sultan of the Ottoman Empire, Mehmet V (Vahideddin), lived here until, on 11 November 1922, he and his retinue, accompanied by trunks full of jewels, gold and antiques, boarded two British Red Cross ambulances for a secret journey to the naval dockyard at Tophane. There they boarded the British battleship HMS *Malaya* for a trip into exile, ending the Ottoman Empire forever. On the way to the quay one of the tyres on the sultan's ambulance went flat; while it was being changed the 'Shadow of God on Earth' quaked, fearing he might be discovered.

In the republican era, the Yıldız Şale has served as a guesthouse for visiting heads of state, including Charles de Gaulle, Pope Paul VI and the Empress Soraya of Iran.

The first room on the tour was used by Abdül Hamit's mother for her religious devotions; the second was her guest reception room with a very fine mosaic tabletop. Then comes a women's resting room and afterwards a tearoom with furniture marked with a gold star on a blue background, which reminds one that this is the 'star' (*yıldız*) chalet.

During the 1898 works the chalet was expanded, and the older section became the harem (with steel doors), while the new section functioned as the *selamlık* (ceremonial suites). In the *selamlık* are a bathroom with tiles from the Yıldız Porcelain Factory and several reception rooms, one of which has furniture made by Abdül Hamit himself.

The grand hall of the *selamlık* is vast, its floor covered by a 7½-tonne Hereke carpet woven just for this room. The rug is so huge that it had to be brought in through the far (north) wall before the building was finished.

Around 500m past the turn-off to Yıldız Şale, you'll come to the Malta Köşkü, now a restaurant and function centre. Built in 1870, this was where Abdül Hamit imprisoned the deposed Murat V and his family. With its views of the Bosphorus, the terrace here makes a great place for a light lunch, tea or coffee.

If you continue walking past the Malta Köşkü for 10 minutes you'll arrive at the Yıldız Porselen Fabrikası (Yıldız Porcelain Factory; ☎ 212-260 2370; ⌚ 9am-3pm). The factory is housed in a wonderful building designed by Italian architect Raimondo D'Aronco, who was to introduce Art Nouveau to İstanbul. Constructed to manufacture dinner services for the palace, it still operates and is open to visitors. There's a small ceramics shop (⌚ 9am-7pm) at the entrance.

If you come to the park by taxi, have it take you up the steep slope to Yıldız Şale. You can visit the other kiosks on the walk down. A taxi from Taksim Square to the top of the hill should cost around YTL7.

ORTAKÖY CAMİİ Map p117
Büyük Mecidiye Camii, Ortaköy; 🚊 **Ortaköy**

Right on the water's edge, this mosque is the work of Nikoğos Balyan, one of the architects of Dolmabahçe Palace (p116). It was built for Sultan Abdül Mecit III between 1853 and 1855. With the super-modern Bosphorus Bridge now looming behind it, the mosque provides a fabulous photo opportunity for those wanting to illustrate İstanbul's 'old meets new' character. Within the mosque hang several masterful examples of Arabic calligraphy executed by the sultan, who was an accomplished calligrapher.

The mosque fronts onto Ortaköy Square, home to a pretty fountain, and popular waterfront cafés and restaurants.

Eating p169

Üsküdar (pronounced 'ooh-skoo-dar') is the Turkish form of the Byzantine name, Scutari, which dates from the 12th century. It comes from the imperial palace of Scutarion, once located on the point of land near Kız Kulesi (p123). The first colonists lived in Chalcedon (modern-day Kadıköy), to the south, and Chrysopolis (now Üsküdar) became its first major suburb; both towns existed about two decades before Byzantium was founded. The harbour at Chrysopolis was superior to that of Chalcedon so that, as Byzantium blossomed, Chrysopolis outgrew Chalcedon to become the largest suburb on the Asian shore. Unwalled and therefore vulnerable, it became part of the Ottoman Empire at least 100 years before the Conquest of 1453.

Judging that Scutari was the closest point in İstanbul to Mecca, many powerful Ottoman figures built mosques here to assist their passage to Paradise. Every year during the Empire a big caravan left from here en route to Mecca and Medina for the Hajj, further emphasising its reputation for piety. Even today, Üsküdar is one of İstanbul's more conservative suburbs. Home to many migrants from rural Anatolia, the mosques are busier here, the families are larger and the headscarf is more obvious than elsewhere in the city. Like Kadıköy and the Western Districts, it's a fascinating and totally un-touristy place to explore.

The main streets radiate from the central square, Demokrasi Meydanı, where the ferry terminal and bus stations are located. The nearby suburbs of Harem and Kadıköy are to the south. *Dolmuş* to Harem travel along the main waterside road, Sahil Yolu, and buses to Kadıköy take Selámi Ali Effendi Caddesi through the hills above town. Upmarket residential suburbs and two public parks, Büyük Çamlıca and Küçük Çamlıca, are located on these hills.

ATİK VALİDE CAMİİ Map p122

Valide Imaret Sokak; ⛴ Üsküdar
This is one of the grandest of Sinan's İstanbul mosques, second only to his Süleymaniye Camii (p80). Experts rate it as one of the most important Ottoman mosque complexes in the country. It was built in 1583 for Valide Sultan Nurbanu, wife of Selim II and mother of Murat III. Nurbanu had been captured by Turks on the Aegean island of Paros when she was 12 years old, ending up as a slave in Topkapı. The poor woman had a lot to bear – first being kidnapped and then taking the fancy of Selim the Sot – but she was his favourite concubine and became a very clever player in Ottoman political life. The Kandınlar Sultanatı (Rule of the Women) under which a succession of powerful women influenced the decisions made by their sultan husbands and sons began with her. Murat adored his mother and on her death commissioned Sinan to build this monument to her on Üsküdar's highest hill. Like the Süleymaniye, it has an impressive courtyard. The tile-adorned mihrab is particularly attractive.

The mosque is located in the neighbourhood of Tabaklar, up the hillside away from Üsküdar's main square.

ÇİNİLİ CAMİİ Map p122

Tiled Mosque; Çinili Mescit Sokak; ⛴ Üsküdar
This little mosque is fairly unprepossessing from the outside, but – boy oh boy – wait till you see the interior! It is brilliant with İznik faïence, the bequest of Mahpeyker Kösem (1640), wife of Sultan Ahmet I (r 1603–17) and mother of sultans Murat IV (r 1623–40) and İbrahim (r 1640–48). It's a 10-minute walk to get here from the Atik Valide Camii.

MİHRİMAH SULTAN CAMİİ Map p122

Dock Mosque; Demokrasi Meydanı; ⛴ Üsküdar
Sometimes called the İskele Camii, this mosque was built between 1547 and 1548 by Sinan for Süleyman the Magnificent's daughter. Though imposing on the outside, it's a bit claustrophobic and dull inside. You'll find it northeast of the Demokrasi Meydanı (main square). Look out for its ablutions fountain in the traffic island, which is particularly attractive.

MİMAR SİNAN ÇARŞISI Map p122

Hakimiyet-i Milliye Caddesi; admission free; ☾ 9am-6pm; ⛴ Üsküdar
Built by Nurbanu Sultan, mother of Sultan Murat III, between 1574 and 1583, this hamam is thought to have been the first designed by Sinan. Having fallen into ruins, part of it was torn down to accommodate construction of the avenue; the remaining half was restored in 1966 and is now cramped and crowded with shops.

ÜSKÜDAR

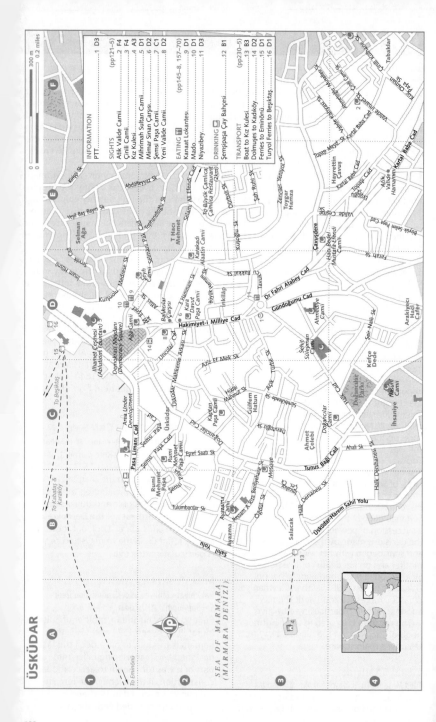

INFORMATION	
PTT	.......1 D3

SIGHTS	(pp121–5)
Atik Valide Camii	.......2 F4
Çinili Camii	.......3 F4
Kız Kulesi	.......4 A3
Mihrimah Sultan Camii	.......5 D1
Mimar Sinan Çarşısı	.......6 D2
Şemsi Paşa Camii	.......7 C1
Yeni Valide Camii	.......8 D2

EATING 🍴	(pp145–8, 157–70)
Kanaat Lokantası	.......9 D1
Mado	.......10 D1
Niyazibey	.......11 D3

DRINKING 🍸	
Şemşipaşa Çay Bahçesi	.......12 B1

TRANSPORT	(pp230–5)
Boat to Kız Kulesi	.......13 B3
Dolmuşes to Kadıköy	.......14 D2
Ferries to Eminönü	.......15 D1
Turyol Ferries to Beşiktaş	.......16 D1

YENİ VALİDE CAMİİ Map p122

**New Queen Mother's Mosque; Demokrasi Meydanı;
🚇 Üsküdar**

Unusual because of the striking 'birdcage' tomb in its overgrown garden, the Yeni Valide Camii was built by Sultan Ahmet III between 1708 and 1710 for his mother, Gülnuş Emetullah. After being captured as a child on Crete and brought to Topkapı, Gülnuş became the favourite concubine of Mehmet IV, and bore him two sons who would become sultan: Mustafa II and his younger brother, Ahmet. Built late in the period of classical Ottoman architecture, it lacks the architectural distinction of many of the suburb's other mosques. The odd wooden additions to the side that faces Demokrasi Meydanı were added as the entrance to the imperial loge.

ŞEMSİ PAŞA CAMİİ Map p122

Sahil Yolu; 🚇 Üsküdar

This charming mosque right on the waterfront was designed by Sinan and built in 1580 for grand vizier, Şemsi Paşa. It is modest in size and decoration – reflecting the fact that its benefactor only occupied the position of grand vizier for a couple of months under Süleyman the Magnificent. Its *medrese* has been stylishly converted into a library. The tomb of Şemsi Paşa, which has an opening into the mosque, is minded by a very friendly attendant, who is happy to show visitors throughout the complex for a small tip.

Next to the mosque you'll find the Şemsipaşa Çay Bahçesi, a great place to recover from a hectic schedule of Üsküdar mosque viewing.

KIZ KULESİ Map p122

**Maiden's or Leander's Tower; ☎ 216-342 4747;
🕑 noon-7pm Tue-Sun; 🚇 Üsküdar**

İstanbul is a maritime city, so it's appropriate that the Kız Kulesi, one of its most distinctive landmarks, is on the water. Arriving at Üsküdar by ferry, you'll notice the squat tower on a tiny island to the right (south), just off the Asian mainland. In ancient times a predecessor of the current 18th-century structure functioned as a tollbooth and defence point; the Bosphorus could be closed off by means of a chain stretching from here to Seraglio Point. Some think its ancient pedigree goes back even further, calling it Leander's Tower after the tragic youth who drowned after attempting to

swim across a strait to Europe to visit his lover, Hero. The object of his desire, who held a torch aloft from a tower to guide his way, is said to have been so distraught when he died that she plunged to her death from the tower. The problem with the story is Kız Kulesi is on the Asian shore – and anyway, it was the strait of the Hellespont (the Dardanelles), 340km away, that Leander swam.

More recently, the tower featured in the 1999 Bond film *The World is Not Enough*.

The tower is open to the public during the day as a café/restaurant. Small boats run from Salacak to the island every 15 minutes from noon to late at night, Tuesday to Sunday; a return ticket costs YTL6. We suggest giving this a miss, as the views from the island aren't great and the tower itself isn't very interesting inside.

BÜYÜK ÇAMLICA off Map p122

☎ 216-443 2198; Turistik Çamlıca Caddesi; admission free; 🕑 9am-11pm; 🚇 Üsküdar, then dolmuş or taxi

The term megalopolis is bandied about a fair bit to describe İstanbul, but it's only when you come to a spot like this that it becomes meaningful. Larger than many sovereign states, the city sprawls further than the eye can see, even when afforded this bird's-eye view. And what a view it is! A hilltop park with a crown of pine trees, Büyük Çamlıca is the highest point in the city and can be seen from miles away (you'll see it as you ferry down the Bosphorus, for example). It's beloved by İstanbullus, who flock here to relax, picnic in the pretty gardens, eat at the Çamlıca Restaurant (p170) and gaze upon their fine city. From the terraces you'll see the minaret-filled skyline of Old İstanbul, as well as the Bosphorus winding its way to the Black Sea.

Once favoured by Sultan Mahmut II (r 1808–39), by the late 1970s the park was a muddy and unkempt car park threatened by illegal and unplanned construction. In 1980 the municipal government leased the land to the Turing group, which landscaped the hilltop and built a restaurant such as Mahmut might have enjoyed. The municipal government took over management of the park in 1995.

To reach the hilltop from Üsküdar's main square, you can take a taxi (YTL9) all the way to the summit, or a *dolmuş* most of the way. For the latter, walk to the *dolmuş* ranks near the ferry terminal, take a *dolmuş* headed for Ümraniye and ask for Büyük Çamlıca. The *dolmuş* will pass the entrance to Küçük Çamlıca and drop you off shortly thereafter in a district called Kısıklı. The walk uphill (pleasant but no great views) following the signs to the summit takes around 30 to 40 minutes.

FLORENCE NIGHTINGALE MUSEUM
Map pp46–7

☎ 216-553 1009; fax 216-310 7929; Selimiye Army Barracks, Nci Ordu Komutanliği 1; admission free; ⏰ 9am-5pm Mon-Fri; 🚢 Harem or 🚢 Üsküdar & 🚇 Harem

The experience of visiting the Selimiye Army Barracks, where this museum is housed, is even better than the museum itself. The barracks, built by Mahmut II in 1828 is on the site of a barracks originally built by Selim III in 1799 and extended by Abdül Mecit I in 1842 and 1853. It is the headquarters of the Turkish First Army, the largest division in the country, and is an extremely handsome building, with 2.5km of corridors, 300 rooms and 300 windows. During the Crimean War (1853–56) the barracks became a military hospital where the famous lady with the lamp and 38 nursing students worked. It was here that Nightingale put in practice the innovative nursing methods that history has remembered her for. Though they seem commonsensical from a modern perspective, it is hard to overstate how radical they seemed at the time. It really is amazing to hear that before she arrived, the mortality rate was 70% of patients and when she left it had dropped to 5%.

The museum is spread over three levels in the northwest tower of the barracks. Downstairs there is a display charting the history of the First Army and concentrating on the Crimean War. On the two upstairs levels you see Nightingale's personal quarters, including her surgery room with original furnishings (including two lamps) and her living room, with extraordinary views across to Old İstanbul. Here there are exhibits such as an original letter explaining how the lady herself defined being a good nurse.

To visit, you need to fax a letter requesting to visit and nominating a time. Include a photocopy of your passport photo page. Do this 48 hours before you

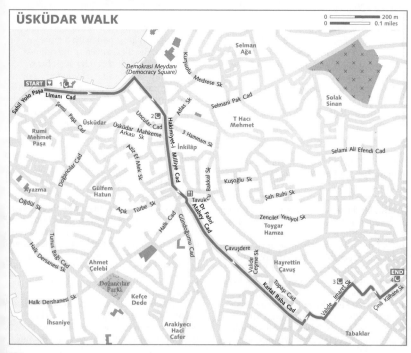

ÜSKÜDAR WALK

wish to visit and make sure you include your telephone number in İstanbul so that someone can respond to your request. The recruits who vet your papers at the entrance, show you from the security check to the museum, and take you on a guided tour are almost all young conscripts counting down the days until their military service is finished. They may not all speak English (although the tour is always in that language) but they are without exception charming and helpful. Their mothers would be proud!

The museum is about half way between Üsküdar and Kadıköy, near the fairytale-like clock towers of the TC Marmara University. To get here, catch a *dolmuş* from outside the ferry terminals in Üsküdar to Harem and ask locals to point you towards the Selimiye Kışlası Harem Kapısı (the barracks' Harem Gate), a short walk away. Alternatively, a taxi from the ferry shouldn't cost more than YTL9.

ÜSKÜDAR WALK
Walking Tour
1 Şemsi Paşa Camii This cute-as-a-button mosque (p123) right on the waterfront was designed by Sinan. It is more modest than his usual work, but is none less pleasing for that

WALK FACTS

Start Şemsi Paşa Camii
End Çinili Camii
Distance 3km
Time 2½ hours
Fuel stop Niyazibey (p169), Şemsi Paşa Çay Bahçesi (p123)

fact. The çay bahçesi next to the mosque complex is a wonderful spot for a glass of tea.

2 Yeni Valide Camii Sultan Ahmet III built this mosque (p123) in memory of his mother Gülnuş Emetullah, an extremely powerful valide sultan. Don't miss the striking 'birdcage' tomb in its overgrown garden.

3 Atik Valide Camii This mosque (p121) is one of the 'big two' – Sinan's greatest İstanbul mosque complexes. Though not as spectacular as the Süleymaniye, it was designed to a similar plan and is also in a commanding location. It was built by Murat III.

4 Çinili Camii Yes, it's a modest and rundown little mosque (p121) but wow, how about those İznik tiles?! These were the bequest of Mahpeyker Kösem (1640), wife of Sultan Ahmet I (r 1603–17).

KADIKÖY

Drinking p177; Eating p170; Shopping p144

Legend has it that the first colonists established themselves at Chalcedon, now modern Kadıköy. Byzas, bearing the oracle's message to found a colony 'Opposite the blind', thought the Chalcedonites blind to the advantages of Seraglio Point (Seray Burnu) as a town site when he arrived in the area, and founded his colony (Byzantium) on the European shore, opposite.

Though there's nothing to show of these historic beginnings and no headline sights, Kadıköy is a neighbourhood well worth visiting, particularly as the half-hour trip here by ferry from Eminönü or Karaköy is so wonderful. There's fabulous fresh produce available in the market precinct near the ferry terminal; cafés and bars galore around Kadife Sokak; and one of the city's largest street markets, the Salı Pazarı (p143).

The two ferry docks – Eminönü and Karaköy & Kızıl Adalar – face a plaza along the south side of Kadıköy's small harbour. To the north is Haydarpaşa Train Station, a 15-minute walk from the ferry terminals. In the early 20th century, when Kaiser Wilhelm of Germany was trying to charm the sultan into economic and military cooperation, he presented the station as a small token of his respect. Resembling a German castle, the neoclassical exterior is a prominent part of Kadıköy's skyline as you approach by ferry. It also has a very pretty, small ferry terminal.

Kadıköy's main street, Söğütlüçeşme Caddesi, runs eastward from the docks into Kadıköy proper; another main road, Serasker Caddesi, runs parallel to it. Busy Bahariye Caddesi runs perpendicular to both of them, around 300m inland, and continues on to the posh residential suburb of Moda.

Near the street market is Rüştü Saraçoğlu Stadium (the home of Fenerbahçe Football Club), and further on from this is the glamorous shopping and café precinct of Bağdat Caddesi, İstanbul's very own Rodeo Drive.

THE INSIDER

If you read *Time Out İstanbul* while you're in town, you'll probably end up chortling over more than a few pieces by local writer, Attila Pelit. As well as his personal byline, he writes under a number of sobriquets – which we wouldn't dream of exposing here – and most of his pieces are written exercises in what is clearly a major preoccupation of his: deconstructing what it is to be an İstanbullu and a Turk. His dedicated (predominantly Western expat) readership can't get enough of his hilarious rants against horrible city phenomena such as Magandas (the local species of beefed-up, thick-as-a-brick petrol-heads) or Nişantaşettes (the local Paris Hilton equivalents, characterised by nasally voices and solarium tans). These readers cheered when he started a campaign against ridiculous tourist entry charges in İstanbul's museums, and collectively sniggered when he took the piss out of the Beyoğlu gallery-opening circuit, describing the 'inexplicable horror' of attending a Con-Art exhibition.

Though Attila's writing is seriously funny, it often has a truly serious – and important – subtext. Take a recent piece titled 'Absurd Istanbul', where he posited that it was truly absurd that in Turkey, Kurds aren't allowed to use letters essential to their own language because those letters don't exist in the official Turkish alphabet. Those letters are X, Q and W. But as he said 'then you look all around you, and you see a store called Queen's House, a company called Winsa and an art gallery called X-Ist... So when our own Kurdish citizens use those letters it's treason, but when Turks use it for good old-fashioned foreign-envy-fuelled catchy commercial gimmickry, it's suddenly okay?'

Attila knows that being opinionated in Turkey can be akin to playing with fire, and acknowledges that there is no tradition of critiquing in Turkish magazines, something that he hopes will change over time. The English version of *Time Out İstanbul* cleverly runs critique masked as humour and can do so because it's published in English and is written predominantly for a Western expat and tourist readership. He says that his aim is to 'throw hard questions out there and encourage Turks to start thinking about those questions and confront some of our national demons'. If he can achieve this through entertainment and humour, he says, he'll be happy.

Though he has lived around the world (his father is a Turkish diplomat, making him one of the 'diplobrats' he loves to lampoon), Attila thinks of İstanbul as home, and says that his favourite thing to do in the city is to catch a ferry to Kadıköy, where he drinks pickle juice in the market, browses for second-hand books, checks out the DVD and CD stores, grabs lunch and then enjoys a few drinks at Karga Bar (p171). And then it's back home to Beyoğlu, to ponder which shibboleth to deconstruct for the next edition.

KADIKÖY

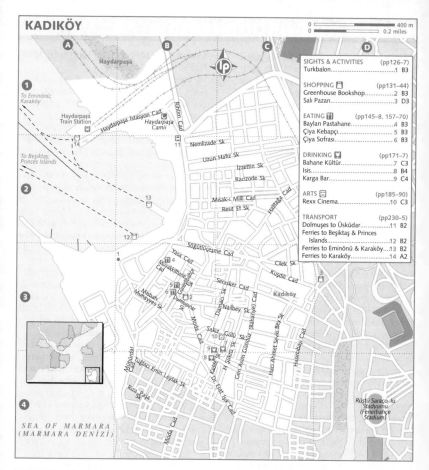

SIGHTS & ACTIVITIES	(pp126–7)
Turkbalon	1 B3

SHOPPING	(pp131–44)
Greenhouse Bookshop	2 B3
Salı Pazarı	3 D3

EATING	(pp145–8, 157–70)
Baylan Pastahane	4 B3
Çiya Kebapçı	5 B3
Çiya Sofrası	6 B3

DRINKING	(pp171–7)
Bahane Kültür	7 C3
Isis	8 B4
Karga Bar	9 C4

ARTS	(pp185–90)
Rexx Cinema	10 C3

TRANSPORT	(pp230–5)
Dolmuşes to Üsküdar	11 B2
Ferries to Beşiktaş & Princes Islands	12 B2
Ferries to Eminönü & Karaköy	13 B2
Ferries to Karaköy	14 A2

TURKBALON Map p127

☎ 0216-347 6703; adult/student YTL15/10;
🕑 9am-8pm; 🚊 Kadıköy

To see İstanbul from the air, head south along the waterfront until you come to the tethered Turkbalon, which will carry you 200m into the air to give you a 360-degree panorama of the city. Weather permitting, of course. The balloon goes up every 15 minutes and stays in the air for 10 to 15 minutes.

OTHER NEIGHBOURHOODS

YEDİKULE HİSARI MÜZESİ Map pp46–7
Fortress of the Seven Towers; ☎ 212-584 4012; Kule Meydanı 4, Fatih; admission YTL5; ☒ 9am-6.30pm; ☒ Yedikule or ☺ Yedikule

If you arrived in İstanbul by train from Europe, or if you rode in from the airport along the seashore, you will probably have noticed this fortress looming over the southern approaches to the city. One of the city's major landmarks, it has a history as substantial as its massive structure.

In the late 4th century Theodosius I built a triumphal arch here. When the next Theodosius (r 408–50) built his great land walls, he incorporated the arch in the structure. Four of the fortress' seven towers were built as part of Theodosius II's walls; the other three, which are inside the walls, were added by Mehmet the Conqueror. Under the Byzantines, the great arch became known as the Porta Aurea (Golden Gate) and was used for triumphal state processions into and out of the city. For a time its gates were indeed plated with gold. The doorway was sealed in the late Byzantine period.

In Ottoman times the fortress was used for defence, as a repository for the Imperial Treasury, as a prison and as a place of execution. In times of war, ambassadors of 'enemy' countries were thrown in prisons; foreign ambassadors to the Sublime Porte often ended up incarcerated in Yedikule. Latin and German inscriptions still visible in the Ambassadors' Tower bring the place's eerie history to light. It was also here that Sultan Osman II, a 17-year-old youth, was executed in 1622 during a revolt of the janissary corps. The kaftan he was wearing when he was murdered is now on display in Topkapı Palace's costumes collection.

The spectacular views from the battlements are the highlight of a visit here. Note that the lack of handrails or barriers on the steep stone staircases can be offputting for some visitors.

While you're in the neighbourhood, consider a trip to Istanbul's best kebapçı, Develi (p163), one station east at Mustafa Paşa.

RAHMİ M KOÇ MÜZESİ Map pp46–7
Rahmi M Koç Industrial Museum; ☎ 212-369 6600; www.rmk-museum.org.tr; Hasköy Caddesi 27; adult/child & student YTL8/4, submarine adult/child & student YTL4.50/3; ☒ 10am-5pm Tue-Fri, 10am-7pm Sat & Sun; ☺ Hasköy

Located on the Beyoğlu side of the Golden Horn, Hasköy was for centuries a small, predominantly Jewish village. In the Ottoman period it also became home to a naval shipyard and a sultan's hunting ground. Today, its main claim to fame is a splendid industrial museum. Founded by the head of the Koç industrial group, one of Turkey's most prominent conglomerates, it exhibits artefacts from İstanbul's industrial past. Its collection is highly eclectic, giving the impression of being a grab-bag of cool stuff collected over the decades or donated to the museum by individuals, organisations or companies who didn't know what else to do with it. This might sound like we're damning the place with faint praise, but this is far from the case. In fact, this is a corker of a museum that children in particular will love.

The museum is in two parts: a new building on the Golden Horn side of the road and a superbly restored and converted Byzantine stone building opposite. Exhibits are largely concerned with forms of transport: Bosphorus ferry parts and machinery; a horse-drawn tram; an Amphicar (half car, half boat) that crossed the English Channel in 1962; Sultan Abdül Aziz's ornate railway coach with its duck-egg-blue stain upholstery; cars (everything from ugly Turkish Anadol models to fabulous pink Cadillacs); a 1960 Messerschmitt; and even much of the fuselage of 'Hadley's Harem', a US B-24D Liberator bomber that crashed off Antalya in August 1943. Other exhibits look at how appliances and electronic devices work – the exhibition of how whitegoods work is particularly fascinating.

Wheelchair access is offered throughout the complex. What's more, excellent interpretive panels in Turkish and English are provided. Experts demonstrate twice a day (at 11am and 5pm) how the machines work. There are buttons galore to push, a lovely café right on the water, a convivial bar and an upmarket French brasserie. The submarine exhibit, from which children under eight years of age are barred, requires an extra ticket.

The museum is near the northern end of the old Galata Bridge (near where Hasköy Caddesi changes into Kumbarahane

Caddesi). A taxi from Beyoğlu will cost around YTL7.

MINIATURK Map pp46–7

☎ 212-222 2882; www.miniaturk.com.tr; Imrahor Caddesi, Sütlüce; adult/child YTL10/3; ⊙ 9am-5pm; ⊚ Sütlüce or ⊚ Sütlüce

We can't explain why this new museum has been such a hit with locals. Marketed as a miniature park that showcases 'all times and locations of Anatolia at the same place at the same time', it's a bizarre tiny town stocked with models of Turkey's great buildings – everything from the Celsus Library at Ephesus to Atatürk International Airport – set in manicured lawns dotted with fake rocks blasting a distorted recording of the national anthem. Children aren't interested in the models but love the miniature train that traverses the paths and the playground equipment. It's tacky and only really interesting as a demonstration of how greatly Turks revere their heritage, even when kitsch-coated.

The museum is a five-minute bus ride further on from the Rahmi M Koç Museum (opposite). It's easily accessed via the Haliç ferry from Eminönü.

BLUELIST[1] (blu,list) *v.*
to recommend a travel experience.
What's your recommendation? www.lonelyplanet.com/bluelist

SHOPPING

top picks

- **Cocoon** (Sultanahmet; p135)
- **Mehmet Çetinkaya Gallery** (Sultanahmet; p135)
- **Ali Muhiddin Hacı Bekir** (Topkapı Palace & Around; p136)
- **Sofa** (Topkapı Palace & Around; p136)
- **Derviş** (Bazaar District; p138)
- **Abdullah Natural Products** (Grand Bazaar; p138)
- **Muhlis Günbattı** (Grand Bazaar p139)
- **art.i.choke** (İstiklal & Around; p141)
- **Gönül Paksoy** (Teşvikiye; p143)
- **Kanyon** (Levent; p143)

SHOPPING

Over centuries, İstanbullus have perfected the practice of shopping, and then shopping some more. Trading is in their blood and they've turned making a sale or purchase into a true art form. Go into any carpet shop and you'll see what we mean – there's etiquette to be followed, tea to be drunk, conversation to be had. And, of course, there's money to be spent and made.

Whether you're after a cheap souvenir or a family-heirloom-to-be, İstanbul is the city to find it. Rugs (carpets and kilims), textiles, ceramics and jewellery are just a few of the temptations laid out in more arcades, bazaars and stores than you could ever hope to flash a credit card in. There's also fashion, decorative arts and homewares that can hold their own against the stock of any concept store or designer boutique in London, LA or Lisbon. And we won't even begin to rhapsodise about the delectable foodstuffs on offer…

BARGAINING

Traditionally, when customers enter a Turkish shop to make a significant purchase, they're offered a comfortable seat and a drink (coffee, tea or a soft drink). There is some general chitchat, then discussion of the shop's goods (carpets, apparel, jewellery etc) in general, then of the customer's tastes, preferences and requirements. Finally, a number of items in the shop are displayed for the customer's inspection.

The customer asks the price; the shop owner gives it; the customer looks doubtful and makes a counteroffer 25% to 50% lower. This procedure goes back and forth several times before a price acceptable to both parties is arrived at. It is considered very bad form to offer an amount, have the shopkeeper agree and then change your mind. If no price is agreed upon, the customer has absolutely no obligation and may walk out at any time.

To bargain effectively you must be prepared to take your time, and you must know something about the items in question, not to mention their market price. The best way to do this is to look at similar goods in several shops, asking prices but not making counteroffers. Shopkeepers will give you a quick education about their wares by demonstrating to you what's good about them and telling you what's bad about their competitors' goods. Soon you will discover which shops have the best quality for the lowest asking prices and you can then proceed to bargain. Always stay good-humoured and polite when you are bargaining – if you do this, the shopkeeper will too. And remember, shopkeepers know their own bottom line and will only bargain up to a certain point.

When bargaining, you can often get a discount by offering to buy several items at once, or by paying in cash and not requesting a receipt.

If you don't have sufficient time to shop around, follow the age-old rule: find something you like at a price you're willing to pay, buy it, enjoy it and don't worry about whether or not you received the world's lowest price.

OPENING HOURS

The most common shopping hours are from 9am to 6pm Monday to Saturday, but this is by no means always the case. We have indicated specific hours in all reviews.

TAXES & REFUNDS

Turkey has a value-added tax (VAT) known as the *katma değer vergisi* (KDV). This means that 18% tax is added to (and hidden in) the price of most goods and services.

If nonresidents buy an expensive item such as a carpet or a leather garment from a shop that participates in the national 'Global Refund: Tax Free Shopping' scheme and then take the item out of the country within three months, they are entitled to a refund of the KDV. Unfortunately, there aren't many shops participating in this scheme. Still, it's always worth asking the shopkeeper if it is possible to get a *KDV iade özel fatura* (special VAT refund receipt). Ask for this when you're haggling over the price, rather than after you've made your purchase. Some shops display a blue, grey and white 'Tax Free Shopping' sign in their window, conveniently signalling that they are participants in the refund scheme.

If the shopkeeper issues the refund receipt, take it with you to the airport when you leave. Before going through immigration, take the receipt and the goods that you have purchased to the 'Global Refund: Tax Free Shopping' desk, where staff will stamp the receipts to confirm that you are leaving the country. You then collect your refund from one of two booths in the departure lounge after you have gone through immigration. The refund is available in the form of cash (Turkish lira) on the spot or a credit to your chosen credit-card account.

WHAT TO BUY

While Turkey's rugs have the highest shopping profile, there are plenty of other souvenir possibilities.

Antiques

The grand Ottoman-era houses of İstanbul are still surrendering fascinating stuff left over from the empire. You'll find these treasures – furniture in the Ottoman baroque style, jewellery, crockery, paintings and more – in the antique shops of Çukurcuma and Nişantaşı.

Ceramics

After carpets and kilims, ceramics would have to be Turkey's most successful souvenir industry. This is for good reason: the ceramics are beautiful and the standard fare fits within most budgets. Many of the tiles you see in the tourist shops have been painted using a silk-screen printing method and this is why they're cheap. One step up are the ubiquitous hand-painted bowls, plates and other pieces; these are made by rubbing a patterned carbon paper on the raw ceramic, tracing the black outline and filling in the holes with colour. The most expensive ceramics for sale are hand-painted – without the use of a carbon-paper pattern – and derived from an original design. Note that many of the ceramics have lead in the glaze, so it's probably safest to use them as ornaments only.

Copper

Some copper vessels on sale in the bazaars are old, most are handsome and some are still eminently useful. The new copperware tends to be of a lighter gauge; that's one of the ways you tell the new from old. But even the new stuff will have been made by hand. Copper vessels should not be used for cooking in or eating from unless they are tinned inside: that is, washed with molten tin that covers the toxic copper. If you intend to use a copper vessel, make sure the interior layer of tin is intact, or negotiate to have it *kalaylamak* (tinned). If there is a *kalaycı* shop nearby, ask about the price of the tinning in advance, as tin is expensive.

Glassware

İstanbul produces some unique glasswork, a legacy of the Ottoman Empire's affection for this delicate and intricate art. Paşabahçe, a large factory on the Asian side, has been producing glass for 150 years and still churns out some good stuff. If you're after tea sets, the Grand Bazaar (Kapalı Çarşı) has many shops selling plain, colourful and gilded sets. Note that most of the ornate, curvy perfume bottles you see in the touristy shops are Egyptian, despite what the seller might say.

Inlaid Wood

Local artisans make jewellery boxes, chess and backgammon (*tavla*) boards, and other items that are inlaid with different coloured woods, silver or mother-of-pearl. Make sure the piece really does feature inlay. These days, alarmingly accurate decals exist. Also, check the silver: is it really silver, or does it look like aluminium or pewter? And what about that mother-of-pearl – is it in fact 'daughter-of-polystyrene'?

Jewellery

İstanbul is a wonderful place to buy jewellery, especially antique stuff. New gold work tends to be flashy, featuring yellow gold and a surfeit of decoration – it won't appeal to everyone. Silverware is more refined and there is an incredible variety of styles and designs, including many inspired by Ottoman and Byzantine jewellery. Gold shops should have a copy of the newspaper that bears the daily price for unworked gold of so many carats. Serious gold buyers should check this price, watch carefully as the jeweller weighs the piece in question, and then calculate what part of the price is for

ANTIQUITIES & THE LAW

When shopping for antiques, it's important to remember that antiquities – objects from Turkey's Hittite, Greco-Roman, Byzantine and early Ottoman past – may not be sold, bought, or taken out of the country under penalty of law. A century-old painting, lampshade or carpet usually poses no problems, but a Roman statuette, Byzantine icon or 17th-century İznik tile means trouble and quite possibly time in jail.

SHOPPING STRIPS

Every tourist has heard of İstanbul's Grand Bazaar (Kapalı Çarşısı; p76), and many will find their way to Sultanahmet's Arasta Bazaar (Map p50), but few know about the various speciality shopping areas in the city. Those who are serious about their shopping or who want specific items should follow the locals and go to the retail neighbourhood specialising in goods of a particular type.

- Antiques – Çukurcuma in Beyoğlu
- Books & Maps – Sahaflar Çarşısı (Old Book Bazaar; Map p78) near the Grand Bazaar; around İstiklal Caddesi (Map p107)
- Ceramics – Grand Bazaar; Sultanahmet
- Fashion – Around Teşvikiye Caddesi in Nişantaşı (Map p115); Kanyon (p143); Çukurcuma in Beyoğlu (Map p107)
- Handicrafts – Grand Bazaar; Sultanahmet
- Jewellery – Grand Bazaar; Sultanahmet; Nuruosmaniye Caddesi in Cağaloğlu (near the Grand Bazaar; Map p63)
- Leather – Grand Bazaar
- Music – Galipdede Caddesi in Tünel (Map p107)
- Rugs & Textiles – Grand Bazaar; Sultanahmet

gold and what part for labour. Silver will also be weighed. There is sterling-silver jewellery (look for the hallmark), but nickel silver and pewterlike alloys are much more common. Serious dealers don't try to pass off alloy as silver. Some shops will pass off plastic, glass and other stones as real gemstones – if you don't know what you're looking for, steer clear.

Leather

On any given Kurban Bayramı (Sacrifice Holiday; see p239), more than 2½ million sheep get the chop in Turkey. Add to that the normal day-to-day needs of a cuisine based on mutton and lamb and you have a huge amount of raw material to be made into leather items, hence the country's thriving leather industry. If you've always wanted a leather coat or jacket, İstanbul may be the place to purchase it, but look out for shoddy workmanship.

Old Books, Maps & Prints

Collectors will have a field day with İstanbul's wealth of antique books – some immaculate, some moth-eaten. The city and its inhabitants have been immortalised in maps, illustrations and engravings throughout the years, and many of these are available as prints, which make excellent souvenirs. You'll also see illuminated pages, supposedly from Ottoman manuscripts. These are usually modern reproductions, but they're attractive nevertheless and, again, make excellent souvenirs.

Silk

Bursa, south of the Sea of Marmara, is the silk centre of Turkey. Silkworms are raised,

their cocoons are sold in Bursa and there the silk is crafted into scarves and other items. Here in İstanbul you can get your hands on Bursa's beautiful scarves; many have ornate hand-painted patterns and/or marbled colouring.

Spices, Potions & Turkish Delight

The Spice Bazaar (Mısır Çarşısı; p82) was once the centre of the spice and medicinal herb trade in İstanbul. It's still an important outlet, though these days locals are more likely to shop in the surrounding streets, leaving the market for tourists. Do what the locals do and shop along Hasırcılar Caddesi (Map p78) for spices, tea, herbs and sweets. Prices are clearly marked and you are encouraged to taste goods before you buy.

SULTANAHMET

DESIGN ZONE Map p50   Art
☎ 212-527 9285; Alibaba Türbe Sokak, Nuruosmaniye; ⏰ 10am-7pm Mon-Sat
Contemporary Turkish designers and artists show and sell their work here. There's nifty jewellery (we love the *lale* motifs), ceramics, furniture and homewares, as well as some less impressive painting and sculpture work.

GALERİ KAYSERİ Map p50   Books
☎ 212-512 0456; Divan Yolu Caddesi 11; ⏰ 9am-9pm; 🚊 Sultanahmet
Sultanahmet's most famous bookshop has two stores on Divan Yolu near the Sultanahmet tram stop. The reasons for this

store's success are simple: the staff know and love their stock and the stock itself is extensive – thousands of English-language titles about Turkey and the Middle East.

İZNİK CLASSICS & TILES Map p50 Ceramics
☎ 212-517 1705; Arasta Bazaar 67, 73 & 141, Cankurtaran; ⏰ 9am-8pm; 🚇 Sultanahmet
İznik Classics & Tiles is the best place in town to source collector-item ceramics, including hand-painted pieces by accredited masters including Adnan Hoca, whose plates, vases and tiles are made with real quartz and metal oxides for pigments and retail for anything up to YTL5000. It also stocks some mass-produced stock, which is a lot cheaper but still beautiful. There's another store around the corner at 17 Utangaç Sokak, and a third in the Old Bazaar at the Grand Bazaar.

CAFERAĞA MEDRESESİ Map p50 Handicrafts
☎ 212-513 3601; Caferiye Sokak, near Topkapı Palace; ⏰ 8.30am-7pm; 🚇 Gülhane
The rooms around this pretty *medrese* (Islamic seminary; see p73) are used as art-teaching studios and some of the products – jewellery, miniatures, *ebru* (marbled paper) – are sold here for reasonable prices. There isn't a lot to choose from, but it's certainly worth wandering in for a peek at what's on offer.

İSTANBUL HANDICRAFTS MARKET
Map p50 Handicrafts
İstanbul Sanatlar Çarşısı; ☎ 212-517 6782; Kabasakal Caddesi 23; ⏰ 9am-6.30pm; 🚇 Sultanahmet
Set in the small rooms surrounding the leafy courtyard of the 18th-century Cedid Mehmed Efendi Medresesi, this handicrafts centre next door to the hotel Yeşil Ev is unusual in that local artisans sometimes work here and don't mind if visitors watch while they do so. Their creations are available for purchase; it's a great place to source beautiful calligraphy, glassware, hand embroidery, miniature paintings, ceramics and fabric dolls.

GALERİ CENGİZ Map p50 Rugs
☎ 212-518 8882; Arasta Bazaar 155-157, Cankurtaran; ⏰ 9am-9pm; 🚇 Sultanahmet
One of the many rug shops in the Arasta Bazaar, Galeri Cengiz stocks a colourful range of carpets and kilims that are sure to place your baggage allowance for the flight home in jeopardy.

HASEKİ HAMAM CARPET & KILIM SALES STORE Map p50 Rugs
Haseki Hürrem Hamamı; ☎ 212-638 0035; Aya Sofya Square 4; ⏰ 8.30am-5.30pm Tue-Sun; 🚇 Sultanahmet
Located in the historic Baths of Lady Hürrem (p53), which are worth a visit in their own right, this Ministry of Culture carpet shop sells new carpets replicated from museum pieces. Prices are set and clearly marked, so it's a good place to compare prices.

COCOON Map p50 Rugs & Textiles
☎ 212-638 6271; Küçük Aya Sofya Caddesi 13, Küçük Aya Sofya; ⏰ 8.30am-7.30pm; 🚇 Sultanahmet
There are so many rug and textile shops in İstanbul that isolating individual stores is usually particularly difficult. We had no problems whatsoever in singling this one out, though. In Cocoon's flagship store, four floors of felt hats and antique costumes and textiles from Central Asia are artfully displayed; its next-door rug outlet sells items from Persia, Central Asia, the Caucasus and Anatolia. The owners here really know their stuff, and most of their sales are international and dealer-based. Put simply, it is one of the most beautiful shops in the city and we love it to bits. There's another, smaller store in the nearby Arasta Bazaar.

ER & NE & MET Map p50 Rugs & Textiles
☎ 212-516 8082; Küçük Aya Sofya Caddesi 1, Küçük Aya Sofya; ⏰ 9am-9pm; 🚇 Sultanahmet
Need a few rugs for your palazzo? This is where to get them. Specialising in over-sized rugs, it stocks a large range of new, old, antique and silk examples of the craft, all of which are top quality.

MEHMET ÇETİNKAYA GALLERY
Map p50 Rugs & Textiles
☎ 212-517 6808; Tavukhane Sokak 7, Küçük Aya Sofya; ⏰ 9.30am-8.30pm; 🚇 Sultanahmet
When rug experts throughout the country meet for their annual shindig, this is where they come to check out the good stuff. You won't find any rubbish here, and you could quite possibly find a family heirloom or two. Just remember: quality never comes cheaply. It has a second shop selling textiles and objects in the Arasta Bazaar.

A CARPET-BUYER'S PRIMER

There's no right or wrong way to go about buying a carpet when you're in Turkey. There are only two hard-and-fast rules. The first is that you should never feel pressured by anyone to buy – the decision is yours and yours alone. The second is to only ever pay a price that you feel comfortable with. When you return home, you want to do so with a piece that you love and that isn't going to bankrupt you.

A good-quality, long-lasting carpet should be 100% wool (yüz de yüz yün): check the warp (the lengthwise yarns), weft (the crosswise yarns) and pile (the vertical yarns knotted into the matrix of warp and weft). Is the wool fine and shiny, with signs of the natural oil? More expensive carpets may be of a silk and wool blend. Cheaper carpets may have warp and weft of mercerised cotton. You can tell by checking the fringes at either end; if the fringe is of cotton or 'flosh' (mercerised cotton) you shouldn't pay for wool. Another way to identify the material of the warp and weft is to turn the carpet over and look for the fine, frizzy fibres common to wool, but not to cotton. But bear in mind that just being made of wool doesn't guarantee a carpet's quality. If the dyes and design are ugly, even a 100% woollen carpet can be a bad buy.

Check the closeness of the weave by turning the carpet over and inspecting the back. In general, the tighter the weave and the smaller the knots, the higher the quality and durability of the carpet. The oldest carpets sometimes have thick knots, so consider the number of knots alongside the colours and the quality of the wool.

Compare the colours on the back with those on the front. Spread the nap with your fingers and look at the bottom of the pile. Are the colours brighter there than on the surface? Slight colour variations could occur in older carpets when a new batch of dye was mixed, but richer colour deep in the pile is often an indication that the surface has faded in the sun. Natural dyes don't fade as readily as chemical dyes. There is nothing wrong with chemical dyes, which have a long history of their own, but natural dyes and colours tend to be preferred and therefore fetch higher prices. Don't pay for natural if you're getting chemical.

New carpets can be made to look old, and damaged or worn carpets can be rewoven (good work but expensive), patched or even painted. There is nothing wrong with a dealer offering you a patched or repainted carpet, of course, provided they point out these defects and price the piece accordingly. And note that some red Bukhara carpets (Bukhara is a city region in Uzbekistan) will continue to give off colour, even though they're of better quality than cheap woollen carpets that don't.

When you are examining the carpet, look at it from one end, then from the other. The colours will differ because the pile always leans one way or the other. Take the carpet out into the sunlight and look at it there. Imagine where you might put the carpet at home and how the light will strike it.

It's all very well taking measures such as plucking some fibres and burning them to see if they smell like wool, silk or nylon, or rubbing a wet handkerchief over the carpet to see if the colour comes off, but unless you know what you're doing you're unlikely to learn much from the exercise – and you may well end up with an irate carpet-seller to deal with!

In the end the most important consideration should be whether or not you like the carpet.

YÖRÜK COLLECTION
Map p50   Rugs & Textiles
☎ 212-511 7766; Yerebatan Caddesi 35-37, Sultanahmet; ⏰ 9am-9pm; ⛴ Sultanahmet
It's worth entering this shop to see the building. It formerly housed an Ottoman library and has been beautifully restored. It sells rugs, silk, miniatures, textiles, ceramics, jewellery and quirky handmade glass light fittings. For a bit of fun, ask to go upstairs and check out 'Mike's Museum', which is filled with a colourful jumble of rugs, pottery, costumes, tassels, jewellery and textiles.

TOPKAPI PALACE & AROUND

SOFA Map p63   Art & Antiques
☎ 212-520 2850; Nuruosmaniye Caddesi 85, Cağaloğlu; ⏰ 9.30am-7pm Mon-Sat

What a treasure-trove of a shop! As well as its eclectic range of prints, textiles, calligraphy and Ottoman miniatures, Sofa sells contemporary Turkish art. The pricey jewellery made out of antique Ottoman coins and 24-carat gold is particularly alluring.

VAKKO İNDİRİM Map p63   Clothing
Vakko Sale Store; ☎ 212-522 8941; Yenicamii Caddesi 1/13, Eminönü; ⏰ 9.30am-6pm Mon-Sat; ⛴ Eminönü
If you've checked out Vakko's style at one of the malls or in Teşvikiye but have concerns about the price tags, this remainder store may be for you. There's a good selection of quality women's and men's clothing, as well as shoes and accessories.

ALİ MUHİDDİN HACI BEKİR
Map p63   Food & Drink
☎ 212-522 0666; Hamidiye Caddesi 83, Eminönü; ⏰ 8am-8pm Mon-Sat, 9am-8pm Sun; ⛴ Eminönü

Pricing & Payment

When it comes to buying, there's no substitute for spending time developing an 'eye' for what you really like. You also need to be realistic about your budget. These days carpets are such big business that true bargains are hard to come by unless there's something (like gigantic size) that makes them hard to sell for their true value. Prices are determined by age, material, quality, condition, demand, the enthusiasm of the buyer and the debt load of the seller. Bear in mind that if you do your shopping on a tour or when accompanied by a guide, the price will have been inflated to include a commission of up to 35% for the tour operator or guide.

It may be wiser to go for something small but of high quality rather than for a room-sized cheapie. And it's worth remembering that kilims (pileless woven rugs) are usually cheaper than carpets. Another way to make your money stretch further is to opt for one of the smaller items made from carpet materials: old camel bags and hanging baby's cradles opened out to make rugs on which food would be eaten, decorative grain bags, even the bags that once held rock salt for animals.

Most dealers prefer to be paid with cash. Most will accept credit cards, but some require you to pay the credit-card company's fee and the cost of the phone call to check your credit-worthiness. They will rarely be participants in the Global Refund Scheme (tax-free shopping; see p132). A few dealers will let you pay in instalments.

All of this is a lot to remember, but it will be worth it if you get a carpet you like at a decent price. You'll have something to take home that will give you pleasure for the rest of your life.

Beware of the Carpet Bait & Switch

Here's the scenario: you make friends with a charming Turk, or perhaps a Turkish-American/European couple. They recommend a friend's shop, so you go and have a look. There's no pressure to buy. Indeed, your new friends wine and dine you (always in a jolly group with others). Before you leave İstanbul you decide to buy a carpet. You go to the shop, choose one you like and ask the price. So far so good; if you can buy that carpet at a good price, everything's fine. But if the owner strongly urges you to buy a 'better' carpet, more expensive because it's 'old' or 'Persian' or 'rare' or 'makes a good investment', beware. You may return home to find you've paid many times more than it is worth. If the shopkeeper ships the carpet for you, the carpet that arrives may not be the expensive carpet you bought; instead it could be a cheap copy.

To avoid this rip-off, you should choose a carpet, inspect it carefully, then shop around. Compare prices for similar work at other shops, then buy the best-value one: not necessarily the one from your friends' shop. Finally take the carpet with you or ship it yourself; don't have the shopkeeper ship it.

It's best to buy *lokum* (Turkish delight) in specialist shops and you can't find one more specialised than this. The stuff was invented by Ali Muhiddin in the 18th century and it's now sold from this (the original) shop by his descendants. Pre-packed gift boxes range in cost from YTL2.75 to YTL14. There's another store on İstiklal Caddesi in Beyoğlu and one in Kadıköy.

HAFİZ MUSTAFA ŞEKERLEMELERİ
Map p63   Food & Drink

☎ 212-526 5627; Hamidiye Caddesi 84-86, Eminönü; ⏰ 8am-8pm Mon-Sat, 9am-8pm Sun; 🚊 Eminönü

Opposite Ali Muhiddin Hacı Bekir (opposite), this shop also sells excellent Turkish delight. You can buy a small bag of freshly made treats to sample, plus gift boxes to take home. Best of all, they're happy to let you taste before buying (within reason, of course). There's also a small café/börekçi (above) upstairs.

BAZAAR DISTRICT

ZİYA AYKAÇ Map p77   Antiques

☎ 212-527 6082; Tekkeciler Sokak 68-72, Old Bazaar, Grand Bazaar; ⏰ 9am-7pm Mon-Sat; 🚊 Beyazıt

Established in 1910, Ziya Aykaç stocks antique watches, silk prayer rugs, silver jewellery and old porcelain. If you can't find something great to take home, you're just not looking hard enough.

KURUKAHVECİ MEHMET EFENDİ
MAHDUMLARI Map p78   Food & Drink

☎ 212-522 0080; Tahmis Sokak 66, Eminönü; ⏰ 9am-6.30pm Mon-Fri, 9am-2pm Sat; 🚊 Eminönü

Caffeine addicts are regularly spotted queuing outside this, the flagship store of İstanbul's most famous coffee purveyor. You can join them in getting a fix of the freshest beans in town, and also purchase a cute little set of two signature coffee cups and saucers, a copper coffee pot and a jar of coffee – it's a great gift to take back home.

ABDULLA NATURAL PRODUCTS
Map p77   Homewares
☎ 212-527 3684; Halıcılar Caddesi 62, Grand Bazaar; ☺ 9am-7pm Mon-Sat; ⓐ Beyazıt
The first of the Western-style designer stores that are starting to appear in this ancient marketplace, Abdulla sells cotton bed linen, handspun woollen throws from Eastern Turkey, cotton *peştemals* (bath wraps) and pure olive-oil soap. It's all quality stuff, but you do pay a premium. There's another store in the Fes Café (p172) in Çemberlitaş.

DERVİŞ Map p77   Homewares
☎ 212-514 4525; Keseciler Caddesi 33-35, Grand Bazaar; ☺ 9am-7pm Mon-Sat; ⓐ Beyazıt
The owner of this shop was in partnership with the crew at Abdulla Natural Products before striking out on his own and he is selling almost identical stock, though with a greater emphasis on village textiles. It's a great place to pick up a souvenir hamam bowl, a felt rug or pair of slippers, cotton and silk towels or dowry shirts in silk or cotton. There's another store at Halıcılar Caddesi 51.

AK GÜMÜS Map p77   Jewellery
☎ 212-527 6648; Gani Çelebi Sokak 8, Grand Bazaar; ☺ 9am-7pm Mon-Sat; ⓐ Beyazıt

Lapis lazuli has a long history, including being used as a gemstone in Mesopotamia and as a finely ground pigment in top-quality Ottoman-era miniatures and calligraphy. Here at Ak Gümüs, the deep-blue stone features in a wide array of jewellery.

MILANO GÜZELIŞ Map p77   Jewellery
☎ 212-527 6648; Kalpakçılar Caddesi 103, Grand Bazaar; ☺ 9am-7pm Mon-Sat; ⓐ Beyazıt
We've received a number of enthusiastic recommendations of this shop from travellers, meaning that we're confident in recommending this long-established store in the bazaar's main street. It makes jewellery to order using every gold grade and every conceivable gem, precious or otherwise.

NECEF Map p77   Jewellery
☎ 212-513 0372; Şerifağa Sokak 123, Old Bazaar, Grand Bazaar; ☺ 9am-7pm Mon-Sat; ⓐ Beyazıt
This is where to come for a gorgeous Byzantine-style piece of jewellery in gold or silver with semiprecious stones. The earrings and rings are particularly elegant and are very well priced when one considers their quality. It also sells antique pieces.

KOÇ DERİ Map p77   Leather
☎ 212-527 5553; Kürkçüler Çarşısı 22-46, Grand Bazaar; ☺ 8.30am-8pm; ⓐ Beyazıt
If you fancy a leather jacket or coat, Koç is bound to have something that suits.

MAKING A LIVING IN THE GRAND BAZAAR

İlhan Güzeliş is the owner and chief designer at Milano Güzeliş (above), a well-known jewellery store in the Grand Bazaar. The family-owned business was established by his great-grandfather in Mardin, in Turkey's southeast, and his father moved it to İstanbul in 1957. At that time there were fewer than 10 jewellery stores in the bazaar – these days 1500 of the bazaar's 4000 shops sell jewellery and the surrounding streets are littered with jewellery workshops. İlhan began learning his trade from his father when he was seven years old, but he fears that his own sons won't be following in his footsteps – it's hard to make a good living from individually designed and handcrafted jewellery these days due to competition from glitzy mega-stores and malls, which sell relatively inexpensive mass-produced jewellery. He fears that the days of jewellers and their customers interacting over individual pieces are about to end.

One aspect of the bazaar that İlhan likes to discuss is its cultural and religious diversity. He points out that Muslims and Christians have always worked together harmoniously here, and that most of the diamonds the jewellers use are supplied by Jewish diamond traders. İlhan himself is a member of the Assyrian Orthodox Church – in İstanbul, half of the church's 15,000 members are involved in the jewellery business. Like many of the bazaar's shopkeepers he speaks a number of languages (in his case Turkish, English, German, French, Italian, Spanish, Portuguese and Arabic), but he and around 50% of his fellow Assyrian Christians can also speak Aramaic, one of the world's oldest languages.

İlhan will stay on in the bazaar for as long as he can keep on making a good livelihood and paying his rent. This is calculated separately for each store according to how much space the store occupies and where it is – all of the stores on Kalpakçılar Caddesi, where Milano Güzeliş is located, pay hefty rents because their street is perhaps the busiest in the bazaar. The rent is paid in gold (which seems particularly appropriate for jeweller tenants!), and can cost anywhere between half a kilogram to 8kg of the precious metal per year.

It's one of the bazaar's busiest stores and certainly the most stylish of the leather outlets here.

KÜÇÜK KÖŞE Map p77   Leather Handbags
Little Corner; ☎ 212-513 0335; Kalpakçılar Caddesi 89-91, Grand Bazaar; ⏱ 9am-7pm Mon-Sat; 🚇 Beyazıt
If you've always wanted a Kelly or Birkin but can't afford Hermès, this place is for you. Its copies of the work of the big-gun designers are good quality and they're a lot more affordable than the originals. The next-door store, Pako, is owned by the same people.

DHOKU Map p77   Rugs
☎ 212-527 6841; Tekkeciler Sokak 58-60, Grand Bazaar; ⏱ 9am-7pm Mon-Sat; 🚇 Beyazıt
One of the new generation of rug stores opening in the bazaar, Dhoku (texture) sells artfully designed wool kilims in resolutely modernist designs. Its sister store, EthniCon (Tekkeciler Sokak, Grand Bazaar), sells similarly stylish rugs in vivid colours and can be said to have started the current craze in contemporary kilims. Brits may have seen some of this store's products in the Conran Shop.

ŞİŞKO OSMAN Map p77   Rugs
☎ 212-528 3548; Zincirli Han 15, Grand Bazaar; ⏱ 9am-7pm Mon-Sat; 🚇 Beyazıt
The Osmans have been in the rug business for four generations and are rated by many as the best dealers in the bazaar. Certainly, their stock is a cut above many of their competitors. Most of the rugs on sale are dowry pieces and all have been hand woven and coloured with vegetable dyes. There's another store at Halıcılar Caddesi 49.

YÖRÜK Map p77   Rugs
☎ 212-527 3211; Kürkçüler Çarşısı 16, Grand Bazaar; ⏱ 8.30am-7pm Mon-Sat; 🚇 Beyazıt
This narrow store has a selection of top-quality rugs from the Caucasus and Central Asia, most of them dowry pieces. The owners are friendly and knowledgeable – best of all, they refrain from the hard sell.

MEHMET KALMAZ BAHARATÇI
Map p78   Spices & Tonics
☎ 212-522 6604; Spice Bazaar 41, Eminönü; ⏱ 8am-7pm Mon-Sat; 🚇 Eminönü
One of the few shops in the Spice Bazaar (Mısır Çarşısı; p76) that specialises in po-

tions and lotions, this old-fashioned place sells remedies to make women younger, others to make men stronger, and a royal love potion that, we guess, is supposed to combine the two. It also stocks spices, bath accessories, teas and medicinal herbs.

ANTIQUE OBJET Map p77   Textiles
☎ 212-526 7451; Zenneciler Caddesi 48-50, Grand Bazaar; ⏱ 9am-7pm Mon-Sat; 🚇 Beyazıt
The cute embroidered slippers sold here make great gifts for friends and family, and the *suzani* (needlework) pieces are the stuff that we all like to treat ourselves to once in a while. You'll need to rummage, as this place is jam-packed.

AZAD TEKSTIL Map p77   Textiles
☎ 212-512 4202; Yağlıkçılar Caddesi 16, Grand Bazaar; ⏱ 9am-7pm Mon-Sat; 🚇 Beyazıt
Simple but stylish cotton bedspreads, tablecloths and *peştemals* (hamam towels) are sold at bargain prices at this busy store. Check out the range here before buying up big at Derviş (opposite) or Abdullah Natural Products (opposite).

MUHLİS GÜNBATTI Map p77   Textiles
☎ 212-511 6562; Parçacilar Sokak 48, Grand Bazaar; ⏱ 9am-7pm Mon-Sat; 🚇 Beyazıt
One of the most famous stores in the bazaar, Muhlis Günbattı specialises in *suzani* fabrics from Uzbekistan. These spectacularly beautiful bedspreads, tablecloths and wall hangings are made from fine cotton embroidered with silk. As well as the textiles, it stocks top-quality carpets, brightly coloured kilims and a small range of antique Ottoman fabrics richly embroidered with gold. Its second shop at Tevkifhane Sokak (Map p50) in Sultanahmet sells a wider range of costumes at truly stratospheric prices.

SEMERKAND SUZANİ Map p77   Textiles
☎ 212-526 2269; Yağlıkçılar Caddesi, Astarcı Han 25, Grand Bazaar; ⏱ 9am-7pm Mon-Sat; 🚇 Beyazıt
If you fancy the idea of swanning around at home wearing an old kaftan from Uzbekistan or a dowry shirt from Anatolia, this is where you can source them. There are caps, fabrics and lots of lovely pieces to choose from.

DELİ KIZIN YERİ JUNIOR Map p77   Toys
☎ 212-511 1914; Halıcılar Caddesi 42, Grand Bazaar; ⏱ 9am-7pm Mon-Sat; 🚇 Beyazıt

In Turkish, the name of this shop is 'The Crazy Lady's Place'. There's nothing nutty about buying the wonderful toys sold here, though. Dolls, marionettes, hand puppets and cute clothes are on offer, all featuring Anatolian motifs, materials and designs. Perfect gifts for the little ones in your life.

EKİNCİOĞLU TOYS & GIFTS Map p78   Toys
☎ 212-522 6220; Kalçın Sokak 5, Eminönü; 9am-7pm; Eminönü
If your junior travelling companion's behaviour is on the skids and some urgent bribery is called for, this place should provide the answer.

GALATA & TOPHANE
İSTANBUL MODERN GIFT SHOP
Map p103   Souvenirs & Gifts
☎ 212-334 7300; Meclis-i Mebusan Caddesi, Karaköy; 10am-6pm Tue-Wed & Fri-Sun, 10am-8pm Thu; Tophane
Sometimes it can be difficult to source well-priced souvenirs to take home to one's nearest and dearest. Fortunately the gift shop at this top-notch contemporary art gallery sells desirable items aplenty – niftily designed T-shirts, CDs, coffee mugs, homewares and jewellery are on offer, as are cute gifts for kids. We particularly like the paint-your-own T-shirts, painting sets and stationery.

İSTİKLAL & AROUND
ANADOL ANTİK Map p107   Art & Antiques
☎ 212-251 5228; Turnacıbaşı Sokak 65, Çukurcuma; 9am-7pm Mon-Sat; Kabataş then funicular to Taksim
Fancy a wooden door from an Ottoman house? Or perhaps a ceramic-clad wood stove? This cavernous shop is filled with a hodgepodge of curios and collectables. If you brave the dust and the dim lights you just might find yourself a treasure.

ARTRIUM Map p107   Art & Antiques
☎ 212-251 4302; Tünel Square 7; 9am-7pm Mon-Sat; Karaköy then funicular to Tünel
This Aladdin's cave of a shop is crammed with antique ceramics, Ottoman miniature paintings, maps, prints and jewellery. It also has occasional pieces of Ottoman cloth-

ing and fabric. If you're after anything in particular, ask the owner, as she'll be happy to rummage upstairs in the storage area where excess stock is kept. Pricey but nice.

GALERİ ALFA Map p107   Art & Antiques
☎ 212-251 1672; Faikpaşa Sokak 47, Çukurcuma; 11am-5.30pm; Kabataş then funicular to Taksim
What makes this store special is its range of charming toy Ottoman soldiers and court figures – even Süleyman the Magnificent has been shrunk to 10cm tall. It also stocks old maps and prints.

HİKMET + PİNAR Map p107   Art & Antiques
☎ 212-293 0575; Faikpaşa Yokuşu 36A, Çukurcuma; 10am-6pm Mon-Sat; Kabataş then funicular to Taksim
An opulently decorated store filled to the brim with top-class Ottoman-era furniture, mirrors, glassware, textiles and paintings, Hikmet + Pinar is the type of place you enter only if you're ready to spend the cash equivalent of a second mortgage. We bet they furnish more than their fair share of İstanbul mansions.

ŞAMDAN Map p107   Art & Antiques
☎ 212-245 4445; Altıpatlar Sokak 20, Çukurcuma; 11am-5.30pm; Kabataş then funicular to Taksim
Located on one of Beyoğlu's main antique strips, this small shop stocks quality antique furniture, china and glassware, specialising in Ottoman and Art Deco pieces.

DENİZLER KİTABEVİ
Map p107   Antique Books, Maps & Prints
☎ 212-249 8893; İstiklal Caddesi 395; 9.30am-7.30pm; Kabataş then funicular to Taksim
A charmingly eccentric shop specialising in old maps and books, Denizler Kitabevi also stocks antique prints and quirky chess sets with different historical figures.

HOMER KİTABEVİ Map p107   Books
☎ 212-249 5902; Yeniçarşı Caddesi 28/A, Galatasaray; 10am-7.30pm Mon-Sat; Kabataş then funicular to Taksim
Homer has an excellent selection of history, architecture and art books – all about Turkey and İstanbul and all in English. It also has a large range of English-language fiction.

İSTANBUL KITAPÇISI Map p107   Books

☎ 212-292 7692; İstiklal Caddesi 379; ☼ 10am-7pm Mon-Sat, 11am-7pm Sun; 🚇 Karaköy then funicular to Tünel

This bookshop is run by the municipality and as a consequence prices are very reasonable. It stocks some English-language books about İstanbul, and a good range of maps, CDs, postcards and prints.

PANDORA Map p107   Books

☎ 212-243 3503; Büyükparmakkapı Sokak 3, off İstiklal Caddesi; ☼ 10am-8pm Sun-Thu, 10am-10pm Fri & Sat; 🚇 Kabataş then funicular to Taksim

Unreconstructed lefties and self-confessed postmodernists are equally at home in this excellent bookshop. Though most of the stock is in Turkish, there are a fair few titles in English, including novels, guidebooks, histories, and art and politics texts. If you can't find what you're looking for on the ground floor, climb two floors up.

ROBINSON CRUSOE Map p107   Books

☎ 212-293 6968; İstiklal Caddesi 389; ☼ 9am-9.30pm Mon-Sat, 10am-9.30pm Sun; 🚇 Karaköy then funicular to Tünel

There are few more pleasant fates than being marooned here for an hour or so. With its classy décor, good magazine selection and wide range of English-language novels and books about İstanbul, it's one of the best bookshops around. Staff speak English and know their books.

BEYOĞLU HALI EVİ Map p107   Ceramics

☎ 212-293 9990; İstiklal Caddesi 388; ☼ 9am-8pm; 🚇 Karaköy then funicular to Tünel

The ceramics on sale here aren't of the highest quality, but they're well priced and worthy of a browse. Tea glasses and copies of Ottoman originals are the best bets.

ART.I.CHOKE Map p107   Clothing

☎ 212-293 7410; Faikpaşa Sokak 4, Çukurcuma; ☼ 10am-7pm Mon-Sat; 🚇 Kabataş then funicular to Taksim

Some places are as much art gallery as they are shop, and art.i.choke is most certainly one of them. A shrine to the wonderful art of felt, it creates and sells unique objects made from the fuzzy stuff. The clothes, slippers, cushions, shawls and rugs on offer here are truly exquisite. If there's no-one in the shop, try the upstairs studio.

BIS Map p107   Clothing

☎ 212-292 292 9700; Aznavur Pasajı 212-213, Galatasaray; ☼ 9am-7pm; 🚇 Kabataş then funicular to Taksim

Its good line in funky urban wear, including clubbing wear, makes Bis a favourite with bright young things. There's another store at Çukurcuma (Hayriye Sokak 18A).

LEYLA SEYHANLI Map p107   Clothing

☎ 212-293 7410; Altıpatlar Sokak 10, Cihangir; ☼ 10am-7pm; 🚇 Kabataş then funicular to Taksim

If you love old clothes, you'll adore Leyla Seyhanlı's boutique. Filled to the brim with piles of Ottoman embroidery and outfits, it's a rummager's delight. It stocks everything from 1890s cashmere and velvet coats to 1950s taffeta party frocks to silk-embroidery cushion covers that would have been at home in the Dolmabahçe Palace linen cupboard.

MAVİ JEANS Map p107   Clothing

☎ 212-293 4332; İstiklal Caddesi 91; ☼ 10am-10pm; 🚇 Kabataş then funicular to Taksim

The dress code of choice for İstanbul's youth is a pair of worn jeans (usually tight and low-slung) and a fair percentage of these would have been purchased from local company Mavi. Among the most popular ranges are those designed by internationally recognised fashion designer, Rıfat Özbek. Prices are at least half of those of foreign imports. There are other branches at İstiklal Caddesi 195 and 425.

SEDEF ÇALARKAN Map p107   Clothing

☎ 212-292 5948; Hayriye Sokak 2, Çukurcuma; ☼ 11am-5pm Mon-Sat; 🚇 Kabataş then funicular to Taksim

Here you'll find a fabulously funky range of T-shirts and leather bags decorated with images of sultans. We were particularly taken with the design featuring Murad III wearing a Bluetooth headset!

MUDO PERA Map p107   Clothing & Gifts

☎ 212-251 8682; İstiklal Caddesi 401; ☼ 10am-7.30pm Mon-Sat; 🚇 Karaköy then funicular to Tünel

Housed on the bottom two floors of an Art Nouveau building, the interior of this boutique is all gleaming wood and cunning lighting – very 1920s Pera. It stocks good-quality clothing made from cashmere, cotton and silks, as well as an eclectic range of gifts and tableware. There's another store in Teşvikiye Caddesi (Map p115).

AMBAR Map p107 — Food & Drink

☎ 212-292 9272; Kallavi Sokak 12; ⏰ 9am-7.30pm Mon-Sat, 12.30-7.30pm Sun; 🚋 Karaköy then funicular to Tünel

This small organic-produce store smells as good as it looks. It stocks free-range eggs, tofu, soy milk and other health foods, as well as a range of stylish earthenware pottery and quality olive-oil soap.

LA CAVE WINE SHOP Map p107 — Food & Drink

La Cave Şarap Evi; ☎ 212-243 2405; Sıraselviler Caddesi 207, Cihangir; ⏰ 9am-9pm; 🚋 Kabataş then funicular to Taksim

Its enormous selection of local and imported wine makes La Cave a good stop for tipplers. The staff can tell a Chablis from a Chardonnay and will be happy to give advice on the best Turkish bottles to add to your cellar.

PAŞABAHÇE Map p107 — Glassware

☎ 212-244 0544; İstiklal Caddesi 314; ⏰ 10am-8pm; 🚋 Karaköy then funicular to Tünel

Established in 1957, this local firm manufactures excellent glassware from its factory on the Bosphorus. Three floors of glassware, vases and decanters feature here and prices are very reasonable. Styles are both traditional and contemporary.

MOR TAKI Map p107 — Jewellery

☎ 212-292 8817; Turnacıbaşı Sokak 16, off İstiklal Caddesi; ⏰ 10.30am-8.30pm Mon-Sat; 🚋 Kabataş then funicular to Taksim

The gals of this city love their jewellery, and this funky little store keeps many of their collections topped up with costume pieces by local designers.

LALE PLAK Map p107 — Music

☎ 212-293 7739; Galipdede Caddesi 1, Tünel; ⏰ 9am-7pm Mon-Sat; 🚋 Karaköy then funicular to Tünel

This small shop is crammed with CDs of jazz, Western classical and Turkish classical and folk music. It's a popular hang-out for local bohemian types.

MEPHISTO Map p107 — Music

☎ 212-249 0687; İstiklal Caddesi 197; ⏰ 9am-midnight; 🚋 Kabataş then funicular to Taksim

If you manage to develop a taste for local music while you're in town, this popular store is the place to indulge it. As well as a huge CD collection of Turkish popular music, there's a select range of Turkish folk, jazz and classical music.

ELVIS Map p107 — Musical Instruments

☎ 212-293 8752; Galipdede Caddesi 35; Tünel; ⏰ 10am-6pm; 🚋 Karaköy then funicular to Tünel

If you thought Elvis was hiding in the Bahamas, you're wrong. He's here, selling a good range of traditional stringed instruments.

A LA TURCA Map p107 — Rugs

☎ 212-245 2933; Faikpaşa Sokak 4, Çukurcuma; ⏰ 10am-6pm Mon-Sat; 🚋 Kabataş then funicular to Taksim

If you fancy an antique Anatolian kilim to brighten up your home (and who doesn't?) A la Turca may be the place to get it. In the trendy Çukurcuma district, which is one of the best areas in the city to browse for antiques and curios, its small but interesting selection of stock is certainly worth a second or third look.

İPEK Map p107 — Silk

☎ 212-249 8207; İstiklal Caddesi 120; ⏰ 9am-6pm; 🚋 Kabataş then funicular to Taksim

The silk ties and scarves sold at this long-established store make great presents, as they don't take up much of your baggage allowance and are keenly priced. Check out the colourful scarves featuring Ottoman calligraphy.

İYİGÜN OYUNCAK Map p107 — Toys

☎ 212-243 8910; İstiklal Caddesi 415; ⏰ 9am-9pm; 🚋 Karaköy then funicular to Tünel

These guys know what little kids like. And unlike the other stores in town, stock isn't dominated by toy weapons. There's everything from Brio to Teenage Mutant Ninja Turtles, with a few educational parent-pleasers thrown in for good measure.

TAKSİM, HARBİYE & NİŞANTAŞI

The city's serious shoppers gravitate towards the upmarket suburbs of Teşvikiye and Nişantaşı, about 2km north of Taksim Square. This is where international fashion and design

MARKETS & MALLS

With one foot planted in the East and another in the West, İstanbul's shopping has more than its fair share of contradictions: ritzy shopping plazas dot posh suburbs, while the mass of shoppers elbow for goods at the weekly street markets.

Street Markets

On Tuesday there is a massive market in Kadıköy, on the Asian side: the Salı Pazarı (Map p127). The cheapest clothes in town are on sale here, so if you've been on the road for a while and your underwear needs replenishing, this is the place to do it! To get there, get off the ferry and move straight ahead along the major boulevard of Söğütlüçeşme Caddesi for about 500m until you come to a busy intersection, Altıyol Square. Cross over, take the right fork and continue eastward along Kuşdili Caddesi for another 250m (three cross streets). At Hasırcıbaşı Caddesi turn left and you'll see the tent-city market spread out before you. It's open between 8am and 6pm. On Sunday the market is taken over by stall-keepers selling a motley collection of antiques, furniture and jewellery.

On Saturday and Sunday the laneways around the waterfront mosque in Ortaköy host a flea market. Merchandise is tacky – most seems to come from the Subcontinent and Africa and is found in flea markets worldwide – and the handicrafts on offer are firmly in the hippy camp, but it's still a pleasant spot to while away a weekend hour or two.

On Wednesday the grounds, courtyard and surrounding streets of the Fatih Camii (p95) in the Western Districts host the Fatih Pazarı, a great market selling fresh produce, clothes and household items.

Malls

Western-style mall culture has well and truly taken off on İstanbul.

The ritzy Kanyon (☎ 212-353 5300; www.kanyon.com.tr; Büyükdere Caddesi 185, Levent; ⏰ 10am-10pm; ⛴ Kabataş then funicular to Taksim then metro to Levent) is home to multinational names such as Harvey Nichols, Wagamama, Georg Jensen, Le Pain Quotidien, Birkenstock, Mango and Mandarina Duck. It also has a few locally based stores, including Vakko, Ottoman Empire (funky T-shirts screen-printed with Ottoman influenced motifs) and Remzi Kitabevi (an excellent chain bookstore with a big English-language selection).

Next door is Metrocity (☎ 212-344 0660; www.metrocity.com.tr in Turkish; Büyükdere Caddesi 171, Levent; ⏰ 10am-10pm; ⛴ Kabataş then funicular to Taksim then metro to Levent), which isn't anywhere near as glam as Kanyon but is still extremely popular. It hosts high-street labels such as Zara, Benetton, Nike, Levi's and Mavi Jeans.

These two malls are large, but they're nowhere near the size of the massive Cevahir (☎ 212-380 0893/4; www.istanbulcevahir.com in Turkish; Büyükdere Caddesi 22, Şişli; ⏰ 10am-10pm; ⛴ Kabataş then funicular to Taksim then metro to Şişli), which advertises itself as Europe's largest mall. It's home to many of the same stores that you'll find in Metrocity and Akmerkez, as well as familiar UK-based outlets such as Topshop and Miss Selfridge.

Once the jewel in the shopping crown, Akmerkez (☎ 212-282 0170; www.akmerkez.com.tr; Nispetiye Caddesi, Etiler; ⏰ 10am-10pm; ⛴ Kabataş then funicular to Taksim then bus 559C to Etiler) has lost some of its shine, but it still boasts an impressive array of shops, including Beyman, Vakko, Zara, Mothercare and Remzi Kitabevi.

labels have traditionally set up shop (though some are now decamping to Kanyon, see above) and where top-drawer local designers show off their creations.

GÖNÜL PAKSOY Map p115 · Clothing
☎ 212-261 9081; Atiye Sokak 6/A & 1/3, Teşvikiye; ⏰ 10am-7pm Mon-Sat; ⛴ Kabataş then funicular to Taksim then metro to Osmanbey
Paksoy creates and sells pieces that transcend fashion and step into art. She works in a number of forms, and these two shops stock her distinctive silk and cotton knits, jewellery based on traditional Ottoman designs, and silk and cotton clothing in rich fabrics with feature trimming.

VAKKO Map p115 · Clothing & Gifts
☎ 212-251 4092; Adbilpekçi Caddesi, Nişantaşı; ⏰ 9.30am-6pm Mon-Sat; ⛴ Kabataş then funicular to Taksim then metro to Osmanbey
İstanbul's most famous boutique department store stocks a quality range of clothing for men and women, fabrics, shoes, homewares and scarves made from Bursa silk. It even produces its own perfume and chocolate.

YARGICI Map p115 · Clothing & Gifts
☎ 212-225 2952; Vali Konaği Caddesi 30, Teşvikiye; ⏰ 9.30am-7.30pm Mon-Sat, 1-6pm Sun; ⛴ Kabataş then funicular to Taksim then metro to Osmanbey

Whether they're aged 15 or 50, İstanbul's men and women love buying clothes, toiletries and accessories at Yargıcı. The clothes are affordable high-street styles that are made in Turkey and the accessories are so good they're exported internationally.

SEMA PAKSOY Map p115   Jewellery
☎ 212-241 5533; Atiye Sokak 9, Teşvikiye; ⊗ 10am-7pm Mon-Sat; ⛴ Kabataş then funicular to Taksim then metro to Osmanbey
If your jewellery is more statement than investment, Sema Paksoy is your woman. Her chunky pieces crafted from antique silver and semiprecious stones are Ottoman-

inspired and lovely. They're pricey but worth it.

KADIKÖY

GREENHOUSE BOOKSHOP CAFE
Map p127   Books & Toys
Sera Kitapevi Kafe; ☎ 216-550 4961/2; Moda Caddesi 28; ⊗ 10am-6.30pm Mon & Wed-Sat; ⛴ Kadıköy
This friendly bookshop stocks the city's best range of books in English about İstanbul and Turkey. There's a huge kids section and a decent fiction section. It's where most of the expats in the know buy their reading matter.

EATING

top picks

- **Mikla** (p165) Top dining
- **Hamdi et Lokantası** (p161) Top view
- **Şehzade Mehmed Sofrası** (p162) Top setting
- **Asitane** (p163) Top Ottoman cuisine
- **Çiya Sofrası** (p170) Top lokanta
- **Sofyalı 9** (p167) Top meyhane
- **Tarıhı Karaköy Balık Lokantası** (p164) Top seafood
- **Develi** (p163) Top kebapçı
- **Saf' Organic Bistro** (p166) Top vegetarian
- **Karaköy Güllüglu** (p165) Top pastane

EATING

İstanbul is a food-lover's paradise. Teeming with affordable fast-food joints, cafés and restaurants, it leaves visitors spoiled for choice when it comes to choosing a venue. Best of all, it's proud of its national cuisine. And oh, what a great cuisine it is! The city's restaurants vie with each other to produce the best damn meze, the freshest possible seafood and the most succulent kebabs in town, all appreciated by legions of locals for whom eating out is a way of life and a true passion. There are other cuisines on offer (you can eat fusion dishes in Western-style brasseries and sample cuisines as diverse as Russian, Italian and Thai), but the best places to eat are the lokantas, meyhanes and Ottoman-style restaurants that the locals frequent.

Unfortunately, Sultanahmet has the least impressive range of eating options in the city. Rather than eating here at night, we recommend crossing the Galata Bridge and joining the locals in Beyoğlu, Ortaköy and the Bosphorus suburbs. Absolutely nothing can beat the enjoyment of spending a night in a meyhane on Nevizade Sokak or in the Asmalımescit quarter (both in Beyoğlu), or dining at one of the swish restaurants on the Bosphorus. There are other pockets of town worth investigating – Eminönü has the enjoyable Hamdi et Lokantası (p161) and Zinhan Kebap House at Storks (p161), Samatya is home to the best kebabs in town at Develi (p163), and Edirnekapı has the excellent Asitane (p163) – but on the whole you will be well served by making your way across the Galata Bridge every night. As the Turks say, *afiyet olsun!* (*bon appétit!*).

For recommendations of places to eat on the Bosphorus, see the Excursions chapter.

HOW İSTANBULLUS EAT

Mealtime in İstanbul is treated with respect. The idea of eating in front of a TV or from a freezer is absolute anathema to Turks. Friends, family and communal tables are as essential to the cuisine as its staple foodstuffs and signature dishes. Restaurants in İstanbul are always full of large groups sharing not only mezes, but conversation and belly laughs, usually over a bottle or two of the national tipple, rakı.

The day starts with *sabahları* (morning food) or *kahvaltı* (breakfast), usually eaten between 6am and 8am. *Öğle yemeği* (lunch) kicks off around noon, is usually consumed quickly and is often enjoyed in a lokanta, pideci or kebapçı. *Akşam yemeği* (dinner), which is eaten any time after 6pm, is where the meyhane or *restoran* comes into its own; in İstanbul many of these places serve until midnight and meals can be drawn out over a long period.

ETIQUETTE

It's not considered very important that everyone eats the same courses at the same pace, so the kitchen will deliver dishes as they are ready: it's quite normal for all the chicken dishes to arrive and then, five minutes later, all the lamb. You don't have to wait for everyone's food to arrive to begin eating.

Turkish waiters have a habit of snatching your plate away before you've finished. This may be due to a rule of Eastern etiquette that holds that it's impolite to leave a finished plate sitting in front of a guest. Saying *kalsın* (let it stay) may slow them down. When you have finished, put your knife and fork together to indicate that the waiter can take the plate. If this has no effect (or you don't have a knife), say '*biti, alabilirsin*' (finished, you can take it) to the waiter.

It's not unusual for people to smoke while others are eating, and you will rarely find non-smoking areas in restaurants. Opting for outdoor seating can be a good way of avoiding the fug.

Toothpicking should be done behind your hands, but you don't need to be particularly discrete. Try to avoid blowing your nose in public; sniff or excuse yourself if you need to do this.

WHERE TO EAT
Balık Restoran

Near the city's fish markets and along the Bosphorus you'll find the popular *balık* (fish) restaurants. Sometimes the fish on offer is displayed, but usually you'll need to ask the waiter what's fresh and ask to see the fish. This is important, as the occasional dodgy restaurant may try to serve you old fish. This trick is not just pulled out for foreigners – most locals ask to check the fish is fresh, so don't be embarrassed to do the same. The eyes should be clear and the flesh under the gill slits near the eyes should be bright red, not burgundy. After your fish has been given the all clear, ask the approximate price. The fish will be weighed, and the price computed at the day's per-kilogram rate.

Börekçi

Börek (sweet and savoury pastries) are distinguished by their filling, cooking method and shape: they are square and cheesy, cigar shaped and meaty, plain and moist, pointy and potato chunky. *Kol böreği* is long and arm-shaped, and comes filled with cheese (*peynirli börek*), spinach (*ıspanaklı börek*), potatoes (*patates börek*) or meat. For the juicy *su böreği* (water börek), *yufka* (filo pastry) is boiled first, making it very soft. Then the *yufka* and the filling are layered into a round metal tray that revolves over a flame. As the *börek* cooks, it's flipped to a golden brown. *Su böreği* are a cross between a pastry and a lasagne – the good ones are succulent, not too oily and full of punchy flavour.

First-time visitors to İstanbul often become deeply infatuated with *börekçis*. Often a tiny window in the wall or a cupboard-sized kiosk with a few stools and benches, they offer a few types of *börek*, tea, instant coffee and a small selection of cold drinks, *ayran* always among them. They're a great place for a quick dirt-cheap breakfast or lunch, or a between-meal carbo tweak. *Börekçi* stock is often sold out by mid-afternoon, and the best time to sample their wares is in the early morning, when the pastries have just come out of the oven.

Büfes

The büfe is a kiosk, a food stand and a shop all rolled into one. It's a place where you can buy cigarettes, crisps, ice cream and confectionary, but where you can also snack on a *tost* (toasted sandwich), döner kebap, freshly squeezed orange juice, *ayran* and even alcohol. Many have stools where you can perch while eating your snack.

Cafés

Chic café-bars are nearly as easy to find in İstanbul as they are in Paris, London or New York. Most are clustered in Beyoğlu, but others are dotted in the suburbs on both sides of the Bosphorus and in other well-heeled neighbourhoods. Finding one in the Old City can be a challenge, though. Most serve coffee,

a variety of teas (including herbal infusions) and food such as sandwiches, salads and pasta. Some also serve alcohol.

The ubiquitous *çay bahçesi* (tea garden) is found throughout the city. It is usually an outdoor, leafy garden serving tea, coffee and occasionally snacks (no alcohol), frequented by clusters of moustached gents playing backgammon, students lazing around a nargileh (water pipe), courting couples and families.

The Drinking chapter recommends cafés and *çay bahçesi* throughout the city.

Kebapçıs & Köftecis

Kebapçıs are low-key, cheap eateries focused on grilled or roasted meat, but usually offering soup, simple salads, cold drinks and *ayran* as well. Don't expect tablecloths or waiterly flourishes – these are quick-fire joints, specialising in high turnover and no-frills nourishment. A köfteci is similar in style, but the food staple is grilled meatballs rather than grilled kebaps. If you spot the word *ocakbaşı* in the menu or the eatery's signage, it means the food will be cooked in front of you. Order your main meat course by the portion: *bir porsyon* (one portion) if you're not overly hungry; *bir buçuk porsyon* (one and a half) if you are, and *duble porsyon* (double) if you're ravenous.

Lokantas

This is the basic Turkish restaurant, varying from starkly simple to homely and charming. The food on offer is mostly cheap *hazır yemek* (ready food) laid out in dishes kept warm in a bain-marie. More often than not the kitchen is open and visible, right behind the food.

Your table may be covered with butcher's paper or a tablecloth; water and bread will arrive and keep on coming as long as you sit there. Even if there is a menu (and usually there isn't), you should go up and choose whatever takes your fancy. Don't feel the need to pile up a plate straight away. It's fine to choose one or two dishes and go back for more as you feel like it.

Most of the time the dishes won't be labelled, so you can practise your Turkish or take pot luck. A normal spread will include a soup, an eggplant dish, a chickpea stew, maybe some beans, a few meat stews (perhaps one chicken and a couple of lamb) and roast chicken. Look out for seasonal vegetable dishes, which are delicious with garlic yogurt. There will always be *pilav* available, either rice,

FANCY SOME BACTERIA WITH THAT?

Street vendors pound pavements across İstanbul, pushing carts laden with artfully arranged snacks to satisfy the appetites of commuters. You'll see these vendors next to ferry and bus stations, on busy streets and squares, even on the city's bridges.

Some of their snacks are innocuous – freshly baked *simit,* golden roasted corn on the cob, refreshing chilled and peeled cucumber – but others score high on the 'you must be mad!' scale. Sample these local treats and you're risking a major dose of the sultan's revenge (diarrhoea). Major offenders:

Midye dolma (stuffed mussels) Delicious, exotic and packed with more bacteria than a Petri dish. Only for those who want to live very, very dangerously.

Pis pilav (rice and chickpeas) Displayed in a glass cabinet, this rice dish often comes with boiled chicken. The direct translation is 'dirty rice', which gains a whole new meaning when you realise that the stuff often sits in the sun all day.

Çiğ köfte (raw meatball) Raw meat kneaded by hand for hours with wheat, onion, clove, cinnamon, salt and hot black pepper and then formed into patties, usually by a profusely perspiring man with a cigarette in his other hand. Enough said.

Kokoreç (lamb's intestines cooked with herbs and spices) The Turkish version of black pudding; locals love to snack on this smelly stuff. We feel queasy even thinking about it.

Balık ekmek (fish sandwich) Best sourced on the quay at Eminönü, this is the quintessential İstanbul snack. They're innocuous and utterly delectable when freshly prepared, dangerous when not. Worth the risk.

---

bulgur or both. Though you can't count on getting dessert in a lokanta, it's fairly common to find *kadayıf* (shredded pastry baked in syrup and often filled with nuts, clotted cream or cheese) and *fırın sütlaç* (rice pudding).

The core trade of lokantas in İstanbul is working people and shoppers looking for lunch. Some lokantas close in the late afternoon or offer a smaller selection for dinner (often left-overs from lunch).

Meyhanes

Imagine an Irish pub crossed with a tapas bar and a dash of Turkish wedding party thrown in and you've conjured up a meyhane in İstanbul. Carousing at a meyhane is something that all visitors to the city should do (see p167). Packed on weekends, these are the places where groups of locals gather to spend the evening, usually ending up drunk as sailors. Musicians strumming fasıl (folk music) sometimes move from table to table entertaining the guests and playing requests. Revellers sing along, throw their arms around each other, clap boisterously and break into dance. Food is usually ordered a couple of dishes at a time – always mezes, often fish and occasionally meat dishes, too. There are usually no menus, so you'll need to look and point. Everything will taste delicious, particularly after you've downed a few of the obligatory glasses of rakı that accompany a meyhane meal.

Pideci

The Turkish version of the pizza parlour is a slice of heaven if you're after a quick and tasty meal. Choose from cheese and various meat toppings and sit back with an *ayran* or a cola, or get a *pide paket* (wrapped to go). Look for woodfire ovens – the *pide* always tastes better. *Pidecis* in İstanbul often also function as kebapçıs, in which case there will be a sign on the shopfront saying '*Pide ve Kebap*'.

Restoran

The line between a *restoran* and a lokanta can be blurry – a low-end *restoran* is pretty much a lokanta under an alias. But, as you move up the price scale, closed kitchens, menus and alcohol will appear. And where there is alcohol, there is usually meze. There's a lot of cross-over between main dishes at a lokanta and a *restoran,* but you're more likely to find *pirzola* (chops), *biftek* (steak) and 'international' meat dishes such as schnitzel at a *restoran*.

At the upper end of the scale are the many classy restaurants around town serving Ottoman, fusion, Mediterranean-influenced dishes and more. Ottoman restaurants specialise in *saray* (palace) cuisine refined over centuries in the kitchens of the sultans. It's delicately flavoured, beautifully presented and if done well, totally delectable.

(Continued on page 157)

FOOD & DRINK

Live dangerously and eat stuffed mussels from the Bosphorus.

FOOD & DRINK

More than anything else, İstanbullus love to eat. Their national cuisine has been refined over centuries and is treated more reverently than any museum collection in the country. What differentiates Turkish food from other national noshes is its rustic and honest base. Here meze (hors d'oeuvres) are simple, kebaps uncomplicated, salads unstructured and seafood unsauced. Flavours explode in your mouth because ingredients are used when they are in season and are treated with respect.

The dishes served in restaurants throughout İstanbul are the same as those in eateries around the country in all but one respect – they're better. This is where the country's best chefs come to perfect their art and where the greatest range of cuisines – both regional and international – are showcased. In Beyoğlu, you're as likely to encounter an innovative take on an Italian pasta dish as you are a classic meze selection or a fabulously fresh grilled fish. Feel like sushi or a Thai red curry? You'll get it here. Have a yen to challenge your tastebuds with an edgy fusion dish conceived and prepared by a European- or Australasian-trained master of the kitchen? No problem – the city has plenty of options.

Dine on fish soup and meze at Balıkçı Sabahattın (p158) while gazing at the Aya Sofya

Available everywhere, simit will get you going in the morning

BREAD

Bread *(ekmek)* is an essential part of any Turkish meal. The day will start with a sesame-encrusted *simit* (bread ring) or crusty white loaf to accompany cheese and olives. Lunch may be a *pide* or *lahmacun* – both are Turkish versions of the pizza: *lahmacun* has a thin, crispy base; *pide* has a standard pizza base. Dinner is always served with baskets of bread to mop up meze and wrap around morsels of meat. Light and airy *lavaş* (thin crispy bread) is often served with the house speciality at kebap restaurants.

MEZE

Meze isn't just a type of dish, it's an eating experience. In a household, your host may put out a few lovingly prepared dishes to nibble on before the main meal. If you choose to spend a few hours in a Beyoğlu meyhane, beckoning the waiter over so that you can choose 'just a few more' inevitably means that the meze will comprise most of your meal.

Turks credit Süleyman the Magnificent with introducing meze into the country. While campaigning in Persia, Süleyman learned from the Persian rulers that food tasters were a good idea for every sultan who wanted to ensure his safety. Once home, Süleyman decreed that *çesnici* (taste) slaves be given small portions of his meals before he tucked in. These portions became known as meze, the Persian word for 'pleasant, enjoyable taste'.

MEZE: TURKISH TAPAS

Mezes are usually vegetable-based, though seafood dishes also feature in meyhanes (see p148). You will probably encounter the following dishes:

Ançüz Pickled anchovy
Barbunya pilaki Red-bean salad
Beyaz peynir White goat's cheese
Çacik Yogurt with cucumber and mint
Enginar Cooked artichoke
Fava salatası Mashed broad-bean paste
Haydari Yogurt with roasted eggplant (aubergine) and garlic
Kalamares Fried calamari
Lakerda Sliced and salted tuna fish
Patlıcan kızartması Fried eggplant with tomatoes
Semizotu Green purslane with yogurt and garlic
Yaprak sarma Vine leaves stuffed with rice, herbs and pine nuts

What is fine dining without dips?

Eat your köfte like a local

MEAT DISHES

There are more *et* (meat) dishes in the Turkish culinary repertoire than you can poke a *şiş* (skewer) at. The most famous of these is the kebap – *şiş* and *döner* – but *köfte* (meat balls), *saç kavurma* (stir-fried cubed-meat dishes), *güveç* (meat and vegetable stews) and *tandır* (meat cooked in a clay oven) dishes are just as common. Offal dishes are also popular, particularly *çiğer* (grilled liver) – if you're a bit squeamish about the yucky bits steer clear of *işkembe* (tripe), *kelle* (head) and *koç yumurtası* (ram's balls). The most popular sausage is the spicy beef *sucuk*. Chicken is extremely popular; you'll find it roasted, boiled, stewed and skewered.

My kebap is bigger than your kebap

KEBAPS & KÖFTE

The national dish is undoubtedly the kebap (kebab), and it comes in many forms. In İstanbul you'll find the following dishes everywhere:

Döner kebap Compressed meat (usually lamb) cooked on a revolving upright skewer and thinly sliced

Şiş kebab Small pieces of lamb grilled on a skewer and usually served with a side of grilled peppers

Fıstıklı kebap Minced suckling lamb studded with pistachios

İskender (Bursa) kebap Döner lamb served on crumbled *pide* and yogurt, topped with tomato and butter sauces

Patlıcan kebap Cubed or minced meat grilled with eggplant

Tokat kebap Lamb cubes grilled with potato, tomato eggplant and garlic

Tavuk şiş Chicken pieces grilled on a skewer

Tasty *köfte* (meatballs) are nearly as common, and are mainly in the following forms:

Şiş köfte Wrapped around a flat skewer and barbecued

Adana kebap A spicy version of *şiş köfte,* with paprika and chillies

Çiğ köfte Raw ground-lamb mixed with pounded bulgur, onion, spices and pepper

İçli köfte Ground lamb and onion with a bulgur coating, often served as a meze

Tekirdağ köftesi *Köfte* served with rice and peppers

SEAFOOD

İstanbullus have always made the most of the city's seaside position, falling hook, line and sinker for fresh fish (*balık*) in any form. There are a number of excellent but pricey fish restaurants along the Bosphorus, the most impressive of which include Poseidon (p220), Körfez (p219), Kordon at the Sumahan on the Water (p209) and Rumeli İskele (p220). In town, the army of meyhanes in Beyoğlu, Kumkapı, Florya and Yeşilköy are often run by restaurateurs from the Black Sea, where the quality of fish is famous. These serve up

THE FISH SANDWICH – AN İSTANBUL INSTITUTION

The cheapest way to enjoy fresh fish from the waters around İstanbul is to buy a fish sandwich from a boatman. Go to the Eminönü end of the Galata Bridge (Map p63) and you'll see bobbing boats tied to the quay. In each boat, men tend to a cooker loaded with fish fillets. The quick-cooked fish is crammed into a quarter loaf of fresh bread and served with salad. It will set you back a mere YTL3.

lightly fried *kalamares* (calamari) as a meze; mains are usually simply grilled fresh fish of the day served with salad. A few fish restaurants are known for their delicious fish soup – try Tarıhı Karaköy Balık Lokantası (p164) near the Karaköy *balık pazarı* (fish market) or Balıkçı Sabahattın (p158) in Sultanahmet.

Kalkan (turbot) and *uskumru* (mackerel) are best consumed between March and June. Mid-July to August is the best time to feast on *levrek* (sea bass), *lüfer* (bluefish), *barbunya* (red mullet) and *istravrit* (horse mackerel), while winter means the delectable and slightly oily *hamsi* (European anchovy).

VEGETABLES

If it weren't for the Turks' passionate love affair with the kebab, they'd probably all be vegetarians. They're sensible about their vegetables, too. There's none of the silly Western fixation

Sample a city speciality – a fresh fish sandwich, right off the boat

with preparing vegetables that are out of season – here tomatoes are eaten when they're almost bursting out of their skins and peppers are stewed when they're so ripe they're downright sexy. Look for what's on the vendors' carts when you're walking around town – you'll see the same produce in restaurant dishes. There are two particularly Turkish ways of preparing them: the first is *zeytinyağlı* (sautéed in olive oil) and the second *dolma* (stuffed with rice or meat).

SALAD

Simplicity is the key to Turkish *salata* (salads), with crunchy fresh ingredients being caressed by a shake of oil and vinegar at the table and eaten with gusto as a meze or as an accompaniment to a meat or fish course. The most popular salad in İstanbul's restaurants in summer is *çoban salatası* (shepherd's salad), a colourful mix of chopped tomatoes, cucumber, onion and pepper.

Vegetarians may have to hunt, but they certainly won't go hungry

IN PRAISE OF PATLICAN

If there's one vegetable that Turks adore more than any other, it is *patlıcan* (eggplant or aubergine). It features in countless dishes and menus across the city and inevitably tastes wonderful. To prove the point, consider what is probably the most famous of all Turkish dishes – *imam bayıldı* (the imam fainted). A simple dish of eggplant slowly cooked with onion and garlic and served cold, it is so named because legend has it that an imam fainted with pleasure on first tasting it. Sample it at Hacı Abdullah (p167) in Beyoğlu, and you'll know how he felt. A dish that has a similar effect is the decadent *hünkar beğendi*, braised lamb cubes served on a bed of creamy puréed eggplant. Unquestionably swoon-inducing.

TURKISH DELIGHT

You'll be making a mistake if you leave İstanbul without sampling real *lokum* (Turkish delight). The stuff you get here is the best in the world, and you can even buy it from the original shop (p136) of Ali Muhiddin Hacı Bekir, its creator.

Ali Muhiddin came to İstanbul from the town of Kastamonu and established himself as a confectioner in the Ottoman capital in the late 18th century. Dissatisfied with hard candies and traditional sweets led him to invent a new confection that would be easy to swallow. He called his creation *rahat lokum*, the 'comfortable morsel'. *Lokum*, as it came to be called, was an immediate hit in the imperial palace, and soon the translucent jellied jewels had fans all over the country.

Ali Muhiddin elaborated on his original confection, as did his offspring (the shop, which was established in 1777, is still owned by his descendants). As well as enjoying it *sade* (plain), you can buy *lokum* with various fillings, including *cevizli* (walnut) and *şam fıstıklı* (pistachio), or flavoured with *portakallı* (orange), *bademli* (almond) or *roze* (rosewater).

Gorgeous globs of Turkish delight

DESSERT & SWEETS

If you have a sweet tooth, prepare to put it to good use when in İstanbul. Though the locals aren't convinced of the idea of dessert to finish a meal, they love a mid-afternoon sugar hit and will pop into a *muhallebici, baklavacı* or *pastane* for a piece of baklava, a plate of chocolate-drenched profiteroles or a *fırın sütlac* (rice pudding) tasting of milk, sugar and just a hint of exotic spices. Turkish specialities worth sampling are *dondurma,* the local ice cream; *fırın sütlaç,* a rice pudding; *kadayıf,* dough soaked in syrup and topped with a layer of *kaymak* (clotted cream); and *künefe,* layers of *kadayıf* cemented together with sweet cheese, doused in syrup and served with a sprinkling of pistachio.

Sweet treats

NON-ALCHOHOLIC DRINKS

Drinking *çay* (tea) is the national pastime. Sugar cubes are the only accompaniment and they're needed to counter the effects of long brewing. Surprisingly, *Türk kahve* (Turkish coffee) isn't widely consumed. A thick and powerful brew, it's drunk in a couple of short sips. If you order a cup, you will be asked how sweet you like it – *çok şekerli*' means 'very sweet', *orta şekerli* 'middling', *az şekerli* 'slightly sweet' and *sade* 'not at all'. Though you shouldn't drink the grounds in the bottom of your cup, you may want to read your fortune – check the website of İstanbul's longest-established purveyor of coffee, Kurukahveci Mehmet Effendi (www.mehmetefendi .com), for a guide.

Freshly squeezed *portakal suyu* (orange juice) is an extremely popular drink, as is *ayran,* a refreshing yogurt drink made by whipping yogurt with water and salt.

If you're in İstanbul during winter, you should try delicious and unusual *sahlep,* a hot drink made from crushed tapioca-root extract.

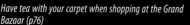
Have tea with your carpet when shopping at the Grand Bazaar (p76)

Something to spout about: drinks poured at your table Turkish-style

ALCOHOLIC DRINKS

Rakı is certainly the most popular of all alcoholic beverages, but *bira* (beer) claims second place. The local drop, Efes, is a perky pilsener.

Served in long thin glasses, rakı fires the passions and ensures a good evening at a meyhane. Its aniseed taste perfectly complements meze and fish and its powerful punch assures many a convivial evening. It's drunk with water, which turns the clear liquid chalky white.

Turkey grows and bottles its own *şarap* (wine). If you want red wine ask for *kırmızı şarap;* for white ask for *beyaz şarap.* Decent tipples include Sarafin Chardonnay, Fumé Blanc, Sauvignon Blanc, Cabernet Sauvignon and Cabernet Merlot; Karma Cabernet Sauvignon; Duluca Özel Kav (Special Reserve) red, white and *lal* (rosé); Antik red and white; and Çankaya white.

(Continued from page 148)

Tatlıcı & Pastane

It's considered normal for a main meal at a restaurant to lead onto the *tatlıcı*, a specialist dessert place. As well as the classic *tatlıcı*, where you can overdose on baklava, *helva* (sweet prepared with sesame oil, cereals and honey or syrup) and *lokum* (Turkish delight), look out for the pastane (or *pastanesi* or *baklavacı*), which tempts you with its baklava, European-style cakes and ice cream, and the *muhallebici*, which specialises in milk-based puddings.

VEGETARIANS & VEGANS

Though it's normal for Turks to eat a vegetarian meal, the concept of vegetarianism is quite foreign. Say you're a vegan and Turks will either look mystified or assume that you're 'fessing up to some strain of socially aberrant behaviour. There is a sprinkling of vegetarian restaurants in Beyoğlu, a couple of which serve some vegan meals, but the travelling vegetarian certainly can't rely on specialist restaurants.

Meze is usually vegetable-based, and meat-free salads, soups, pastas, omelettes and *böreks*, as well as hearty vegetable dishes, are all readily available. Ask '*etsiz yemekler var mı?*' (is there something to eat that has no meat?) to see what's on offer.

The main source of inadvertent meat eating is *et suyu* (meat stock), which is often used to make otherwise vegetarian *pilavs*, soups and vegetable dishes. Your hosts may not even consider *et suyu* to be meat, so they will reassure you that the dish is vegetarian; ask '*et suyu var mı?*' (is there meat stock in it?) to check.

COOKING COURSES

Cooking Alaturca (☎ 0536 338 0896; www.cookingalaturka .com; classes €45) runs excellent, hands-on Turkish cooking classes. The delicious results are enjoyed over lunch.

The well-regarded İstanbul Food Workshop (Map p94; ☎ 212-534 4788; www.istanbulfoodworkshop.com; Yıldırım Caddesi 111, Fener) runs walking tours for foodies as well as cooking classes focusing on both Turkish and Ottoman cuisine.

PRACTICALITIES

Opening Hours

Most eateries in İstanbul are open for long hours every day of the week; occasionally they will close on a Sunday or Monday. Some lokantas and all *börekçis* and büfes open for early breakfasts; cafés open around 9am and serve into the night; and *pidecis,* kebapçıs, meyhanes, cafés and restaurants all open for lunch and dinner. Their average closing time will be 11pm, though many stay open later, particularly on Friday and Saturday evenings.

How Much?

You can spend a fortune or a pittance on a meal in İstanbul, but most visitors will spend something in between. The cheapest meals are those served in *pidecis,* kebapçıs and lokantas – it's quite usual for a meal to cost under YTL10 in these joints. A toasted sandwich or döner kebap and fresh juice in a büfe will usually cost even less. And one of the city's most famous meals – a delicious fish sandwich on the quay at Eminönü or Üsküdar – costs a bargain basement YTL3. Cafés are pricey in comparison, with a cappuccino costing as much as a lokanta meal in some instances. Restaurants where alcohol is served are in another league again; a meyhane meal will cost around YTL40 including alcohol, and a meal in one of the swish Western-style eateries in town can cost up to double that.

Booking Tables

İstanbullus like to eat out and they often book ahead, which means that you should, too. On Friday and Saturday nights it's very difficult to get a table anywhere popular if you haven't booked. Restaurants with views almost inevitably expect diners to reserve; if you want to ensure a table with a view, be very sure to specify this when you book.

Some of the more glamorous places in town will have more than one sitting in an evening. This means that you may be offered a table at 6pm or 10pm, and be told that there's nothing available in between. Fortunately this is quite uncommon.

Price Guide

Our guide to the per-person price of a meal consisting of meze/starter and main dish without alcohol is as follows:

€€€	more than YTL50
€€	YTL16 to YTL50
€	YTL15 or under

Tipping

Tipping is expected in all places where table service is given. Ten per cent is the norm. A few of the more touristy establishments include an extra service charge in the bill (look for the words *servis dahil*), but as is the case in many European countries, you are usually expected to tip on top of this.

Self-Catering

İstanbul has many small supermarkets (eg DIA, Gima, Makro) sprinkled through the streets around Beyoğlu, with giant cousins (eg Migros) in the suburbs. These sell most of the items you will need if you plan to self-cater. Then there is the ubiquitous *bakkal* (corner shop), which stocks bread, milk, basic groceries and usually fruit and vegetables. Some of these also sell *süt* (fresh milk) – look for the term 'pasteurised' on the label and you'll know it's fresh rather than long-life.

The best places to purchase fresh produce are undoubtedly the street markets. Down in Eminönü, the streets around the Spice Bazaar (Map p78) sell fish, meats, vegetables, fruit, spices, sweets and much more. The best stuff is available at the street stalls on Tahmis Caddesi on the market's west wall. In Beyoğlu, the Balık Pazar (Fish Market) next to the Çiçek Pasajı (Map p107) on İstiklal Caddesi is a great, if expensive, little market. As well as its many fish stalls, it has small shops selling freshly baked bread, greengrocers selling a wide range of fruit and vegetables, and delicatessens (*şarküteri*) selling cheeses, dried meats such as *pastırma* (pastrami), pickled fish, olives, jams and preserves. You can even get imported goods such as French jams, Iranian caviar and English tea here. Larger produce markets are found opposite the ferry terminals in Kadıköy and Beşiktaş – Kadıköy is known for its delicatessens and bakeries, and Beşiktaş for its fruit and vegetable stalls.

SULTANAHMET

It really is a shame that the quality of food served up in Sultanahmet's eateries is so mediocre. Some of the local restaurants have lovely settings and great views, but boy-oh-boy their food is disappointing (disgraceful is a word that frequently comes to mind). We've eaten our way through the neighbourhood, and are forced to limit our recommendations to those below. Once or twice, we have listed a place because its setting is so wonderful that

it doesn't matter too much that its food isn't. Around here places close early and there is no food strip as such.

BALIKÇI SABAHATTIN
Map p50   Seafood €€€

☎ 212-458 1824; Seyit Hasan Koyu Sokak 1, Cankurtaran; mains YTL28-50; ☯ noon-1am; ☒ Sultanahmet

The solid stream of chauffeur-driven limousines stopping outside Balıkçı Sabahattın is testament to its enduring popularity with the city's establishment. One of the few top-notch restaurants in Sultanahmet, it's set in a restored wooden Ottoman house tucked away in a ramshackle street just near the train line. The menu comprises a limited range of mezes and top-quality fresh fish, and there's also a delicious *buğlama* (fish soup). In summer, grab a table in the garden with the politicians and industrialists, and try to guess whether the glamorous women at their tables are wives, daughters or mistresses. We know where we'd put our bets.

GİRİTLİ Map p50   Seafood €€€

☎ 212-458 2270; Keresteci Hakkı Sokak, Cankurtaran; set menu YTL75; ☯ 11am-11pm; ☒ Sultanahmet

You'll find this restaurant tucked away in a deathly quiet corner of Cankurtaran. Serving top-notch Cretan seafood dishes, it's the type of place that polarises people – some don't mind the idea of paying this much money for a huge seafood set menu with alcohol included; others baulk at the idea and are affronted by the fact that the waiters can be very rude if you ask to order à la carte (been there, done that…). Summer service is in a pretty garden; winter meals are enjoyed in a dilapidated Ottoman building.

TERAS RESTAURANT
Map p50   Modern Turkish €€€

☎ 212-638 1370; Hotel Armada, Ahırkapı Sokak, Cankurtaran; degustation menu YTL58, starter tray YTL21, mains YTL19-31; ☯ 7-11pm; ☒ Sultanahmet

The chef at this posh hotel (p199) restaurant came up with an inspired idea when he devised his Turkish degustation menu. Six sampling courses of 'İstanbul cuisine' feature, and they are wonderfully complemented by an excellent (and affordable)

wine list. If you decide to order à la carte, you can expect treats such as *bademli patlıcan çorbaşi* (aubergine soup with almonds) and can order specialities such as the *şefin çilinger sofrası* (chef's traditional starters tray), which features eight different seasonal mezes. With a killer view of the Blue Mosque and Sea of Marmara, as well as very comfortable seating and occasional live Turkish music, this place is quite possibly the best eating option in Sultanahmet.

RAMİ Map p50   Anatolian & Ottoman €€
☎ 212-517 6593; Utangaç Sokak 6, Cankurtaran; starters YTL13-17, mains YTL27-28; ☒ noon-11pm; ☒ Sultanahmet

This restored Ottoman house has several quaint dining rooms that are decorated with impressionist-style paintings by Turkish painter Rami Uluer (1913–88), but the favoured spot for dinner is the rooftop terrace, which has a full view of the Blue Mosque. Make sure you request a table there when you book. Ottoman specialities such as *kağıt kebap* (lamb and vegetables cooked in a paper pouch) dominate the menu and although the food is nothing to get excited about, the view and the decent wine list certainly compensate. No credit cards.

HOUSE OF MEDUSA Map p50   Anatolian €€
☎ 212-511 4116; Muhtereme Fendi Sokak, off Yerebtan Caddesi, Sultanahmet; meze YTL9-16, mains YTL18-28; ☒ noon-10pm; ☒ Sultanahmet

Medusa's charming shaded courtyard beckons guests off Yerebatan Caddesi. It's a lovely spot to relax after a morning spent sightseeing, which is why we've decided to include it here. The food's nothing special – acceptable executions of Turkish dishes such as kebaps and stews – but if you order a mixed meze plate and an ice-cold beer, you'll be happy.

ALBURA CAFÉ & RESTAURANT
Map p50   Modern Turkish & International €€
☎ 212-517 9031; Akbıyık Caddesi 26, Cankurtaran; starters YTL9-18.50, mains YTL16-21; ☒ noon-11pm; ☒ Sultanahmet

This newcomer is a welcome addition to the otherwise mediocre array of restaurants along Akbıyık Caddesi. Its pretty streetside tables are usually occupied by tourists sampling Turkish dishes such as *hünkar beğendi* (lamb or beef goulash served on a mound of rich aubergine puree) or opting for

international favourites such as tortellini with mushrooms and basil. The food is decent, but we've been unimpressed by the house wine (dreadful and overpriced) – stick to bottles, and check that the prices on the bill match those on the menu.

DUBB Map p50   Indian €€
☎ 212-513 7308; İncili Çavuş Sokak, Alemdar; mains YTL8.30, curries YTL11.50-21.50, thalis YTL29.50-32.50; ☒ noon-3pm & 6-10.30pm; ☒ Sultanahmet

One of İstanbul's few Indian restaurants and the only one worthy of a recommendation, Dubb is a little piece of the Subcontinent slap-bang in the middle of İstanbul. Specialising in tandoori dishes (the breads are great, as are the tandoori kebabs), it also serves the full complement of fragrant curries, including a wide range of vegetarian choices. Its *thalis*, which offer small serves of a number of dishes including dessert, are particularly popular. The outdoor terrace on the 4th floor offers fabulous views of Aya Sofya and the Sea of Marmara – request a table there when you book.

MOZAIK
Map p50   Modern Turkish & International €€
☎ 212-512 4177; İncirli Çavuş Sokak 1, off Divan Yolu Caddesi; pastas YTL12-16, mains YTL15-27; ☒ 9am-midnight; ☒ Sultanahmet

Over the years Mozaik has built a reputation as the most stylish restaurant in this part of town. Housed in a romantic Ottoman building dating from 1878 and with plenty of streetside tables, it has a huge menu that offers pastas and international dishes but specialises in dishes from different regions of Turkey – try the *kara erık yahnısı* (black plum and lamb stew) or the *kuzu sultan* (lamb marinated with thyme and served with a pilaf of rice, lamb liver, cinnamon, pinenuts and raisons). There's a great salad selection (perfect for lunch), a good wine list and attentive service.

LALE RESTAURANT (PUDDING SHOP)
Map p50   Lokanta €€
☎ 212-522 2970; Divan Yolu Caddesi 6; portion YTL5-9; ☒ 7am-11pm; ☒ Sultanahmet

It's a long time since the Pudding Shop served up fare to the hippies who made it famous, but its fame still drags in backpackers travelling in their parents' footsteps.

Appearing for the prosecution: the stodgy, badly cooked food. For the defence: the fact that it has wi-fi and booze.

AYASOFYA KEBAP HOUSE
Map p50   Kebapçı €

☎ 212-458 3653; Küçük Aya Sofya Sokak; kebaps YTL7-12; ☾ 11am-11pm; ⓐ Sultanahmet

This neighbourhood kebapçı serves lots of tourists, but it also provides plenty of locals with belly fuel. You can grab a table on the street or order to take-away – either way you'll get a perfectly adequate kebap dinner for under YTL10, or a quick lunch of *mercimek çorbası* (lentil soup) or *sulu köfte* (meat balls filled with rice and cooked in a tomato-based sauce) for considerably less. You can also order a beer or glass of wine here.

TARİHİ SULTANAHMET KÖFTECİSİ
SELİM USTA Map p50   Köfteci €

☎ 212-511 3960; Divan Yolu Caddesi 4; meal YTL13; ☾ 11am-11pm; ⓐ Sultanahmet

This is one of the most famous eateries in the city, and to be frank, we're at a total loss to understand why. The ever-present queues of locals obviously adore its rubbery *köfte* (meatballs) served with bread, beans, salad and pickled chillies, but we have always been underwhelmed. Why not try it yourself, though? The place is certainly clean, cheap and cheerful.

KARADENİZ AİLE PİDE VE KEBAP
SALONU Map p50   Pideci & Kebapçı €

☎ 212-528 6290; Hacı Tahsinbey Sokak 1, off Divan Yolu Caddesi; pides YTL7-8.50; ☾ 11am-11pm; ⓐ Sultanahmet

This friendly place serves super-fresh soup, kebaps and *pide*. If you sit inside you'll be able to watch the cooks make your food; sit on the street tables and you'll have to put up with passers-by hungrily eying off your delicious-looking meal. Either way, you should order a *karaşik* (mixed) *pide* and prepare to enjoy a great cheap eat.

CANKURTARAN SOSYAL TESİSLERİ
Map p50   Anatolian €

Saraçhane Sokak, Cankurtaran; soup YTL2, salads YTL2.50, kebaps YTL6-9; ☾ 9am-10pm; ⓐ Sultanahmet

Literally built into Theodosius' walls, with views over busy Sahil Yolu to the Sea of Marmara, this terrace restaurant and *çay*

bahçesi near the Cankurtaran train station is very popular with families. It's set in a landscaped garden and has a small playground. Simple dishes such as soup, salads and kebaps feature.

ÇİĞDEM PASTANESİ Map p50   Pastane €

☎ 212-526 8859; Divan Yolu Caddesi 62A; cappuccino YTL4, tea YTL1.50, pastries YTL0.50-3.50; ☾ 8am-11pm; ⓐ Sultanahmet

Customers have been ordering tea and baklava here since 1961. Çiğdem serves a cappuccino that could hold its head high on the Via Veneto in Rome, well-priced *portakal suyu* (fresh orange juice) and a wide range of cakes, pastries and puddings. No wonder it's always crammed with students from nearby İstanbul University.

TOPKAPI PALACE & AROUND

Eating options around the palace are relatively thin on the ground, but Sultanahmet and Eminönü are only a hop, skip and jump away.

KONYALI Map p64   Anatolian €€

☎ 212-513 9696; Topkapı Palace; mains YTL21-26; ☾ 10am-5pm Wed-Mon; ⓐ Gülhane

Fabulously positioned in the grounds of Topkapı Palace (p62) and emanating a charmingly down-at-heel Riviera feel, Konyalı is usually swamped with tourists but is still worth a visit, particularly as it's the only eatery in the palace. Try and bag a table overlooking the Golden Horn and Sea of Marmara (phone ahead and reserve one) and consider sampling an Ottoman sherbet with your meal – you'll see their bright colours glinting from the large glass decanters on display. Food is stock-standard cafeteria-style fare.

SULTANAHMET FISH HOUSE
Map p63   Seafood €€

☎ 212-527 4445; Prof. Kazım İsmail Gürkan Caddesi 14, Cağaloğlu; fish soup YTL4, mains YTL15-30; ☾ noon-11pm; ⓐ Gülhane

If you're the fishy type, traditionally there have been only three viable dining options in the Old City: heading down to Kumkapı (see boxed text, p163), grabbing a fish sandwich on the dock at Eminönü or booking a table at the pricey Balıkçı Sabahattin (p158). But with the opening of this casual restaurant in Cağaloğlu, another option has been un-veiled, and an interesting one at that. What makes this joint distinctive are its prices, which are remarkably low for what's on offer. Take the set lunch for example – fish soup, salad, fresh fish of the day and a dessert for YTL9! Wine is also well priced, and everything is squeaky clean. Wow.

CAFERAĞA MEDRESESİ
Map p63   Anatolian €

☎ 212-513 3601; Caferiye Sokak; soup YTL2.50, köfte YTL9; ☩ 8.30am-6pm; ⓔ Sultanahmet
In Sultanahmet, it's rare to nosh in stylish surrounds without paying through the nose for the privilege. That's why this teensy lokanta in the gorgeous courtyard of this Sinan-designed *medrese* near Topkapı Pal-ace is such a find. The food isn't anything to write home about, but it's fresh and cheap as chips, so who's complaining?

SEFA RESTAURANT Map p63   Lokanta €

☎ 212-520 0670; Nuruosmaniye Caddesi 17, Cağaloğlu; soup YTL2.50, portion YTL5-11, kebabs YTL6.50-16; ☩ 8am-7pm Mon-Sat; ⓔ Sultanahmet
Locals rate this place near the bazaar highly, and after sampling the dishes on offer you'll realise why. It describes its cui-sine as Ottoman, but what's really on offer here are top-quality lokanta dishes and kebaps at extremely reasonable prices. You can order from an English menu or choose from the bain marie – the vegetable dishes are particularly appetising and they'll let you order half portions if you ask nicely.

BUHARA RESTAURANT & OCAKBAŞI
Map p63   Kebapçı €

☎ 212-527 5133; Nuruosmaniye Caddesi 7A, Cağaloğlu; kebabs YTL7-11; ☩ 11am-10pm; ⓔ Sultanahmet
It ain't glam (quite the contrary), but Buhara has built a loyal local following over many years for its well-cooked kebaps. It's busy at lunch but usually quiet at night, so you shouldn't have trouble bagging a table. You can order an Efes to accompany your meal.

HAFİZ MUSTAFA ŞEKERLEMELERİ
Map p63   Pastane & Börekçi €

☎ 212-526 5627; Hamidiye Caddesi 84-86, Eminönü; ☩ 8am-9pm Mon-Sat, 9am-9pm Sun; ⓔ Eminönü
If you walk up the steep staircase at the rear of this excellent *börek*, pastry and

Turkish-delight shop, you'll find a tiny café secreted under the roof. Here locals eat all-day snacks of melt-in-your-mouth cheese *börek*, peppery *ıspanaklı börek* (spinach *börek*) and delicious biscuits and sweet pastries, all washed down with tea and coffee. Breakfast will set you back a mere two or three lira.

BAZAAR DISTRICT

Generations of shoppers have worked up an appetite around the Grand Bazaar, and fortu-nately there have always been eateries to meet this need, including a range of great lokantas such as Havuzlu and Subaşı. A little further away is the tranquil Şehzade Mehmed Sofrası, one of our favourite spots in the Old City. Down near the water there aren't too many choices – a delicious fish sandwich on the quay at Eminönü is your best bet. At night, make sure you a meal served with views at Hamdi et Lokantası or Zinhan Kebap House.

ZİNHAN KEBAP HOUSE AT STORKS
Map p78   Anatolian & International €€

☎ 212-512 4275; Ragıpgümüşpala Caddesi 2-5, Eminönü; meze YTL4-6, kebabs YTL13-21; ☩ noon-11pm; ⓔ Eminönü
Zinhan's regal position next to the Galata Bridge (p74) means that every İstanbullu knows it. Unfortunately (for them, that is) most haven't eaten here. If you buck this trend, you'll enjoy an excellent meal on one of the most impressive roof terraces in the city – the views from here are simply sen-sational. Best is the fact that there are lots of tables in prime positions, meaning that you won't have to book weeks ahead as is often the case at places such as Hamdi (below). You'll sit on comfortable chairs at huge, well-spaced tables to enjoy tasty mezes such as *humus pastırmalı* (hummus with *pastırma*) and sophisticated kebap dishes such as *ali nazik* (spicy kebap on a bed of broiled egg-plant salad with garlic yogurt). Also on offer are international dishes such as Tournados Rossini and a well-priced wine list.

HAMDİ ET LOKANTASI
Map p78   Anatolian €€

Hamdı Restaurant; ☎ 212-528 0390; Kalçın Sokak 17, off Tahmis Caddesi, Eminönü; kebabs YTL12-16; ☩ noon-11pm; ⓔ Eminönü
It's a hard call to make in a city with as many fabulous eateries as İstanbul, but if

forced to list our top five Turkish restaurants, Hamdi would certainly be one of them. Its setting (on a rooftop with panoramic views across to Galata, down the Golden Horn and back to the Old İstanbul skyline) is wonderful, and its food is among the best in town. Try the *hayari* (yogurt with roasted eggplant and garlic), the *içli köfte* (meatballs rolled in *bulgur*) and the *patıcanlı kebab* (lamb kebab with eggplant) and you'll see what we mean. Any place this good is always going to be busy, so make sure you book, and don't forget to request a rooftop table with a view (outside if the weather is hot). If you get there early (around 6pm), you might be able to score one of these without booking. Enter through the ground-floor baklava shop.

ŞEHZADE MEHMED SOFRASI

Map p78   Anatolian €€

☎ 212-526 2668; Şehzadebaşı Caddesi, Fatih; kebaps & mains YTL10-19, pides YTL8-12; ☾ 9am-10pm; 🚇 Üniversite

Locations don't come any better than this. You'll find this welcoming restaurant and *çay bahçesi* in the magnificent *külliye* (mosque complex) of the Şehzade Mehmed Camii (p81). After a tasty meal of *köfte*, *tavuk kavurma* (roast chicken), kebap or *pide* you can settle back on one of the Turkish couches and relax over a *Türk kahvesi* (Turkish coffee) and narghile. Enter from the garden at the rear of the mosque.

BAB-İ HAYAT Map p78   Anatolian €

☎ 212-520 7878; Mısır Çarşısı, 47; pides YTL6.50-7.50, kebaps YTL8-12.50; ☾ 7.30am-7.30pm Mon-Sat; 🚇 Eminönü

It took seven months for a team headed by one of the conservation architects from Topkapı Palace to restore and decorate this vaulted space over the eastern entrance to the Spice Bazaar. Hand-painted ceilings and tiled window frames provide an atmospheric setting in which to sample decent kebaps and adequate *pides* and *hazır yemek* dishes. The ultra-friendly service stands in stark contrast to that at neighbouring Pandeli (which we've elected not to review), and you can even get a beer if you ask discreetly. Enter through the Serhadoğlu fast-food shop.

SUBAŞI LOKANTASI Map p77   Lokanta €

☎ 212-522 4762; Kiliçcilar Sokak 48; portion YTL5-12; ☾ 11am-5pm Mon-Sat; 🚇 Çemberlitaş

This place first opened its doors in 1959 and it's been feeding a constant stream of the Grand Bazaar's shopkeepers and customers ever since. Choose from the spread of excellent hot food in the kitchen on the right as you enter and then grab a seat at a table on one of the two floors. Don't let the waiters cajole you into ordering an expensive mixed plate; instead check out the price list at the door and order by the portion. You'll find it near the Nuruosmaniye gate.

HAVUZLU RESTAURANT

Map p77   Anatolian €

☎ 212-527 3346; Gani Çelebi Sokak 3, Grand Bazaar; portions YTL4-10, kebaps YTL10-12; ☾ 8am-7pm Mon-Sat; 🚇 Beyazıt

There are few more pleasant experiences than parking your shopping bags and enjoying a meal at the best eatery at the Grand Bazaar. A lovely space with a vaulted ceiling, pale lemon walls and an ornate central light fitting, Havuzlu serves up excellent fare to hungry hordes of tourists and shopkeepers. Try the spinach and yogurt dish or the one of the excellent kebaps, and don't even *think* of leaving without sampling the delights of the figs stuffed with walnuts and served with *kaymak* (clotted cream).

MESHUR KURU FASÜLYECI

Map p78   Anatolian €

Prof. Sıddık Sokak 11, Süleymaniye; fasülyeci YTL5.50; ☾ 11am-4pm; 🚇 Üniversite

This popular local lokanta in the former *medrese* of the Süleymaniye Camii (p80) serves its famous spicy *fasülyeci* (broad beans) and rice to hordes of hungry locals from the theological college and nearby commercial areas.

NİMLA PASTIRMACI Map p78   Delicatessen €

☎ 212-511 6393; Hasırcılar Caddesi 14, Eminönü; ☾ 7am-7pm Mon-Sat; 🚇 Eminönü

Nimla's mouth-watering selection of cheese, *pastırma* (pastrami) and mezes is known throughout the city. The take-away *pastırma* rolls are delicious and there's also an upstairs cafeteria where you can grab a tasty light lunch.

İMREN LOKANTASI Map p78   Lokanta €

☎ 212-513 3601; Kadırga Meydanı; soup YTL2, portion YTL3-6; ☾ 8.30am-6pm; 🚇 Sultanahmet

We've eaten here many times and have always been the only non-Turk doing so (something that's bound to change now that we're listing it here). A neighbourhood lokanta with only five (shared) tables, it's a fab place to grab a delicious quick lunch. You can order a portion of döner kebap or choose from the range of hot dishes on offer – the *guveç* (stew) cooked in a terracotta pot is our favourite. Waiters will bring you a towering basket of bread so that you can mop up your food à la Turca, and you can finish up with a speedy glass of *çay*. Great stuff.

WESTERN DISTRICTS

There aren't too many eateries of note in this area, but it is home to one of the city's best restaurants, Asitane. The suburbs here are quiet at night, so you're probably best off sampling the delights of this place at lunch after visiting the Chora Church (p93).

ASITANE Map p94   Ottoman €€
☎ 212-534 8414; Kariye Oteli, Kariye Camii Sokak 18, Edirnekapı; mains YTL22-35; ☺ 8am-11pm; ⊕ Edirnekapı
It's not often that you'll get the opportunity to sample Ottoman dishes devised especially for a 16th century royal circumcision feast, but this is what's on offer at this popular restaurant. The food is magnificent – try the *vişne yalanci dolmasi* (vine leaves stuffed with morello cherries) and *yufkada kuzu incik marmarina'li* (baked lamb with pureed spinach and cheese on a plate of flaky pastry); we're sure that Süleyman the Magnificent would have approved of them as much as we do. The surrounds are mod-

ern and elegant, featuring a pale-lemon colour scheme, comfortable seating, pristine napery and an outdoor courtyard for summer dining. Vegetarians are well catered for.

DEVELİ Map pp46–7   Kebapçi €
☎ 212-529 0833; Gümüşyüzük Sokak 7, Samatya; kebabs YTL10-15; ☺ noon-midnight
Near the Wall at Samatya, on the Sea of Marmara, the five floors (including a roof terrace) of Develi are always full of happy punters enjoying the flavours of southeastern Anatolia. It's been serving up kebabs to hungry locals since 1912, so Develi really knows what it's doing when it comes to the national dish. Try the *çiğ köfte* (raw ground lamb, *bulgur*, onions and spices) and the *fıstıklı* (pistachio) *kebab* and you'll feel happy too. To get there from Sultanahmet, catch a taxi along Kennedy Caddesi or take the train from Cankurtaran Station (get off at Mustafa Paşa Station). You'll find Develi inland from the station on a plaza filled with parked cars.

GALATA & TOPHANE

This part of town once had a very unsavoury reputation; it's still reasonably quiet at night, so be a bit careful walking around after dark. The enclave of eateries near the Karaköy ferry terminal is well worth checking out, as is the café at the stylish İstanbul Modern (p102). There are also a few good eateries around Galata Tower.

İSTANBUL MODERN CAFE
Map p103   Modern International €€
☎ 212-249 9680; İstanbul Modern, Meclis-i Mebusan Caddesi, Tophane; sandwiches YTL13-15, salads YTL11-20, mains YTL13-45; ☺ 10am-6pm Tue-Sun, 10am-8pm Thu; ⊛ Tophane

KUMKAPI

In Byzantine times, the fishers' harbour called Kontoscalion was due south of Beyazıt. The gate into the city from that port came to be called Kumkapı (Sand Gate) by the Turks. Though the gate is long gone, the district is still filled with fishermen, who moor their boats in a more modern version of the old harbour. And around this harbour cobbled laneways are filled with seafood restaurants and meyhanes. A few years ago the district was always packed with large groups of locals enjoying a boozy night on the town, but these days the attractions of Nevizade and Soyalı Sokaks in Beyoğlu (p165) have caused its star to wane and its streets are only full of hawkers trying to lure passers-by into establishments that are rarely even half full. Still, the surrounds and the quality of the seafood in a few of the longer-standing eateries make it worth a visit when you're in town. On the Sea of Marmara just inside the Wall, it's a quick taxi ride from Sultanahmet. Alternatively, you can walk all the way down Tiyatro Caddesi from Beyazıt. When there, wander around and see which establishment takes your fancy. We usually gravitate towards Kör Agop Restaurant (Map p78; ☎ 212-517 2334; Ördekli Bakkal Sokak 7, Kumkapı; fish meze YTL8-13, fish YTL15-40; ☺ 11am-2am), which was established in 1938 and has one of the best fasıl bands around. It also serves excellent fresh fish.

A New York–style 'industrial arty' vibe and great views over the water to Sultanahmet (when there are no moored cruise ships in the way), make the café at İstanbul's pre-eminent contemporary art museum a perfect place for lunch. Some dishes have a Turkish influence – try the grilled eggplant puree with aged parmesan cheese cracker – but most have an international flavour, with snacks such as chicken club sandwiches with caesar sauce.

TARIHI KARAKÖY BALIK LOKANTASI
Map p103   Seafood €€

☎ 212-251 1371; Karaköy; fish soup YTL5, mains YTL24; ⏰ 11.30am-3.30pm Mon-Sat; 🚇 Karaköy
Walk through the run-down quarter behind the Karaköy Balıkçılar Çarşısı (Karaköy Fish Market) and you'll come upon this utter gem, one of the few old-style fish restaurants left on the Golden Horn. There's no other word for the food here except fabulous, with the dirt-cheap fish soup possibly being the best you'll ever eat. Everything is so fresh it's almost writhing and the staff are happy to point out what's particularly good on the day. With seafood being such an expensive proposition in most of İstanbul's restaurants, it's incredibly refreshing to encounter top class, perfectly prepared dishes that are within everyone's budget. Go.

GALATA HOUSE Map p103   Georgian €€
☎ 212-245 1861; Galata Kulesi Sokak 61, Galata; mains YTL14-18; ⏰ noon-midnight Tue-Sun; 🚇 Karaköy
This would have to be one of the most eccentric restaurants in town. Run by the utterly charming husband-and-wife team of Nadire and Mete Göktuğ, it is housed in the Old British Jail, just down from Galata Tower. The jail functioned from 1904 to 1919, and has been sympathetically but comfortably restored by Mete, who is one of İstanbul's most prominent heritage architects. Nadire uses recipes handed down from her Georgian mother to concoct great comfort food – the hingali (meat-filled dumplings in tomato sauce) are absolutely delicious. She also plays the piano for guests.

GALATA KONAK PATISSERIE CAFÉ
Map p103   Anatolian & Pastane €€
☎ 212-252 5346; Hacı Ali Sokak 2/2, Galata; breakfast YTL5-13, cakes YTL6-7, pastas YTL10-12, kebabs YTL13-22; ⏰ 9am-9pm; 🚇 Karaköy

After checking out the pastries and cakes on sale in the ground-floor patisserie, make your way up the stairs to the roof terrace café, where you can order anything that has taken your fancy downstairs or choose from a large and varied menu. For breakfast try the excellent menemen (eggs cooked with tomatoes, peppers and white cheese) or the super-fresh poğaca (breakfast buns); there are also decadent cakes for morning and afternoon pick-me-ups and kebabs and pastas for lunch. The view, which includes the Sultanahmet skyline, down the Bosphorus and over the Golden Horn, is fabulous.

KARAKÖYÜM CAFÉ & RESTAURANT
Map p103   Anatolian €€
☎ 212-244 6808; Kemeraltı Caddesi 4, Karaköy; mains YTL6-11; ⏰ 10.30am-midnight; 🚇 Karaköy
The elegant lady owners will greet you personally when you enter this popular rooftop restaurant. Everyone in town knows the secret of the success here – put simply, the women in the kitchen are wonderful home-style cooks. Try Anatolian favourites such as the utterly delicious dürüm köfte (köfte wrapped in pastry and served with yogurt and tomato sauce) and we're confident that you'll become an instant devotee. There's a terrace with views of Topkapı Palace, and a wine list that is well priced.

GÜNEY RESTAURANT Map p103   Lokanta €€
☎ 212-249 0393; Kuledibi Şah Kapısı 6, Tünel; soup YTL2.50, portions YTL3.50-7, kebaps YTL7-18; ⏰ 7am-10pm Mon-Sat; 🚇 Karaköy
You'll be lucky if you can fight your way through the crowds of hungry locals to claim a lunchtime table at this bustling eatery directly opposite Galata Tower. Friendly waiters will set you up with a basket of fresh bread and point you towards the array of meze and hot dishes on offer. It's also a great place to grab a hearty bowl of çorba (soup) for breakfast.

NAMLI Map p103   Delicatessen €
☎ 212-293 6880; Rıhtım Caddesi, Karaköy; ⏰ 7am-10pm; 🚇 Karaköy
As well as being one of the best delicatessens in the city (check out that cheese selection!), Namlı also stocks hard-to-find Asian ingredients, imported tea and other treats. Take away your choice from the impressive salad and meze selection, or grab one of the tables at the front and eat in.

KARAKÖY GÜLLÜGLU Map p103 Pastane €

☎ 212-249 9680; Mumhane Caddesi 171, Karaköy; YTL20-25 per kilo; ⏰ 10.30am-midnight; 🚇 Karaköy

This is a place where waistlines are destroyed and dentists get rich, but no-one cares because they're all sitting at the funky 1960s Arabesque-style outdoor seating and gobbling the best baklava in the city, washed down by tea or coffee. Utter bliss.

SEBO BÖREK Map p103 Börekçi €

☎ 212-244 8787; Rıhtım Caddesi 9, Karaköy; ⏰ 7am-6pm; 🚇 Karaköy

This Karaköy branch of a popular *börek* chain serves an array of freshly made *börek* that makes a perfect mid-morning snack.

İSTİKLAL & AROUND

The streets in the Asmalımescit district, with their raft of good-quality meyhanes packing the crowds in every Friday and Saturday night, are giving the famous Nevizade Sokak a run for its money these days, but they're not the only establishments off İstiklal doing well. This is, without doubt, the best neighbourhood in town in which to eat, drink and be merry. You would be mad if you didn't make your way here at least once during your visit.

CHANGA Map p107 Modern International €€€

☎ 212-249 1348; Sıraselviler Caddesi 47, Taksim; starters YTL19-25, mains YTL32-55; ⏰ 6pm-1am Mon-Sat Nov-Jun; 🚇 Kabataş, then funicular to Taksim

İstanbul's most controversial eatery has fans and detractors. At issue is Peter Gordon's handling of fusion dishes: do they work? Try the salmon and wasabi tortellini with grilled porcini and creamed lemongrass sauce and see what you think. One dish that no-one would question is the soft meringue of strawberries, lychees and fresh cheese with a strawberry and raspberry sauce – delicious. The décor is stark modern, featuring Eames chairs and a stylish bar, with the quirky touch of a glass floor looking down on the kitchen. The wine list is superb. In summer all action moves to Changa's second restaurant, the wonderful Müzedechanga (p220).

MİKLA Map p107 Modern Mediterranean €€€

☎ 212-293 5656; Marmara Pera, Meşrutiyet Caddesi 1, Tepebaşı; starters YTL17-27, mains YTL29-55; ⏰ noon-11.30pm; 🚇 Karaköy, then funicular to Tünel

Among the big guns of İstanbul's top-end dining scene, one place reigns supreme in our minds, and that's Mikla. On the top floor of the Marmara Pera hotel, this sleek operation serves up excellent Mod Med cuisine to a truly international clientele. The chefs here embrace top-notch ingredients and simple execution and the results speak for themselves: try the absolutely delicious grilled tenderloin with roasted garlic potato cream, parmesan baked fennel and goat's cheese butter; or the wonderful lightly smoked lamb loin with pinenut-sauteed French beans, walnut pistou and white bean puree. Service and the wine list are impressive, and the view is quite simply to die for. Ask for a table on the terrace overlooking the Old City.

360 Map p107 Modern International €€

☎ 212-251 1042; Mısır Apartmenti, İstiklal Caddesi 311, Kat 8; pizzas YTL17-23, pastas & risottos YTL17-30, mains YTL21-32; ⏰ lunch Mon-Fri, dinner daily; 🚇 Kabataş, then funicular to Taksim

It's the most hyped restaurant-bar in the city, and quite frankly we don't think it deserves its reputation. Though its stylish fitout and knockout views make it a fabulous spot for a drink, the food here is trying too hard – and falling flat as a result. If you order simply you'll enjoy your meal, but beware the fussy mains, which often have flavours that clash. We suggest opting for the Miss Piggy pizza, which features prosciutto, fresh rocket, parmesan, tomato and mozzarella, or for an uncomplicated risotto or pasta. Fortunately, the desserts live up to the hype – try the sensational crystallised coconut rice pudding with mango-ginger parfait.

NU TERAS Map p107 Modern Mediterranean €€

☎ 212-245 6070; Meşrutiyet Caddesi 149/7, Tepebaşı; pizzas YTL19-23, pasta YTL18-23, mains YTL22-34; ⏰ noon-11.30pm July-Oct; 🚇 Karaköy, then funicular to Tünel

Nu Teras is the summer project of the much-loved Lokanta (p166), a long-standing showcase of casual chic and Mod Med food. On the roof of the Lokanta building, this terrace bar-restaurant isn't quite as glam as it was in its heyday, but that's good news because it means ordinary

165

mortals can now score a table. The extraordinary views over the Golden Horn should be appreciated over a pre-dinner drink at the bar before you move onto a table and make your choice from the menu of huge and very tasty pizzas, a wide array of pasta dishes and mains such as roasted cod with tomatoes, capers, currents and pine nuts served with potato salad. We suggest opting for the pizzas and pastas, as mains can sometimes be disappointing.

LOKANTA Map p107   Modern Mediterranean €€
☎ 212-245 6070; Meşrutiyet Caddesi 149/1, Tepebaşı; pizzas YTL19-23, pasta YTL18-23, mains YTL22-34; ☟ noon-11.30pm Nov-Jun; ⛴ Karaköy, then funicular to Tünel
This cool-weather venue is the twin of Nu Teras (p165), and serves an almost identical menu.

CEZAYİR Map p107   Modern Turkish €€
☎ 212-245 9980; Hayriye Caddesi 16, Galatasaray; starters YTL9-15, mains YTL18-28; ☟ noon-11.30pm; ⛴ Kabataş, then funicular to Taksim
After reading that Cezayir showcased 'experimental Turkish cuisine' we visited with a great deal of trepidation; fortunately, our delicious meal would more rightly be categorised as Modern Mediterranean with Turkish accents. One of the most popular restaurant-bars in Beyoğlu, this place is housed in an old school building that has been sympathetically and glamorously renovated to provide inside and outside dining areas and two bars. The décor is traditional with a twist and the crowd is middle-aged and arty. Great fun.

LEB-I DERYA Map p107   Modern Turkish €€
☎ 212-244 1886; Kumbaracı Yokuşu 115/7; starters YTL9-23, mains YTL17-28; ☟ 11am-2am Mon-Fri & 8.30am-3am Sat & Sun; ⛴ Karaköy, then funicular to Tünel
The magnificent views are here to stay, but some of our recent meals here have been disappointing. It's still a great spot for a weekend brunch, though, particularly when the food is washed down by a therapeutic Bloody Mary or two.

SAF' ORGANIC BISTRO
Map p107   Vegetarian & Vegan €€
☎ 212-245 9515; Ensiz Sokak 1A; starters YTL12-17, mains YTL20-24, tasting menus YTL40-70; ☟ noon-11pm Mon-Sat; Ⓥ; ⛴ Karaköy, then funicular to Tünel

Supremely stylish Saf' is planets away from the earnest but oh-so-boring tofu-dominated restaurants that vegetarians often have to make do with. Here, the menu is creative and delicious in equal parts, with dishes such as mushroom ravioli with marinated beetroot, wild mushrooms, porcini cream and a balsamic fig compote featuring. There are five- and three-course tasting menus that match each course with a glass of organic wine, as well as a fabulous array of cocktails – try the expat harem (vodka, fresh cucumber, home-made ginger beer and fresh apple juice, YTL18). All ingredients are organic and vegans are catered for.

REFİK Map p107   Meyhane €€
☎ 212-245 7879; Sofyalı Sokak 7; meze YTL5-12, fish YTL15-30; ☟ noon-midnight Mon-Sat, 6.30pm-midnight Sun; ⛴ Karaköy, then funicular to Tünel
Refik is the original meyhane in the Asmalımescit area and it's always full of large groups of liquored-up locals enjoying the convivial (and noisy) atmosphere and decent meyhane food. There are two dining areas (on each side of the street) and loads of streetside tables. Try the excellent çacık (yogurt and mint salad).

KREPENDEKI İMROZ RESTAURANT
Map p107   Meyhane €€
☎ 212-249 9073; Nevizade Sokak 24; meze YTL4-9, fish YTL15-25; ☟ noon-midnight; ⛴ Kabataş, then funicular to Taksim
The minute you see the waiters heaving around their enormous meze-laden trays in this popular meyhane you'll know you've made the right dinner choice. With outdoor tables on both sides of the street, you'll also have a slightly better chance of scoring a spot in the middle of the action – to make sure, ring ahead and book. The food is typical of the island of Gökceada (İmroz) and is top-class; those in the know always include the octopus salad and pickled anchovies in their meze choices.

BONCUK RESTAURANT
Map p107   Meyhane €€
☎ 212-243 1219; Nevizade Sokak 19; meze YTL4-9, fish YTL15-25; ☟ noon-2am; ⛴ Kabataş, then funicular to Taksim
Armenian specialities differentiate Boncuk from its Nevizade neighbours. Try the excellent topik (meze made with chickpeas,

MEYHANES – THE BIGGEST PARTY IN TOWN

If you only have one night out on the town when you visit İstanbul, make sure you spend it at one of the meyhanes on Nevizade or Sofyalı Sokaks in Beyoğlu. On any night of the week, meyhanes such as Sofyalı 9 (below), Refik (opposite), Boncuk (opposite) and Krependeki İmroz (opposite) will be full of chattering locals sampling the dizzying array of meze and fresh fried fish on offer, washed down with a never-ending supply of raki. On Friday and Saturday summer evenings the streets literally heave with people looking for a table, grabbing a drink at one of the many bars along the strips or just wandering past. You'd be mad if you didn't join them.

pistachios, onion, flour, currants, cumin and salt) and the very tasty *börek*. To ensure that you get a table on the street, where all the action is, get there early or call ahead and book.

SOFYALI 9 Map p107   Meyhane €€

☎ 212-245 0362; Sofyalı Sokak 9; cold meze YTL1.50-3.50, hot meze YTL2-8, kebabs YTL8-13; ☯ noon-midnight Mon-Sat; ⊠ Karaköy, then funicular to Tünel

Tables here are hot property on a Friday or Saturday night, and no wonder. This gem of a place serves up some of the best meyhane food in all of İstanbul, and does so in surroundings that are as welcoming as they are attractive. It's a bit like eating in a close friend's home, except here you're offered a large array of meze and a wealth of grills and fresh fried fish along with the bonhomie. The *köpeoğlu* (eggplant and tomato with yogurt and garlic) and *semizotu* (green purslane with yogurt and garlic) are among the best we've ever eaten and the *kaşaril börek* (cheese pastries) and *kalamar* (fried calamari with garlic sauce) are damn fine, too. Regulars swear by the *Anavut ciğeri* (Albanian fried liver).

HOUSE CAFÉ Map p107   Modern International €€

☎ 212-2459515; Sofyalı Sokak 9/1; sandwiches YTL16.50-20, mains YTL14.50-28; ☯ 8am-2am Mon-Sat, 8am-11pm Sun; ⊠ Karaköy, then funicular to Tünel

This stylish café would look equally at home in Soho, Seattle or Sydney. On the city's most happening street, its casual but chic interior is invariably packed with ladies

lunching, young couples courting and businesspeople meeting over coffee. The food is resolutely international in flavour and execution; you can choose from a menu including sandwiches, pizzas, salads and light dishes such as Thai chicken noodle soup and a 'House burger' with wedges. We'd describe the food as adequate rather than inspired and feel compelled to say that the waiters can display more attitude than aptitude. Sunday brunch is the best bet.

KAFE ARA Map p107   Modern International €€

☎ 212-245 4104; Tosbağ Sokak 8A; pastas YTL11-12.50, mains YTL16-18; ☯ 8am-midnight; ⊠ Karaköy, then funicular to Tünel

In the Beyoğlu popularity stakes one café stands head and shoulders above the rest – Kafe Ara. A converted garage with tables and chairs spilling out into a wide laneway opposite the Galatasaray Lycée, this is boho central, a casual and welcoming place where you can sample well-priced paninis, salads and pastas in a convivial atmosphere. The emphasis here is on top-quality, super-fresh ingredients and simple Mediterranean-slanted dishes, though it's also possible to order Turkish favourites such as *mantı* (Turkish-style ravioli filled with minced meat and served with a sauce of yogurt, garlic, hot butter and spices). There's no alcohol.

LOKAL Map p107   Modern International €€

☎ 212-245 5743/4; Müeyyet Sokak 9, off İstiklal Caddesi; Thai soups TYL8-21, salads YTL12-19, mains YTL12-20; ☯ noon-10.30pm; ⊠ Karaköy, then funicular to Tünel

This funky place just off İstiklal Caddesi has only seven tables inside and five outside, and these are always full of bright young things ordering from the eclectic menu and admiring the Warhol-clone screenprints on the walls. Some of the cooks are Asian and this is reflected in the number of curries that feature – try the Thai green chicken curry with its creamy coconut base and fragrant herbs or the succulent tandoori lamb chops with yogurt and tamarind sauce. The weekday lunch menus (YTL10 to YTL15) are fabulous value. We concur with the restaurant's slogan: 'Think global, eat Lokal'.

HACI ABDULLAH Map p107   Lokanta €€

☎ 212-293 8561; Sakızağacı Caddesi 17; meze YTL5-7, portions YTL5-15; ☯ 11am-10pm; ⊠ Kabataş, then funicular to Taksim

Just contemplating the sensational *imam bayildi* (the imam fainted) at Hacı Abdullah's makes our tastebuds go into overdrive. This İstanbul institution – it was established in 1888 – is probably the best lokanta in the city and is one of the essential gastronomic stops you should make when in town. You'll find all the traditional favourites, as well as a wide selection of desserts, including home-bottled fruit compote and a damn fine *künefe* (shredded wheat pastry with pistachios, honey and sugar). The elegant surrounds feature bottle upon bottle of pickled vegetables and comfortable banquette seating. No alcohol is served.

ZENCEFİL NATURE & PEACE
Map p107   Vegetarian €

☎ 212-243 8234; Kurabiye Sokak 8; salads YTL7.50-10.50, mains YTL9-10.50; ☺ 10am-10.30pm Mon-Sat; Ⓥ ; Ⓖ Kabataş, then funicular to Taksim

We're not surprised that this new-wave vegetarian café has a loyal following. Its interior is comfortable and stylish, with a lovely glassed courtyard and funky lime-green colour scheme, and its food is fresh, cheap and varied. Bread is home-made and there's a wide range of herbal teas. Proof that it's not a haven for old-style hippies lies in its drinks menu, which includes treats such as freshly made *limonata* (lemonade) with Absolut vodka. Anyone hoping for a non-smoking area will be disappointed – this is Turkey, after all.

FLAMM Map p107   Anatolian €

☎ 212-245 7604; Sofyalı Sokak 16/1; mains YTL8-12; ☺ 11am-midnight; Ⓖ Karaköy, then funicular to Tünel

Once a stylish Mod Med bistro, Flamm has morphed into a well-priced Turkish eatery that has retained its sense of style but lowered its prices. In the centre of the hopping Asmalımescit precinct, its outdoor tables are good spots to soak up the scene and sample simple dishes such as *mantı* and *ızgara köfte* (grilled meatballs).

CANIM CİGERIM İLHAN USTA
Map p107   Anatolian €

☎ 212-252 6060; Minare Sokak 1; fixed menu YTL12; ☺ 10am-midnight; Ⓖ Karaköy, then funicular to Tünel

The name means 'my soul, my liver', and this small place behind the Ali Hoca Türbesi

specialises in grilled liver served with herbs, *ezme* (spicy tomato sauce) and grilled vegetables. If you can't bring yourself to eat offal, fear not – you can substitute the liver with beef if you so choose. Locals rate this place highly and no wonder, as this is fabulous, cheap food served in a really friendly atmosphere. No alcohol, but *ayran* is the perfect accompaniment.

KONAK Map p107   Pideci & Kebapçı €

☎ 212-244 4281; İstiklal Caddesi 259; kebabs YTL8-12, pide YTL6-8; ☺ 9am-9pm; Ⓖ Kabataş, then funicular to Taksim

The waiters run rather than walk at this frantically busy place on İstiklal Caddesi. You'll understand why they're so busy as soon as you taste the sensational *İskender kebap*, the excellent *yoğurtlu kebab* and the melt-in-your-mouth *pide*. The setting is a cut above, too, with ornate gilded ceiling, chandeliers and banquettes covered in rich brocade.

HELVETICA LOKANTA Map p107   Lokanta €

☎ 212-245 8780; Sümbül Sokak; soup YTL3, salads YTL4.50-5.50; ☺ 8am-10pm Mon-Sat, 8am-11am Sun; Ⓥ ; Ⓖ Karaköy, then funicular to Tünel

This hip *lokanta* is popular with locals (particularly of the vegetarian variety), who pop in here for fresh, tasty and cheap-as-chips soups, salads and bean dishes. Start with a yogurt or tomato soup and follow up with your choice from the daily salads spread.

İNCİ PASTANESI Map p107   Pastane €

İstiklal Caddesi 124; ☺ 9am-9pm; Ⓖ Karaköy, then funicular to Tünel

A Beyoğlu institution, İnci is famous throughout the city for its delicious profiteroles. You'll have to fight through the crowds to reach the counter at this tiny shop but believe us, it's worth the effort.

SARAY MUHALLEBİCİSİ
Map p107   Muhallebİci & Pastane €

☎ 212-292 3434; İstiklal Caddesi 102-104; ☺ 8am-11pm; Ⓖ Kabataş, then funicular to Taksim

A *muhallebici* (pudding purveyor) that's been serving puddings to appreciative sweet-tooths since 1935, Saray is still going strong. You can pop in for a *poğaça* (breakfast bun) in the morning and a köfte sandwich for lunch, but it's most famous for sweet milk-based puddings such as *fırın sütlaç* and *tavuk göysü* (chicken pudding).

There's also a recently opened branch in Eminönü (Map p63).

BEŞİKTAŞ & ORTAKÖY

The cafés, bars and restaurants around the waterside road İskele Square in Ortaköy form a bustling entertainment precinct that's particularly busy on Friday and Saturday evenings and on weekend days. Be aware that getting here by taxi during these times can be a nightmare due to the horrendous traffic along Çirağan Caddesi.

BANYAN Map p117   Asian €€€
☎ 212-259 9060; Salhane Sokak 3, Ortaköy; starters YTL12-20, mains YTL25-40; ✆ noon-2am; V ; ⌂ Ortaköy

The menu here travels around Asia, featuring Thai, Japanese, Vietnamese and Chinese dishes. There is even the occasional fusion number: why not try the grilled vegetables and warm goat's cheese with pea *paratha* and green mandarin and ginger-infused olive oil and see if it works for you? If it does – and the food here claims to be good for the soul – you can enjoy it while soaking up the exceptional views of the Ortaköy mosque and Fatih Bridge from the terrace. There's another branch on Abdi İpekçi Caddesi (Map p115) in Nişantaşı.

HOUSE CAFÉ Map p117   Modern International €€
☎ 212-227 2639; Salhane Sokak 1, Ortaköy; sandwiches YTL18.50-21.50, mains YTL17-29.50; ✆ 9am-2am Mon-Thu & Sun, 8am-2am Fri & Sat; ⌂ Ortaköy

This is İstanbul's hottest spot for Sunday brunch. A huge place right on the waterfront at Ortaköy, it offers a good-quality all-you-can-eat buffet spread for YTL45 between 9am and 2pm. The style here is casual chic and the clientele is young professional, though everyone will feel welcome.

ÇINAR Map p117   Seafood €€
☎ 212-261 5818; İskele Square 42, Ortaköy; meze YTL5-11, mains YTL15-35; ✆ noon-2am; ⌂ 56

With loads of outdoor tables and waiters running around with loaded trays, this long-standing favourite resembles a busy French brasserie. The views over the water and of the bustling square are great, and the food is quite good, too. Seafood mezes feature and you can choose your own fish

for mains. The perfect place to spend a summer's evening.

MADO Map p117   Ice-Cream Parlour €
☎ 212-227 3876; İskele Square, Ortaköy; ✆ 7am-2am; ⌂ Ortaköy

Next to Çınar, this branch of the popular ice-cream chain is packed on weekends, when locals stop by after checking out the flea market. The views are great and the people-watching opportunities unrivalled. Oh, and the ice cream goes down a treat. There are also Mado branches in locations such as Üsküdar (Selmanípek Caddesi) and Beyoğlu (☎ 212-244 1781; 188 İstiklal Caddesi).

ÜSKÜDAR

One of the city's most conservative areas, Üsküdar is not the place to come if you're looking for a boozy night on the town. During the day, the myriad kebab joints and pastanes in the street around the ferry terminal do a bustling trade.

NİYAZİBEY Map p122   Anatolian €
☎ 216-310 4821; Ahmediye Meydanı; perde pilavı YTL5, kebaps YTL9-16, pides YTL2-9; ✆ 11am-9pm; ⌂ Üsküdar

Niyazibey specialises in *perde pilavı*, a dish that it describes as hen and rooster meat (symbolising the bride and groom) cooked with rice (for blessing) and almonds (for children) and encased in pastry sheets (symbolising the home). Anything so loaded with Turkish symbolism immediately whets our interest, and when we first tasted this very traditional dish we were beside ourselves with excitement because it was delicious as well. A problem arose on our second visit, though. Would we reprise our first meal, or opt for an alterative such as *fırın şış kebap* (kebap and cheese cooked in *pide* dough) or a *dürüm döner* (thin slices of lamb cooked in pastry)? Everything at this comfortable place is great, and it's fantastic value as well. There's another branch at Halıtağa Caddesi 5B (Map p122) in Kadıköy – neither sell alcohol.

KANAAT LOKANTESI Map p122   Lokanta €
☎ 216-310 4821; Ahmediye Meydanı; soup YTL2.50-3, portions YTL4.50-10, kebaps YTL7.50-10; ✆ 11am-9pm; ⌂ Üsküdar

This barn-like place near the ferry terminal has been serving up competent *hazır yemek* (bistro food) since 1933. It's recently been spruced up, and now has an understated but pleasing décor featuring framed photographs of old street scenes. Service is brusque but efficient and the food passes our 'do we want seconds?' test, but only just. There's a huge dessert list.

ÇAMLICA RESTAURANT
off Map p122   Anatolian €

Küçük Çamlıca Köşkleri; ☎ 216-443 2199; Büyük Çamlıca; ⏰ 9am-midnight; 🚇 Üsküdar
Should you take the time to visit Üsküdar, this charming kiosk on the hill is a great spot to savour a coffee or a snack. Marble floors are covered by rugs, and seating is on small stools clustered around brass tray tables. In winter there's a log fire, and in summer the windows looking out over the park provide an attractively airy feel.

KADIKÖY

We reckon that when you add the lure of a meal at Çiya to a lovely ferry trip and a wander around one of the city's best fresh produce markets, you have the ingredients for a perfect İstanbul day.

ÇIYA SOFRASI Map p127   Lokanta €

☎ 216-330 3190; Güneşlibahçe Sokak 43; meze plate YTL5-10; ⏰ 10am-midnight; 🚇 Kadıköy

We're going to go out on a limb here, and say that this is our favourite lokanta in the city. We love the simple modern interior and ever-friendly staff, and we adore the food – everything from the yogurt soup to the stuffed artichokes to the *perde pilavı* (traditional chicken dish). The self-service meze array is a fabulous idea (and so cheap!) and the milk puddings and crystallised fruit are perfect finales to a meal. Next-door Çiya Kebapçı is owned and run by the same people, and is just as impressive. If these places served alcohol, we'd move in permanently.

BAYLAN PASTAHANE
Map p127   Pastane €

☎ 216-336 2881; Muvakkithane Caddesi 19; coffee YTL5-7, cakes YTL3-6.50; ⏰ 10am-10pm; 🚇 Kadıköy

Baylan has been serving its home-made pastries, *dondorma* (Turkish ice cream) and cakes to appreciative İstanbullus since 1923. This branch dates from 1925, but had its last facelift in 1961, making it a truly funky decorative time capsule. To the rear of the shop there's a courtyard complete with astroturf and a profusion of hanging baskets – a great spot to scoff a fabulous *caffe glace* (iced coffee with *dondurma*), a top-notch espresso or a plate of profiteroles.

BLUELIST[1] (blu,list) *v.*
to recommend a travel experience.
What's your recommendation? www.lonelyplanet.com/bluelist

DRINKING

top picks

- Hotel Nomade Terrace Bar (p172)
- Java Studio (p173)
- Café Meşale (p173)
- Set Üstü Çay Bahçesi (p173)
- Leb-i Derya Richmond (p176)
- Leyla (p176)
- Mikla (p176)
- Nu Teras (p176)
- 360 (p176)
- The raft of nargileh joints at Tophane (p174)

DRINKING

It may be the biggest city in an officially Muslim country, but İstanbul's population likes nothing more than a drink or two. If the raki-soaked atmosphere in the city's meyhanes isn't a clear enough indicator, a foray into Beyoğlu's thriving bar scene will confirm this fact. If you're in the mood for a drink, we suggest you go out on the town on a Thursday, Friday or Saturday night. Alternatively, you could check out the alcohol-free, atmosphere-rich çay bahçesis (tea gardens) or kahvehanes (coffee houses) dotted around Sultanahmet and over the Galata Bridge in Tophane. These are great places to relax and sample a Turkish institution, the nargileh (water pipe), and a cup of Türk kahvesi (Turkish coffee) or çay (tea).

SULTANAHMET

Sadly, there are few pleasant bars in Sultanahmet. The joints along Akbıyık Caddesi are great for backpackers and unthinkable for everyone else. Don't despair, though. Why not substitute tobacco or caffeine for alcohol and visit one of the many atmospheric çay bahçesis dotted around the neighbourhood?

CHEERS BAR Map p50 Bar
Akbıyık Caddesi 20; ☾ 10am-2am; 🚇 Sultanahmet
Slap-bang in the middle of backpacker central, this raucous bar is not for the faint-hearted. If you can imagine nothing better than sinking a skinful, listening to Men at Work's Land Down Under and bragging about how cheaply you're managing to live while on the road, this place is for you. The nearby Just Bar offers more of the same.

HOTEL NOMADE TERRACE BAR
Map p50 Bar
☎ 212-513 8172; www.hotelnomade.com; Ticarethane Sokak 15, Alemdar; ☾ noon-11pm; 🚇 Sultanahmet
Guests aren't the only ones to enjoy the rooftop bar at this chic boutique hotel. Management is happy for everyone to claim a comfortable banquette seat and soak up the view of Aya Sofya and the Blue Mosque while enjoying a cold beer, fresh juice or cocktail.

KYBELE HOTEL BAR Map p50 Bar
☎ 212-511 7766; Yerebatan Caddesi 35; ☾ 8am-10pm; 🚇 Sultanahmet
The lounge bar at this charming but vaguely eccentric hotel is chock-full of antique furniture, richly coloured rugs and old etchings and prints, but its signature style comes courtesy of the hundreds of colour-

ful glass lights that are suspended from the ceiling. It's a wonderfully atmospheric spot for a pre-dinner drink.

SEVEN HILLS TERRACE BAR Map p50 Bar
☎ 212-516 9497; Tevkifhane Sokak 8A; ☾ noon-midnight; 🚇 Sultanahmet
We agonised about whether to include this rooftop bar-restaurant in the book or not. Its amazing views are certainly worthy of comment, but like everyone in Sultanahmet, we're deeply disturbed as to how the place managed to get a permit to build so high, dominate the skyline (not felicitously) and obscure the views of so many other businesses. On top of this, the waiters here can be spectacularly disinterested in serving guests who only want a drink – the money (and tips) are clearly in the substandard fish dishes the place serves and not in the pricey drinks. Hmm.

SULTAN PUB Map p50 Bar
☎ 212-528 1719; Divan Yolu Caddesi 2; ☾ 9.30am-1am; 🚇 Sultanahmet
Sultanahmet's version of Ye Olde English Pub, the Sultan has been around for years and continues to attract the crowds due to its peerless position close to Aya Sofya, the Blue Mosque and the Basilica Cistern. The pub grub is what you would expect from a place like this (ie stodge), but the outdoor tables are a great spot to watch the world go by and the beer is served in iced glasses, just the way it should be.

FES CAFÉ Map p50 Café
☎ 212-526 3071; Ali Baba Türbesi Sokak 25-27, Nuruosmaniye; ☾ 9am-10pm; 🚇 Beyazıt
A relaxed atmosphere prevails in this sister establishment of the well-known Grand Bazaar café. It's a good spot for a post-bazaar

recovery, with good-quality Illy coffee and home-made lemonade on offer.

JAVA STUDIO Map p50   Café
☎ 212-517 2378; Dalbastı Sokak 13; ⏰ 7am-11pm; 🚇 Sultanahmet
Celebrating the 'fine art of coffee', this laid-back café in the shadow of the Blue Mosque is run by Canadian Jennifer Gaudet, who takes her beans and brews very seriously. You can choose from an extensive list of coffees, teas, milkshakes and lassis, accompanying your choice of tipple with a slice of freshly baked lemon poppyseed cake or a chocolate brownie. There's comfortable seating, free wi-fi and a book exchange. A true traveller's haven.

CAFÉ MEŞALE Map p50   Çay Bahçesi
☎ 212-518 9562; Arasta Bazaar, Utangaç Sokak, Cankurtaran; ⏰ 24hr; 🚇 Sultanahmet
Meşale, located in a sunken courtyard behind the Blue Mosque, is a tourist trap *par excellence*, but we still love it. Generations of backpackers have joined locals in claiming one of its cushioned benches under coloured lights and enjoying a tea and nargileh. There's sporadic live Turkish music in the evening and a dervish performance at 8pm and 10pm.

DERVİŞ AİLE ÇAY BAHÇESİ
Map p50   Çay Bahçesi
Dervish Family Tea Garden; Mimar Mehmet Ağa Caddesi, Cankurtaran; ⏰ 9am-11pm, closed winter; 🚇 Sultanahmet
The Derviş' paved courtyard, which is superbly located directly opposite the Blue Mosque, beckons patrons with its comfortable cane chairs and shady trees. Efficient service, reasonable prices and peerless people-watching opportunities make it a great place for a leisurely tea, nargileh and game of backgammon.

NARGILEHS: NAUGHTY BUT NICE

When ordering a nargileh, you'll need to specify what type of tobacco you would like. Most people opt for *elma* (when the tobacco has been soaked in apple juice, giving it a sweet flavour and scent), but it's possible to order it unadulterated (*tömbeki*). The water pipe will be brought to your table, hot coals will be placed in it to get it started and you will be given a disposable plastic mouthpiece to slip over the pipe's stem. Just draw back and you're off. Bliss!

TÜRK OCAĞI KÜLTÜR VE SANAT MERKEZI İKTISADİ İŞLETMESI ÇAY BAHÇESİ Map p50   Çay Bahçesi
Crn Divan Yolu & Babıalı Caddesis, Çemberlitaş; ⏰ 8am-midnight, later in summer; 🚇 Çemberlitaş
Tucked into the rear right-hand corner of a shady courtyard filled with Ottoman tombs, this enormously popular tea garden is a perfect place to escape the crowds and relax over a *çay* and nargileh. You can even score a cheap and tasty *gözleme* (Turkish crepe filled with cheese, spinach or potato) here.

YEŞİL EV GARDEN BAR/CAFÉ
Map p50   Café/Bar
☎ 212-517 6785; Kabasakal Caddesi 5, Cankurtaran; ⏰ noon-10.30pm; 🚇 Sultanahmet
Most of the bars in Cankurtaran are rowdy backpacker establishments, so the elegant rear courtyard of this historic hotel is a real oasis for those wanting a quiet drink. In spring flowers and blossom fill every corner; in summer the fountain and shady trees keep the temperature down; and in the cooler months a flower-filled conservatory provides shelter. The drinks are expensive – a fresh juice or a beer will cost YTL9, for instance – but as the old adage says, quality doesn't come cheaply.

YENİ MARMARA Map p50   Nargileh Café
Marmara Café; ☎ 212-516 9013; Çayıroğlu Sokak, Küçük Aya Sofya; ⏰ 8am-midnight; 🚇 Sultanahmet
This is the genuine article: a neighbourhood teahouse packed to the rafters with backgammon-playing locals, who play while sipping tea and puffing on nargilehs. The place has bucket loads of character, featuring rugs, wall hangings, low brass tables and fasıl music on the CD player. In winter a wood stove keeps the place cosy; in summer patrons sit on the rear terrace and look out over the Sea of Marmara.

TOPKAPI PALACE & AROUND

SET ÜSTÜ ÇAY BAHÇESİ
Map p63   Çay Bahçesi
Gülhane Parkı; ⏰ 10am-11pm; 🚇 Gülhane
Those who appreciate the ceremony of proper tea service will love this terraced tea

garden overlooking Seraglio Point. Here, you can watch the ferries plying the route from Europe to Asia, while at the same time enjoying an excellent cup of tea served in a teapot and accompanied by hot water (such a relief after the fiendishly strong brews that are common in Turkey). It's so pleasant that you may decide to stay for a lunch of a cheap *köfte ekmek* (meatball sandwich) or a *tost* (toasted cheese jaffle).

BAZAAR DISTRICT

Like most parts of the Old City, the area around the Grand Bazaar is conservative and there are few places serving alcohol. There are a number of *çay bahçesi*s that are worth checking out though, as well as the city's most famous *boza* (tonic) bar.

VEFA BOZACISI Map p78   Boza Bar
☎ 212-519 4922; Katip Çelebi Caddesi 104/1, Kalenderhane; ☯ 7am-midnight; 🚇 Laleli
This famous *boza* bar was established in 1875 and locals still flock here to drink the stuff, which is made from water, sugar and fermented grain. The viscous mucous-coloured beverage has a reputation for building up strength and virility – it won't be to everyone's taste, but the bar itself, with its blue tiles, mirrored columns, marble tables and wooden bar, is worth a visit in its own right. If the *boza* is too confrontational for you, the bar also serves *şıra*, a fermented grape juice.

BALKAN TÜRKLERİ DAYANIŞMA VE KÜLTÜR DERNEĞİ Map p78   Çay Bahçesi
☎ 212-511 2618; Yeniçeriler Caddesi 84, Çemberlitaş; ☯ 7am-midnight, later in summer; 🚇 Çemberlitaş
This club, set in the pleasant courtyard of the Koca Sinan Paşa Medrese, is a pretty spot in which to enjoy a cup of *Türk kahvesi* or *çay*. Enter through the gate to Koca Sinan Paşa's tomb.

ERENLER ÇAY BAHÇESİ
Map p78   Çay Bahçesi
☎ 212-528 3785; Yeniçeriler Caddesi 36/28, Çemberlitaş; ☯ 7am-midnight, later in summer; 🚇 Çemberlitaş
Packed to the rafters with students from nearby İstanbul University who are doing their best to live up to their heritage (ie develop a major tobacco addiction), this

nargileh establishment is set in the leafy courtyard of the Çorlulu Ali Paşa Medrese and has a row of carpet shops down its side.

LALE BAHÇESİ Map p78   Çay Bahçesi
Sifahane Sokak, Süleymaniye; ☯ 8am-midnight; 🚇 Üniversite
In a sunken courtyard that was once part of the Süleymaniye *külliye* (mosque complex), this charming outdoor teahouse is always full of students from the nearby theological college and İstanbul University, who come here to sit on cushioned seats under trees and relax while watching the pretty fountain play. It's one of the cheapest places in the area to enjoy a *çay* and nargileh.

ETHAM TEZÇAKAR KAHVECİ
Map p77   Kahvehanesİ
Halıcılar Caddesi, Grand Bazaar; ☯ 8.30am-7pm Mon-Sat; 🚇 Beyazıt
This tiny tea and coffee stop is found smack-bang in the middle of Halıcılar Caddesi. Its traditional brass-tray tables and wooden stools stand in stark contrast to the funky and more-expensive Fes Café opposite.

ŞARK KAHVESİ Map p77   Kahvehanesİ
☎ 212-512 1144; Yaglikcilar Caddesi 134, Grand Bazaar; ☯ 8.30am-7pm Mon-Sat; 🚇 Beyazıt
The Şark's arched ceiling betrays its former existence as part of a bazaar street; years ago some enterprising *kahveci* (coffeehouse owner) walled up several sides and turned it into a café. The nicotine colour on the walls is testament to its long pedigree as a popular tea and cigarette spot for the bazaar's stall-holders. These days they have to fight for space with tourists, who love the quirky 'flying dervish' murals, the old photographs on the walls, and the cheap tea and coffee.

GALATA & TOPHANE
There aren't too many bars and cafés around this area, but you'll find a raft of incredibly popular nargileh cafés in the park behind the Tophane tram stop (Map p103). There's nothing gained by us singling out one of these joints at the expense of the others – they're all redolent with the smell of apple tobacco and packed with trendy teetotallers.

ANEMON GALATA BAR Map p103   Bar
☎ 212-293 2343; cnr Galata Meydani & Büyükhendek Caddesi, Tünel; ⏱ 6pm-midnight; 🚇 Karaköy
As yet undiscovered by the İstanbul bar set, this eyrie on top of a recently restored Ottoman hotel is one of the best places in the city to watch the sun set while enjoying a cocktail. Views over to Old İstanbul and across the Golden Horn are stunning.

İSTİKLAL & AROUND
Whether you want to drink a few quiet ales in a cosy pub, down a martini or two in a sophisticated bar or party the night away in its pumping next-door neighbour, the streets and lanes off İstiklal Caddesi will have the drinking spot for you. This is where the city's barflies and party set hang out (when they're not down on the shores of the Bosphorus) and it's great fun.

Coffee culture is also something that is embraced on this side of the Galata Bridge. In fact, we will go so far as to say that Beyoğlu has gone batty over its beans, and really needs to calm down. At the time of research there were seven multinational coffee-chain franchises on İstiklal Caddesi. In our view, that's caffeine addiction that's got truly out of hand…

See the Eating chapter for reviews of cafés that serve good food.

ADA Map p107   Bar/Café
☎ 212-251 6682; İstiklal Caddesi 158A; ⏱ 8am-midnight; 🚇 Karaköy, then funicular to Tünel
The side streets off İstiklal may be full of great cafés and bars, but the grand boulevard itself possesses a motley range of choices. Fortunately, Ada is the exception. A cavernous place that's half book and music store and half bar/café, it has style and substance in equal measure. The house wine by the glass is Antik, an excellent quaffing drop, and the coffee is good too.

BADEHANE Map p107   Bar
☎ 212-249 0550; General Yazgan Sokak 5, Tünel; ⏱ 9am-2am; 🚇 Karaköy, then funicular to Tünel
This tiny neighbourhood bar is a favourite with Beyoğlu's bohemian set. In fine weather patrons chain smoke, sip beer and play backgammon in the laneway. When it's cold, dark or wet, the action moves inside and is often accompanied by live music. Dress down and come ready to enjoy an attitude-free evening.

BÜYÜK LONDRA OTELİ BAR Map p107   Bar
☎ 212-245 0670; Meşrutiyet Caddesi 117, Tepebaşı; ⏱ noon-11pm; 🚇 Kabataş, then funicular to Taksim
This is a true time-warp experience. We'd hazard a guess that the décor at this historic hotel has remained untouched for close on a century, and we're pleased to report that the prices haven't hiked up much during that time (an Efes is YTL4). The gin and tonics are pricey but lordy, they're strong!

5 KAT Map p107   Bar
☎ 212-293 3774; Soğancı Sokak 7/5, Cihangir; ⏱ 10am-2am Mon-Fri, 10.30am-3am Sat & Sun; 🚇 Kabataş, then funicular to Taksim
Run by glamorous red-haired film actress Yasemin Alkaya, 5 Kat is one of the city's original glamour bars. The 'boudoir chic' décor features deep red walls, satin ceiling, velvet chairs and candles galore – it's amusingly over the top. The Bosphorus views from the full-length windows are simply breathtaking and in the warmer months there's a rooftop terrace bar as well.

JAMES JOYCE IRISH PUB Map p107   Bar
☎ 212-224 2013; Irish Centre, Balo Sokak 26, off İstiklal Caddesi; ⏱ 1pm-2am Sun-Thu, 1pm-4am Fri & Sat; 🚇 Kabataş, then funicular to Taksim
The only authentic Irish bar in town, this popular place is a good spot to enjoy a pint and a *craic*. There's a mixed crowd and a popular all-day breakfast. It occasionally organises live sessions of traditional Irish folk music and performances by Irish singers.

KEVE Map p107   Bar
☎ 212-251 4338; Tünel Geçidi 10, Tünel; ⏱ 8.30am-2am; 🚇 Karaköy, then funicular to Tünel
Is this the most atmospheric bar in the city? In a plant-filled Belle Époque arcade just opposite the Tünel station, Keve is invariably full of 30-somethings who've just been to a gallery opening on İstiklal and need a drink before moving on to see a new arthouse release at the cinema. The twinkling lights and wrought-iron tables add mightily to the atmosphere.

LEB-İ DERYA Map p107   Bar
☎ 212-293 4989; Kumbaracı Yokuşu 115/7; ⏱ 11am-4am; 🚇 Karaköy, then funicular to Tünel

On the 7th floor of a building off İstiklal Caddesi, this much-loved place is friendly, stylish and always buzzing. And oh, the views! Sip a cocktail or cold beer while gazing over to the Asian side and you'll never want to leave. There's also food on offer (see p166).

LEB-İ DERYA RICHMOND Map p107 Bar
☎ 212-243 4375; Richmond Hotel, İstiklal Caddesi 445, Kat 6; ⏰ 7pm-2am Mon-Sat; 🚋 Karaköy, then funicular to Tünel

This glam younger sister of perennial favourite Leb-i Derya (p175) has managed to wheedle her way into many hearts since she opened in 2007. The views are to die for, and the surrounds are incredibly chic. A wonderful spot for a pre-dinner cocktail or two.

LEYLA Map p107 Bar
☎ 212-244 5350; Akarsu Yokuşu Sokak 46, Cihangir; ⏰ 8am-4am; 🚋 Kabataş, then funicular to Taksim

The bar de jour in trendy Cihangir when this book went to print, Leyla has a casually stylish interior, a DJ who really knows his stuff (every night except Sunday) and a reasonably priced drinks list.

MİKLA Map p107 Bar
☎ 212-293 5656; Marmara Pera, Meşrutiyet Caddesi 167/185; ⏰ noon-2am; 🚋 Karaköy, then funicular to Tünel

This is the classiest bar in town. Sink into the Alvar Aalto–designed chairs and watch the twinkling lights of Beyoğlu while you down a wonderfully dry martini or good-quality glass of house wine. After your drinks, we highly recommend you stay for dinner. See p165 for a restaurant review.

NU TERAS Map p107 Bar
☎ 212-245 6070; Meşrutiyet Caddesi 149/7; ⏰ 6.30pm-2am Mon-Thu & Sun, 6.30pm-4am Fri & Sat Jun-Oct only; 🚋 Karaköy, then funicular to Tünel

With its glass bar, tables full of beautiful people dining alfresco and panoramic views, Nu Teras is one of the places to be seen in town. Go at sunset and frock up. See p165 for a restaurant review.

PASİFİC HOUSE Map p107 Bar
Sofyalı Sokak, Asmalımescit; ⏰ noon-2am; 🚋 Karaköy, then funicular to Tünel

There are loads of bars on this side of town, but not too many that are both cheap and well located. Ultra-casual Pasific scores on both of these counts (a beer is only YTL3.50), so there's no wonder that it's constantly packed. The fact that it's on one of the city's most happening streets is a plus, too.

PANO Map p107 Bar
☎ 212-292 6664; Hamalbaşı Caddesi 26, Tepebaşı; ⏰ 11am-1am; 🚋 Kabataş, then funicular to Taksim

You'll have to fight your way through the throngs at this extraordinarily popular wine bar on a Thursday, Friday or Saturday night. Serious drinkers prop themselves on the high bar tables at the front and swig the cheap house wine; others take a table at the back or upstairs and pace themselves while sampling good-quality hot and cold meze.

SMYRNA Map p107 Bar
☎ 212-244 2466; Akarsu Yokuşu Sokak 29, Cihangir; ⏰ 10.30am-midnight; 🚋 Kabataş, then funicular to Taksim

Smyrna is known for its long bar, collection of antique toys, couch-filled back corner and candle-lit tables. The atmosphere is laid back, the music is unobtrusive and the crowd is early 30s 'Beyoğlu Arty'. If you decide to make a night of it here (and many do) there's good simple food available, too.

360 Map p107 Bar
☎ 212-251 1042; Mısır Apartmenti, İstiklal Caddesi 311, Kat 8; ⏰ noon-2am Mon-Thu & Sun, noon-4am Fri & Sat; 🚋 Kabataş, then funicular to Taksim

Its 'industrial chic' interior design and knock-out views have made 360 the darling of the city's beautiful people, who love nothing more than perching at one of its terrace bars and ordering from the huge drinks menu. A martini will set you back YTL20, but it will be oh-so-worth-it. The place morphs into a nightclub on Friday and Saturday nights. See p165 for a restaurant review.

URBAN Map p107 Bar
Kartal Sokak 6A; ⏰ noon-2am; 🚋 Kabataş, then funicular to Taksim

In a quiet and leafy laneway near the Galatasaray Lycée, this place makes a perfect pitstop in the late afternoon or early evening. In warm weather, sit outdoors under the grapevine to enjoy a beer or freshly made limonata (lemonade); in cold or wet weather, the mezzanine seating is nearly as nice. There's free wi-fi.

KAFFEEHAUS Map p107 Café

☎ 212-245 4028; Tünel Meydanı 4, Tünel; ⏰ 8am-11pm; 🚋 Karaköy, then funicular to Tünel

This place is popular with locals, who monopolise its tables for long breakfasts and lingering coffees every day of the week. In warmer weather, the front of the space opens to Tünel Square and provides great people-watching opportunities; when it's cooler, the velvet-upholstered armchairs are the perfect place to curl up with a coffee and a newspaper.

HACO PULO Map p107 Çay Bahçesi

☎ 212-2444210; Hacopulo Pasajı; ⏰ 9am-11pm; 🚋 Kabataş, then funicular to Taksim

Set in a picturesque cobbled courtyard, this was one of original tea-and-nargileh joints to open in the side streets off İstiklal Caddesi. Locals love it, and we hazard a guess that you will, too.

CLUB 17 Map p107 Gay Bar

Zambak Sokak 17; cover charge YTL10 (Fri & Sat only, includes one free drink); ⏰ 11pm-4am Sun-Thu, 11pm-5:30am Fri & Sat; 🚋 Kabataş, then funicular to Taksim

Attractive young men looking for hormonal release or patronage pack this small, narrow bar as aggressive techno beats accompany wafting sexual energies. At closing, the veritable meat rack in the street makes final hook-up attempts possible.

BEŞİKTAŞ & ORTAKÖY

ÇIRAĞAN PALACE HOTEL KEMPINSKI
Map p117 Bar

☎ 212-326 4646; www.ciragan-palace.com; Çırağan Caddesi 32, Beşiktaş; 🚋 Yıldız

This is where the botox brigade comes to show off its bling. Nursing a mega-pricey drink at one of its terrace tables and watching the scene around the city's best swimming pool, which is right on the Bosphorus, makes us feel like Diane Fossey observing her chimps. Some similar habits, perhaps, but definitely a different species...

KADIKÖY

This is where the city's grunge set comes to party, and party it certainly does. The length of Kadife Sokak is filled with unpretentious bars and cafés that are busy from late morning to late at night. During the day, coffee and games of Scrabble, Monopoly and backgammon are on the agenda; at night, cheap beer, live music and conversation take over. Karga Bar (see below) is the most famous of the street's establishments, but Isis and Bahane Kültür and a host of others are great back-ups. Dress down and don't forget that the last ferry back to Karaköy leaves at midnight (8.40pm to Eminönü) – if you want to stay later, a *dolmuş* to Taksim will be your only public transport option.

KARGA BAR Map p127 Bar

☎ 216-449 1725; Kadife Sokak 16; ⏰ 11am-2am; 🚇 Kadıköy

Karga is one of the most famous bars in the city, offering up cheap drinks, loud music and avant-garde art on its walls and in the upstairs gallery. It doesn't have a street sign – look for a green and cream building with a wooden door. There's a small courtyard downstairs that's a great spot to enjoy a late-afternoon beer. Nearby Isis and Bahane Kültür are also good bets.

BLUELIST[1] (blu˺list) *v.*
to recommend a travel experience.
What's your recommendation? www.lonelyplanet.com/bluelist

top picks

- **Q Jazz by Les Ottomans** (p182)
- **360** (when there's an imported DJ spinning or a special event; p176)
- **Crystal** (p181)
- **Kokosh By Asmali** (p184)
- **Ghetto** (p181)
- **Love Dance Point** (p181)
- **Sortie** or **Reina** (any time in summer; p181)
- **Tonique** (p181)

NIGHTLIFE

There's an entertainment option for everyone in İstanbul. You can while away the night in glamorous nightclubs on the Bosphorus – where you'll spend your entire holiday budget in one night if you're not careful – or you can drink rakı while listening to live fasıl music at one of the city's many cheap and rowdy meyhanes. With an almost religious devotion to all forms of music and a great love of dance, it's rare to have a week go by when there's not a special event, festival or performance scheduled (see also p16) in İstanbul. In short, the only thing you can't do in this town is be bored.

Tickets & Reservations

If you can't make it to the box office, or if there isn't one for the venue, try Biletix (☎ 216-454 1555, 216-556 9800; www.biletix.com). It's a major ticket seller for all kinds of events from festivals and big-name concerts to football matches. Biletix outlets are found in many spots throughout the city, but the most convenient for travellers is probably the one at the İstanbul Kitapçısı (☎ 212-292 9518; İstiklal Caddesi 79-81, Beyoğlu). Alternatively, you can buy tickets by credit card on Biletix's website and collect them from the venue before the concert.

CLUBBING

Who cares if İstanbul's in Europe or Asia? All we know is that it's developing a great club and live-music scene. The horrible 1980s covers and saccharine Turkish pop that used to be inflicted on club-goers are increasingly being replaced by Middle Eastern fusion beats, techno and jazz-influenced tracks. If you're like us, you'll rarely see the daylight during your stay.

When İstanbullus go out clubbing they dress to kill. If you don't do the same, you'll be unlikely to get past the door bitches (usually buffed young hunks) at the mega-venues on the Bosphorus. Fortunately, you'll have no trouble in venues in other parts of town as these cater to the transient crowd and couldn't give a toss what labels you're wearing.

As is the case with bars and restaurants, most of the clubbing action is in Beyoğlu or along the Bosphorus. The only thing to do at night in Sultanahmet is leave. Clubs are busiest on Friday and Saturday nights, and the action doesn't really kick off until 1am. Many of the clubs close down from June or July – when the party crowd moves down to Turkey's southern coasts – until the end of September. Those clubbers who stay in town tend to flock to the open-air waterfront spots such as Sortie and Reina.

As well as the clubs reviewed here, Angelique (☎ 212-327 2844/45; www.istanbuldoors.com/en/; Salhane Sokak 5, Ortaköy; ☼ 7pm-3am summer only; 🚌 Ortaköy), Blackk (☎ 212-236 7256; www.blackk.net; Muallim Naci Caddesi 71, Kuruçeşme; ☼ 10.30pm-4am; 🚌 25E, 25T, 40) and 360 (p176) are safe bets if you want to have dinner, a few drinks and a dance or two.

ARAF Map p107

☎ 212-244 8301; Balo Sokak 32, Kat 5, Beyoğlu; no cover charge; ☼ 5pm-4am; 🚇 Kabataş, then funicular to Taksim

This is grungy fun central for English teachers and Turkish language students, who shake their booties to the in-house gypsy band and swill the cheapest club beer around (a mere YTL5). To avoid the locals' weekend mating madness, go on Tuesday or Wednesday.

BABYLON Map p107

☎ 212-292 7368; www.babylon.com.tr; Şehbender Sokak 3, Tünel; cover charges & performance times vary, bookings at Biletix or at the box office (open 10am-6pm); ☼ 9.30pm-2am Tue-Thu, 10pm-3am Fri & Sat; 🚇 Karaköy, then funicular to Tünel

Recent developments have seen Babylon devoting itself exclusively to live performances; in this regard, it's truly a city institution. The eclectic program often features big-name international music acts, particularly during the festival season. DJ chill-out sessions have been moved to its restaurant/lounge right behind the concert hall.

BALANS MUSIC HALL Map p107

☎ 212-251 7020; www.balansmuzik.com; Balo Sokak 22, Beyoğlu; cover charge varies, sometimes free; ☼ closed summer, from 10pm Wed-Sat in winter; 🚇 Kabataş, then funicular to Taksim

After enjoying the city's best locally brewed beer (the caramel brew) on the 1st floor, the lively multinational crowd here separates. Rock aficionados gravitate to the upper floors and the rest of the crowd moves to the impressive 1500-person-capacity performance hall, which features a glass-encased winter garden that is as magical as it is acoustically enhancing. This is the outpost of the new crop of gig-goers. Check the website for details.

CRYSTAL Map p117
☎ 212-278 4578; www.clubcrystal.org; Muallim Naci Caddesi 65, Ortaköy; cover charge Fri & Sat YTL35; 🕒 midnight-5.30am Thu-Sat; 🚌 56
This is home to the city's techno aficiona-dos, who come here to appreciate sets put together by some of the best DJs from Tur-key and the rest of Europe. There's a great sound system, a crowded dance floor and a lovely covered garden bar. The Friday and Saturday cover charge includes one drink.

DÉJÁ VU Map p107
☎ 212-252 6131; Sadri Alışık Sokak 26, off İstiklal Caddesi; cover charge YTL10; 🕒 10pm-4am Sun-Thu, 10pm-5am Fri & Sat; 🚡 Kabataş, then funicular to Taksim
Progressive electronica and hip-hop lasso in the youthful dancers contorting on the dance floor, while other dance enthusiasts egg them on. This is the place to go with the musical flow. The cover charge includes one drink.

GABILE Map p107
☎ 0538-277 1699; www.clubgabile.com; Hüseyinağa Mah, Yeşilcam Sokak 7, Beyoğlu; free entry; 🕒 11pm-5am; 🚡 Kabataş, then funicular to Taksim
A circus atmosphere prevails in Gabile's three floors and rooftop terrace. Circuit clones, fey young things, lipstick lesbians and straying straights mix to enjoy the amateurishly staged drag and erotic shows. It's unbridled fun to the max. Drinks cost YTL8.

GHETTO Map p107
☎ 212-251 750/2; www.ghettoist.net; Kalyoncu Kulluk Caddesi 10, Beyoğlu; cover charge varies; 🕒 8pm-4am; 🚡 Kabataş, then funicular to Taksim
Décor-wise, this three-story club behind Çiçek Pasajı (p110) makes a bold postmodern state-ment, with Renaissance-style painted high ceilings and a long, back-illuminated bar with bottles that seem to glow in the dark. The musical program is equally interesting,

comprising creative foreign or local live acts. At Ghetto Terras (reached via a back stair-case) techno and house music rule.

LOVE DANCE POINT Map p115
☎ 212-296 3357; www.lovedancepoint.com; Cumhuriyet Caddesi 349/1, Harbiye; cover charge YTL20; 🕒 11:30pm-4am Wed, 11:30pm-5am Fri & Sat; 🚡 Kabataş, then funicular to Taksim
Going into its eighth year and wresting the plum as the major player in the gay club scene, Love DP often partners with major London/Amsterdam/Berlin clubs to host wild, pan-European circuit parties. Here, gay anthems are thrown in with hard-cutting techno and Turkish Pop. This place attracts the well-travelled and the un-impressionable, even some straight hipsters from nearby Nişantaşı. The cover charge includes one drink.

ROXY Map p107
☎ 212-245 6539; www.roxy.com.tr; Arslan Yatağı Sokak 1-3, off Sıraselviler Caddesi, Taksim; cover charge YTL35 Fri & Sat; 🚡 Kabataş, then funicular to Taksim
Bright young things flock to this dance-and-performance club that's been around since 1994. It recently expanded its premises to include a gallery, a party space and YAN Gastro Bar (🕒 4pm-1am Mon-Sat, 4pm-4am Fri & Sat). It works to your advantage if you eat here before clubbing because you get a free pass, dodging the long line outside. If you come late you might not get in. The cover charge on Friday and Saturday in-cludes one drink.

SORTIE Map p215
☎ 212-327 8585; www.sortie.com.tr; Muallim Naci Caddesi 141, Kuruçeşme; 🚌 25E, 25T, 40
Sortie vies with Reina (☎ 212-259 5919/21; www .reina.com.tr; Muallim Naci Caddesi 44, Kuruçeşme; Mon-Thu & Sun free, Fri & Sat 50YTL; 🕒 dining 6pm-midnight, dancing midnight-4am; 🚌 25E, 25T, 40) for title of queen of the Ortaköy gold coast nightclub row. It pulls in the city's glamour-pussies and poseurs, most of whom are on the lookout for celebrities and other tabloid fodder.

TONIQUE Map p107
☎ 212-251 7020; www.balanstonique.com; Balo Sokak 22, Beyoğlu; cover charge Mon-Fri YTL10, Sat & Sun YTL20; 🚡 Kabataş, then funicular to Taksim

Perched as a part-open-air penthouse duplex on the top floor of the Balans building, this has been the scene of many recent memorable electronic music and MTV happenings in the city. Resident and foreign guest DJs creatively vie to captivate beautiful scenesters.

LIVE JAZZ

İstanbul has seen an increase in the number of dedicated jazz venues in recent years, all of which have very different styles. These include the smoky atmosphere and unpretentious décor of Nardis, the opulent trappings of Q Jazz by Les Ottomans and dinner sessions at the Istanbul Jazz Center. During the popular International İstanbul Jazz Festival (p17) and Akbank Jazz Festival (p17), other live-music sites host events.

İSTANBUL JAZZ CENTER Map p117

☎ 212-327 5050; www.istanbuljazz.com; next to Radisson SAS Bosphorus Istanbul Hotel, Salhane Sk 10, Ortaköy; music charge YTL40, set menu YTL40; ☾ dinner 7pm-midnight, shows at 9pm & 12:30am; ᗒ 56

Owner Kerem Görsev, a popular Turkish jazz icon, has a free hand when it comes to booking the jazz world's who's who. The club's stylish setting makes up for the dinner plus music plus drinks bill, which is steep (domestic beer YTL13).

JAZZ CAFÉ Map p107

☎ 212-245 0516; Hasnun Galip Sokak 20, Beyoğlu; cover varies, dinner per person approx YTL40; ☾ 8pm-4am Tue-Fri, sets at 10:30pm & 1am; ᗕ Kabataş, then funicular to Taksim

Bathed in mood lighting, this mellow place boasts expat hosts and loads of 30-something jazz-heads. Live music kicks off at 10pm. The programme changes and isn't always jazz. Beer costs YTL6.

NARDIS JAZZ CLUB Map p103

☎ 212-244 6327; www.nardisjazz.com; Galata Kulesi Sokak 14, Galata; cover varies; ☾ 8pm-1am Mon-Thu with sets at 9:30pm & 12:30am, 8pm-2am Fri & Sat with sets at 10:30pm & 1:30am; ᗕ Karaköy, then funicular to Tünel

Just down the hill from the Galata Tower, this venue, named after a Miles Davis track, is where the real jazz aficionados go. Run by jazz guitarist Önder Focan and his wife Zuhal, a director of the local magazine

Jazz, Nardis is small but big in atmosphere. Its line-up of performers is exceptionally good; some come from the winners' ranks of its yearly amateur contest and others are visiting international artists. Different daily performers make every visit fresh and serendipitous – book ahead.

Q JAZZ BY LES OTTOMANS Map p215

☎ 212-359-1582; www.lesottomans.com; Muallim Naci Caddesi 163, Kuruçeşme; ☾ from 7pm, live performances 11pm-3am; ᗒ 25E, 25T, 40

This luxury hotel on the Bosphorus, which aims to replicate an Ottoman pasha's splendiferous surroundings, offers the chance to enjoy first-rate international jazz vocalists for a cover of only YTL30. The bar menu isn't outrageously priced, either.

LIVE TURKISH MUSIC

Turks are proud of their traditional music (see p33) and, whether young or old, will usually be familiar enough with the most popular folk and fasıl numbers to sing along in bars or meyhanes. One of the most entertaining experiences you can possibly have while visiting İstanbul is to have dinner at a fasıl venue where the guests take turns in serenading the restaurant with their favourite songs. Several restaurants in the Balık Pazarı (p110) and on Nevizade Sokak (p167) are among a number of places in Beyoğlu that now offer this type of sing-and-dance-along entertainment with their reasonably priced menus. Others have a set meal deal with either limited or unlimited booze. Make sure to tip when the musicians come to your table, nothing extravagant but substantial enough to be appreciated (YTL5 to YTL 10 per person is about right). When booking at a meyhane (it's not necessary to book at bars), try to opt for a Friday or Saturday night – on other nights restaurant management might tell musicians not to come in if numbers are low.

ANDON Map p107

☎ 212-251 0222; Sıraselviler Caddesi 89, Taksim; set menu incl all drinks YTL60, ☾ 2pm-4am Mon-Sat, live music 9pm-2am; ᗕ Kabataş, then funicular to Taksim

In addition to a rooftop restaurant with fine views over the Bosphorus, a wine bar with a rowdy soloist, a disco in the ground floor and a 3rd floor dedicated to the socalled İstanbul sanat (art) music, Andon is known for the fasıl music performed in its excellent 4th-floor meyhane. Come prepared to sing along.

CUMHURİYET Map p107

☎ 212-293 1977; Sahne Sokak No. 4 (in the Balık Pazarı), Beyoğlu; meze YTL4-6, beer YTL4; ☾ 9am-2am, fasıl music 8:30pm-midnight; ⓖ Kabataş, then funicular to Taksim

The drinks and à la carte dishes at this three-storey meyhane are incredibly reasonably priced. Atmosphere is nostalgic, as befits a place that was known to have been a favourite watering hole of Atatürk (check out the photos of him on the walls). The name is Turkish for 'Republic'.

DEGUSTASYON Map p107

☎ 212-292 0667; Sahne Sokak No. 41 (in the Balık Pazarı), Beyoğlu; mains YTL10-18, beer YTL4; ☾ 10am-1am, fasıl music 8:30pm-1am; ⓖ Kabataş, then funicular to Taksim

This place has three stories with a summer terrace, and can accommodate 180 persons, meaning that you can usually just walk in off the street. Good cheap food and lively music are dished up – a real find in the Fish Market.

DESPINA Map pp46–7

☎ 212-247 3357; Açıkyol Sokak 9, Kurtuluş; meals YTL45; ☾ noon-12:30am Mon-Sat, fasıl music 8:30pm-midnight; ⓐ taxi

Established in 1946 by the glamorous Madame Despina, whose faded photograph greets guests at the entrance, Despina is mainly patronised by neighbourhood locals, who come for its superb Armenian/Greek food (à la carte only) and the live fasıl music played by very accomplished musicians. On a warm evening the garden is a great setting for musical carousing.

GAY & LESBIAN İSTANBUL

All gay and lesbian listings in this book (clubs, hamams and bars) were written by René Ames, an İstanbul resident and freelance writer for *Time Out İstanbul*. René also updated the sections on clubbing, live jazz and live Turkish Music.

Having previously lived in New York, Switzerland, London and Spain, René is well qualified to assess how the gay and lesbian scene stacks up against its equivalents in the world's other big cities. He describes it as being just as lively and energy-sapping, but adds that the current impetus towards Europe makes it even more dynamic. 'People have that feeling of liberation, knowing that the European Union is hovering and showing interest in Turkey's human rights situation. It's like being in the cusp of a major historical turnover; very similar to the La Movida moment before Spain joined the rest of Europe, a truly exhilarating time when you can feel and live the possibilities.'

Asked about how the scene differs to those of its European sister cities he says, 'There are more tranny bars here than in New York or London or any other European capital. Leather and fetish clubs are the only ones absent in this mosaic, except when held as party themes. And we don't have dark rooms and naughty nooks like in some Western gay venues, meaning that most action needs to be done in private. The only public sex available is in a seedy cinema on İstiklal Caddesi showing heterosexual erotic films, or via furtive flings in dark alleys.'

The furtiveness may be due in part to the ambiguous legal status of homosexuality here; René points out that while Turkey has no laws against homosexuality, it has none in favour of it, either. 'In other words, it's neither legal nor illegal and that's where the problem is, because gays can be prosecuted or just plain harassed by the authorities under other legal statutes. Most telling is the fact that there are no antidiscriminatory laws covering sexual identity in this country; this is what the EU wants changed.' René is yet to witness police action leading to a closure of a gay venue, but he has been present when police visit and check everyone's *kimlik* (identity cards). He also notes that the hamam scene is changing: 'Police have been pretty vigilant against lewdness in hamams, too, so much so that bathhouse habitués say that the traditional homoerotic undercurrents in these bathhouses have changed considerably'.

Unfortunately, there are few organisations fighting for gay rights in Turkey. René describes the best known of these, Lambda Istanbul (www.lambdaistanbul.org in Turkish), as 'a far cry from their counterparts elsewhere', and comments that when he recently visited to try and gauge its political stance on the present situation in Turkey regarding the ascent of AKP, the implications of a Gül presidency and the impact of an impending socio-cultural overhaul after the last elections, the organisation's spokespeople had no comments to make: 'Either they were timid and not prone to open their mouths or they haven't done their homework... When I was in their office they were decorating and they seemed more interested in that task than to put their agenda out through a sympathetic member of the media.'

Asked to nominate an İstanbul gay icon, René is emphatic: 'That would have to be Ahmet Kural, one of my *Time Out* interviewees, who is credited with establishing the first gay bar in İstanbul. His bar (1001 Gece in Taksim) is still popular, though it now predominantly caters for chicks-with-dicks chasers.'

NIGHTLIFE RIP-OFFS

Foreigners, especially single foreign males, are targets for a classic İstanbul rip-off that works like this. You're a single male out for a stroll in the afternoon or evening. A well-spoken, well-dressed Turk strikes up a conversation and says he knows a 'good place where we can have a drink and chat' or a 'great nightspot' etc. You enter, sit down and immediately several women come to your table and order drinks. When the drinks come, you're asked to pay – anywhere from YTL200 to however much money you have with you. It's a mugging and if you don't pay up, they take you into the back office and take it from you.

A variation is a single foreign male having a drink and a meal at the Çiçek Pasajı. Several Turkish friends strike up a conversation, then suggest you all take a taxi to another place. In the taxi, they forcibly relieve you of your wallet.

How do you avoid such rip-offs? As many Turks are generous, hospitable, curious and gregarious, it's difficult to know whether an invitation is genuine (as it most often is) or the prelude to a mugging. Tread carefully if there's any reason for suspicion. As for nightclub recommendations, take them from a trusted source, such as your hotel clerk.

GARIBALDI Map p107
☎ 212-245 2522; İstiklal Caddesi Perukar Çikmazi (Odakule Yani) 11, Beyoğlu; www.garibaldibar.com; set menu YTL60 incl all drinks; ☾ 7:30pm-midnight Mon-Wed, 8pm-12:30am Thu-Sat, fasıl music from 8:30pm-closing; 🚇 Karaköy, then funicular to Tünel

Garibaldi is tucked into the side alley of an old Armenian Catholic church in Odakule, along the same street side as the big Collezione store. Its set menu means that you don't have to make any decisions other than to enjoy yourself, something that is ensured by the pleasing six-member fasıl group. There's a garden area if you don't feel like joining the action in the dining hall.

KOKOSH BY ASMALI Map p107
☎ 212-243 7678; Meşrutiyet Caddesi 193, Tepebaşı; set menu incl all drinks YTL80, unlimited

drinks at bar YTL50; ☾ 6pm-2am Tue-Thu, 6pm-4am Fri & Sat, live music from 8pm; 🚇 Karaköy, then funicular to Tünel

This place opposite the Pera Palas Hotel (p110) is famous for its entrancing sounds created by the zither and kettledrum, which supply the background for serious drinking and vociferous singing.

LEVENDIZ GREEK MEYHANE Map p117
☎ 212-236 7256; www.blackk.net; Muallim Naci Caddesi 71, Ortaköy; set menu incl all drinks YTL80; ☾ 7:30pm-12:30am, live music 9:30pm-midnight; 🚌 56

Part of the luxury supper club complex, Blackk, and offering a great Bosphorus view to accompany its inspired Greek cuisine, Levendiz is easily the most upscale meyhane hereabouts for the money-is-no-object crowd. Come dressed accordingly.

BLUELIST[1] (blu‚list) *v.*
to recommend a travel experience.
What's your recommendation? www.lonelyplanet.com/bluelist

THE ARTS

top picks

- Proje4l/Elgiz Museum of Contemporary Art (p186)
- Atatürk Cultural Centre (p188)
- Akbank Culture & Arts Centre (p188)
- Aya İrini (p188)
- Galerist (p186)
- santralistanbul (p186)

THE ARTS

When the EU designated İstanbul one of its European Cultural Capitals for 2010, no-one here was surprised. Pleased, yes, but İstanbullus hadn't failed to note the fact that over the past decade their city had built considerably on its formidable cultural infrastructure and been gifted a whole new generation of museums and galleries, including the İstanbul Modern (p102), Pera Museum (p110), Sakıp Sabancı Museum (p218), Proje4L/Elgiz Museum of Contemporary Art (below) and santralistanbul (below). Fortunately, this proliferation of venues isn't short of exciting new work to show, with the city's contemporary arts practice going from strength to strength and its visual artists finally starting to take their place on the international stage alongside their musician, writer and filmmaker peers.

ART GALLERIES

İstanbul has a thriving art scene. As well as cultural centres (p188), most of which have excellent exhibition spaces, numerous small independent galleries exhibit the work of local and international visual and multimedia artists. Most upmarket private galleries are in the shopping areas of Teşvikiye and Nişantaşı, whereas the high-profile contemporary spaces funded by banks and other companies are on İstiklal Caddesi in Beyoğlu. Small galleries exhibiting the work of young local and international artists are often found in the sidestreets off İstiklal Caddesi (Map p107). For larger art museums, such as İstanbul Modern (p102), see individual entries in the Neighbourhoods chapter.

The big visual arts event on the calendar is the International İstanbul Biennial (p17).

GALERI NEV Map p107

☎ 212-252 1525; Meşrutiyet Caddesi 59, Tepebaşı; www.galerinev.com; ☺ 11am-6.30pm Mon-Sat; ☒ Karaköy, then funicular to Tünel

This long-established commercial gallery shows painting, sculpture and installation works by contemporary Turkish artists.

GALERIST Map p107

☎ 212-244 8230; www.galerist.com.tr; İstiklal Caddesi 311/4, Galatasaray; ☺ 10am-6pm Mon-Sat; ☒ Karaköy, then funicular to Tünel

In the fashionable Mısır Apartmentı Building on İstiklal (home to 360, see p165), this excellent commercial gallery shows young Turkish artists living at home and abroad working in a variety of media.

PLATFORM GARANTİ CONTEMPORARY ART CENTRE Map p107

☎ 212-293 2361; www.platformgaranti.blogspot.com; İstiklal Caddesi 136, Beyoğlu; ☺ 1-8pm

Tue-Thu, 1-10pm Fri & Sat; ☒ Kabataş, then funicular to Taksim

A minimalist space funded by the Garanti Bank, Platform shows the very best of international contemporary art, with an emphasis on installation and multimedia work.

PROJE4L/ELGIZ MUSEUM OF CONTEMPORARY ART

Elgiz Çağdaş Sanat Müzesi, İstanbul; ☎ 212-281 5150; www.elgizmuseum.org; Harman Sokak, Harmancı Giz Plaza, Levent; ☺ 11am-7pm Tue-Sat; ☒ Kabataş, then funicular to Taksim, then metro to Levent

Established by local architect and property developer Can Elgiz to further the understanding of experimental art in the city, Proje4L is super cool and programmes cutting-edge exhibitions mainly sourced from Europe. It occupies an annex of a tower block in Levent and is well worth a visit. You'll find it near Kanyon (p143).

SANTRALİSTANBUL

Eski Silahtarağa Elektrik Santrali; ☎ 212-311 5000; www.santralistanbul.com; Kazım Karabekır Caddesi 1, Eyüp; ☺ 10am-10pm Tue-Sun; ☒ Eyüp

İstanbul's version of the Tate Modern, santralistanbul is a contemporary art gallery housed in a converted power station. It opened in September 2007 with an exhibition entitled 'Modern and Beyond' surveying the history of Turkish art from 1950 through to 2000, and promises to deliver an ongoing program of survey shows, artist-in-residence programs and workshops. Get there on the Haliç (Golden Horn) ferry from Eminönü or catch the free shuttle bus from the Atatürk Cultural Centre in Taksim; these leave every 30 minutes from 9am to 8pm.

SCHNEIDERTEMPEL ART CENTER
Map p103

Schneidertempel Sanat Merkezi; ☎ 212-252 5157;
Felek Sokak 1, Karaköy; ⏱ 10.30am-5.30pm Tue-
Sat, noon-4pm Sun; 🚊 Karaköy

Housed in an old synagogue, the Schneidertempel exhibits work by local Jewish
artists, as well as frequent exhibitions from
abroad. Quality varies, but we've seen
some excellent photographic exhibitions
here, as well as extremely moving exhibitions of historical work from the Holocaust.
Security here is tight and opening hours
are irregular. Treat those given above as a
guide only.

CINEMAS

İstiklal Caddesi is the centre of İstanbul's cinema (sinema) district. During April's İstanbul
International Film Festival (p16) every corner
of Beyoğlu is filled with enthusiastic cinema-
goers keen to see the latest Hollywood blockbuster or major European release, as well as
home-grown products. Tickets to this festival
are hot numbers – you'll need to book way
in advance.

During the rest of the year, the enthusiasm
for flicks remains. Films are mostly shown in
English with Turkish subtitles, but double-
check at the box office in case the film has
Turkish (Türkçe) dubbing, as this sometimes
happens with blockbusters. For movie listings,
see the Turkish Daily News.

When possible, buy your tickets a few
hours in advance. Depending on the venue,
tickets cost between YTL10 and YTL15 –
many places offer reduced rates before 6pm,
to students, and all day on Monday and
Wednesday.

The usher will expect a small tip for showing you to your seat.

AFM AKMERKEZ

☎ 444 1 AFM; Akmerkez Shopping Centre,
Nispetiye Caddesi 76/1, Etiler; 🚊 Kabataş, then
funicular to Taksim, then metro to Akmerkez

This multiplex is pricey, but its comfortable
surrounds are a good place to rest after a
big day shopping.

AFM FİTAŞ Map p107

☎ 444 1 AFM; İstiklal Caddesi 24-26, Fitaş Pasajı,
Beyoğlu; 🚊 Kabataş, then funicular to Taksim

This multiplex has 11 screens and all the
Hollywood trimmings.

ALKAZAR SİNEMA MERKEZİ Map p107

☎ 212-293 2466; İstiklal Caddesi 179; 🚊 Kabataş,
then funicular to Taksim

First a porn cinema, then an arthouse joint,
Alkazar has now given in to Hollywood,
though it still occasionally programmes an
arthouse hit. There are three screens and a
plush and cosy interior.

ATLAS SINEMALARI Map p107

☎ 212-252 8576; İstiklal Caddesi 209, Atlas Pasajı;
🚊 Kabataş, then funicular to Taksim

On the 1st floor of one of the historic arcades along İstiklal, Atlas is always bustling.
There are three screens and the program-
ming is eclectic. Istanbul Film Festival
screenings also happen here.

EMEK Map p107

☎ 212-293 8439; Yeşilçam Sokak 5, Beyoğlu;
🚊 Kabataş, then funicular to Taksim

Functioning since the 1920s, this barn of a
cinema is one of the oldest in the city. It's
not the most comfortable on offer, but has
managed to retain a bit of the glamour it
had during Pera's heyday. It's another venue
for the İstanbul International Film Festival.

KANYON MARS CINEMA

☎ 212-353 0814; www.marssinema.com; Kanyon
Shopping Mall, Levent; 🚊 Kabataş, then funicular
to Taksim, then metro to Levent

In the city's most glamorous shopping
mall, this multiplex is a comfortable place
to enjoy a flick. It screens some, but not all,
films in original languages.

REXX Map p127

☎ 216-336 0112; Sakızgülü Sokak 20-22, Kadıköy;
🚊 Kadıköy

We've sheltered here from bad weather
before risking a ferry back to town more
than once. On the Asian side of İstanbul,
the Rexx's program usually lacks surprises.
The only exception is in April, when it
screens part of the İstanbul International
Film Festival.

ŞAFAK SİNEMALARI Map p50

☎ 212-516 2660; Divan Yolu Caddesi 134,
Çemberlitaş; 🚊 Çemberlitaş

This seven-screen cinema is the closest to
Sultanahmet, only a 10-minute walk along
Divan Yolu. It screens Hollywood blockbusters and is beloved of heavy petters, who sit
at the back.

CLASSICAL MUSIC & OPERA

İstanbul has a lively Western classical music scene and its own headline act, the İstanbul State Symphony Orchestra. There are also regular visits by international orchestras and chamber ensembles (for venues, see below).

In summer, concerts are also held in the atmospheric amphitheatre at Rumeli Hisarı, (p217), at Yedikule Hisarı Müzesi (p128) and in the watery cavern of the Basilica Cistern (p58).

During the International İstanbul Music Festival (p16) there is a wealth of classical music and opera on offer, including performances in the extraordinarily atmospheric Aya İrini (p65).

The İstanbul State Opera & Ballet has a season running from October to May, with some extra performances during the International İstanbul Music Festival. Most performances take place at the Atatürk Cultural Centre (right).

CULTURAL CENTRES & PERFORMANCE VENUES

There's big money behind the arts in İstanbul, with banks leading the way in funding the major arts companies and festivals. There are also plenty of impressive venues around town where the sponsors can schmooze and the dignitaries can party after the performance. Most of these venues are cultural centres hosting a number of different art forms – it's not unusual for these places to host an opera one night, a jazz performance the next, a ballet on the night after that and an exhibition in the foyer the whole time.

To get an overview of what's on where, refer to the monthly listings in *Time Out Istanbul*. Tickets are usually available through Biletix (☎ 216-454 1555, 216-556 9800; www.biletix.com).

AKBANK CULTURE & ARTS CENTRE
Map p107

☎ 212-252 3500; www.akbanksanat.com; Zambak Sokak 1, Beyoğlu; ⛴ Kabataş, then funicular to Taksim

This small venue, funded entirely by the Turkish bank of the same name, hosts classical and jazz music recitals, as well as exhibitions of the work of local artists.

ATATÜRK CULTURAL CENTRE Map p107

AKM, Atatürk Kültür ve Sanat Merkezi; ☎ 212-251 5600; www.idobale.com in Turkish; Taksim Square; ⏰ box office 10am-6pm; ⛴ Kabataş, then funicular to Taksim

At night the lights of the city's major cultural centre glow behind its stylised steel grill, providing a welcome sight in the otherwise unprepossessing Taksim Square. Unfortunately, during the day the building isn't quite as beguiling. Being the home of the city's major theatre, ballet and opera companies, it hosts more than its fair share of opening nights and acclaimed performances. The centre includes five performance halls in addition to a gallery and a cinema. Tickets are almost always affordable.

AYA İRİNİ Map p63

Hagia Eirene, Church of Divine Peace; First Court of Topkapı Palace; ⛴ Sultanahmet

Big-name classical events make the most of the acoustics in this ancient venue (see p62), particularly during the International İstanbul Music Festival. During the festival a board outside lists upcoming events and contact details; tickets are available through Biletix or at the festival ticket box at the Atatürk Cultural Centre.

BORUSAN ARTS & CULTURE CENTER
Map p107

Borusan Kültür ve Sanat Merkezi; ☎ 212-292 0655; www.borusansanat.com; İstiklal Caddesi 421; ⏰ gallery 10.30am-7pm Tue-Sat; ⛴ Kabataş, then funicular to Taksim

This well-regarded arts centre has an established gallery showcasing the work of local artists, with the occasional high-profile international show. It also hosts concerts and recitals by artists of the calibre of world-famous Turkish pianist, Fazıl Say.

CEMAL REŞİT REY CONCERT HALL
Map p115

Cemal Reşit Rey Konser Salonu; ☎ 212-232 9830; www.crrks.org in Turkish; Gümüş Sokak, Harbiye; ⏰ box office 10am-7.30pm; ⛴ Kabataş, then funicular to Taksim

With its great acoustics and comfortable chairs, this concert hall is a popular venue for dance, classical and Ottoman music, and the occasional jazz gig. Its handy monthly guides list upcoming events and prices in English, and are available around town (they're everywhere on İstiklal Caddesi).

İŞ ART & CULTURAL CENTRE

İş Sanat Kültür Merkezi; ☎ 212-316 1083; www
.issanat.com; İş Kuleleri 4, Levent; ⏰ box office
9am-6pm; 🚇 Kabataş, then funicular to Taksim,
then metro to Levent (Plazalar exit)

This sleek venue in the İş Towers hosts
international acts, poetry readings and performances of live jazz, Ottoman music and
world music. A free shuttle service to here
leaves from outside the Atatürk Cultural
Centre (opposite) in Taksim at 6.30pm.

ITALIAN CULTURAL CENTRE Map p107

İtalyan Kültür Merkezi, Istituto Italiano di Cultura;
☎ 212-293 9848; www.iicist.org.tr; Meşrutiyet
Caddesi 161, Tepebaşı; 🚇 Karaköy, then funicular
to Tünel

In summer this centre hosts low-key performances and recitals mainly organised by
the Borusan Arts & Culture Centre (opposite).

LÜTFI KIRDAR CONCERT HALL Map p115

Convention Centre, Lütfi Kırdar Kongre ve Sergi Sa-
lonu; ☎ 212-296 3055; Darülbedai Sokak, Harbiye;
🚇 Kabataş, then funicular to Taksim

Originally built for the 1948 World Wres-
tling Championships, this huge refurbished
concert hall hosts conferences, the Borusan İstanbul Philharmonic Orchestra, and
events for the International İstanbul Music
Festival and İstanbul Film Festival (p16).

TARIK ZAFER TUNAYA KÜLTÜR
MERKEZİ Map p107

Tarık Zafer Tunaya Cultural Centre; ☎ 212-293
1270; Şahkulu Bostanı Sokak 8, Tünel; 🚇 Karaköy,
then funicular to Tünel

As well as its regular screenings of Turkish
flicks and informative lectures on Turkish
culture, this centre hosts music events,
including occasional performances of Ottoman music.

DANCE
FOLK DANCE

Many people immediately think of belly dancing when they hear the term 'Turkish folk
dance', but there are other, far more authentic,
traditional dance forms in the country. Although belly dancing has a long, wobbly and
undulating history, contrary to popular belief
it's not strictly a Turkish dance. It's said to have
originated in Egypt as a meditative-erotic dance
to entertain the elite in life and death, and was

brought to Turkey during the Ottoman Empire.
Today in İstanbul it's mainly tourist fodder, and
although it's entertaining – and pretty sexy –
the dancers are usually second-rate and you
won't see a performance of the art at anywhere
near its best.

As well as belly dancing, other dances can
be seen at the cheesy, touristy 'Turkish Shows'
around town. These provide a snapshot of
Turkey's folk dances (with belly dancing),
usually accompanied by dinner. Beloved by
package-tour operators, they are expensive
and the food is usually mediocre at best. Still,
if you are keen to see some folk dance while
you're in town these are usually the only
places you'll be able to do it.

Finally, check with the cultural centres to
see if any special folk dance performances are
programmed. If you're lucky enough to be in
town when they are, snap up a ticket.

DANCE OF COLOURS Map p78

☎ 212-517 8692; www.danceofcolours.com;
FKM Fırat Culture Centre, Divan Yolu Caddesi,
Çemberlitaş; YTL31; ⏰ 7.30pm Tue, Thu & Sat;
🚇 Çemberlitaş

This popular performance features dances
from 10 different regions of Turkey. If you
want to see a dervish whirl, a belly dancer
undulate and lots more, this one-hour
show is for you. Colourful costumes and
professional dancers make for a good
evening's fun, with the added bonus that
you don't have to fork out for an indifferent
meal. It's possible to arrange a hotel pick-
up if you request this when booking.

ORIENT HOUSE Map p78

☎ 212-517 6163; www.orienthouseistanbul.com;
Tiyatro Caddesi 27, Beyazıt; adult/child 5-9/child under
5 YTL128/64/free; ⏰ 8.30pm-midnight; 🚇 Beyazıt

Orient House is popular mainly because it's
close to Sultanahmet and its spruikers have
sprinkled brochures and the promise of attractive commissions around many Sultanahmet hotels. Still, its live Ottoman janissary
band, ersatz traditional wedding and Sufi
sema, belly dancers and folk dancers seem
to be exactly like its audiences like. The
price includes a three-course dinner with
drinks.

BALLET

Like opera, ballet has a keen following among
the moneyed elite in İstanbul. There are occasional performances by home-grown and

international artists, usually at the Atatürk Cultural Centre (p188). The city's major company is the İstanbul State Opera & Ballet (☎ 212-251 1023; www.idobale.com), based at the Atatürk Cultural Centre.

THEATRE

The Turks are enthusiastic theatregoers and have a special genius for dramatic art. The problem for the foreign visitor is language, as most performances are in Turkish. Your best chance of seeing theatre in English is during April's International İstanbul Theatre Festival (p16), where some English-language plays are staged, often sponsored by cultural organisations such as the British Council.

One form of theatre that is accessible to foreign visitors is the famous *karagöz* (shadow-puppet theatre). Although the country's main troupe is based in Bursa, it also performs in İstanbul. The puppets (10cm to 50cm tall) are cut from hide pieces, coated with oil to promote translucency and decorated with colourful paints. Most have movable arms and legs, and some have movable heads. During the performances they prance behind a white sheet enacting stories. The best time to see *karagöz* is in May each year, when the city hosts the International Ülker Puppet Festival İstanbul (p16).

SPORTS & ACTIVITIES

top picks

- **Çırağan Palace Hotel Kempinski** (p192) Top pool
- **Orsep Royal Hotel** (p192) Top gym
- **Ambassador Hotel Spa Center** (p192) Top massage
- **Çemberlitaş Hamamı** (p193) Top hamam
- **Yeşildirek Hamami** (p195) Top gay hamam

SPORTS & ACTIVITIES

There's plenty to do in İstanbul when you want a break from the sights. You can check out the summer social scene beside a five-star hotel swimming pool, succumb to the steam and a soapy scrub in one of the city's historic hamams, or scream yourself hoarse with the rest of the crowd at a Super League football match. Whichever you choose, you're bound to enjoy yourself.

HEALTH & FITNESS

In summer, going to a swimming pool here is more about seeing and being seen than getting fit, which is why the pools at the five-star hotels are so popular with locals. These hotels probably offer the best options for those travellers craving a gym workout, too.

SWIMMING

Swimming in the Bosphorus is only an option for those who have a death wish. Those with a hankering for the water can head to the beaches at Yeşilköy and Florya (you can get to these by train from Sirkeci Railway Station) – but only to paddle. The water around the Princes' Islands is relatively clean, though the tiny beaches are crammed bottom-to-bottom in summer.

Most of İstanbul's pool facilities are privately owned and open to members only. However, it's possible to organise a pricey day pass to use the leisure facilities at many of the city's luxury hotels, and there's much to be said for the idea of spending a day poolside at one of these places, particularly when good eateries, a health club and Bosphorus views come as part of the package. Here's a list of top hotel pools:

Çırağan Palace Hotel Kempinski (Map p115; ☎ 212-326 4646; Çırağan Caddesi 32, Beşiktaş; weekdays YTL115, weekends YTL175; ⏰ 7am-11pm; 🚌 56).

Hotel Les Ottomans (☎ 212-359 1500; Muallim Naci Caddesi 68, Kuruçeşme; YTL100; ⏰ 9am-7pm; 🚌 25E, 25T, 40)

İstanbul Hilton (Map p115; ☎ 212-3156000; Cumhuriyet Caddesi, Harbiye; weekdays YTL70, weekends YTL110; ⏰ 8am-8pm; 🚌 Kabataş then funicular to Taksim)

Swissôtel İstanbul the Bosphorus (Map p117; ☎ 212-326 1100; Bayıldım Caddesi 2, Maçka; weekdays YTL80, weekends YTL100; ⏰ 8am-7pm; 🚌 25E, 25T, 40)

GYMS

Many of the local gyms are testosterone-packed joints full of muscles and attitude.

The equipment is usually fairly limited too, so it's probably worth forking out a bit more and paying for a day pass at one of the big international hotels.

ORSEP ROYAL HOTEL Map p63

☎ 212-511 8585; www.orseproyalhotel.com; Nöbethane Caddesi 10, Sirkeci; day pass YTL30; ⏰ 9am-9pm; 🚇 Sirkeci

Conveniently located behind Sirkeci Railway Station, this hotel has an excellent gym and wellness centre with an indoor pool, hamam, sauna, steambath, Jacuzzi and new exercise equipment. There's also a rooftop pool with fabulous panoramic views.

ACTIVITIES

Sightseeing is the activity you'll indulge in most while in İstanbul, but while you're here it's worth forgoing the sights for a few hours and surrendering your body to the steamy environs of the hamam. If you're here over a weekend, it's also worth thinking about attending a football match. Just try to make sure it's one where Galatasaray, Fenerbahçe or Beşiktaş are playing, because these are the most exciting.

HAMAMS

We run the danger of sounding like your mum here, but frankly, we just don't think it's advisable for you to leave İstanbul without having a bath. A Turkish bath, that is…

AMBASSADOR HOTEL SPA CENTER
Map p50

☎ 212-512 0002; www.hotelambassador.com; Ticarethane Sokak 19, Sultanahmet; Turkish bath with soap & oil massage YTL50; ⏰ 8am-10pm; 🚇 Sultanahmet

We reckon the best hamam experience in the city is on offer at this shabby modern hotel just off Divan Yolu. There's no atmosphere to speak of, but the bath and massage packages are excellent value. Best of all, you get the pretty (but small) hamam all to yourself. The 75-minute Turkish massage treatment gives you the same package that you get in the big hamams (bath, scrub and soap massage), but what makes this place superior is the 30-minute oil massage after the bath, which is given by Zeki Ulusoy. Zeki is trained in sports, remedial and aromatherapy massage and he really knows his stuff – you'll float out of here at the end of your session. You can also book the hamam for private use (YTL17 per person per hour).

CAĞALOĞLU HAMAMI Map p63
☎ 212-522 2424; www.cagalogluhamami.com.tr; Yerebatan Caddesi 34, Cağaloğlu; standard/luxury bath, scrub & massage YTL54/72, bath only YTL24; ✆ 8am-10pm men, 8am-8pm women; 🚇 Sultanahmet

Built over three centuries ago, this is one of the city's most beautiful hamams. It boasts (without evidence) that King Edward VIII, Kaiser Wilhelm II, Franz Liszt, Cameron Diaz and Florence Nightingale have enjoyed its pleasures, no doubt at the same time and with Elvis in attendance. It's pricey, but the surroundings are so impressive that they've featured in everything from soap ads to an *Indiana Jones* film. Separate baths each have a large *camekan* (reception area), where it's possible to have a nap or a tea at the end of your bath. Be warned: staff here have a reputation for hassling for tips.

ÇEMBERLİTAŞ HAMAMI Map p50
☎ 212-522 7974; Vezir Hanı Caddesi 8, Çemberlitaş; bath, scrub & soap massage YTL40, bath YTL28, 30-min oil massage YTL28; ✆ 6am-midnight; 🚇 Çemberlitaş

There won't be too many times in your life when you'll get the opportunity to have a Turkish bath in a building dating back to 1584, so now might well be the time to do it. Commissioned by Nurbanu Sultan, wife of Selim II and mother of Murat III, this hamam was designed by the great architect Sinan and is among the most beautiful in the city. Just off Divan Yolu near the Grand Bazaar, it's a double hamam (separate baths for men and women) that's particularly popular with tourists. Although the splendid *camekan* is unfortunately for men only (women must put up with a utilitarian corridor filled with lockers and

benches), the *sıcaklık* (hot room) in each section is a glorious space with a large marble *göbektaşı* (raised platform above the heating source) and domed ceilings with star-like apertures admitting filtered light. In the women's *sıcaklık* it's not unusual for one of the masseuses to break into song. For your money you'll get lots of heat and a thorough and very soapy massage. There's a 20% discount for ISIC student-card holders.

SÜLEYMANİYE HAMAMI Map p78
☎ 212-519 5569; www.suleymaniyehamami .com; Mimar Sinan Caddesi 20, Süleymaniye; from the Old City YTL51, from Beyoğlu YTL60; ✆ 6am-midnight; 🚇 Beyazıt

Another hamam designed by Sinan, though this one's not as impressive as the Çemberlitaş and is a mixed bath with only male masseurs, meaning that some women will not feel comfortable here. The price includes bath, scrub and soap massage, as well as a free pick-up and drop off from your hotel. It has to be said that the fact that the hamam proudly advertises that life insurance is included in the price of its hamam treatment is slightly disconcerting!

TARİHİ GALATASARAY HAMAMI Map p107
Historic Galatasaray Turkish Bath; ☎ 212-252 4242; Turnacıbaşı Sokak 24, Çukurcuma; full treatment YTL63, bath YTL30; ✆ men 6am-10pm, women 8am-8pm; 🚇 Kabataş, then funicular to Taksim

Though not as pretty as many Old İstanbul hamams (it dates from 1964), this quiet place off İstiklal Caddesi is one of the city's best, with lots of marble decoration, small cubicles for resting and sipping tea after the bath, pretty fountains and even a shoeshine service. Parts of the building date from 1481, but it has been rebuilt several times. The interiors are much nicer in the men's section than the women's. It's famous for having one of the hottest *göbektaşı* in town (that sounds rude but we mean it literally).

GAY HAMAMS & SAUNAS
Stuff goes on at these places that the *imam* sure ain't going to approve of. All are for men only.

HAMAM ETIQUETTE

The concept of the steam bath was passed from the Romans to the Byzantines and then on to the Turks, who named it the hamam and have relished it ever since. They've even exported the concept throughout the world, hence the term Turkish bath. Until recent decades, many homes in İstanbul didn't have washing facilities and, due to Islam's emphasis on personal squeaky-cleanness, the community relied on the hundreds of hamams that were constructed throughout the city, often as part of the mosque complex. Of course, it wasn't only personal hygiene that was attended to in the hamam. It was the perfect place for a prospective mother-in-law to eye off, and pinch and prod a prospective daughter-in-law, for instance, and it was equally good for catching up on the neighbourhood gossip. Now that many people have bathrooms in İstanbul, hamams are nowhere near as popular as they used to be, but some carry on, no doubt due to their role as local meeting places. Others have become extremely successful tourist attractions.

The city's hamams vary enormously. Some are dank dives where you may come out dirtier than you went in (remember – Turks call cockroaches 'hamam insects'); others are plain and clean, servicing a predominantly local clientele. An increasing number are building a reputation as gay meeting places (we're talking truly steamy here) and a handful are geared exclusively towards tourists. If you're only going to visit one or two when you're in town, we suggest you choose the 'Big Two' – Cağaloğlu and Çemberlitaş (see p193). Sure, they're touristy, but they're also gorgeous, historic buildings where most of the clientele will be having their first experience of a hamam, so you won't feel out of place. They're also clean and have some English-speaking staff.

Bath Procedure

Upon entry you are shown to a *camekan* (entrance hall or space) where you will be allocated a dressing *halvet* (cubicle) or locker and given a *peştemal* (bath-wrap) and *nailn* (wooden sandals). Store your clothes and don the *peştemal* and *nailn*. An attendant will then lead you through the *soğukluk* (intermediate section) to the *sicaklik* (hot section), where you sit and sweat for a while, relaxing and loosening up, perhaps on the *göbektaşı* (central, raised platform atop the heating source).

Soon you will be half-asleep and as soft as putty from the steamy heat. The cheapest bath is the one you do yourself, having brought your own soap, shampoo and towel. But the real Turkish bath experience is to have a *tellak* (attendant) wash, scrub and massage you.

If you have opted for the latter, an attendant douses you with warm water and lathers you with a sudsy swab. Next you are scrubbed with a coarse cloth mitten loosening dirt you never suspected you had. After a massage (these yo-yo between being enjoyable, limp-wristed or mortally dangerous) comes a shampoo and another dousing with warm water, followed by one with cool water.

When the scrubbing is over, stay in the *sicaklik* relaxing or head for the cool room and grab a towel. You then go back to your locker or cubicle to get dressed – if you've got a *halvet* you can even have a rest or order something to drink. If you want to nap, tell the attendant when to wake you. The average hamam experience takes around one hour.

Modesty

Traditional Turkish baths have separate sections for men and women, or have only one set of facilities and admit men or women at different times. Bath etiquette requires that men remain clothed with the bath-wrap at all times. In the women's section, women sometimes wear their underwear (but not their bra). It's up to you – most tourists seem not to do this. During the bathing, everyone washes their private parts themselves, without removing the bath-wrap or underclothes.

In touristy areas, some baths now accept that foreign men and women like to bathe together. No Turkish woman would let a masseur touch her (it must be a masseuse), but masseurs are usually the only massagers available in these foreign-oriented baths. We suggest that women willing to accept a masseur should have the massage within view of male companions or other friends.

Practicalities

Soap, shampoo and towels are provided at all of the hamams we've reviewed; if you're just having a bath, you'll need to pay for the soap and shampoo separately – it's usually included in the cost of full treatments. Çemberlitaş is the only hamam where the price includes tips; others will tell you that tipping is at your discretion, but frankly, you've got as much of a chance of leaving without tipping as you have of approaching the Blue Mosque and being ignored by the touts selling postcards. We suggest giving 10% to 20% of the total fee (depending on service). You'll get drenched, so make sure you take a comb, toiletries, make-up and (if you choose to wear underwear during the massage) a dry pair of replacement knickers.

AĞA HAMAMI Map p107

☎ 212-249 5027; Turnacıbaşı Sokak 66, Çukur-cuma, Beyoğlu; bath YTL20, with massage YTL30; ⏱ 5pm-5am; 🚋 Kabataş, then funicular to Taksim

This historical hamam is down the street from Istanbul's premier chicks-with-dicks club, Sahra. Though it has been closely and beautifully restored to its original Otto-man glory, we have to say that it's not the antique ambience that brings the boys here in the early morning hours, especially during the weekend – the attraction is undoubtedly what they can do under the sleepy eyes of the bathhouse attendants.

AQUARIUS Map p107

☎ 212-251 8925; Sadri Alisik Sokak 29/1, Beyoğlu; admission YTL30, massage per hr YTL50; ⏱ 24hr; 🚋 Kabataş, then funicular to Taksim

Unabashedly proclaiming itself as 'the only gay sauna in Istanbul', Aquarius can also lay claim to having the only swimming pool in its premises, which means it comes closest to what most Western gay sauna habitués are used to – most notably a clean environ-ment. An added attraction is the stable of 14 hunky, delicious masseurs who take you into the private cubicles for a massage – be sure to negotiate the price and the service parameters clearly. Note: what goes on here should remain here.

ÇEŞME HAMAMI Map p103

☎ 212-252 3441; Yeni Çeşme Sokak 9, off Perşembe Pazari Caddesi, Karaköy; with/without massage YTL15/25; ⏱ 8am-7pm; 🚋 Karaköy

Its maze-like location in a backstreet be-hind the hardware stores that litter this part of town often discourages the non-local bathhouse action seekers. But this favourite hamam of bears and pot-bellied mousta-chioed types is worth finding because of the relaxed attitude of the management. Just be careful you don't stick out like a pink thumb or you'll incite a feeding frenzy.

YEŞİLDİREK HAMAMI Map p103

Tersane Caddesi 74, Azapkapi; bath YTL20, with massage YTL30; ⏱ 6am-9pm; 🚋 Karaköy

This spacious, well-maintained hamam (located across from Azapkapı Sokollu Mehmet Paşa Camii at the base of the Atatürk Bridge) with all the traditional trap-pings is crowded with testosterone-laden bathhouse lovers – among them expats

and in-the-know tourists – who have been displaced from other bathing areas in the city where vigilance has become the norm. The need for discretion cannot be over-emphasised here.

SPECTATOR SPORTS

In İstanbul, there's only one spectator sport worth mentioning, and that's the football (soccer). If you're a football fan, attending a match here will be one of the highlights of your stay. And even if you're not sport-mad, these events can provide a fascinating insight into the city's psyche.

FOOTBALL

The Big Three (*Üç Büyükler*) teams in the national Super League (*Turkcell Süper Lig*) are Galatasaray, Fenerbahçe and Beşiktaş. All are based in İstanbul, and locals are extravagantly proud of them. Indeed, when Galatasaray be-came the first Turkish team to win a UEFA Cup (in 2000), locals went wild with excite-ment – in many eyes it was probably the most significant event since the Conquest. When the national team reached the semifinals of the World Cup in 2002 and ended up in third place, an estimated 1.5 million people came out on İstanbul's streets to congratulate the players on their return. As most of the team members were sourced from the ranks of the city's big three clubs, it was seen as a local triumph as well as a national victory.

There are two other teams based in the city: Kasımpaşa SK and İstanbul Büyükşehir Belediyespor.

Many of the İstanbul teams have strong roots in local or ethnic communities. Trans-lated, Fenerbahçe means 'Garden of the Lighthouse', a clear reference to the Greek community in old Phanar (today's Fener); and Galatasaray was formed by Muslim students of the French-run Galatasaray Lycée.

For the 24 hours preceding a big match, team scarves are worn, flags are aflutter and hotted-up testosterone-motors bounce up and down at red lights before screeching off drag-ging team colours behind them. At the end of the game, traffic around Beyoğlu crawls to a halt as merrymakers head to Taksim Square to celebrate. Here, the crowds sway, chant club anthems, wave club flags and clamber all over each other, while many still find time to ogle passing women (football is strictly a male concern).

THE BIG THREE

- Beşiktaş (www.bjk.com.tr) Home stadium: İnönü Stadyumu, Beşiktaş. Colours: black and white.
- Fenerbahçe (www.fenerbahce.org.tr) Home stadium: Rüştü Saraçoğlu Stadyumu, Kadıköy. Colours: yellow and blue.
- Galatasaray (www.galatasaray.org.tr) Home stadium: Ali Sami Yen Stadyum, Mecidiyeköy (about 3km northeast of Taksim). Colours: yellow and red.

Eighteen teams from all over Turkey compete from August to May. Each season three move up from the second league into the first and three get demoted. The top team of the first league plays in the UEFA Cup. Matches are usually held on the weekend, often on a Saturday night. Tickets are sold at the stadium (*stadyum*) on the day of the match, but most fans purchase them ahead of time through Biletix (☎ 216-454 1555, 216-556 9800; www .biletix.com). Open seating is affordable; covered seating – which has the best views – can be very pricey.

Although violence at home games is not unknown, most matches are fine. If you're worried, avoid the Galatasaray and Fenerbahçe clashes, as the supporters of these arch rivals can become overly excited and throw a few punches around.

SLEEPING

top picks

- **Four Seasons Hotel Istanbul** (p199) Top luxury hotel
- **Hotel Empress Zoe** (p200) Top Ottoman boutique hotel
- **Hotel Nomade** (p201) Top budget boutique hotel
- **Hotel Peninsula** (p202) Top cheap sleep
- **İstanbul Holiday Apartments** (p206) Top apartments
- **Tria Hotel İstanbul** (p200) Top mid-range option
- **Hotel Şebnem** (p201) Top value for money
- **Eklektik Guest House** (p206) Top gay-friendly sleep
- **Leb-i Derya Richmond** (at the Richmond Hotel; p176) Top hotel bar

SLEEPING

Accommodation Styles

Every possible accommodation style is available in İstanbul. You can live like a sultan in a world-class luxury hotel, doss in an anonymous hostel dorm or relax in a simple but stylish boutique establishment. We've labelled each hotel's type next to its name to help you in your choice. By 'Ottoman Boutique Hotel' we mean a small-to-medium-sized hotel, usually but not always in an old building, that places great emphasis on décor (usually with Ottoman or Anatolian touches) and friendly service. By 'Boutique Hotel' we mean a stylish modern hotel with great service and amenities. The 'Hotel' tag alone means that the place would be at home in any international city, and doesn't make any real gestures to traditional Turkish decoration or services.

With the exception of the hostels listed, all hotels reviewed offer rooms with en suite bathroom. The prices we've given include breakfast, usually of the Turkish variety (fresh bread, jams, sheep's milk cheese, olives, tomatoes, cucumber and tea or coffee). Exceptions to these norms are noted in the reviews.

Keep in mind that the appearance of a hotel's lobby doesn't always reflect the quality of its rooms. Look at several rooms if possible. If you're not impressed with the first one you are shown, ask 'Başka var mı?' ('Are there others?').

Room Rates

You can bag a mattress on a roof terrace for as little as €7 per night or splurge on the Presidential Suite at the Four Seasons Hotel for €3000. Most of us will opt for something between the two.

A double room in an Ottoman Boutique hotel in Sultanahmet will cost from €45 to €280; you'll pay a bit more to sleep on the other side of the Galata Bridge and lots more to luxuriate on the Bosphorus.

All prices in this book have been cited in euros, are high season prices and include the 18% KDV (value-added tax). During the low season (October–April, but not the Christmas period) you should be able to negotiate a discount of at least 20% on the room price. Be warned that during the Formula 1 Grand Prix (May) prices often skyrocket.

If booking direct, ask if the hotel will give you a discount for a cash payment (this will usually be 10%), whether a pick-up from the airport is included (it often is if you stay more than three nights) and whether discounts are offered for extended stays. Many of the luxury hotels offer special packages; ask when you make reservations.

We recommend that you refrain from booking accommodation at the airport hotel booking desks, as you'll inevitably pay a premium. If you arrive at the airport and have no accommodation booked, the Tourist Information Office (24 hr) is usually happy to let you use its phone to call one of the hotels reviewed in this chapter and see if a room is available.

SULTANAHMET

The Sultan Ahmet Camii, more commonly known as the Blue Mosque, gives its name to the quarter surrounding it. This is the heart of Old İstanbul and the city's premier sightseeing area, so the hotels here, and in the adjoining neighbourhoods to the east (Cankurtaran), west (Küçük Aya Sofya) and north (Binbirdirek), are supremely convenient. The area's only drawbacks are the number of carpet touts around and the lack of decent places to eat and drink.

Akbıyık Caddesi in Cankurtaran is the backpacker hub, home to thumping bars and

PRICE GUIDE

For a double room:

€€€	over €300 per night
€€	€51 to €300 per night
€	under €50 per night

drunken carousing by night and street cafés by day. Other streets in the area are low key. Küçük Aya Sofya is a charming, old-fashioned and quiet area, just downhill from the south-western end of the Hippodrome; while just uphill and to the west, Binbirdirek is a quiet residential district named after the Byzantine cistern of that name.

Every imaginable hotel type can be found around this neighbourhood: the city's best luxury hotel (the Four Seasons); innumerable boutique Ottoman hotels decorated in a pleasing style that we've dubbed 'Cankurtaran Modern'; comfortable but relatively characterless midrange options; and a host of budget choices, including most of the city's hostels. Almost every place has a roof terrace with views of the Blue Mosque, Aya Sofya and/or the Sea of Marmara.

FOUR SEASONS HOTEL ISTANBUL
Map p50   Luxury Hotel €€€
☎ 212-638 8200; www.fshr.com; Tevkifhane Sokak 1, Cankurtaran; s €330-510, d €360-530; ☒ ☒ ☐ ☖ ; ☒ Sultanahmet

This used to be the infamous Sultanahmet prison (remember *Midnight Express*?), and boy oh boy, we couldn't imagine anything better than being forced to do some serious time here these days. A regular entry in 'Best Hotel in the World' lists, this place oozes quality and comfort. Rooms are country club-elegant, with king-sized beds, enormous marble bathrooms and antique-style work desks. Location is ideal – the hotel is literally in the shadow of the Blue Mosque and Aya Sofya – but the fact that an extension is currently being built at the rear of the hotel site (on top of an important archaeological site – how on earth was that approved?!) means that building noise could be a slight problem until 2010. Breakfast costs an extra €30.

YEŞİL EV Map p50   Ottoman Boutique Hotel €€
☎ 212-517 6785; www.istanbulyesilev.com; Kabasakal Caddesi 5, Cankurtaran; s €160, d €220-280; ☒ ☐ ; ☒ Sultanahmet

This place has either a proud history or a lot to answer for – it depends on your point of view. The model for hundreds of Ottoman boutique hotels across Turkey, it has been one of the city's most famous places to sleep since it opened in 1984. Brass beds and chintz furnishings feature, as do cramped bathrooms. Despite adoring

its idyllic rear courtyard, overall we prefer the slightly cheaper Ayasofya Konakları (p204), which was restored and is run by the same organisation.

HOTEL ARMADA Map p50   Hotel €€
☎ 212-455 4455; www.armadahotel.com.tr; Ahırkapı Sokak 24, Cankurtaran; r standard/superior €295/354; ☒ ☒ ☐ ☖ ; ☒ Sultanahmet

Fresh flowers and a pond full of tortoises greet guests when they check in to this comfortable hotel. Rooms feature pale green furnishings and are very well equipped; superior ones come with a sea view. Though the location – very near the Cankurtaran suburban train station and a few steps from the Bosphorus shore – isn't great, it's only a 10-minute walk uphill to Sultanahmet. The hotel's major selling point is the Teras Restaurant (p158), with its wonderful view and very pleasant surrounds. Check the website for special offers, as room rates can vary wildly.

İBRAHİM PAŞA OTELİ
Map p50   Ottoman Boutique Hotel €€
☎ 212-518 0394; www.ibrahimpasha.com; Terzihane Sokak 5, Binbirdirek; s/d €135/190; ☒ ☒ ☐ ; ☒ Sultanahmet

The owners of this small designer hotel just off the Hippodrome have managed to straddle the divide between sleek modernist and antique Ottoman with great success. Parquet floors, crisp white linen, marble bathrooms and gold mirrors make the smallish, well-equipped rooms distinctive, and the building's common areas ooze class. After enjoying the excellent breakfast, served in a downstairs kitchen with stainless-steel bench and olive-green walls, guests often have to be encouraged to leave the building – the alternative option of sinking into one of the foyer lounge's leather couches and enjoying a quiet read is just too tempting. It's worth paying for one of the four deluxe rooms, as the 12 standard ones are verging on being too expensive for what they offer.

DERSAADET OTELİ
Map p50   Ottoman Boutique Hotel €€
☎ 212-458 0760; www.dersaadethotel.com; Kapıağası Sokak 5, Küçük Aya Sofya; r €105-110; ☒ ☒ ; ☒ Sultanahmet

Roughly translated, the name of this hotel means 'The Place of Happiness' in Turkish, and we're confident that guests will be more than happy with this comfortable mid-sized hotel. In a painstakingly restored Ottoman wooden house, the interior features exquisitely painted ceilings and custom-designed wooden furniture throughout. Rooms, which have four-star amenities, are extremely comfortable, sporting a gold and russet-red colour scheme that gives a sense of luxury. Those with sea views cost a little bit extra. There's a lift, a roof terrace with Sea of Marmara and Blue Mosque views, and a charming breakfast café. Best of all, levels of service are extremely high.

SARI KONAK OTELİ
Map p50   Ottoman Boutique Hotel €€

☎ 212-638 6258; www.istanbulhotelsarikonak .com; Mimar Mehmet Ağa Caddesi 42-46, Cankurtaran; r standard/deluxe €89/129, ste €149-219; ✗ ⊠ 🖳 ; 🚇 Sultanahmet

The type of place that could fit just as easily in Washington as in this city of sultans, the Sarı Konak is a truly classy joint. The spacious deluxe rooms are beautifully decorated with soothing colour schemes, top-notch linens and attractive prints, embroideries and etchings on the walls; try and snaffle number 303, which is pretty as a picture. The standard rooms are considerably smaller, but are just as attractive, and the suites are total knockouts – perfect for families. Guests enjoy relaxing on the roof terrace with its Sea of Marmara and Blue Mosque views, but seem to be equally partial to hanging out in the downstairs lounge and courtyard.

HOTEL EMPRESS ZOE
Map p50   Ottoman Boutique Hotel €€

☎ 212-518 2504; www.emzoe.com; Adliye Sokak 10, Cankurtaran; s €85, d €100-135; ✗ ⊠ 🖳 ; 🚇 Sultanahmet

Named after the feisty Byzantine Empress whose portrait adorns the gallery at Aya Sofya, this fabulous place is owned and managed by American Ann Nevens and her sister Cristina, who really know their stuff when it comes to running a hotel. The prototype for 'Cankurtaran Modern', the now almost ubiquitous decorative style utilised in myriad Sultanahmet boutique hotels, the Empress Zoe is unusual in that it is constantly being changed and improved – hence the recent opening of the stylish

Maison Zoe and Villa Zoe garden suites (€225 to €250). These join the Chez Zoe garden suites (€150 to €200) in overlooking a gorgeous flower-filled garden where breakfast is served. Equally fabulous is Room 42, which has a private terrace and views over the Sea of Marmara (€135). All rooms are individually and charmingly decorated, and although some rooms in the main building are tiny, these are available at discounted rates (s/d €60/70). The rooftop lounge-terrace has excellent views.

HOTEL TURKOMAN
Map p50   Ottoman Boutique Hotel €€

☎ 212-516 2956; www.turkomanhotel.com; Asmalı Çeşme Sokak 2, Binbirdirek; s €79, d €99-139; ⊠ 🖳 ; 🚇 Sultanahmet

You'll feel as if you've booked into a private club when you walk into the Turkoman. In a fantastic position up the hill a few steps off the Hippodrome, this renovated 19th-century building features rooms that are simply but tastefully decorated with kilims, reproduction antique furniture and brass beds. Ask for room 4A, which has a balcony and Blue Mosque view. The roof terrace has good views.

TRIA HOTEL İSTANBUL
Map p50   Ottoman Boutique Hotel €€

☎ 212-518 4518; www.triahotelistanbul.com; Turbıyık Sokak 7, Cankurtaran; standard s/d €75/95, deluxe s/d €100/120; ✗ ⊠ 🖳 ; 🚇 Sultanahmet

The old adage that handsome is as handsome does certainly applies to the Tria. This totally terrific hotel opened in 2007 and has already built a formidable reputation for its service and style. Extremely comfortable rooms offer tea-and-coffee making equipment, satellite TV, work desk and large bed; all are attractively decorated with polished floorboards, silk curtains, embroidered bedspreads and objets d'art. There's a comfortable lounge on the ground floor and a wonderful roof terrace furnished with cane armchairs and huge umbrellas – a perfect spot to view the Sea of Marmara, Aya Sofya and the Blue Mosque.

HOTEL DAPHNE
Map p50   Hotel €€

☎ 212-638 7060; www.hoteldaphne.com; Su Terazisi Sokak 10, Binbirdirek; standard s/d €75/95, deluxe s/d €100/120; ✗ ⊠ 🖳 ; 🚇 Sultanahmet

A hop, skip and jump away from the Hippodrome and close to the Grand Bazaar (p76), this small hotel is particularly notable for its lovely roof terrace, which has great Sea of Marmara views. Rooms have a pretty décor in shades of burnished orange and emerald green – ask for one with a sea view. Bathrooms are large (with baths), which is a definite plus, but some of the air-con units can be noisy – ask to check this out before you unpack.

HOTEL ARARAT

Map p50   Ottoman Boutique Hotel €€

☎ 212-516 0411; www.ararathotel.com; Torun Sokak 3, Cankurtaran; r €75-95, ste €110; ✗ ⊠ 💻 ; 🚇 Sultanahmet

Another hotel decorated by Nikos Papadakis, who did such an inspired job with the initial rooms at the Empress Zoe (opposite), the Ararat is tiny, but its charming host Haydar Sarigul and cosy rooftop terrace-bar in the shadow of the Blue Mosque make it a popular choice. Dark wooden floors, textile bedspreads and clever space-enhancing mirrors are the decorative hallmarks; quality linen and homemade *börek* (savoury pastry) for breakfast are quality touches. It's not worth paying the extra euros for a view, particularly as the two terrace rooms are the smallest in the hotel.

HOTEL NOMADE Map p50   Boutique Hotel €€

☎ 212-513 8172; www.hotelnomade.com; Ticarethane Sokak 15, Alemdar; s/d €70/85; ✗ ⊠ ; 🚇 Sultanahmet

Mega style and budget pricing don't often go together, but the Nomade bucks the trend. A few years ago the owners brought in French designer Dan Beranger to give the place a total overhaul and all we can say is 'ooh la la'. Just a few steps off busy Divan Yolu, the hotel's 16 small rooms and three suites are très, très chic, with great bathrooms, stylish bedlinen and satellite TV. With one of the best roof-terrace bars in town (smack-bang in front of Aya Sofya) and a Philippe Stark feel, this place is about as hip as Sultanahmet gets.

HOTEL UYAN İSTANBUL

Map p50   Ottoman Boutique Hotel €€

☎ 212-518 9255; www.uyanhotel.com; Utangaç Sokak 25, Cankurtaran; s €50, d standard/deluxe €99/130; ✗ ⊠ 💻 ; 🚇 Sultanahmet

The Uyan is in a close race with the Tria Hotel (opposite), Tan Otel (p204) and Ottoman Hotel Imperial (p204) for the title of best new

midrange addition to the Old City's sleeping scene. Like its competitors, it offers comfortable and attractive rooms with a good range of amenities and high levels of service. The extremely elegant décor nods towards the Ottoman style, but never goes over the top – everyone will feel comfortable here. The view from the spacious roof terrace is one of the best in the area.

ARTEFES HOTEL

Map p50   Ottoman Boutique Hotel €€

☎ 212-516 5863; www.artefes.com; Çayıroğlu Sokak 25, Küçük Aya Sofya; s €50-60, d €70-80; ✗ ⊠ 💻 ; 🚇 Sultanahmet

A large wooden house adorned with flower-filled window boxes, the Artefes is almost a prototype of a safe midrange accommodation choice. It offers clean, sun-drenched rooms featuring amenities such as satellite TV and hairdryer. The foyer and roof terrace are impressive and the location is blissfully quiet.

HOTEL ŞEBNEM

Map p50   Ottoman Boutique Hotel €€

☎ 212-517 6623; www.sebnemhotel.net; Adliye Sokak 1, Cankurtaran; s €50, d €65-75; ⊠ 💻 ; 🚇 Sultanahmet

Simplicity is the rule at the Şebnem, and it works a treat. Run by a wonderfully friendly young team, its rooms have rose-pink walls, wooden floors and extremely comfortable canopy beds. Stylish linen and framed Ottoman prints provide a touch of class. The large terrace upstairs has views over the Sea of Marmara (as do the more expensive double rooms), and the downstairs rooms, though a tad dark, have a private courtyard garden. All of this, plus one of the best breakfast spreads in Sultanahmet, mean that this place is hard to beat.

HOTEL POEM

Map p50   Ottoman Boutique Hotel €€

☎ 212-638 9744; www.hotelpoem.com; Terbıyık Sokak 12; s/d €45/70; ✗ ⊠ 💻 ; 🚇 Sultanahmet

Many guests end up waxing lyrical about their stays in this cute hotel. Rooms are named after poems by well-known Turkish poets, and the tranquil rear garden is a perfect spot to linger over an anthology and a glass of tea. Book into the 'All of a Sudden' room (€130) and you'll be able to sit on a private balcony looking towards the Princes' Islands; score 'Listening to Istanbul' (€130) and you'll appreciate its large windows, sea views and king-sized bed. Other rooms are on the small side and lack style, but they're clean and have amenities such as satellite TV and hairdryer. There's also a terrace with good views.

HOTEL HALI Map p50 Hotel €€
☎ 212-516 2170; www.halihotel.com; Klodfarer Caddesi 20, Çemberlitaş; s/d €45/70; ✗ ✗ ; ⑨ Sultanahmet

All the rugs in Turkey couldn't hide this hotel's institutional feel. That said, it's worth considering due to its roof terrace, which has amazing views, its huge bathrooms and its quiet position. Third- and 4th-floor rooms have views of the Sea of Marmara and Aya Sofya.

HOTEL ALP GUESTHOUSE
Map p50 Ottoman Boutique Hotel €€
☎ 212-517 7067; www.alpguesthouse.com; Adliye Sokak 4, Cankurtaran; s/d/f €45/65/90; ✗ ✗ ; ⑨ Sultanahmet

The Alp lives up to its location in Sultanahmet's premier small-hotel enclave, offering a range of attractive and well-equipped rooms at reasonable prices. Rooms have four-poster beds with white linen and gold hangings, wooden floorboards scattered with rugs, and extras such as satellite TV and work desks. The spacious front rooms are the pick of the bunch (ask for 301 or 401) because though some rear rooms have sea views, they also look onto the minaret of a local mosque, meaning that early-morning noise can be a problem. The roof terrace is lovely, with great sea views and comfortable indoor and outdoor set-ups.

HOTEL SULTAN'S INN
Map p50 Ottoman Boutique Hotel €€
☎ 212-638 2562; www.sultansinn.com; Mustafa Paşa Sokak 50, Küçük Aya Sofya; s €35-70, d €50-100; ✗ ✗ ; ⑨ Sultanahmet

One of a growing number of good-value, reasonably stylish hotels in the Küçük Aya Sofya area, the Sultan's Inn is a safe if uninspired choice. The well-equipped rooms are pretty but small, and bathrooms could do with a lavish application of anti-mould agent. The roof terrace is home to flowerpots and plants galore; it's a lovely spot for breakfast. The owners also run

the nearby Naz Wooden House and Deniz Konak hotels; rooms at these are slightly more comfortable and attractive than those on offer here (they're also a tad more expensive), but neither of their roof terraces are as impressive.

HANEDAN HOTEL
Map p50 Ottoman Boutique Hotel €€
☎ 212-516 4869; www.hanedanhotel.com; Adliye Sokak 3, Cankurtaran; s/d/f €35/55/75; ✗ ✗ ; ⑨ Sultanahmet

Recent renovation works have endowed this small and very clean hotel with the ubiquitous 'Cankurtaran aesthetic', and it's very pleasant as a result. Pale lemon walls and polished wooden floors give the rooms a light and elegant feel, as do the white marble bathrooms (with hairdryer) and the firm beds covered with crisp white linen. The huge Byzantium Room with its Sea of Marmara views is perfect for families. A pleasant roof terrace overlooks the sea and Aya Sofya.

HOTEL PENINSULA
Map p50 Ottoman Boutique Hotel €
☎ 212-458 6850; www.hotelpeninsula.com; Adliye Sokak 6, Cankurtaran; s/d €35/45; ✗ ✗ ; ⑨ Sultanahmet

The management of this unassuming hotel could quite possibly be the friendliest we've ever encountered. And we're talking friendly in a good, non-pushy, we-really-like-meeting-people type of way, not the hi-I'm-your-new-best-friend-please-visit-my-carpet-shop type of way. There are 12 simple but comfortable rooms that are slated for renovation in the near future, as well as a lovely terrace with sea views and comfortable hammocks. We like the breakfast room with its traditional low stools and brass tables and we love the fact that the owner's mum makes cakes, jam and yogurt for everyone's breakfast. Great value.

SIDE HOTEL & PENSION
Map p50 Hotel & Apartments €
☎ 212-517 2282; www.sidehotel.com; Utangaç Sokak 20, Cankurtaran; hotel s/d €45/60, pension s/d without bathroom €25/35, pension s/d with bathroom €35/45, 4-person apt €80-95; ✗ ✗ 🖳 ; ⑨ Sultanahmet

A sprawling place that has built a reputation for providing cheap, clean and comfortable rooms, the Side has hotel rooms with TV and en suite; pension rooms with shared or private bathrooms; and fully equipped but dark apartments sleeping one to six people. The picks of the bunch are the front hotel rooms with private balcony overlooking the Blue Mosque and Aya Sofya. The rooftop garden-lounge has decent views and a welcoming atmosphere. Note that air-con costs an extra €10 per room per night.

ORIENT INTERNATIONAL HOSTEL
Map p50   Hostel €

☎ 212-518 0789; www.orienthostel.com; Akbıyık Caddesi 13, Cankurtaran; dm €10-13, s/d without bathroom €27/33, d with bathroom €42; ☒ ▣ ; ▣ Sultanahmet

The Orient should be considered if you don't care about creature comforts and are ready to party. There's a shower for every 12 guests and an array of dorms, some of which are light and relatively quiet, and others that are unpleasantly dark and have the most uncomfortable mattresses that we've ever encountered (and considering our job, that's really saying something). The cheapest option is a barracks-style 30-bed dorm. The rooftop terrace bar has fabulous views and is a good place to relax, unlike the noisy cafeteria and internet area. Private rooms are overpriced for what they offer.

MAVİ GUESTHOUSE Map p50   Hostel €
☎ 212-517 7287; www.maviguesthouse.com; Kutlugün Sokak 3, Sultanahmet; dm €10-11, s €20, d €24-30; ▣ ; ▣ Sultanahmet

Mavi's management is very friendly, which is just as well since some rooms at this tiny place are cramped and windowless, and all share bathrooms that could do with a thorough scrub. Mattresses on the rooftop cost €7 (including breakfast) but the best value is provided by front rooms, one of which has an Aya Sofya view. Breakfast is served downstairs or at streetside tables.

SULTAN HOSTEL Map p50   Hostel €
☎ 212-516 9260; www.sultanhostel.com; Akbıyık Sokak 21, Cankurtaran; dm €9-15, d without/with bathroom €30/36; ☒ ▣ ; ▣ Sultanahmet

Next door to – and clearly in hot competition with – the Orient, this place is currently undergoing a staged renovation. As a result, it offers accommodation that is far more comfortable than that provided by

its raffish neighbour. The freshly painted dorms have new bunk beds and good mattresses; linen is clean and crisp and towels are provided. Shared bathrooms are very clean and there are female-only dorms for those gals who want to steer clear of smelly socks. The pick of the rooms on offer is number 48, a double with lovely Sea of Marmara views and its own cubicle bathroom. Views from the terrace bar aren't as impressive as those at the Orient, but its set-up is much more relaxed and stylish. There's a 10% discount for HI cardholders.

BAHAUS GUESTHOUSE Map p50   Hostel €
☎ 212-638 6534; www.travelinistanbul.com; Kutlugün Sokak 3, Cankurtaran; dm €9-14, d without bathroom €34, d with shower €44; ☒ ▣ ; ▣ Sultanahmet

When it comes to hostels, word of mouth is the most reliable gauge of quality. And this place generates great word of mouth. Friendly and knowledgeable staff run a professional operation that's miles away from the institutional feel of some of its nearby and much larger competitors. Dorms have bunks with good mattresses and curtains to provide a skerrick of privacy; some have their own bathroom and all have ceiling fans. There's one shared bathroom for every seven beds and a constant supply of lukewarm water. Top marks go to the rooftop terrace, with its sea view, beanbags, cheap evening meals (YTL8), beers (YTL5) and nargilehs (YTL5).

BIG APPLE HOSTEL Map p50   Hostel €
☎ 212-517 7931; www.hostelbigapple.com; Bayram Fırını Sokak 12, Cankurtaran; dm €9-12; ▣ Sultanahmet

Though a newcomer to the competitive Cankurtaran hostel scene, we reckon this well-run place is likely to be a stayer. Dorms on the ground floor are a bit dingy, but those above are light, freshly painted and clean. There's a foyer with large-screen satellite TV and a rooftop bar with beanbags, lounges and good views where you can enjoy a nargileh (YTL6) and a cheap beer (YTL3).

TOPKAPI PALACE & AROUND

There aren't too many hotels in this area. Fortunately, the two below – one near Gülhane

Park and the other close to the Spice Bazaar – are both sound choices.

AYASOFYA KONAKLARI
Map p63   Ottoman Boutique Hotel €€
☎ 212-513 3660; www.ayasofyakonaklari.com; Soğukçeşme Sokak; s €85-100, d €110-130, ste €190; 🄗 🖳 ; 🚇 Gülhane
If you're keen to play out Ottoman fantasies, come here. A row of 19th-century wooden houses occupying an entire cobbled street abutting Topkapı Palace (Topkapı Sarayı; p62), Ayasofya Konakları is about as authentic as the Ottoman boutique hotel comes and it's picturesque to boot. Choose from a total of 52 rooms, all of which are charmingly decorated with brass beds, and enjoy the most glamorous breakfast in town, served in a glass conservatory complete with chandeliers.

KONUK EVİ Map p63   Ottoman Boutique Hotel €€
☎ 212-513 3660; www.ayasofyapensions.com; Soğukçeşme Sokak; s €85-100, d €110-130; 🄗 🖳 ; 🚇 Gülhane
Part of the Ayasofya Konakları (above), this annex set in a spectacular private garden overlooking the Caferağa Medresesi (p73) is even more impressive than its parent. Rooms are large and extremely elegant, with parquet floors, luxurious rugs and velvet-upholstered furniture. The building itself is a replica of a large Ottoman house that was on this site, so it has all the mod cons as well as more than its fair share of period charm. The foyer features gilt mirrors and a grand piano. An undeniably classy option.

KYBELE HOTEL
Map p63   Ottoman Boutique Hotel €€
☎ 212-511 7766; www.kybelehotel.com; Yerebatan Caddesi 35, Alemdar; s €70-80, d €90-120; 🄗 🖳 ; 🚇 Sultanahmet
The gilded exterior of this small hotel (peacock blue with loads of gold) reflects the décor inside, which features hundreds of coloured lights, wooden floors covered in rugs, and antique furniture and curios. Run by three brothers in a personable and professional style, it's got bucketloads of charm and lots of added extras, including a great café and bar, a charming rear garden patio and a library for guests. The location near Aya Sofya is central, and the rooms, which feature cute marble bathrooms, are smallish but comfortable. Try

and score room number 201, which is a corker.

OTTOMAN HOTEL IMPERIAL
Map p63   Ottoman Boutique Hotel €€
☎ 212-513 6150/1; www.ottomanhotelimperial.com; Caferiye Sokak 6/1; standard s/d €89/109, superior s/d €129/149; 🄧 🄗 🖳 ; 🚇 Gülhane
This recently opened four-star hotel is in a wonderful location just outside the walls of Topkapı Palace (Topkapı Sarayı; p62). Once the city's main youth hostel, the building has been extensively renovated and features large rooms decorated with Ottoman-style ceramics, textiles and *ebru* (traditional Turkish marbling). Comfort and amenity levels are high, and some rooms have Aya Sofya views (try and snaffle number 406). There's a lift, a lovely rear garden with restaurant and bar, and excellent levels of service.

TAN OTEL Map p63   Boutique Hotel €€
☎ 212-520 9130; www.tanhotel.com; Dr Emin Paşa Sokak 20, Alemdar; s/d/ste €80/99/139; 🄧 🄗 🖳 ; 🚇 Sultanahmet
Run by an enthusiastic brother-and-sister team, this newly opened hotel off Divan Yolu is a showcase of understated style and high-level service. Everything here is brand spanking new and generously sized – the beds in some rooms are so large we can only describe them as Sheikh-sized. Bathrooms are excellent (all have Jacuzzis) and are so clean they gleam. There's even a terrace bar sporting excellent views of the Blue Mosque, Aya Sofya and the Sea of Marmara.

WORLD PARK HOTEL Map p63   Hotel €€
☎ 212-527 6767; www.worldparkhotel.com; Hamidiye Caddesi 64, Eminönü; s/d/ste €199/229/369; 🄧 🄗 🖳 🄫 🄬 ; 🚇 Sirkeci
Occupying the architecturally significant 4 Vakif Han (p92), this recently opened five-star hotel conversion is a mass of contradictions. The 'Kulliye' rooms are massive and wonderfully full of light, whereas the 'Atrium' rooms are relatively small and dark – bizarrely, there's no difference in price. And the architects have done an absolutely wonderful job renovating the grand foyer, but have totally missed the opportunity to capitalise on what could have been a fabulous top-floor terrace, instead offering a bland and unwelcoming function room-cum-buffet restaurant

area. We like the pool, hamam and fitness centre in the basement, though, and find the location next to the Spice Bazaar (p82) excellent.

HOTEL ERBOY Map p63   Hotel €€
☎ 212-513 3750; www.erboyhotel.com; Ebussuut Caddesi 32, Sirkeci; s/d €54/64; ✂ ☒ ; 🚇 Sirkeci
The Vegas-style furniture and marble floors in its lobby are the Erboy's only attempts at glamour. The rest of the place is resolutely mom-and-pop style, with small rooms that are clean but without frills. On the plus side, the location, near Topkapı, is central and quiet, and the rooms are reasonably priced. There's a roof terrace with so-so views and a pleasant restaurant spilling into the cobbled street.

BAZAAR DISTRICT

This part of town is noisy and doesn't have the charm of the rest of Old İstanbul, but its close proximity to the Grand Bazaar will be drawcard enough for some visitors.

HOTEL NILES Map p78   Hotel €€
☎ 212-517 3239; www.hotelniles.com; Dibekli Cami Sokak 19, Beyazıt; s/d €55/65; ✂ ☒ ; 🚇 Beyazıt
Serious shoppers seduced by the prospect of bunking down close to the Grand Bazaar could do a lot worse than stay in this well-run and reasonably priced place. Rooms are characterless but extremely clean, and there's a pleasant rooftop terrace and restaurant.

HOTEL TÜRKUAZ
Map p78   Ottoman Boutique Hotel €€
☎ 212-518 1897; www.hotelturkuaz.com; Kadırga Cinci Meydanı 36, Kumkapı; s €35, d €40-45, ste €65-80; ☒ ; 🚇 Beyazıt
If you're the type of traveller who is happy to trade comfort for character, this eccentric place will be right up your alley. In a local neighbourhood near Küçük Aya Sofya (p57), it occupies an atmospheric 150-year-old timber mansion that once would have been the grandest place on the block but now is in urgent need of a facelift. The owners have plans to replace the antiquated bathrooms and hot-water system, sagging beds and patchy plasterwork in the near future, but are fortunately intent on retaining the crystal chandeliers, velvet curtains and ornate furniture.

GALATA & TOPHANE

In many ways, this is the best location in İstanbul. Halfway between the major sights of Old İstanbul and the main entertainment and eating strip of İstiklal Caddesi, it's rapidly building a reputation as the city's new bohemian centre, with art galleries, cafés, bars and funky boutiques starting to sprout.

ANEMON GALATA
Map p103   Ottoman Boutique Hotel €€
☎ 212-293 2343; www.anemonhotels.com; cnr Galata Meydani & Büyükhendek Caddesi, Karaköy; s/d € 120/140; ✂ ☒ ▯ ; 🚇 Karaköy
Small hotels don't come much better than this, particularly on this side of town. Located on the attractive new square that's been built around Galata Tower, this wooden building dates from 1842 but has been almost completely rebuilt inside. Individually decorated rooms are extremely elegant, featuring ornate painted ceilings, king-sized beds and antique-style desks. Large bathrooms have baths and marble basins. Frankly, we're not sure which of the hotel's features is the best. Is it the classically beautiful foyer with its chandeliers, marble floors and luxurious rugs? Or the stylish modern bar-restaurant sheathed in glass that's been built on the rooftop? Ask for a room with a view.

GALATA RESIDENCE CAMONDO APARTMENT HOTEL
Map p103   Apartments €€
☎ 212-292 4841; www.galataresidence.com; Hacı Ali Sokak, Karaköy; 1-/2-bed apartments €80/120; ☒ ; 🚇 Karaköy
Buried in the maze of narrow streets down from the Galata Tower, this historic building was built in the late 19th century to house indigent Jewish families. It's now an apartment-hotel with a Greek restaurant on the top floor and a modern annex (for the one-bedroom apartments) next door. Perfectly situated between İstiklal Caddesi and Eminönü (to find it, ask taxi drivers to drop you in front of the Yaşar Bank at the corner of Voyvova Caddesi and Haraçci Ali Sokak and walk up the steep stairs – the hotel is right at the top), the fully-equipped apartments are run down but comfortable, with large rooms and a reasonable amount of light. Top marks go to the daily servicing and the helpful staff. To avoid listening to

renditions of *Zorba the Greek* late into the night, avoid the top-floor rooms. Monthly rates are available.

EKLEKTİK GUEST HOUSE
Map p103   Ottoman Boutique Hotel €€

☎ 212-243 7446; www.eklektikgalata.com; Kadrıbey Cıkmazi 4, Galata; r €95-115; ✷ ▯ ; ▣ Karaköy

Advertising itself as offering 'the first and only gay accommodation in Istanbul', this gay-owned-and-managed place offers seven individually decorated rooms with TV. You can enact fantasies in the Pasha Room, chill out after a big night in the Zen Room or just feel funky in the Retro Room. There's a roof terrace for bronzing that buffed bod. It's hard to find – look for the bright pink building (geddit?) in a cul de sac.

İSTANBUL HOLIDAY APARTMENTS
     Apartments €€

☎ 212-251 8530; www.istanbulholidayapartments.com; per night €90-210; ✷ ; ▣ Karaköy

Saying that holiday apartments in İstanbul are easy to find is like saying the sultans were celibate – it just ain't true. So we can say with absolute certainty that the ever-expanding portfolio of apartments run by American Ann Taboroff Uysel is as unique as it is welcome. Now in locations as diverse as Galata, Cihangir, Taksim, Şişli and Beşiktaş, these handsome apartments in residential blocks are perfect for city sojourns of three days or more. Our favourites are the penthouse terrace and top-floor view apartments in the Glorya building near the Galata Tower, but all are impressive, having undergone quality renovations and being fitted out with washer/drier, good kitchens, CD players and satellite TVs; some have aircon and/or dishwashers and some have knock-em-dead views over the Golden Horn and Bosphorus. There's weekly maid service.

WORLD HOUSE HOSTEL Map p103   Hostel €
☎ 212-293 5520; www.worldhouseistanbul.com; Galipdede Caddesi 85, Tünel; dm €10-14, s/d €35/40; ▯ ✷ ; ▣ Karaköy

We like this place. Hostels in İstanbul are usually impersonal hulks with jungle-like atmospheres, but World House is small, friendly and calm. Best of all is the fact that it's located close to Beyoğlu's restaurant, bar and club scene, but not *too*

close – meaning that it's possible to grab a decent night's kip here. The enthusiastic young owners have set up a cheerful café on the ground floor and have plans to build both a terrace on the roof and a second hostel nearby. The small dorms are clean and light, and bathrooms are in plentiful supply. Avoid the private rooms – they're far too expensive for what they offer.

İSTİKLAL & AROUND

If you're in town to party at the nightclubs, take advantage of the city's great restaurant and bar scene or do business, this is a good choice of location. Hotels here are more expensive and generally less impressive than their Sultanahmet alternatives, though.

MARMARA İSTANBUL
Map p107   Luxury Hotel €€€

☎ 212-251 4696; www.themarmarahotels.com; Taksim Square; s €350-400, d €400-480, ste €650-950; ✷ ✷ ▯ ▤ ; ▣ Kabataş, then funicular to Taksim

Right beside busy Taksim Square, the Marmara is an İstanbul institution, having opened to great acclaim in 1976. Its splendid views (10th floor and up) and extremely comfortable rooms make it a good choice for tourists and business people alike. Rooms are large with a classy décor enlivened with royal-blue and gold Ottoman touches. There is a rooftop restaurant and bar, as well as a gym and hamam. Breakfast costs an extra €24.

MARMARA PERA
Map p107   Luxury Hotel €€

☎ 212-251 4646; www.themarmarahotels.com; Meşrutiyet Caddesi 1, Tepebaşı; s €225-260, d €250-285; ✷ ✷ ▯ ▤ ▤ ; ▣ Karaköy, then funicular to Tünel

This funky little sister of the landmark hotel in Taksim Square opened in 2004 and has been a popular choice with glam globetrotters ever since. Rooms are small-ish but extremely well appointed, featuring quality touches such as a magazine selection, pillow menu and stylish white linen. Standout amenities include one of the best restaurants in the city, Mikla (p165), a rooftop pool bar with spectacular views, and a 24-hour fitness centre. It's worth paying extra for a room on a higher floor with sea view.

Note that the hotel website usually has much cheaper deals on offer than the rack rates cited above.

LUSH HIP HOTEL Map p107 Boutique Hotel €€
☎ 212-243 9595; www.lushhiphotel.com; Sıraselviler Sokak 12, Taksim; s €182-244, d €214-278; ✕ ✕ 🖥 ; 🚋 Kabataş, then funicular to Taksim
One of a fast-sprouting crop of boutique hotels around town, this self-consciously hip place has 22 attractive rooms of varying sizes, all of which are individually decorated and presented with nice touches such as L'Occitane toiletries and CD players. There's a strong emphasis on service here – if you want a personal shopper or a limousine, you'll have no trouble getting them – and management claims that its staff possess 'a mastery of speedy problem solving'. Gosh. It's on a busy street near Taksim Square, so front rooms could be a tad noisy.

TAKSİM SQUARE HOTEL Map p107 Hotel €€
☎ 212-292 6440; www.taksimsquarehotel.com.tr; Sıraselviler Caddesi 15, Taksim; s/d €120/130; ✕ ✕ ; 🚋 Kabataş, then funicular to Taksim
This glass-fronted building matches the ugly Taksim surrounds, but inside you'll be pleasantly surprised by the large rooms, which feature a stylish autumn-leaf décor. Most rooms have views (Square or Bosphorus); corner rooms from the fourth floor up have views of both sides at a nice price, so request one of these. The top-floor breakfast salon is a great place to prepare for the day. In all, a bargain four-star choice.

RICHMOND HOTEL Map p107 Hotel €€
☎ 212-252 5460; www.richmondhotels.com.tr; İstiklal Caddesi 445; r €89-119, ste €199; ✕ ✕ 🖥 ; 🚋 Karaköy, then funicular to Tünel
Next to the palatial Russian consulate, the Richmond has a fabulous location right on the city's major boulevard. Behind its 19th-century facade, the place is modern, quite comfortable and well run. Standard rooms are comfortable if characterless, but the suites are knock outs, with modernist décor, excellent views, great workstations, Jacuzzis and plasma TVs. Best of all is the fact that one of the best bars in the city, Leb-i Derya Richmond (p176) is on the top floor, meaning that your bed will only be a short stagger away. A mainly business clientele keeps the place busy so book ahead.

TRIADA RESIDENCE Map p107 Apartments €€
☎ 212-251 0101; www.triadaresidence.com; Meşelik Sokak 10, Taksim; r €60-80; ✕ ; 🚋 Kabataş, then funicular to Taksim
Attracted by the idea of sitting in your own apartment and enjoying a meal and a bottle of wine before kicking off to a nearby club? You can do this at the Triada. These well-appointed apartments, which sleep up to three, are located in a side street off İstiklal Caddesi and are perfect for those who want to self-cater. All have small, clean kitchens and bathrooms, as well as a bedroom and sitting area with satellite TV. The best of the bunch is apartment 601, which has a huge terrace complete with BBQ, outdoor furniture and a view of Taksim Square.

HOTEL RESIDENCE Map p107 Hotel €€
☎ 212-252 7685; www.hotelresidence.com.tr; Sadri Alışık Sokak 19, off İstiklal Caddesi; s/d €44/55; ✕ ; 🚋 Kabataş, then funicular to Taksim
This place is opposite a large police station, so guests will feel extremely safe when returning from a heavy night of partying at the nearby nightclubs. It's very old-fashioned and not at all stylish, but at these prices, who's complaining? Rooms are light and have a small bathroom; most have twin beds.

BÜYÜK LONDRA OTELİ
Map p107 Historic Hotel €€
☎ 212-245 0670; www.londrahotel.net; Meşrutiyet Caddesi 117, Tepebaşı; unrenovated s €35-100, d €50-115, renovated s €75-120, d €85-130; ✕ ; 🚋 Karaköy, then funicular to Tünel
The Büyük's 'gothic house of horrors' feel may not be for everyone. Dating from the same era as the nearby Pera Palas Oteli (p110), it is looking decidedly worse for wear these days. The good news is that its run-down rooms are slowly being renovated – we'd suggest making a booking only if you are guaranteed one of these. The remaining rooms are musty and very scuffed around the edges, with tiny bathrooms and no aircon. Fortunately, you can always escape them and park yourself at a table in the wonderfully atmospheric foyer bar (p175).

VARDAR PALACE HOTEL Map p107 Hotel €€
☎ 212-252 2888; www.vardarhotel.com; Sıraselviler Caddesi 54, Taksim; s €44-64, d €78-90; ✕ ; 🚋 Kabataş, then funicular to Taksim
This old-fashioned small hotel just off Taksim Square offers excellent value for money and

so is well worth considering. Rooms at the rear are darkish and quiet, front rooms are light but face onto a noisy nightclub strip – all are very clean and come with cable TV. There's a roof terrace with great views.

YENİŞEHİR PALAS Map p107 Hotel €€
☎ 212-252 7160; www.yenisehirpalas.com; Oteller Sokak 1-3, Tepebaşı; standard s/d €39/52, renovated s €64-74, d €85-98, deluxe s €74-83, d €95-110; ✗ ✗ 🖳 ♿ ; 🚊 Karaköy, then funicular to Tünel

You could do a lot worse than book into one of the deluxe or renovated rooms here, which are clean, comfortable and well priced. The exterior is unprepossessing, but the interior can hold its own with most of the city's business hotels. There's an English-style pub downstairs that's often crowded with Russian guests.

TAKSİM, HARBİYE & NİŞANTAŞI

Take the metro to Osmanbey, one stop from Taksim Square (or walk 30 minutes), and you'll find the upmarket shopping districts of Harbiye and Nişantaşı, home to some of the city's best luxury hotels.

BENTLEY HOTEL Map p115 Luxury Hotel €€€
☎ 212-291 7730; www.bentley-hotel.com; Halaskargazi Caddesi 75, Harbiye; s €200, d €240-280, ste €400-800; ✗ ✗ 🖳 ; 🚊 Kabataş, then funicular to Taksim

The Bentley features luxurious rooms that look as if they're straight from the pages of *Wallpaper* magazine, sleek suites for those in the mood to splurge and enough staff to cater to your every whim. If you over-indulge in the classy foyer bar, don't worry – the health club and sauna will help you recover.

SOFA HOTEL Map p115 Luxury Hotel €€€
☎ 212-368 1818; www.thesofahotel.com; Teşvikiye Caddesi 123, Nişantaşı; s/d €280/300, ste €390-1000; ✗ ✗ 🖳 ; 🚊 Kabataş, then funicular to Taksim, then metro to Osmanbey

The chichi Sofa Hotel has got the lot: huge rooms, pillow menus, complimentary ironing service, personalised letterhead, rain showers, a spa (with dipping pool) and a fitness room. Once coaxed out of your room, you'll be able to dine in the well-

regarded TuuS restaurant, which serves artfully presented and ruinously expensive 'New Mediterranean' cuisine.

DIVAN TAKSIM SUITES Map p115 Hotel €€
☎ 212-254 7777; www.divan.com.tr; Cumhuriyet Caddesi 49, Taksim; r €250-275; ✗ 🖳 ; 🚊 Kabataş, then funicular to Taksim

The Divan Taksim Suites is a showcase for the Ikea aesthetic. The 14 hotel suites, all with well-equipped kitchens, feature light wooden floors and white furniture: very minimal and about as far away from 'Cankurtaran Modern' as you can get. Front suites on the 4th to 7th floors have Bosphorus views, but overlook manic Cumhuriyet Caddesi and so are very noisy – consider requesting one at the rear. All feature sitting areas, work desks and large beds. There's a downstairs breakfast room, a small gym on the roof and daily maid service.

CENTRAL PALACE Map p115 Luxury Hotel €€
☎ 212-313 4040; www.thecentralpalace.com; Lamartin Caddesi 18, Taksim; s/d €190/230; ✗ ✗ 🖳 ; 🚊 Kabataş, then funicular to Taksim

This boutique hotel has been designed around a 'wellness' concept. Parquet floors feature instead of asthma-inducing carpets, therapeutic fruit juices for every possible complaint are available at the flick of a room-service switch, the restaurant food is all organic, and massage showers and Jacuzzis are installed in every bathroom. Ten rooms even have their own exercise bike. We feel healthy even *thinking* about checking in. The joy is that the place is not at all hippy-dippy: appointments are luxurious, all fabrics are from Vakko (İstanbul's poshest store) and the décor is opulent, with oodles of gilt and marble. The only things missing are views and alcohol service.

RIVA HOTEL Map p115 Hotel €€
☎ 212-256 4420; www.rivahotel.com.tr; Aydede Caddesi 8, Taksim; s/d €120/150; ✗ ; 🚊 Kabataş, then funicular to Taksim

One of a host of similar places around Taksim, the Riva has long been a safe albeit unsexy choice. The rooms are clean, light and roomy, with comfortable beds and a tiny bathroom. There's a bar downstairs and a welcoming breakfast room on the mezzanine. Look out for the regular promotional rates, which are half the rack rate above, that feature on its website.

BOSPHORUS NIGHTS

If you're in Istanbul to relax rather than indulge in an orgy of sightseeing, you should consider staying in one of a grow-ing number of glam boutique hotels in the Bosphorus suburbs. Most of these are housed in painstakingly restored *yalıs* (traditional wooden houses), have incredibly chic fitouts and offer excellent restaurants. They're a long way from the sights of Sultanahmet and the entertainment district of Beyoğlu, but are perfect places for a romantic retreat. We can't in good faith recommend the glitzy and ludicrously overpriced Hotel Les Ottomans (Map p215; ☎ 212-359 1500; www.lesottomans.com; Muallim Nacı Caddesi 68, Kuruçeşme; ✕ ✕ 🖳 🖈 ; 🚍 25E, 25T, 40), which offers rooms priced between €950 and €4130, but we've no hesitation at all in recommending two places on the Asian shore of the Bosphorus: the gorgeous Sumahan on the Water (Map p215; ☎ 216-422 8008; www.sumahan.com, Kuleli Caddesi 51, Çengelköy; r €280, ste €330-490; ✕ ✕ 🖳 🖈 ; 🚊 Kandilli) and Ajia (Map p215; ☎ 216-413 9300; www .ajiahotel.com; Çubuklu Caddesi 27, Kanlıca; r €255-555, ste €655-855; ✕ ✕ 🖳 🖈 ; 🚊 Kanlıca).

BEŞİKTAŞ & ORTAKÖY

If you have cash to spare and don't mind being away from the centres of Sultanahmet and Taksim Square, the suburbs along the Bospho-rus could be just what you're looking for. One thing is sure: the views and hotel restaurants in this golden strip are damn fine. During research, the new Four Seasons Hotel Istanbul at the Bosphorus (www.fourseasons.com) on Çırağan Cad-desi in Beşiktaş was approaching completion. Right on the water, its 166 rooms, pools and spa will no doubt be extremely impressive.

ÇIRAĞAN PALACE HOTEL KEMPINSKI

Map p117   Luxury Hotel €€€

☎ 212-326 4646; www.ciragan-palace.com; Çırağan Caddesi 32, Beşiktaş; r €306-810, ste €810-10,260; ✕ ✕ 🖳 🖳 ; 🚍 Yıldız

Housed in a palace constructed by Sultan Abdülaziz and rebuilt as a hotel in the 1980s, most of the guest rooms in this five-star place are in a modern annexe next door. The recently renovated wedding cake–style palace holds meeting rooms, posh 'palace suites', a ballroom and restau-rants. The best things about the place are its location right on the Bosphorus and its amazing infinity pool. If you've got deep pockets, opt for a sea-facing room with balcony – they're much nicer than the park-view alternatives. We're sure that Abdülaziz would have approved of the hotel boat, which ferries guests from Ataköy near the airport across the water to the hotel's pri-vate landing place, but we doubt he would have got his head around the concept of the hotel's wellness spa and hamam.

EXCURSIONS

EXCURSIONS

If you can bear to tear yourself away from the manifold delights of the city, there are a number of alluring options for day and overnight excursions, including the ubiquitous (but no less fabulous) ferry trip along the Bosphorus; a ferry trip to the summer playground of the Princes' Islands; or an overnight trip to the Dardanelles to discover the historically significant sites of Gallipoli and Troy.

A DAY ON THE BOSPHORUS

A trip along the Bosphorus offers treats galore. See how many times you can make your way to Asia from Europe and back! Highlights include Beylerbeyi Palace (p215), Rumeli Hisarı (p217), the Sakıp Sabancı Müzesi (p218) and Hıdiv Kasrı (p218) and the Sadberk Hanım Müzesi (p218).

We suggest two itineraries to make the most out of your day on the water.

Catch the 10.35am Bosphorus excursions ferry to Anadolu Kavağı (p219). After admiring the view from the ruined castle on the hill, take the No 15A bus down to Kanlıca (p216). Wander around the main square and walk up to Hıdiv Kasrı, where you can admire the fabulous Art Deco building and the gorgeous gardens. You can either have lunch here or choose to walk down to the waterfront and dine in style at Körfez (p219), before taking the 2.50pm ferry to Bebek (p216). Alternatively, take the 1.20pm ferry to Bebek after visiting Hıdiv Kasrı and have lunch at the glamorous Poseidon, Mangerie, or Il Porto (see p220). After lunch, catch a bus or taxi to Rumeli Hisarı (p217). After clamouring over the ramparts, take a bus from outside the nearby restaurants back to town, perhaps stopping at Ortaköy for an early dinner (p169).

Another possibility is to take the 10.35am ferry as far as Sarıyer, wander around the town and visit the Sadberk Hanım Müzesi (p219). After this, catch the No 25E, 40 or 40B bus outside the museum to Emirgan (p218), where you can visit the Sakıp Sabancı Müzesi (p218) and have lunch at the fabulous Müzedechanga (p220). Next, catch a bus towards Taksim, stopping along the way first at Rumeli Hisarı (p217) to see the castle and then at the Çırağan Palace Hotel Kempinski (p177) for a late-afternoon drink on the terrace.

ISLAND ESCAPE

There are few more idyllic escapes than jumping on a ferry and escaping to the tranquil Princes' Islands (p220). Most day-trippers stay on the ferry until Heybeliada, stop there for an hour or so and then hop on another ferry to Büyükada, where they catch a *fayton* (horse-drawn carriage) to the Monastery of St George (p222), have lunch at Yücetepe Kır Gazinosu (p223) and spend the rest of the afternoon admiring the island's many mansions and gardens while walking back to the ferry terminal.

BATTLEFIELDS

The sites of monumental battles over three millennia apart – Troy (p228) and Gallipoli (p225) – make a fascinating overnight trip. If you're keen to sign up for organised tours of both battlefields, you'll need to arrive in the small university town of Çanakkale the night before your day of touring and be ready to see Troy first thing in the morning; the Gallipoli tours start around noon and include lunch. Then you can bus back to İstanbul on the same night.

An alternative is to arrive from İstanbul in the late morning, visit Troy under your own steam that afternoon and then organise a private guide and car to take you to Gallipoli the next morning, before returning to İstanbul in the afternoon. Either way, you'll pack a lot into two days!

BOSPHORUS TOUR

Divan Yolu and İstiklal Caddesi are always awash with people, but neither is the major thoroughfare in İstanbul. That honour goes to the mighty Bosphorus Strait, which runs from the Sea of Marmara (Marmara Denizi) at the Galata Bridge (Galata Köprüsü) all the way to the Black Sea (Karadeniz), 32km north. Over the centuries the Bosphorus has been crossed by conquering armies, intrepid merchants and many an adventurous spirit. These days, thousands of İstanbullus commute daily along its length, fishing vessels try their luck in its waters and tourists ride its ferries from Eminönü to Anadolu Kavağı and back.

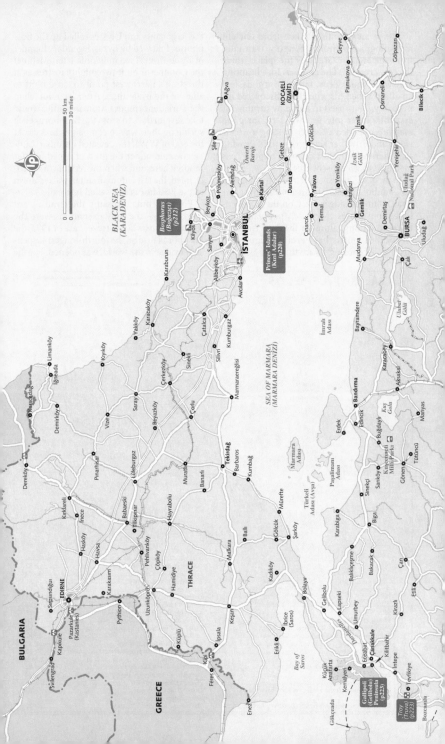

The strait's name is taken from ancient mythology. Bosphorus roughly translates from the ancient Greek as the 'place where the cow crossed'. The cow was Io, a beautiful lady with whom Zeus, king of the gods, had an affair. When his wife Hera discovered his infidelity, Zeus tried to atone by turning his erstwhile lover into a cow. Hera, for good measure, provided a horsefly to sting Io on the rump and drive her across the strait. Proving that there was no justice in Olympus, Zeus managed to get off scot-free.

In modern Turkish, the strait is the Boğaziçi or İstanbul Boğazı (from *boğaz,* throat or strait). On one side is Asia, on the other Europe. Both shores are densely populated and have attractions galore for the day visitor.

The Bosphorus has certainly figured in history. According to myth, both Jason of the Argonauts and Ulysses sailed up the Bosphorus, followed by Byzas, legendary founder of Byzantium. Two millennia later, Mehmet the Conqueror built two mighty fortresses at the strait's narrowest point to close it off to allies of the Byzantines. After İstanbul fell to the Turks, enormous Ottoman armies would take several days to cross the Bosphorus each spring on their way to campaigns in Asia. At the end of WWI, the defeated Ottoman capital cowered under the guns of Allied frigates moored here; and when the republic was proclaimed, the last Ottoman sultan walked down to the Bosphorus and sailed into exile.

For millennia, crossing the strait meant a boat trip – the only exceptions were the few occasions when it froze. Late in 1973, the Bosphorus Bridge, the fourth-longest suspension bridge in the world, was opened. For the

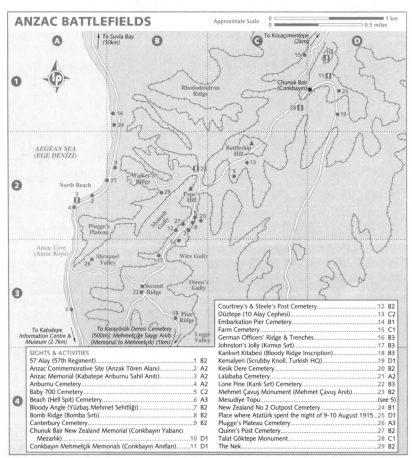

ANZAC BATTLEFIELDS

Approximate Scale — 0 — 1 km / 0.5 miles

SIGHTS & ACTIVITIES
57 Alay (57th Regiment)	1	B2
Anzac Commemorative Site (Anzak Tören Alanı)	2	A2
Anzac Memorial (Kabatepe Arıburnu Sahil Anıtı)	3	A2
Arıburnu Cemetery	4	A2
Baby 700 Cemetery	5	C2
Beach (Hell Spit) Cemetery	6	A3
Bloody Angle (Yüzbaş Mehmet Sehitliği)	7	B2
Bomb Ridge (Bomba Sırtı)	8	B2
Canterbury Cemetery	9	B2
Chunuk Bair New Zealand Memorial (Conkbayın Yabancı Mezarlık)	10	D1
Conkbayın Mehmetçik Memorials (Conkbayın Anıtları)	11	D1
Courtney's & Steele's Post Cemetery	12	B2
Düztepe (10 Alay Cephesi)	13	C2
Embarkation Pier Cemetery	14	B1
Farm Cemetery	15	C1
German Officers' Ridge & Trenches	16	B3
Johnston's Jolly (Kırmızı Sırt)	17	B3
Kanlısırt Kitabesi (Bloody Ridge Inscription)	18	B3
Kemalyeri (Scrubby Knoll, Turkish HQ)	19	D1
Kesik Dere Cemetery	20	B2
Lalababa Cemetery	21	A2
Lone Pine (Kanlı Sırt) Cemetery	22	B3
Mehmet Çavuş Monument (Mehmet Çavuş Anıtı)	23	B2
Mesudiye Topu	(see 5)	
New Zealand No 2 Outpost Cemetery	24	B1
Place where Atatürk spent the night of 9-10 August 1915	25	D1
Plugge's Plateau Cemetery	26	A3
Quinn's Post Cemetery	27	B2
Talat Göktepe Monument	28	C1
The Nek	29	B2

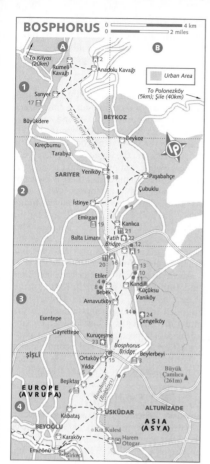

BOSPHORUS
0 |———| 4 km
0 |———| 2 miles

BOSPHORUS

SIGHTS & INFORMATION
Anadolu Hisarı..1 B3
Anadolu Kavağı Kalesi....................................2 A1
Beylerbeyi Sarayı...3 B4
Boğaziçi Üniversitesi.......................................4 A3
Çırağan Sarayı...5 A4
Dolmabahçe Palace..6 A4
Fethi Ahmet Paşa Yalı.....................................7 B4
Former Egyptian Consulate Building.................8 A3
Hıdiv Kasrı..9 B2
Kıbrıslı Mustafa Emin Paşa Yalı......................10 B3
Kırmızı Yalı..11 B3
Köprülü Amcazade Hüseyin Paşa Yalı.............12 B2
Küçüksu Kasrı..13 B3
Kuleli Military School.....................................14 B3
Ortaköy Camii..15 B4
Rumeli Hisarı...16 B3
Rumeli İskele...(see 20)
Sadberk Hanım Müzesi..................................17 A1
Sait Halim Paşa Yalı......................................18 A2
Sakıp Sabancı Müzesi....................................19 A2

EATING
Donjon...20 A3
Hıdiv Kasrı Café.......................................(see 9)
Il Porto..(see 8)
Kale Café & Pastane................................(see 20)
Körfez Restaurant...21 B2
Mangerie...(see 8)
Müzedechanga..(see 19)
Poseidon...(see 8)
Sade Kahve...(see 20)

ENTERTAINMENT
Q Jazz by Les Ottomans...........................(see 23)

SLEEPING
Ajia..22 B2
Hotel Les Ottomans......................................23 A3
Sumahan on the Water..................................24 B3

first time there was a physical link across the straits from Europe to Asia. Traffic was so heavy over the bridge that it paid for itself in less than a decade. Now there is a second bridge, the Fatih Bridge (named after Mehmet the Conqueror, Mehmet Fatih), just north of Rumeli Hisarı. A third bridge, even further north, is planned.

For pleasant places to pit-stop, see p219; and for details on boat and ferry services, bus connections and fares, see the Transport boxed text, p217.

EMINÖNÜ TO ORTAKÖY

As you start your trip up the Bosphorus, watch out for the small island of Kız Kulesi (p123), just off the Asian shore near Üsküdar. Just before the first stop at Beşiktaş, you'll pass the grandiose

Dolmabahçe Palace (p116), built on the European shore of the Bosphorus by Sultan Abdül Mecit between 1843 and 1856. Shortly after Beşiktaş, Çırağan Sarayı (p119), once home to Sultan Abdül Aziz and now a luxury hotel, looms up on the left. On the Asian shore is the Fethi Ahmet Paşa Yalı, built in the late 18th century. The word yalı comes from the Greek word for 'coast', and describes the waterside wooden summer residences along the Bosphorus built by Ottoman aristocracy and foreign ambassadors in the 17th, 18th and 19th centuries, now all protected by the country's heritage laws. This one is known as the 'pink yalı'. To your left a little further on is the pretty Ortaköy Camii (p120), its dome and two minarets dwarfed by the adjacent Bosphorus Bridge, the symbol of modern İstanbul.

BEYLERBEYI PALACE

On the waterfront across the bridge is the grand Beylerbeyi Palace (Beylerbeyi Sarayı; ☎ 216-321 9320;

215

Abdullah Ağa Caddesi, Beylerbeyi; admission YTL8, camera YTL6, video YTL15; ☺ 9.30am-5pm Tue, Wed & Fri-Sun). Look for its whimsical marble bathing pavilions on the shore, one was for men, the other for the women of the harem.

Every sultan needed a little place to get away to, and the 30-room Beylerbeyi Palace was the place for Abdül Aziz (r 1861–76). An earlier wooden palace had burned down here, so Abdül Aziz wanted stone and marble. He ordered architect Sarkis Balyan, brother of Nikoğos, architect of Dolmabahçe, to get to work. Balyan came up with a building that delighted the many foreign dignitaries who visited, including Empress Eugénie of France; Nasruddin, shah of Persia; and Nicholas, grand duke of Russia. The palace's last imperial 'guest' was the former sultan, Abdül Hamit II, who was brought here to spend the remainder of his life (1913–18) under house arrest. He had the dubious pleasure of gazing across the Bosphorus and watching the empire he had ruled for over 30 years crumble before his eyes.

A visit to Beylerbeyi is an attractive alternative to visiting the grander but much more crowded Dolmabahçe. The compulsory guided tour whips you past room after room of Bohemian crystal chandeliers, French (Sèvres) and Ming vases and sumptuous carpets. There's a grand *selamlik* (private quarters) and a small but opulent harem. Highlights include the music room, with its inlaid walnut walls; a sitting room with parquet floors and walls inlayed with ebony and wood; and a dining room with chairs covered in gazelle skin. After the tour you can enjoy a glass of tea in the pretty garden café.

The palace is a few kilometres north of Üsküdar. Catch bus No 15A or a *dolmuş* north along the shore road from Üsküdar's main square, and get out at the Çayırbaşı stop, just north of Beylerbeyi and the Asian pylons of the Bosphorus Bridge. The trip takes 15 minutes.

ORTAKÖY TO BEBEK

Past the small village of Çengelköy on the Asian side is the imposing Kuleli Military School, built in 1860 and immortalised in Irfan Orga's wonderful memoir, *Portrait of a Turkish Family* (see p30).

Opposite Kuleli on the European shore north of Ortaköy is Arnavutköy, a village boasting a number of frilly Ottoman-era wooden houses, including numerous *yalıs*. On the

hill above it are buildings formerly occupied by the American College for Girls. Its most famous alumni was Halide Edib Adıvar, who wrote about the years she spent here in her 1926 autobiographical work, *The Memoir of Halide Edib*.

Arnavutköy runs straight into the glamorous suburb of Bebek, famous for upmarket restaurants such as Poseidon (p220) and waterside cafés such as Mangerie and Il Porto (see p220). It also has the most glamorous Starbucks in the city (right on the water, and with a lovely terrace). Bebek's shops surround a small park and a mosque; to the east of these is the ferry dock, to the south is the former Egyptian consulate building. This gorgeous Art Nouveau minipalace was built by the last khedive of Egypt, Abbas Hilmi II, who also later built Hıdiv Kasrı (p218) above Kanlıca on the Asian side of the Bosphorus. You'll see its mansard roof and ornate wrought-iron fence from the ferry.

Above Bebek you'll notice the New England 19th century–style architecture of the Boğaziçi Üniversitesi (Bosphorus University). Founded by American missionaries in the mid-19th century as Robert College, the college had an important influence on the modernisation of political, social, economic and scientific thought in Turkey. It was donated to the Turkish Republic in the early 1970s.

BEBEK TO KANLICA

Opposite Bebek on the Asian shore is Kırmızı Yalı (Red *Yalı*), constructed in 1790 and one of the oldest mansions still standing; a bit further on, also past the village of Kandilli, is the long, white Kıbrıslı Mustafa Emin Paşa Yalı.

Next to the Kıbrıslı Yalı are the Büyük Göksu Deresi (Great Heavenly Stream) and Küçük Göksu Deresi (Small Heavenly Stream), two brooks that descend from the Asian hills into the Bosphorus. Between them is a fertile delta, grassy and shady, which the Ottoman elite thought perfect for picnics. Foreign residents, referred to the place as 'The Sweet Waters of Asia'.

If the weather was good, the sultan joined the picnic, and did so in style. Sultan Abdül Mecit's answer to a simple picnic blanket was the wedding cake-like Küçüksu Kasrı (☎ 216-332 3303; Küçüksu Caddesi; admission YTL4; ☺ 9am-4pm Tue, Wed & Fri-Sun Nov-Mar, 9.30am-5pm Tue, Wed & Fri-Sun Apr-Oct), an ornate lodge built in 1856–57. Earlier sultans had wooden kiosks here, but architect Nikoğos Balyan designed a rococo gem in marble for his monarch. Take bus No

TRANSPORT – BOSPHORUS

The most popular way to explore the Bosphorus is by ferry. Most day-trippers take the Eminönü-Kavaklar Boğaziçi Özel Gezi Seferleri (Eminönü-Kavaklar Bosphorus Special Touristic Excursions) ferry up its entire length. These depart from the Boğaz Hattı dock (dock No 3; Map p63) at Eminönü daily at 10.35am. From June to September, there are extra services at noon and 1.35pm. A ticket costs YTL12.50 return, YTL6.50 one-way. The ferry stops at Beşiktaş, Kanlıca, Yeniköy, Sarıyer, Rumeli Kavağı and Anadolu Kavağı (the turnaround point). It is not possible to get on and off the ferry at stops along the way using the same ticket.

The boats fill up early in summer – especially on weekends – so buy your ticket and walk aboard at least 45 minutes (preferably an hour) prior to departure to get a seat outside or next to a window. During the trip waiters will offer you fresh orange juice, tea and other drinks. An orange juice costs YTL4, other drinks are cheaper.

Most day-trippers take the ferry all the way to Anadolu Kavağı, stopping at various sights along the way, but some go only as far as Sarıyer, on the European shore. They then make their way back to the city on the bus, stopping at Emirgan (p218) and Rumeli Hisarı (below) on the return trip; sometimes they also stop at Ortaköy (p116), Çırağan Palace (p119) or Dolmabahçe Palace (p116) on the return trip. From Sarıyer, bus No 25E makes the slow trip back to Eminönü, No 40 and 25T to Taksim Square and No 40B to Beşiktaş. Those to Taksim and Beşiktaş go via Emirgan, Rumeli Hisarı, Bebek, Ortaköy and Yıldız. The ferry arrives at Sarıyer at 11.45am, 11.10pm (June to September) and 2.45pm (June to September).

The trip to Anadolu Kavağı takes 1¾ hours and the ferry returns at 3pm and 4.15pm. If you decide to catch the ferry to Anadolu Kavağı and make your way back by bus, catch the No 15A, which leaves from just east of the ferry terminal en route to Kavacik Aktarma. Get off at Kanlıca to visit Hıdıv Kasrı (p218) and then catch the No 101 bus to Beşiktaş. Alternatively, catch the infrequent Nos 15 or 15P to Üsküdar, from where you can catch a ferry to Eminönü; or catch a taxi across the Fatih Bridge to Rumeli Hisarı and catch a bus back to Eminönü, Taksim Square or Beşiktaş.

From Kanlıca it's also possible to catch a passenger ferry back to towards İstanbul. These stop at Anadolu Hisarı, Kandilli, Bebek and Arnavutköy. Departures from Kanlıca are at 8.40am, 10.10am, 1.30pm, 2.40pm, 4.10pm, 5.40pm, 5.05pm and 7pm. The trip to Bebek takes 25 minutes. These are winter times (departure times vary with the seasons).

There is also a passenger ferry service between Sarıyer and Anadolu Kavağı, with 15 ferries a day from 7.15am to 11pm; seven of these ferries stop at Rumeli Kavağı on the way.

Yet another option is a private Bosphorus boat tour. Ticket touts are always to be found around dock No 3 at Eminönü flogging the tickets for these, which cost YTL24 (try bargaining). Tours are on smaller boats (60 to 100 people), each with a small sun deck. They only travel as far as Rumeli Hisarı (without stopping) where they stop for lunch for an hour before returning. The whole trip takes about three hours. The advantage of these trips is they take less time and the boat goes closer to the shore; the disadvantages are the higher price and the fact that you don't get to see the whole of the Bosphorus. These boats leave when they are full, starting from 11am and finishing at 8pm from May to September (4pm at other times).

15A or a *dolmuş* along the shore road north from Beylerbeyi and Üsküdar to reach the Küçüksu Kasrı bus stop, then walk the 300m to the shore and the pavilion.

Just before the Fatih Bridge are the majestic structures of Rumeli Hisarı (Fortress of Europe; ☎ 212-263 5305; Yahya Kemal Caddesi 42, Rumeli Hisarı; admission YTL2; ⏰ 9am-noon & 12.30-4.30pm Thu-Tue) and Anadolu Hisarı (Fortress of Anatolia). Mehmet the Conqueror had Rumeli Hisarı built in a mere four months during 1452, in preparation for his siege of Byzantine Constantinople. For its location, he chose the narrowest point of the Bosphorus, opposite Anadolu Hisarı, which Sultan Beyazıt I had built in 1391. By doing so, Mehmet was able to control all traffic on the strait, so cutting the city off from re-supply by sea.

To speed Rumeli Hisarı's completion (he was impatient to conquer Constantinople),

Mehmet ordered each of his three viziers to take responsibility for one of the three main towers. If the tower's construction was not completed on schedule, the vizier would pay with his life. Not surprisingly, the work was completed on time. The mighty fortress' useful military life lasted less than one year. After the conquest of Constantinople, it was used as a glorified Bosphorus tollbooth for a while, then as a barracks, a prison, and finally as an open-air theatre. Its amphitheatre still functions as a performance venue during the summer months, particularly during the International İstanbul Music Festival (p16).

Within Rumeli Hisarı's walls are parklike grounds, an open-air theatre and the minaret of a ruined mosque. Steep stairs (with no barriers, so beware!) lead up to the ramparts and towers; the views of the Bosphorus from here are magnificent. Just next to the fortress is a clutch of cafés and restaurants, including the hip eatery/bar, Donjon (p220), long-standing favourite Rumeli İskele (p220), and popular cafés such as Sade Kahve (p220) and Kale Café & Pastane (p220).

To get to Rumeli Hisarı by bus, catch No 25E, 40, 40B or 42 from Beşiktaş or No 559C from Taksim. The buses from Beşiktaş stop in front of the cafés next to the fortress; the bus from Taksim terminates in the town above the fortress and you'll have to walk for 10 minutes down the hill.

Though not open as a museum, visitors are free to wander about Anadolu Hisarı's ruined walls.

Just past Anadolu Hisarı (before the Fatih Bridge) is Köprülü Amcazade Hüseyin Paşa Yalı, built right on the water in 1698. It is the oldest mansion on the Bosphorus and is in a deplorable state of repair.

Past the bridge, still on the Asian side, is the charming village of Kanlıca, famous for its rich and delicious yoghurt. You'll be offered some on the ferry and can sample it in the Asırlık Kanlıca Yoğurdu, a café on the shady waterfront village square. The small Gâzi İskender Paşa Camii in the square dates from 1560 and was designed by Sinan.

KANLICA TO İSTİNYE

One of İstanbul's most famous seafood restaurants, Körfez Restaurant (opposite), is on Kanlıca's outskirts, almost directly under the bridge. This is the perfect place to spend an afternoon, eating lunch on its outdoor terrace while watching the ferries and boats sail past. Just near Körfez is the late-19th-century Ethem Pertev Yalı, with its boathouse and ornate wooden decoration.

High on a promontory above Kanlıca is Hıdiv Kasrı (Khedive's Villa; ☎ 216-413 9644; Çubuklu Yolu 32, Kanlıca; admission free; ⏰ 8am-11pm), a grand Art Nouveau villa built by the last khedive of Egypt as a summer residence for use during his family's annual visits to İstanbul.

Having ruled Egypt for centuries, in 1805 the Ottomans lost control to an adventurer named Muhammed Ali (also known as Mehmet Ali), who defied the sultan in İstanbul to dislodge him. The sultan, unable to do so, gave him quasi-independence and had to be satisfied with reigning over Egypt rather than ruling. This was left to Muhammed Ali and his line, and the ruler of Egypt was styled *hıdiv*, 'khedive' (not 'king', as that would be unbearably independent). The khedives of Egypt kept up the pretence of Ottoman suzerainty by paying tribute to İstanbul.

The Egyptian royal family, which looked upon itself as Turkish, often spent its summers in a traditional *yalı* on the Bosphorus shore at Bebek (now the Egyptian consulate, p216). In 1906, Khedive Abbas Hilmi II built himself this palatial villa on the most dramatic promontory on the Bosphorus. In the 1930s it became the property of the municipality.

Restored after decades of neglect, the Hıdiv Kasrı now functions as a restaurant and garden café (p220), much to the delight of İstanbullus and tourists alike. The villa is a gem and the view from the extensive and lovely garden is superb.

The villa is a few minutes by taxi (YTL4) uphill from Kanlıca or a 20-minute walk. To walk, go north from Kanlıca's main square and mosque and turn right at the first street (Kafadar Sokak), which winds up towards the villa car park. Turn left at Dere Sokak and shortly you'll come to a fork in the road. Take the left fork and walk up past Kanlıca Hekimler Sitesi on the corner. You'll soon see the villa's car park and extensive wooded garden.

On the opposite shore is the wealthy suburb of Emirgan, home to the recently opened and extremely impressive Sakıp Sabancı Müzesi (☎ 212-277 2200; www.muze.sabanciuniv.edu; Sakıp Sabancı Caddesi 22; adult/student/child under 14 YTL10/3/free; ⏰ 10am-6pm Tue, Thu, Fri & Sun, 10am-10pm Wed, 10am-7pm Sat), which hosts international travelling art exhibitions. The museum is home to one of İstanbul's hottest eateries, Müzedechanga (p220). In late April to early May, Emirgan Park, just above the town, is decked out in tulips. North of Emirgan, there's a ferry dock near the small yacht-lined cove of İstinye.

İSTİNYE TO SARIYER

Just north of İstinye, Yeniköy is on a point jutting out from the European shore. It was first settled in classical times and later became a favourite summer resort, as indicated by the lavish 19th-century Ottoman yalı of the one-time grand vizier, Sait Halim Paşa. Look for its two small stone lions on the quay. On the opposite shore is the village of Paşabahçe, famous for its glassware factory. A bit further on is the fishing village of Beykoz, which has a graceful ablutions fountain İshak Ağa Çeşmesi, dating from 1746, near the village square, as well as several fish restaurants. Much of the land along the Bosphorus shore north of Beykoz is a military zone.

Originally called Therapia for its healthy climate, the little cove of Tarabya on the

European shore has been a favourite summer watering place for İstanbul's well-to-do for centuries, though contemporary developments such as the horrendous multi-storey Grand Hotel Tarabya right on the promontory have poisoned some of its charm. For an account of Therapia in its heyday, read Harold Nicolson's 1921 novel *Sweet Waters*. Nicholson, who is best known as Vita Sackville-West's husband, served as the third Secretary in the British Embassy in Constantinople between 1912 and 1914, the years of the Balkan wars, and clearly knew Therapia well. In the novel, the main character, Eirene, who was clearly based on Vita, spent her summers here.

North of the village are some of the old summer embassies of foreign powers. When the heat and fear of disease increased in the warm months, foreign ambassadors would retire to palatial residences, complete with lush gardens, on this shore. The region for such embassy residences extended north to the village of Büyükdere, notable for its churches, summer embassies and the Sadberk Hanım Müzesi (☎ 212-242 3813; Büyükdere Caddesi 27-9, Sarıyer; admission YTL7; ☒ 10am-5pm Thu-Tue). Walk south from the ferry docks in Sarıyer for approximately 15 minutes. Named after the wife of the late Vehbi Koç, founder of Turkey's foremost commercial empire in 1926, the museum is a showcase for her extraordinary private collection of antiquities and Ottoman heirlooms. Labels are in English and Turkish.

The original museum building is a graceful old *yalı*, once the summer residence of Manuk Azaryan Efendi, an Armenian who was speaker of the Ottoman parliament. It houses artefacts and exhibits such as beautiful İznik and Kütahya ceramics, and Ottoman silk textiles and needlework. A number of rooms in the great old house have been arranged and decorated in Ottoman style.

The collections in the new building, which is beside the original *yalı*, include an exquisite collection of diadems from the Mycenaean, Archaic and Classical periods, as well as Ottoman and Roman times.

The residents of Sarıyer, the next village up from Büyükdere on the European shore, have occupied themselves for most of their history by fishing. This is still a pastime and the main livelihood here, and Sarıyer is justly noted for its good fish restaurants. It's a busy place. Turn right as you leave the ferry dock, stay as close to the shore as

possible, and you will pass the seabus terminal and several fish restaurants before coming to the Tarihi Balıkçılar Çarşısı, the village's historic fish market.

SARIYER TO ANADOLU KAVAĞI

The ferry's second-last stop is Rumeli Kavağı, a sleepy place that only gets excited with the arrival and departure of the ferry. A public beach named Altınkum, near the village, has a small restaurant serving meze and beer, but not much else. To the south of the town is the shrine of the Moslem saint Telli Baba, reputed to be able to find suitable husbands for young women who pray there.

Anadolu Kavağı is where the Bosphorus excursions ferry finishes its journey. It's a pleasant spot in which to wander and have a seafood lunch at one of the touristy places on the square in front of the ferry terminal.

Perched above the village are the ruins of Anadolu Kavağı Kalesi, a medieval castle that originally had eight massive towers in its walls. First built by the Byzantines, it was restored and reinforced by the Genoese in 1350, and later by the Ottomans. Two more fortresses built by Sultan Murat IV in the 17th century are north of here. It will take you 30 to 50 minutes to walk up to the fortress from the town. Alternatively, taxis wait near the fountain in the town square just east of the ferry dock; they charge YTL12 for the return trip with 30 minutes waiting time. Whichever way you get there, it's worth the effort for the spectacular Black Sea views. Unfortunately, the site is strewn with litter discarded by picnickers.

EATING & DRINKING

There are places for every taste and budget along the shores of the Bosphorus. Many people choose to organise their day's itinerary around their choice of lunch venue, and there's a lot to be said for following their example.

Körfez Restaurant (☎ 216-413 4314; Körfez Caddesi 78, Kanlıca; mains YTL30-75; ☒ 11am-4pm Tue-Sun, 6pm-midnight daily) Famous for its sea bass baked in salt, Körfez is the perfect place for a special meal in İstanbul. To make it even more special, organise for the restaurant's own motor launch to pick you up from Rumeli Hisarı across the strait and drop you back after your meal. Book ahead.

Poseidon (☎ 212-263 3823; Cevdet Paşa Caddesi 58, Bebek; starters YTL4-22, fish by kg YTL65-120; ⏱ noon-midnight) This place evokes class with a capital 'C' – for credit card danger. If you want some of the best seafood in the city served on a stylish deck overlooking the bobbing boats of Bebek Bay, it's the perfect place. You'll be in the company of beautifully groomed women who dote on designer handbags and are often mistaken by their dining partners as said fashion accessory.

Rumeli İskele (☎ 212-263 2997; Yahya Kemal Caddesi 1, Rumeli Hisarı; meze YTL4-20, mains YTL35-65; ⏱ noon-1am) In the old timber ferry terminal building right on the water, this long-standing favourite is a great spot for lunch. Businessmen (sometimes with girlfriend, sometimes with colleagues) are a permanent fixture, ordering delectable meze such as *levrek marine* (sea bass in a creamy but piquant lemon sauce) or *çıroz* (salted and dried thin mackerel). The catch of the day is priced by the kilo (prepare yourself for a hefty outlay) and there are good wine choices by the glass and bottle. There's a cover charge of YTL5 per person – tsk tsk.

Müzedechanga (☎ 212-3230901; Sakıp Sabancı Müzesi, Sakıp Sabancı Caddesi 22, Emirgan; starters YTL14-28, mains YTL19-46; ⏱ 10.30am-1am Tue-Sun) İstanbul was agog when the relatively new Sakıp Sabancı Museum announced that one of the city's top restaurants, Changa (p165), was going to relocate here during the summer months. Many were dubious that the Changa crew would be happy making the transition from Taksim to this sleepy Bosphorus suburb, but it soon became obvious to all that the curators at the museum know how to present a masterpiece, be it an artwork or a restaurant. As well as possessing the most stylish restaurant interior in the city (maybe in Europe?), this place also has a terrace with lovely Bosphorus views. The food is wonderful – brunch favourites include the mixed breakfast plate or the *katmer* (local flaky pastry with goat-cheese cream and marinated green olives with preserved lemons) accompanied by a wasabi Bloody Mary; lunch and dinner highlights include perfectly cooked dishes such as grilled grouper on white-bean purée with fresh broad beans and a mint and green pepper salsa, washed down by a glass of wine from a good list. Well worth the trip from town – go for a weekend lunch or brunch.

Donjon (☎ 212-287 2910; Yahya Kemal Caddesi 40, Rumeli Hisarı; mains YTL20; ⏱ 8am-2am) Hip young things loll on the beanbags downstairs and

listen to the in-house DJ spin his stuff; others seek out the pleasant roof balcony or the terraces with its swimming pool and imposing views over the Bosphorus. It's the second café from the fortress.

Il Porto (☎ 212-263 5199; Cevdet Paşa Caddesi 58, Bebek; mains YTL20; ⏱ 10am-midnight) There are a number of ways to observe the glam Bebek set at play: you can dine at the mega-pricey Poseidon, have a coffee on the terrace at Starbucks or enjoy a casual summer lunch on the terrace here at Il Porto. Built right over the water, this is a good spot to see and be seen – the food is perfectly acceptable, but that's not why the crowds are here. Wear casual designer togs and have a botox shot before you go.

Mangerie (☎ 212-263 5199; Cevdet Paşa Caddesi 69/3, Bebek; mains YTL20; ⏱ 8am-midnight) Mangerie has got the Bebek sheen of casual chic, but isn't at all pretentious. The interior is light and white, with soaring ceilings and a decidedly Scandinavian feel, and there's a terrace with Bosphorus views. Food is simple but more-ish, with sandwiches and salads taking centre stage.

Hıdiv Kasrı Café (☎ 216-320 2036; sandwiches YTL5-10, grills YTL18-24; ⏱ 8am-11pm) Choose from the simple menu at the charming café next to the rose garden or the more extensive choice in the grand dining room and adjoining marble terrace. The food is average but the surroundings are drop-dead gorgeous. No alcohol is served.

At Sade Kahve (☎ 212-358 2324; Yahya Kemal Caddesi 36, Rumeli Hisarı; ⏱ 8am-2am) you have a cheap and cheerful terrace café near the fortress that is a good spot for a tea and snack. It's similar to the Kale Café & Pastane next to the bus stop, which serves Anatolian favourites such as *mantı* (Turkish ravioli served with a yogurt and tomato sauce), *gözleme* (Turkish crepes filled with cheese, spinach or potato and cooked on a griddle) and *menemen* (eggs cooked with tomato, onions and white cheese).

PRINCES' ISLANDS

Most İstanbullus refer to the Princes' Islands (Kızıl Adalar, or 'Red Islands'; Map p213) as 'The Islands' (Adalar), as they are the only islands around the city. They lie about 20km southeast of the city in the Sea of Marmara, and make a great destination for a day escape from the city.

In antiquity the islands were known as Demonisia, the People's Islands. In Byzantine times, refractory princes, deposed monarchs and troublesome associates were interned here in convents and monasteries, hence the name the 'Princes' Islands'. A steam-ferry service from İstanbul was started in the mid 19th century and the islands became popular summer resorts with Pera's Greek, Jewish and Armenian communities. Many of the fine Victorian villas built by these wealthy merchants survive, and make the larger islands, Büyükada and Heybeliada, charming places to explore. There are still significant Armenian and Jewish populations living on the islands, as well as some members of the Greek community, but most of the current island population is Turkish. For excellent historical and architectural background on the islands and their buildings, try to source a copy of John Freely's *The Princes' Isles: A Guide,* which is published by Adalı Islander Editions. You should be able to find it in İstanbul's English-language bookshops.

You'll realise after landing that there are no cars on the islands, something that comes as a welcome relief after the traffic mayhem of the city. Except for the necessary police, fire and sanitation vehicles, transportation is by bicycle, horse-drawn carriage and foot, as in centuries past.

All of the islands are busy in summer, particularly on weekends. For that reason, avoid a Sunday visit. If you wish to stay overnight during the summer months, book ahead. Many hotels are closed during winter.

There are nine islands in the Princes' Islands group and the ferry stops at four of these. Year-round there are 15,000 permanent residents scattered across the six islands that are populated, but numbers swell to 100,000 or so during summer when İstanbullus – many of whom have holiday homes on the islands –

escape the city heat. The small islands of Kınalıada and Burgazada are the ferry's first stops; frankly, neither offers much reward for the trouble of getting off the ferry.

In contrast, the charming island of Heybeliada (Heybeli for short) has much to offer the visitor. It's home to the Deniz Lisesi (Turkish Navel Academy), which was founded in 1773, and which you'll see to the left of the ferry dock as you arrive, and it has a number of restaurants and a thriving shopping strip, with bakeries and delicatessens selling picnic provisions to day-trippers, who come here on weekends to walk in the pine groves and swim from the tiny (but crowded) beaches. The island's major landmark is the hilltop Hagia Triada Monastery (☎ 216-351 8563). Perched above a picturesque line of poplar trees in a spot that has been occupied by a Greek monastery since Byzantine times, this building dates from 1894. It functioned as a Greek Orthodox theological school until 1971, when it was closed on the government's orders, and has an internationally renowned library. There are signs that it may re-open soon. You may be able to visit if you call ahead.

Heybeliada has a couple of hotels, including the comfortable Merit Halki Palace (p222), perched at the top of Rafah Şehitleri Caddesi with wonderful water views. The delightful walk up to this hotel passes an antique shop and a host of large wooden villas set in lovingly tended gardens. Many laneways and streets leading to picnic spots, and lookout points are located off the upper reaches of this street. To find the hotel, turn right as you leave the ferry and head past the waterfront restaurants and cafés to the plaza with the Atatürk statue. From here walk up İsgüzar Sokak, veering right until you hit Rafah Şehitleri Caddesi. If you don't feel

TRANSPORT – PRINCES' ISLANDS

Fourteen ferries run to the islands each day from 6.50am to midnight, departing from Kabataş 'Adalar İskelesi' dock. The most useful departure times for day-trippers are 9.30am, 10am and 11.30am. On summer weekends, board the vessel and grab a seat at least half an hour before departure time unless you want to stand the whole way. The trip costs YTL2 to the islands and the same for each leg between the islands and the return trip. The cheapest and easiest way to pay is to use your Akbil. To be safe, check the timetable at www.ido.com.tr, as the schedule can change.

The ferry steams away from Kabataş and on its journey treats passengers to fine views of Topkapı Palace, Aya Sofya and the Blue Mosque on the right, and Üsküdar and Haydarpaşa on the left. After 20 minutes the ferry makes a quick stop at Kadıköy on the Asian side before making its way to the first island, Kınalıada. This leg takes 30 minutes. After this, it's another 15 minutes to Burgazada; another 15 minutes again to Heybeliada, the second-largest island; and another 10 minutes to Büyükada, the largest island in the group.

Ferries return to İstanbul every 1.5 hours or so. The last ferry of the day leaves Büyükada at 10pm and Heybeliada at 10.15pm.

SEX & DEATH ON THE PRINCES' ISLANDS

For an entertaining take on life in the Princes' Islands, read Lawrence Goodman's series of crime novels set on the archipelago. The cast of characters includes Everett and Lily Blum, an expat American couple with more than a few similarities to William Powell and Myra Loy in the *Thin Man* movies of the 1930s (too many martinis and coy sexual banter). In the books, these amateur sleuths befriend hapless American English-language teacher Ed Wilkie and his no-nonsense Turkish wife, Elif. The plots are silly, but the books evoke life on the islands and in İstanbul well. The first in the series, *Sweet Confusion on the Princes' Islands*, has been followed by *Sour Grapes on the Princes' Islands* and *A Grain of Salt on the Princes' Islands*.

like walking up to the hotel (it's uphill but not too steep), you can hire a bicycle (YTL2 to YTL3 per hour) from one of the shops in the main street or a *fayton* to take you around the island. A 25-minute tour (*küçük tur*) costs YTL20 and a one-hour tour (*büyük tur*) costs YTL30. Some visitors spend the day by the pool at the Merit Halki Palace, which is a good idea, as the waters around the island aren't very clean. Towels and chaise lounges are supplied, and there's a pleasant terrace restaurant for meals or drinks. The charge for non-guests to use the pool is YTL35 on weekdays and YTL50 on weekends.

The largest island in the group, Büyükada (Great Island), is impressive from the ferry, with gingerbread villas climbing up the slopes of the hill and the bulbous twin cupolas of the Splendid Otel providing an unmistakable landmark. It's a truly lovely spot to spend an afternoon.

The ferry terminal is an attractive building in the Ottoman kiosk style; it dates from 1899. Inside there's a pleasant tile-decorated café with an outdoor terrace, as well as a Tourist Information Office. Eateries serve fresh fish to the left of the ferry terminal, next to an ATM.

The island's main drawcard is the Greek Monastery of St George, in the 'saddle' between Büyükada's two highest hills. Walk from the ferry straight ahead to the clock tower in İskele Square (Dock Square). The shopping district is left along Recep Koç Sokak. Bear right onto 23 Nisan Caddesi, then head along Çankaya Caddesi up the hill to the monastery; when you come to a fork in the road, veer right. The walk (at least one hour) takes you past a long progression of impressive wooden villas set in gardens. About a quarter of the way up on the left is the Büyükada Kültür Evi, a charming spot where you can enjoy a tea or coffee in a garden setting. The house itself dates from 1878 and was restored in 1998. After 40 minutes or so you will reach a reserve called 'Luna Park' by the locals. The monastery is a 25-minute walk up an

extremely steep hill from here. Some visitors hire a donkey to take them up the hill and back for YTL10. As you ascend, you'll see countless pieces of cloth tied to the branches of trees along the path – each represents a prayer, most made by female suppliants visiting the monastery to pray for a child.

There's not a lot to see at the monastery. A small and gaudy church is the only building of note, but there are fabulous panoramic views from the terrace, as well as the highly regarded Yücetepe Kır Gazinosu (right), a restaurant with outdoor seating. From its tables you will be able to see all the way to İstanbul and the nearby islands of Yassıada and Sivriada.

Bicycles are available for rent in several of the town's shops, and shops on the market street can provide picnic supplies, though food is cheaper on the mainland. Just off the clock tower square and opposite the Splendid Otel there are *fayton* stands. Hire one for a long tour of the town, hills and shore (one hour YTL45) or a shorter tour of the town (YTL35). It costs YTL16 to be taken to Luna Park. A shop just near the *fayton* stand hires out bicycles (YTL2.50 to YTL3 per hour).

INFORMATION

Tourist Information Office (☎ 0216-382 1092; Ferry Terminal, Büyükada; ⏱ 10am-4pm) Staffed by volunteers, this office offers advice, but no maps or brochures.

SLEEPING

There's not really much of an argument for staying here overnight – it's much more sensible to spend the day and then return to the city, where the sleeping options are better and less expensive.

Merit Halki Palace (☎ 216-351 0025; www.halkipalace hotel.com; Refah Şehitleri Caddesi 94, Heybeliada; s/d €72/95; 🐾) This comfortable hotel was built in the style of an 1852 hotel that was previously on the site but burned down in 1991. With its garden setting and wonderful pool area, if you're going to overnight on the islands, this is the place to do it.

Splendid Palas (☎ 216-382 6950; www.splendidhotel .net; Nisan Caddesi 23, Büyükada; r from €65; ☒) This landmark building is indeed splendid. Rooms aren't quite as impressive as the exterior, but are comfortable enough. Front ones have small balconies and sea views. There's a pool and a restaurant.

EATING

There aren't many eateries of note on the islands, particularly on Heybeliada. A picnic is your best bet there. On Büyükada, we highly recommend the outdoor restaurant at the Monastery of St George's.

Alibaba Restaurant (☎ 216-382 3733; Gülistan Caddesi 20, Büyükada; meze YTL5-12, fish YTL20-35; ☯ noon-11pm) Alibaba is the most popular of the seafood joints on the water near the ferry terminal. The overpriced food is adequate, but nothing more.

Büyükada Kültür Evi (☎ 216-382 8620; Çankaya Caddesi 21, Büyükada; sandwiches YTL5-10, grills YTL10, beer YTL6; ☯ daily Apr-Oct, weekends only Nov-Mar) Set up by the Turing Association in 1998, this garden café serves breakfast, lunch and dinner in its terraced garden. Service can be desultory and the food's not up to much, but it's an undeniably pretty setting and a great spot for a morning glass of tea or a late-afternoon beer.

Yücetepe Kır Gazinosu (Monastery of St George, Büyükada; meze YTL3.50-5, grills YTL6-7, beer YTL3.50; ☯ daily Apr-Oct, weekends only Nov-Mar) What a shame this utterly fabulous eatery is so far out of the city! If it were closer, we'd be eating here morning, noon and night. At the very top of the hill where the Monastery of St George is located, its benches and chairs are set up on a terrace overlooking the sea and İstanbul. Dishes are simple but really impressive – the köfte we enjoyed on our most recent visit was possibly the best we've ever eaten and meze such as the fried *patlican* (eggplant) with yogurt were nearly as good. You can enjoy a beer and will finish the end of your meal having only spent YTL12 or so on the food. Fabulous.

GALLIPOLI & TROY

Few places resonate with history as strongly as Troy and Gallipoli. Both are the locations of great battles and have been the subjects of major works of literature, countless school history texts and Hollywood feature films both good and bad (Brad Pitt as Achilles? *Ay curumba!*). Together, they make a trip to the Dardanelles from İstanbul an enticing prospect.

ÇANAKKALE

This pleasant harbour town is the principal base for people visiting Gallipoli and Troy. Home to Çanakkale University, it's a surprisingly fun place to visit (see Eating & Drinking, p224).

TRANSPORT – GALLIPOLI, TROY & ÇANAKKALE

Çanakkale is the logical base for visits to the Gallipoli battlefields and/or Troy. Truva Turizm (www.truvaturizm .com) and Radar Turizm (www.radarturizm.org) buses depart Kadıköy and then İstanbul's main *otogar* at Esenler regularly between 7.45am and midnight. The only time you'll need to book ahead is around Anzac Day. The trip (six hours, 340km) costs YTL27, with a small discount for children. Buses stop for one rest break. If you're heading back to İstanbul, you can buy bus tickets and board buses from near the ferry docks rather than going to the Çanakkale *otogar*. Truva Turizm buses leave Çanakkale at 7am, 8am. 9am, 10am, 11am, 1pm, 4pm and 1am. Radar Turizm buses follow a similar timetable. Most buses to/from İstanbul travel on the Eceabat–Çanakkale ferry and along the Thracian side of the Sea of Marmara coast.

Atlas Jet (www.atlasjet.com) flies from İstanbul to Çanakkale (YTL72 to YTL162, 35 to 40 minutes) every day except Saturday and flies the other way every day except Sunday. The airport is approximately 8km from the centre of town; a *dolmuş* between the two costs YTL1 and a taxi costs YTL15.

If you are travelling in your own car, there are car ferries between Gelibolu and Lapseki; Eceabat and Çanakkale; and Kilitbahir and Çanakkale. Most depart hourly between 6am and midnight.

Troy is only 25 minutes (36km) by car or *dolmuş* from Çanakkale. The *dolmuş* station is under a small bridge opposite the fairground on Atatürk Caddesi. In high summer, *dolmuşes* go to the small village of Tevfikiye, just outside Troy, every 30 to 60 minutes. A ticket cost YTL5. At other times of the year, you should plan to visit early in the day to be sure of getting a return *dolmuş*.

There is no public transport around the Gallipoli Peninsula, so your only options are to take a tour or have your own car.

Çanakkale is situated at the narrowest point in the Dardanelles; it was from here that Leander swam across what was then called the Hellespont to his lover Hero, and from here too that Lord Byron emulated the feat in 1810.

Today visitors by sea are greeted by a strangely familiar, life-sized Trojan Horse on the waterfront promenade: yes, it is the actual horse from the movie *Troy* (2004).

Information

The Tourist Information Office (☎ 217 1187; ☯ 8am-noon & 1-7pm Mon-Fri) is located by the harbour. There are banks, a PTT and shops around Cumhuriyet Meydanı on the waterfront. Check your emails at Maxi Internet (Fetvane Sokak 51; per hr YTL1; ☯ 10am-1am).

Tours

Hassle Free Tours (☎ 213 5969; www.anzchouse.com; Cumhuriyet Meydanı 61) This well-known outfit is based at the Anzac House hostel in Çanakkale. It runs Gallipoli tours for €30 and Troy tours for €26. The three-hour Troy tour leaves at 8.30am; the 5½-hour Gallipoli tour leaves at 11.30am and includes lunch at the Maydos Restaurant in Eceabat. It's possible to do both tours in one day. Hassle Free also organises round-trip Gallipoli tours from its İstanbul office (Map p50), which includes transport, a Troy tour and one night's accommodation in Çanakkale. There is a tour for the dawn service on Anzac Day. Check the website.

TJ Tours (☎ 286-814 3121; www.anzacgallipolitours.com; Cumhuriyet Caddesi 5/A, Eceabat) Run by a Turkish-Australian couple, TJ's offers a four-to-five-hour Gallipoli tour leaving at 11.30am. The company is based at TJ's Hostel in Eceabat on the Gallipoli Peninsula, across the strait from Çanakkale, and its Gallipoli tour has a good reputation.

Sleeping

All hotels are heavily booked in summer, and the town is insanely crowded around Anzac Day. Unless mentioned, all places listed offer air-conditioned rooms with en suite bathroom.

Hotel Akol (☎ 286-217 9456; www.hotelakol.com; Kordonboyu; s/d €45/67; ✳ 🖥 🖳) This place has large rooms with all the mod cons and is popular with tour groups as a consequence. Though

getting on in years it's aging quite gracefully. All rooms have a balcony, some with water views.

Çanak Otel (☎ 286-214 1582; www.canakhotel.com; Dibek Sokak 1; s/d €43/50; ✳) This relatively new place offers extremely comfortable rooms at reasonable prices. There's a pleasant rooftop restaurant and bar.

Hotel Kervansaray (☎ 217 8192; www.otelkervansaray .com; Fetvane Sokak 13; s/d €25/45; ✳ 🖳) Çanakkale's only boutique hotel lays on loads of Ottoman flourishes and is far and away the best accommodation choice in town. The rooms are beautifully presented and the public areas are impressive, especially the gorgeous courtyard garden. Excellent value.

Maydos Hotel (☎ 213 5970; www.maydos.com.tr; Yalı Caddesi 12; s €22.50-34, d €45-68; ✳ 🖳) The latest venture from the people behind Hassle Free Tours, the Maydos offers clean and comfortable rooms at reasonable prices.

Yellow Rose Pension (☎ 217 3343; www.yellowrose.4mg .com; Yeni Sokak 5; dm €8, s €14, d €20-28; 🖳) This cheerful hostel has a quiet location and lots of extras, from laundry and kitchen to book exchange and video library. All rooms have private bathroom.

Efes Hotel (☎ 217 3256; Aralık Sokak 5; s/d €14/20; ✳) This place near the clocktower is spotlessly clean, has very comfortable beds and is extremely quiet. Two rooms have air-conditioning; the rest have fans. Breakfast costs extra, but is really good.

Eating & Drinking

Good eateries are thin on the ground here, but there's a healthy bar scene.

Hünnaphan (☎ 286-214 2535; Mehmetçik Bulvarı 21; mains YTL8-15; ☯ 11am-11.30pm) Set in an old purple house away from the waterfront, this charming restaurant has a beautiful patio garden and two semiprivate balconies where diners can enjoy park views. Turkish and Western dishes are on offer and there's an extensive wine list.

Rıhtım Restaurant (Eski Balıkhane Sokak; mains YTL5-12; ☯ 11am-11.30pm) This long-established eatery on the waterfront serves a varied menu of Turkish and Western dishes.

Köy Evi (Yalı Caddesi 13; dishes YTL1.5-3; ☯ 8am-9pm) Here, headscarfed local women serve up dirt-cheap home-cooked *mantı*, *börek* and other Anatolian favourites.

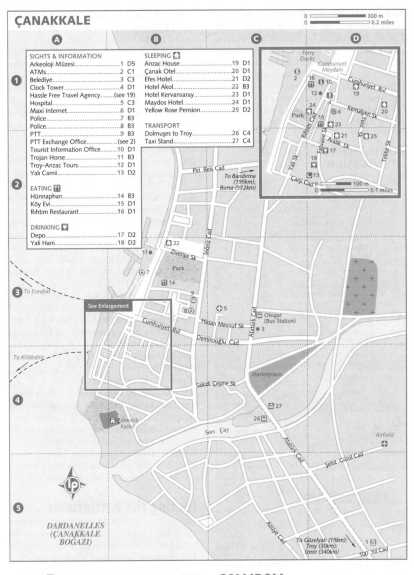

ÇANAKKALE

0	300 m
0	0.2 miles

SIGHTS & INFORMATION
Arkeoloji Müzesi.............................1 D5
ATMs..2 C1
Belediye...3 C3
Clock Tower.....................................4 D1
Hassle Free Travel Agency.........(see 19)
Hospital..5 C3
Maxi Internet...................................6 D1
Police..7 B3
Police..8 B3
PTT...9 B3
PTT Exchange Office.................(see 2)
Tourist Information Office............10 D1
Trojan Horse..................................11 B3
Troy-Anzac Tours..........................12 D1
Yalı Camii......................................13 D2

SLEEPING
Anzac House..................................19 D1
Çanak Otel.....................................20 D1
Efes Hotel......................................21 D2
Hotel Akol.....................................22 B3
Hotel Kervansaray.........................23 D1
Maydos Hotel................................24 D1
Yellow Rose Pension......................25 D2

TRANSPORT
Dolmuşes to Troy...........................26 C4
Taxi Stand.....................................27 C4

EATING
Hünnaphan....................................14 B3
Köy Evi..15 D1
Rıhtım Restaurant..........................16 D1

DRINKING
Depo..17 D2
Yalı Hanı..18 D2

Ferry Docks
Cumhuriyet Meydanı
Cumhuriyet Bul
Kemalyeri Sk
Park
Rıhtım Cad
Fetvane Sk
Yalı Sk
Aralık Sk
Tekke Sk
Çarşı Cad

0	100 m
0	0.1 miles

Piri Reis Cad
To Bandırma (195km); Bursa (312km)

Ziveriye Sk
İnönü Cad
Park

See Enlargement

To Eceabat

Cumhuriyet Bul
Hasan Mevsuf Sk
Atatürk Cad
Otogar (Bus Station)
Demircioğlu Cad

To Kilitbahir

Sakızlı Çeşme Sk

Marketplace

Çimenlik Kalesi
Sarı Çay

Airfield

Şehit Gürol Cad

DARDANELLES (ÇANAKKALE BOĞAZI)

Atatürk Cad
Aziziye Cad
100 Yıl Cad

To Güzelyalı (15km); Troy (30km); İzmir (340km)

Depo (☎ 212-6813; Fetvane Sokak 19; admission YTL5) The biggest and rowdiest joint in a street of similar establishments, Depo has a warehouse vibe and a fantastic open courtyard full of bean-bag chairs. It's the best dance spot in town.

Yalı Hanı (Fetvane Sokak 26; admission YTL5; ⌚ 10.30am-midnight) This atmospheric bar set in an old caravanserai is the town's most popular live-music venue. As well as the bar, there's a pleasant courtyard *çay bahçesi*.

GALLIPOLI

The slender peninsula that forms the north-western side of the Dardanelles (Çanakkale Boğazı; Map p226), across the water from the town of Çanakkale, is called Gallipoli ('Geli-bolu' in Turkish). For a millennium it has been the key to İstanbul – the navy that could force the straits had a good chance of capturing the capital of the Eastern European world. Many fleets have tried to do so. Most, including the Allied fleet mustered in WW1, have failed. Today, the Gallipoli battlefields are peaceful places covered in scrubby brush, pine forests and fields. But the battles fought here nearly a century ago still live in the memories of many people. The annual pilgrimage that Australians and New Zealanders make here on Anzac Day (25 April) has become one of the major events on the Turkish tourism calendar.

Most people know the tragic story of the Gallipoli offensive. With the intention of capturing the Ottoman capital and the road to Eastern Europe during WWI, Winston Churchill, British First Lord of the Admiralty, organised a naval assault on the Dardanelles. A strong Franco-British fleet tried first to force them in March 1915 but failed. Then, in April, British, Australian, New Zealand and Indian troops were landed on Gallipoli, and French troops near Çanakkale. Both Turkish and Allied troops fought desperately and fearlessly. After months of ferocious combat with little progress, the Allied forces were withdrawn.

The Turkish success at Gallipoli was partly due to bad luck and bad leadership on the Allied side, and partly due to the timely provision of reinforcements aiding the Turkish side under the command of General Liman von Sanders. But a crucial element in the defeat was that the Allied troops landed in a sector where they faced Lieutenant-Colonel Mustafa Kemal (Atatürk).

At this time Atatürk was a relatively minor officer, but he had General von Sanders' confidence. He guessed the Allied battle plan correctly when his commanders did not, and disobeyed an order from his commanders to send his troops south to Cape Helles, instead stalling the invasion by bitter fighting that wiped out his regiment. Though suffering from malaria, he commanded in full view of his troops and of the enemy, and miraculously escaped death several times. His brilliant performance made him a folk hero and paved the way for his promotion to *paşa* (general).

The Gallipoli campaign lasted until January 1916, and resulted in a total of more than half a million Allied and Turkish casualties.

Touring the Battlefields

Gallipoli is a fairly large area to tour: it's over 35km as the crow flies from the northernmost battlefield to the southern tip of the peninsula. The principal battles took place on the western shore of the peninsula, near Anzac Cove and Arıburnu Cemetery, and in the hills just to the east.

With a car you can easily tour the major battlefields in a day and be in a Çanakkale hotel by nightfall. If you're in a hurry, a morning or afternoon will be enough time to see the main sites. Most of the tours run by companies in Çanakkale and Eceabat take half a day. The best of these tours are run by Hassle Free in Çanakkale and TJ Tours in Eceabat (see p224).

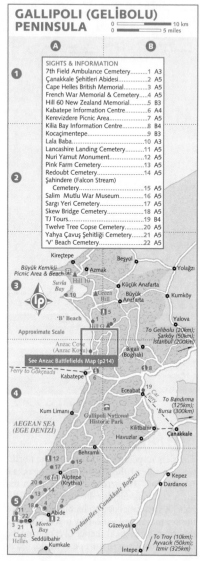

If you're a hiker, and you have lots of time, take a ferry from Çanakkale to Eceabat and a *dolmuş* or taxi to Kabatepe, and follow the trail around the sites described in an excellent map sold at the Kabatepe Information Centre & Museum (Kabatepe Tanıtma Merkezi Müzesi; 🕑 9am-5pm).

Gallipoli National Historic Park (Gelibolu Yarımadası Tarihi Milli Parkı) covers much of the peninsula and all of the significant battle sites. To get to the Information Centre, head north of Eceabat. After about 3km you'll see a road marked for Kabatepe; follow it until you come to the information centre, just east of Kabatepe.

From the information centre, head west and then north for 3km to the Beach (Hell Spit) Cemetery; a bit further on a road goes inland to the Shrapnel Valley and Plugge's Plateau Cemetery.

Further north from the inland turn-off is Anzac Cove (Anzac Koyu). The ill-fated Allied landing was made here on 25 April 1915, beneath and just south of the Arıburnu cliffs. As it is a memorial reserve, the beach here is off limits to swimmers and picnickers.

A few hundred metres south of the Anzac Memorial is the Arıburnu Cemetery. Less than 1km further north along the seaside road are the cemeteries at No 2 Outpost, set back inland from the road, and the New Zealand No 2 Outpost, right next to the road. The Embarkation Pier Cemetery is shortly beyond them.

Retrace your steps and follow the signs to Lone Pine Cemetery (Kanlı Sırt). It's along the same inland road that passes Shrapnel Valley. At Lone Pine, 400m uphill from the Kanlı Sırt Kitabesi (Bloody Ridge Inscription), Australian forces captured Turkish positions on 6 August. In the few days of the August assault, 4000 men died. The trees that shaded the cemetery were swept away by a 1994 fire, leaving only one: a lone pine planted as a memorial years ago from the seed of the original tree that stood here during the battle. The small tombstones carry touching epitaphs: 'Only son', 'He died for his country' and 'If I could hold your hand once more just to say well done'.

The trenches were separated only by the width of the modern road at Johnston's Jolly, 300m beyond Lone Pine; Courtney's & Steele's Post, another 300m along; and especially at Quinn's Post, another 400m uphill. On the western side at Johnston's Jolly is the Turkish monument to the soldiers of the 125th Regiment who died here on 'Red Ridge' (Kırmızı Sırt/125 Alay Cephesi). At Quinn's Post is the memorial to Sergeant Mehmet, who fought with rocks and his fists after he ran out of ammunition; and the Captain Mehmet Cemetery.

Just over 1km uphill from Lone Pine is a monument to Mehmetçik (the Turkish equivalent of GI Joe) on the west side of the road and, on the east side, the cemetery and monument for officers and soldiers of the Ottoman 57th Regiment. As the Anzac troops made their way up the slopes towards Chunuk Bair on 25 April, Atatürk brought up the 57th Infantry Regiment and gave them his famous order: 'I order you not just to attack, but to die. In the time it takes us to die, other troops and commanders will arrive to take our places'. The 57th was wiped out, but held the line and inflicted equally heavy casualties on the Anzacs below.

The statue of an old man showing his granddaughter the battle sites portrays veteran Hüseyin Kaçmaz, who fought in the Balkan Wars, in Gallipoli and in the War of Independence at the fateful Battle of Dumlupınar. He died in 1994 at the age of 110.

A few hundred metres past the 57th Regiment Cemetery, a road goes northwest to the monument to Mehmet Çavuş (another Sergeant Mehmet) and the Nek. It was at the Nek on 7 August 1915 that the 8th (Victorian) and 10th (West Australian) regiments of the 3rd Light Horse Brigade vaulted out of their trenches into withering fire and certain death. Their action was immortalised in Peter Weir's film, *Gallipoli*.

Baby 700 Cemetery on the site of the other object of the assault, is 300m further uphill from Mehmet Çavuş.

At the top of the hill, past the monument to Talat Göktepe, is a 'T' intersection. A right turn takes you to the spot where, having stayed awake for four days straight, Atatürk spent the night of 9–10 August, and to the Kemalyeri (Scrubby Knoll), his command post. A left turn leads after 100m to Chunuk Bair, the first objective of the Allied landing in April 1915, and now the site of the New Zealand memorial. Chunuk Bair was at the heart of the struggle on 6 to 9 August 1915, when 28,000 men died on this ridge. The peaceful pine grove of today makes it difficult to imagine the battlefield of old. The Anzac attack on 6–7 August, which included the New Zealand Mounted Rifle Brigade and a Maori contingent, was deadly, but the attack on the following day was of a ferocity which, according to Atatürk, 'could scarcely be described'.

To the east a road leads up to the Turkish Conkbayırı Mehmetçik Memorial. Here are five gigantic tablets with inscriptions (in Turkish) describing the progress of the battle.

Memorials on the Southern Peninsula can be reached via the road that goes south from near the Kabatepe Information Centre. It's about 18km to the village of Alçıtepe, formerly known as Krythia or Kirte. In the village, signs point out the road southwest to the cemeteries of Twelve Tree Copse and Pink Farm and north to the Turkish cemetery Sargı Yeri and the Nuri Yamut monument.

Heading south, the road passes the Redoubt Cemetery. About 5.5km south of Alçıtepe, just south of the Skew Bridge Cemetery, the road divides, the right fork leading to the village of Seddülbahir and several Allied memorials.

The initial Allied attack was two-pronged, with the southern landing taking place here at the tip of the peninsula on 'V' Beach. Yahya Çavuş was the Turkish officer who led the first resistance to the Allied landing on 25 April 1915, causing heavy casualties. The cemetery named after him, Yahya Çavuş Şehitliği, is between the Helles Memorial and 'V' Beach.

Follow the signs for Yahya Çavuş Şehitliği to reach the Cape Helles British Memorial, 1km beyond the Seddülbahir village square. From the Helles Memorial there are fine views of the Dardanelles, with ships cruising by placidly. Lancashire Landing Cemetery is off to the north along a road marked by a sign.

Retrace your steps to the road division and go east. For Abide and/or Çanakkale Şehitleri Abidesi follow the signs east at Morto Bay. Along the way you pass the French War Memorial and Cemetery. French troops, including a regiment of Africans, attacked Kumkale on the Asian shore in March 1915 with complete success, then re-embarked and landed in support of their British comrades-in-arms at Cape Helles.

Çanakkale Şehitleri Abidesi (Çanakkale Martyrs' Memorial) commemorates all of the Turkish soldiers who fought and died at Gallipoli. It's a gigantic four-legged stone table, almost 42m high and surrounded by landscaped grounds, standing above a war museum. At the foot of the Turkish monument hill is a fine pine-shaded picnic area.

TROY

The approach to Troy Archaeological Site (Truva; Map p213; ☎ 286-283 0536; admission YTL10; ☯ 8.30am-6pm), 36km from Çanakkale, is across rolling grain fields. This is the ancient Troad, all but lost to legend until German-born Californian treasure-seeker and amateur archaeologist Heinrich Schliemann (1822–90) excavated atop a promising hill in 1871. He uncovered four superimposed ancient towns, destroying three others in the process.

The window where you buy your admission ticket is just past the village of Tevfikiye, 500m before the site. Guidebooks (with maps) to the site are available at souvenir shops near the ticket box. The author of one of the guidebooks, Mustafa Askin, is a highly regarded local guide. Check out his website (www.thetroyguide.com) or inquire through Hassle Free Tours (p224).

There are few structures here, but visitors can clearly trace the excavations and can get an idea of what the ancient town must have looked like. With a good guide, it makes a fascinating excursion. The views around the countryside and over to the Dardanelles are a bonus, too.

In Homer's *Iliad,* Troy was the town of Ilium. The Trojan War took place in the 13th century BC, with Agamemnon, Achilles, Odysseus (Ulysses), Patroclus and Nestor on the Achaean (Greek) side, and Priam with his sons Hector and Paris on the Trojan side. Rather than suggesting commercial rivalries as a cause for the war, Homer claimed that Paris had kidnapped the beautiful Helen from her husband, Menelaus, King of Sparta (his reward for giving the golden apple for most beautiful woman to Aphrodite, goddess of love), and the king asked the Achaeans to help him get her back.

During the decade-long war, Hector killed Patroclus and Achilles killed Hector. Paris knew that Achilles' mother had dipped her son in the River Styx to make him invincible. However, to do so she had held him by his heel, the one part of his body that remained unprotected. Hence Paris shot Achilles in the heel and bequeathed a phrase to the English language.

When 10 years of carnage couldn't end the war, Odysseus came up with the idea of the wooden horse filled with soldiers, against which Cassandra warned the Trojans in vain. It was left outside the west gate for the Trojans to wheel inside the walls. At the site there is a wooden replica that children love to climb.

One theory has it that the earthquake of 1250 BC aided the Achaeans by bringing down Troy's formidable walls and allowing them to battle their way into the city. In gratitude to Poseidon, the earth-shaker, they built a monumental wooden statue of his horse. So there may well have been a Trojan horse, even though Homer's account is not historical.

Excavations by Schliemann and others have revealed nine ancient cities, one on top of another, dating back to 3000 BC. The first people lived here during the early Bronze Age. The cities called Troy I to Troy V (3000–1700 BC) had a similar culture, but Troy VI (1700–1250 BC) had a different character, with a new population of Indo-European stock related to the Mycenaeans. The town doubled in size and carried on a prosperous trade with Mycenae.

Troy VII lasted from 1250 to 1050 BC, then languished for four centuries. It was revived as a Greek city (Troy VIII; 700–85 BC) and then as a Roman one (Troy IX; 85 BC–AD 500).

The Kazı Evi (Excavation House) near the wooden horse replica was used by earlier archaeological teams. Today it holds exhibits on work in progress, as well as historical interpretations and a history of the site's excavation that is particularly unkind to Schliemann. The models and illustrations show what Troy looked like at different points in its history.

Of the remaining structures at the site, the oldest still-standing wall in the world; the bouleuterion (council chamber) built circa 800 BC; the stone ramp from Troy II; and the Temple of Athena from Troy VIII, rebuilt by the Romans, are of particular interest.

TRANSPORT

As it's the national capital in all but name, getting to İstanbul is easy. There are two international airports, two *otogars* (bus stations) from which international services arrive and depart, and two international rail stations.

Flights, tours and rail tickets can be booked at www.lonelyplanet.com/travel_services.

AIR
Airlines

Most of İstanbul's airline offices are in the streets around Taksim Square, particularly Cumhuriyet Caddesi (see Map p115), but Turkish Airlines has offices around the city. Travel agencies can also sell air tickets and make reservations. The two major airlines flying domestic routes are Turkish Airlines (www .thy.com) and Onur Air (www.onurair.com.tr), though newcomers Atlasjet (www.atlasjet.com), Fly Air (www .flyair.com.tr) and Pegasus Airlines (www.flypgs.com) are also flying routes.

Airports

The city's main airport, Atatürk International Airport (Atatürk Hava Limanı; flight information ☎ 212-465 3000, 212-465 5555; www.ataturkairport.com), is in Yeşilköy,

23km west of Sultanahmet (the heart of Old İstanbul). The international terminal (Dış Hatlar) is polished and organised. Close by, the domestic terminal (İç Hatlar) is smaller but no less efficient. The city's second international airport, Sabiha Gökçen International Airport (☎ 216-585 5000; www.sgairport.com) at Kurtköy on the Asian side of the city, is popular with low-cost European airlines, but is nowhere near as convenient to get to and from.

There are car-hire desks, exchange offices, a pharmacy, ATMs and a PTT at the international arrivals area at Atatürk International Airport. There is also a 24-hour Tourist Information Office (☎ 212-663 0793) that can supply maps, advice and brochures. A 24-hour supermarket is found in the walkway to the metro. The 24-hour left-luggage service charges YTL12 to YTL15 per suitcase per 24 hours; you'll find the booth to your right as you exit customs.

One of the few annoying things about Atatürk Airport is that travellers must pay to use a trolley on either side of immigration. You can pay in lira (YTL1) or euros (€1), which you get back when you return the trolley.

There's a bank, mini-market and PTT at Sabiha Gökçen. Use of trolleys there is free of charge.

CLIMATE CHANGE & TRAVEL

Climate change is a serious threat to the ecosystems that humans rely upon, and air travel is the fastest-growing contributor to the problem. Lonely Planet regards travel, overall, as a global benefit, but believes we all have a responsibility to limit our personal impact on global warming.

Flying & Climate Change

Pretty much every form of motorised travel generates carbon dioxide (the main cause of human-induced climate change) but planes are far and away the worst offenders, not just because of the sheer distances they allow us to travel, but because they release greenhouse gases high into the atmosphere. The statistics are frightening: two people taking a return flight between Europe and the US will contribute as much to climate change as an average household's gas and electricity consumption over a whole year.

Carbon Offset Schemes

Climatecare.org and other websites use 'carbon calculators' that allow travellers to offset the level of greenhouse gases they are responsible for with financial contributions to sustainable travel schemes that reduce global warming – including projects in India, Honduras, Kazakhstan and Uganda.

Lonely Planet, together with Rough Guides and other concerned partners in the travel industry, support the carbon offset scheme run by climatecare.org. Lonely Planet offsets all of its staff and author travel.

For more information check out our website: www.lonelyplanet.com.

GETTING INTO TOWN
Atatürk International Airport

A taxi from the airport to Sultanahmet or Taksim Square costs around YTL25, more if it's between midnight and 6am or if there's heavy traffic.

There's a quick, cheap Light Rail Transit (LRT) service from the airport to Zeytinburnu, from where it's easy to connect with the tram to Sultanahmet, Eminönü and Kabataş (for Taksim Square). The station is on the lower ground floor beneath the international departures hall – follow the 'Rapid Transit' signs down the escalators and right to the station. A ticket to Aksaray costs a mere YTL1.30. Services depart every 10 minutes or so from 5.40am until 1.40am. When you get off the light rail, the tram platform is right in front of you. You'll need to buy another ticket (YTL1.30) and pass through the turnstiles to board. If you miss the stop at Zeytinburnu (try not to), you can continue on the LRT to Aksaray and then walk to the Yusufpaşa tram stop. To find this, exit the station, cross over busy Adnan Menderes Bulvarı and turn right at the Murat Paşa mosque. A short walk will bring you to another major street, Turgut Özal Caddesi (Millet Caddesi), where the tram stop is located. Cross to the stop near the opposite side of the road. Ticket kiosks are located at the tram stop. The tram makes its way down Divan Yolu to Sultanahmet and then terminates at Eminönü. The entire trip from the airport takes around 50 to 60 minutes to Sultanahmet, 60 to 70 minutes to Eminönü and 85-95 minutes to Taksim.

If you are staying near Taksim Square, the Havaş airport bus (☎ 212-243 3399; www.havas.com.tr) from Atatürk International Airport is your best bet. This departs from outside the arrivals hall. Buses leave at 5am, 6am and then every 30 minutes until 1am; the trip takes between 40 minutes and one hour, depending on traffic. Tickets cost YTL9 (25% more after midnight or before 6am) and the bus stops outside the Havaş ticket office (Map p115) on Cumhuriyet Caddesi, just off Taksim Square.

Many hotels will provide a free pick-up service from Atatürk Airport if you stay with them for three nights or more. There are also a number of cheap (but very slow) shuttle bus services from hotels to the airport for your return trip. These charge around YTL7 – check details with your hotel.

Sabiha Gökçen International Airport

Taxis from this airport to the city are expensive. To Taksim you'll be looking at between YTL50 and YTL60; more if it's after midnight or if the traffic is heavy. To Sultanahmet you'll be looking at anywhere between YTL60 and YTL80 depending on the time of day and the traffic conditions.

The Havaş airport bus (☎ 212-243 3399; www.havas.com.tr) travels from the airport to the Yapı Kredi Plaza in Levent 25 minutes after the arrival of many, but not all, flights. Tickets cost YTL9.50 and the trip takes approximately one hour. From Levent, you can catch a metro to Taksim Square. If you're heading towards the Old City, you'll then need to take the funicular to Kabataş and the tram from Kabataş to Sultanahmet. The service occasionally travels to Taksim – check with the driver.

Hotels rarely provide free pick-up services from Sabiha Gökçen. Shuttle bus services from hotels to the airport for return trips charge around YTL26 but only leave once or twice per day – check details with your hotel.

BOAT
Cruise Ships

Cruise ships arrive at the Karaköy International Maritime Passenger Terminal (Map p103; ☎ 212-249 5776), just near the Galata Bridge.

Ferries & Seabuses

The most enjoyable way to get around town is by ferry. Crossing between the Asian and European shores, these vessels are as efficient as they are popular with locals. The İstanbul Deniz Otobüsleri (☎ 212-444 4436; www.ido.com.tr) has fare and timetable information or you can pick up a printed timetable at any of the ferry docks.

On the European side, the major ferry docks are at the mouth of the Golden Horn (Eminönü, Sirkeci and Karaköy), and at Kabataş, 2km past the Galata Bridge, at the end of the tram line from the airport and Sultanahmet.

Information regarding ferry service times is found throughout the Transport chapter and in the Excursions chapter (p217). The ferries run to two annual timetables: winter (mid-September to mid-June) and summer (mid-June to mid-September). Printed timetables are available from all ferry terminals and an online timetable (in Turkish) is available at www.tdi.com.tr. Tickets (*jetons*) are cheap (usually YTL1.30) and it's possible to use Akbil (see p233) on most routes.

FERRY TRAVEL

Ferries ply the following routes:

- Eminönü–Üsküdar
- Eminönü–Kadıköy (some stop at Haydarpaşa)
- Sirkeci–Harem (daily car ferry from 7am, then every half-hour until 9.30pm)
- Üsküdar–Karaköy–Eminönü–Kasımpaşa–Fener–Balat–Hasköy–Ayvansaray–Sütlüce–Eyüp
- Eminönü–Moda–Bostancı
- Eminönü–Anadolu Kavağı (Bosphorus Excursions Ferry)
- İstinye–T.Burnu–Emirgan–Kanlıca–Anadolu Hisarı–Kandilli–Bebek–Arnavutköy–Çengelköy
- Kabataş–Kadıköy–Kınalıada–Burgazada–Heybeliada–Büyükada (Princes' Islands ferry)
- Kabataş–Üsküdar
- Kabataş–Kadıköy
- Beşiktaş–Üsküdar
- Beşiktaş–Kadıköy
- Karaköy–Kadıköy (some stop at Haydarpaşa)
- Karaköy–Üsküdar
- Sarıyer–Rumeli Kavağı–Anadolu Kavağı–Poyraz
- Sirkeci–Harem

There are also *deniz otobüsü* (fast catamaran or seabus) services, but these ply routes that are of less interest to the traveller; they are also more expensive than the ferries. The most useful seabus routes are Bostancı–Karaköy–Eminönü and Bostancı–Princes' Islands.

BUS

The International İstanbul Bus Station (Uluslararası İstanbul Otogarı; ☎ 212-658 0505) is the city's main bus station for both intercity and international routes. Called simply the *otogar* (bus station), it's in the western district of Esenler, just south of the expressway and about 10km west of Sultanahmet. The LRT service from Aksaray stops here (Otogar stop) on its way from the airport; you can catch this to Aksaray and then connect with a tram to Sultanahmet. If you're going to Beyoğlu, bus 830 leaves from the centre of the *otogar* between 5.45am and 1.40am every three to 25 minutes (depending on the time of day) and takes about an hour to reach Taksim Square. A taxi will cost approximately YTL20 to Sultanahmet, YTL25 to Taksim.

Many bus companies offer a free *servis* (shuttle bus) between the *otogar* and Taksim Square or Sultanahmet. If you're booking a ticket out of İstanbul from a bus office in Taksim (or elsewhere), ask about this service. You'll be asked to front up at the bus office around an hour before your bus is due to leave and a minibus will pick you up and take you from the office to your bus at the *otogar*. If you've just arrived by bus in İstanbul, ask your bus driver about the *servis*. One should be waiting close by to drop you at Sultanahmet or Taksim Square.

There's a smaller bus station on the Asian shore of the Bosphorus at Harem (Map pp46–7; ☎ 216-333 3763), south of Üsküdar and north of Haydarpaşa train station. If you're arriving in İstanbul by bus from anywhere on the Asian side of Turkey, it's always quicker to get out at Harem and take the car ferry to Sirkeci/Eminönü (every 30 minutes from 7.30am to 9.30pm); if you stay on the bus until the *otogar,* you'll add at least an hour to your journey. If you're going the other way, you may want to *catch* your bus here, instead of at the *otogar;* check if this is possible at the bus office.

City Buses

The bus system in İstanbul is extremely efficient. The major bus stands are at Taksim Square, Beşiktaş, Aksaray, Rüstempaşa (Eminönü), Kadıköy and Üsküdar, and most services run between 6.30am and 11.30pm. Destinations and main stops on city bus routes are shown on a sign on the right (kerb) side of the bus (*otobüs*) or on the electronic display at its front.

İETT buses are run by the city and you must have a ticket (YTL1.30) before boarding. Buy tickets from the white booths near major stops and bus, tram and metro stations, or from some nearby shops for a small mark-up (look for 'İETT *otobüs bileti satılır*'). Think about buying enough to last you throughout your stay in the city. You can also use your Akbil (p233) and save some money. Blue private buses regulated by the city called *Özel Halk Otobüsü* run the same routes; these accept cash (pay the conductor) and some accept Akbil.

İETT

İstanbul Elektrik Tramvay ve Tünel (İETT) is responsible for running the public bus, tram, LRT and metro systems in the city. Its excellent website (www.iett.gov.tr) has useful timetable and route information in Turkish and English. The site also has information on the Akbil system.

AKBIL

İstanbul's public transport system is excellent and the Akbil system is one of its best features. If you're staying in the city for a week or more you should consider getting yourself one of these computerised debit fare tags and save yourself time and money when hopping on and off trams, trains, ferries and buses all around the city. Daily (*günlük*), weekly (*haftalık*), 15-day (*15 günlük*) and monthly (*aylık*) Akbil tags are available at the Akbil Gişesi booths at Sirkeci, Eminönü, Aksaray or Taksim Square bus stands for a deposit of YTL7.50 (daily), YTL40 (weekly), YTL60 (15-day) and YTL100 (monthly). When you have your tag, you can charge it with any amount from YTL4 (daily), YTL20 (weekly), YTL30 (15-day) and YTL50 (monthly) at any Akbil booth or at machines at the Tünel, funicular or metro stations. Press the card's metal button into the fare machine on a bus, ferry, LRT, train or tram and – beep – the fare is automatically deducted from your line of credit. Some turnstiles have a display that shows your Akbil's credit balance as you pass through. Akbil fares are 10% lower than cash or ticket fares. You'll get your deposit back when you return the device.

Intercity & International Buses

Many bus offices are in Beyoğlu, near Taksim Square, on Mete and İnönü Caddesis, as well as at the *otogar* (see opposite). This is a list of the top national lines:

Kamil Koç (Map p107; ☎ 252 7223; www.kamilkoc .com.tr in Turkish; İnönü Caddesi 31, Taksim) Services most major cities throughout Turkey.

Ulusoy (Map p107; ☎ 244 6375; www.ulusoy.com .tr; İnönü Caddesi 59, Taksim) Ulusoy runs twice-weekly buses to and from Greece, Germany and France, as well as services to most major cities in Turkey.

Varan Turizm (Map p107; ☎ 212-251 7474; www.varan .com.tr; İnönü Caddesi 29B, Taksim) Varan is a premium line with routes to major Turkish cities and to several points in Europe, including Athens.

CAR
Driving

It makes no sense to drive in İstanbul. The traffic is hectic, free parking is scarce and drivers can be aggressive. If you have a car, we suggest leaving it at your hotel or in a car park (*otopark*) and using public transport, except perhaps for excursions out of the city.

Drivers must have a valid driving licence. An International Driving Permit (IDP) is required for stays of more than three months, or if your licence is from a locality that a Turkish police officer is likely to find obscure. Drive on the right-hand side of the road. The speed limit is 50km/h in urban areas and 120km/h on motorways.

The Türkiye Turing ve Otomobil Kurumu (Turkish Touring & Automobile Club; ☎ 212-282 81 40; www.turing.org.tr; Oto Sanayi Sitesi Yanı, Çamlık Caddesi 4, Levent) has licence and other information you'll need to hire a car or bring your own vehicle into the country.

Between 9am and 5pm it offers a breakdown service (☎ 212-278 6214).

Hire

You need to be at least 21 years old, with a year's driving experience, to be able to rent a car. You must pay with a major credit card, or you will be required to make a large cash deposit. Most rental cars have standard gearshift; you'll pay more to have automatic transmission and air-conditioning.

Rental cars are moderately expensive in Turkey, partly due to huge excise taxes paid when the cars are purchased. A week's rental will be between YTL490 and YTL560, depending on the type of car and the time of year. Child safety seats are usually available for an extra charge.

Mandatory third-party liability insurance and KDV (value-added tax) are included in the standard charge. Optional collision damage waiver, theft protection and SOS personal accident and health insurance are also offered by all companies for an extra cost.

If your car incurs any accident damage, or if you cause any, do not move the car before finding a police officer and asking for a *kaza raporu* (accident report). The officer may ask you to submit to a breath-alcohol test. Contact your car-rental company within 48 hours. Your insurance coverage may be void if it can be shown that you were operating under the influence of alcohol or other drugs, were speeding, or if you did not submit the required accident report within 48 hours.

The agencies listed below are among many with 24-hour booths at the arrivals hall in Atatürk Airport's international terminal:

Avis (Map p115; head office ☎ 212-246 5256; www .avis.com.tr; Hilton Hotel Arcade, Cumhuriyet Caddesi 107, Elmadağ); Atatürk International Airport (☎ 212-662 0852)

MARVELLOUS MARMARAY

Marmaray (www.marmaray.com) is an ambitious public transport infrastructure project aimed at relieving İstanbul's serious traffic congestion. It involves rebuilding the rail line that currently stretches between Yeşilköy on the coast and Sirkeci Station on the Golden Horn; the stretch between Yedikule and Sirkeci will go underground. The line will continue from Sirkeci underneath the Bosphorus to another new underground station in Üsküdar, on the Asian side of the city, before terminating at Söğütlüçeşme, past Kadıköy.

The project's completion date is slated as 2010, but this is proving a challenge due to the many important archaeological finds that have been made during excavation works, which are slowing the process down. These include the site of a Byzantine harbour complete with boats at Yenikapı and an ancient port and bazaar at Üsküdar.

Budget (Map p115; head office ☎ 212-296 3196; www .budget.com; Cumhuriyet Caddesi 12, Gezi Apartımanı Kat 4, Elmadağ); Atatürk International Airport (☎ 212-663 0808)

Hertz (Map p127; head office ☎ 216-349 3040; www .hertz.com; Bağdat Caddesi 146, Feneryolu, Kadıköy); Atatürk International Airport (☎ 212-465 5999)

National (Map p115; Taksim office ☎ 212-254 7719; www .nationalcar.com; Şehit Muhtar Mah Aydede Sokak 1/2, Taksim); Atatürk International Airport (☎ 212-465 3546)

DOLMUŞ

A dolmuş is a shared minibus; it waits at a specified departure point until it has a full complement of passengers (in Turkish, dolmuş means full), then follows a fixed route to its destination. Destinations are displayed in the window of the dolmuş. Passengers flag down the driver to get on and indicate to the driver when they want to get off, usually by saying 'inecek var'. Fares vary (pay on board) and are slightly more expensive than those on the municipal buses, but dolmuşes are almost as comfortable as taxis, run later into the night in many instances and sometimes ply routes that buses don't service.

FUNICULAR & CABLE-CAR

There are two funiculars (funıküleri) and one cable-car (teleferic) in the city.

An antique funicular called the Tünel carries passengers between Karaköy, at the base of the Galata Bridge, to Tünel Square, the southwestern end of İstiklal Caddesi. It was closed for restoration at the time of research.

The second funicular carries passengers from Kabataş – at the end of the tram line from Zeytinburnu, through the Old City and over the Galata Bridge – to Taksim Square in Taksim, where it connects to the metro.

A cable-car runs between the waterside at Eyüp to the Pierre Loti Café.

All are short trips (approximately three minutes) and cost YTL1.30. Akbil can be used.

LIGHT RAIL TRANSIT (LRT)

The excellent LRT service connects Aksaray with the airport, stopping at 15 stations, including the otogar, along the way. Trains leave every 10 minutes or so from 5.40am to 1.40am. There are plans to extend the service to Yenikapı. Tickets cost YTL1.30 and Akbil can be used.

METRO

From Taksim there is a service stopping at Osmanbey, Şişli, Gayrettepe, Levent and Levent 4. The full trip takes 25 minutes. Services run every five minutes or so from 6.15am to 12.30am Monday to Thursday, 6.15am to 1am on Friday and Saturday and 6.30am to 12.20am on Sunday. Tickets cost YTL1.30 and Akbil can be used.

See left for details of the one-stop Tünel underground system between Karaköy and Tünel Square and the new funicular from Kabataş to Taksim Square.

TAXI

İstanbul is full of taxis. Some drivers are lunatics; others are con artists – most are neither. If you're caught with the first category and you're about to go into meltdown, say 'yavaş!' (careful/slow down!). Drivers in the second of these categories – the con artists – are unfortunately reasonably common. All taxis have digital meters and must run them, but some of these drivers ask for a flat fare, or pretend the meter doesn't work so they can gouge you at the end of the run. The best way to counter this is to tell them no meter, no ride.

A base rate (drop rate, flag fall) is levied during the daytime (*gündüz*); the night-time (*gece*) rate, from midnight to 6am, is 50% higher. Meters, with LCD displays, flash '*gündüz*' or '*gece*' when they are started. Occasionally, drivers try to put the night-time (*gece*) rate on during the day, so watch out.

Few taxis have seatbelts. If you catch a taxi over either of the Bosphorus Bridges, it is your responsibility to cover the toll. The driver will add this to your fare.

TRAIN
Long-Distance Trains
All trains from Europe terminate at Sirkeci Railway Station (Map p63; ☎ 212-527 0051; Ankara Caddesi, Sirkeci), right next to Eminönü. Outside the station's main door there's a convenient tram up the hill to Sultanahmet, Beyazıt and Zeytinburnu and across the Galata Bridge to Kabataş, from where you can catch a funicular to Taksim Square.

International services from Sirkeci include the Bosfor Ekspres service leaving at 10pm on Monday, Wednesday, Friday and Saturday, going to Budapest (YTL185.40, 33 hours). There is also a slow daily service (the Dostlu/ Filia Ekspres) to Thessaloniki (YTL89.30, 16 hours) departing at 8pm, where you can connect with trains to Athens.

Trains from the Asian side of Turkey, and from points east and south, terminate at Haydarpaşa Railway Station (Map p127; ☎ 216-336 4470; Haydarpaşa İstasyon Caddesi, Kadıköy), on the Asian shore of the Bosphorus close to Kadıköy. Ignore anyone who suggests you should take a taxi to or from Haydarpaşa. The ferry from the station is cheap, convenient, pleasant and speedy. Taxis across the Bosphorus are expensive and slow.

Services from Haydarpaşa include eight daily departures to Ankara (YTL11.75

to YTL100). International services from Haydarpaşa include the Transasya Espress to Tehran (YTL98), leaving at 10.55pm on Wednesday; and the Toros Espress to Aleppo (YTL57), leaving at 8.55pm on Sunday.

Haydarpaşa has a left-luggage room (*emanet*), a restaurant serving alcoholic beverages, numerous snack shops, left-luggage lockers, bank ATMs and a small post office (PTT).

Local Trains
There are two suburban train lines (*banliyö treni*) in İstanbul. The first rattles along the Sea of Marmara shore from Sirkeci Railway Station, around Seraglio Point to Cankurtaran, Kumkapı, Yenikapı and a number of stations before it terminates past Atatürk International Airport at Halkalı. This is currently being rebuilt (see the Marvellous Marmaray boxed text, opposite). The second runs from Haydarpaşa railway station to Gebze, via Bostancı. The trains are dirty and decrepit but reasonably reliable (nearly every half-hour) and cheap (YTL1.30 to YTL1.50). Akbil can be used.

TRAM
An excellent tramway (*tramvay*) service runs from Zeytinburnu (where it connects with the airport LRT) to Sultanahmet and Eminönü, and then across the Galata Bridge to Karaköy (to connect with the Tünel) and Kabataş (to connect with the funicular to Taksim Square). Trams run every five minutes from 6am to midnight. The fare is YTL1.30 and Akbil can be used.

A two-stop antique tram runs along İstiklal Caddesi between Tünel and Taksim Squares in Beyoğlu.

A tram also runs between Kadıköy Square on the Asian side and the exclusive residential suburb of Moda.

DIRECTORY

BUSINESS HOURS

Opening hours vary wildly across businesses and services in İstanbul. Actual opening hours are cited with every restaurant, bar, shop and museum listing throughout this book. The following is a very general guide:

Banks 8.30am to noon and 1.30pm to 5pm Monday to Friday.

Grocery shops 6am or 7am to 7pm or 8pm.

Offices Government and business hours are usually 8am or 9am to noon and 1.30pm to 5pm Monday to Friday; however during Ramazan (p239) the work day is shortened.

Post Offices 8.30am to 12.30pm and 1.30pm to 5.30pm.

Shops 9am to 6pm or 7pm Monday to Saturday; some shops close for lunch (noon to 1.30pm or 2.30pm); some stay open late and others are open seven days.

CHILDREN

Your child (çocuk) or children (çocuklar) will be treated indulgently in İstanbul. Given the high Turkish birth rate, they'll have lots of company, too. The larger hotels can arrange for day-care (kreş) and baby-sitting services. Charges are usually negotiated directly with the childcare centre or baby-sitter. Chains like Mothercare have opened large stores in major shopping malls such as Cevahir and Akmerkez, and stock everything you could possibly need. Disposable nappies (bebek bezi) and formula are sold at supermarkets. The best brands of nappies are Prima and Huggies.

Lonely Planet's *Travel with Children* offers useful general advice for families travelling with children.

CLIMATE

The best times to visit İstanbul are around spring and autumn, roughly from April to May and from September to October, when the climate is perfect. During July and August it is hot and steamy; a lot of İstanbullus head for the west and south coasts over these months. Chill winter winds and snow are common in winter.

CONSULATES

Embassies (büyükelçiliği) are in Ankara, the national capital. The following countries are among many who have consulates (konsolosluğu) in İstanbul:

Australia (☎ 212-243 1333; Asker Ocağı Caddesi 15, Suzer Plaza Kat 2, Elmadağ, Şişli)

Canada (Map p107; ☎ 212-251 9838; İstiklal Caddesi 373/5, Beyoğlu)

Egypt (☎ 212-324 2180; Akasyalı Sokak 26, 4 Levent)

France (Map p107; ☎ 212-334 8730; İstiklal Caddesi 8, Taksim)

Germany (Map p107; ☎ 212-334 6100; İnönü Caddesi 16/18, Taksim)

Greece (Map p107; ☎ 212-245 0596; Turnacıbaşı Sokak 32, Galatasaray)

Iran (Map p107; ☎ 212-513 8230; Ankara Caddesi 1/2, Cağaloğlu)

Israel (☎ 212-317 6500; Yapı Kredi Plaza, Blok C, Kat 7, Levent)

Italy (Map p107; ☎ 212-243 1024; Palazzo di Venezia, Tomtom Kaptan Sokak 15, Galatasaray)

Japan (☎ 212-317 4600; Büyükdere Caddesi, Tekfen Tower 4, Levent)

Netherlands (Map p107; ☎ 212-393 2121; İstiklal Caddesi 393, Tünel)

Spain (☎ 212-270 2465; Karanfil Aralığı Sokak 16, Levent)

Syria (Map p115; ☎ 212-232 6721; Maçka Caddesi 59, Ralli Apt 3, Nişantaşı)

UK (Map p107; ☎ 212-334 6400; Meşrutiyet Caddesi 34, Tepebaşı)

USA (☎ 212-335 9000; Kaplıcalar Mevkii 2, İstinye)

COURSES
Belly Dancing

Les Arts Turcs (Map p50; ☎ 212-458 1318, 212-520 7743; www.lesartsturcs.com; İncili Çavuş Sokak 37, Kat 3, Sultanahmet;

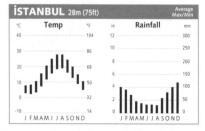

İSTANBUL 28m (75ft) — Average Max/Min — Temp / Rainfall

10am-8pm) can organise private lessons in Turkish-style belly dancing for YTL80 per hour for one or two participants.

Cooking

See p157 for details of cooking courses in İstanbul.

Handicrafts

The historic Caferağa Medresesi (Map p63; ☎ 212-513 3601; www.tkhv.org; Caferiye Sokak, Sultanahmet) is the home of the Turkish Cultural Services Foundation, which runs courses for locals and travellers in techniques such as calligraphy, miniature painting, marbling, binding and glass painting. Courses are organised into 2½-hour sessions one day per week over three months and cost YTL360. It also occasionally organises day courses costing YTL36.

Language

The best-known Turkish-language courses for native English speakers are run by Taksim Dilmer (☎ 212-292 9696; www.dilmer.com; Tarık Zafer Tunaya Sokak 18, Taksim). On offer are eight-week courses (96 hours total) costing YTL670; four-week courses (80 hours total) costing YTL560; and eight-week evening courses (72 hours total) costing YTL500. Classes have a maximum of 14 students. Other language schools include EF Language School (www.turkishlesson.com), Spoken Turkish (ww.spokenenglish.com) and Tömer (www.tomer.com.tr).

CUSTOMS REGULATIONS

İstanbul's Atatürk International Airport uses the red and green channel system, randomly spot-checking passengers' luggage. Items valued over US$15,000 must be declared and may be entered in your passport to guarantee that you take the goods out of the country. You're allowed to bring two bottles of wine, one carton (200) of cigarettes, 1.5kg of coffee and 10 cigars (100 cigars if they are purchased from the duty-free shop at the airport arrivals hall). There's no limit to the amount of Turkish liras or foreign currency you can bring into the country. It's illegal to take antiquities out of the country. Check www.gumruk.gov.tr for more information.

ELECTRICITY

Electricity in İstanbul is supplied at 220V, 50Hz, as in Europe. Plugs (fiş) are of the European variety, with two round prongs. There are infrequent power cuts across the city, so it's a good idea to travel with a torch (flashlight) in your bag or pocket. Check www.kropla.com for more information.

EMERGENCY

Ambulance (☎ 112)

Fire (☎ 110)

Police (☎ 155)

Tourism police (☎ 212-527 4503)

GAY & LESBIAN TRAVELLERS

Homosexuality isn't illegal in Turkey, but neither is it officially legal. There's an ambivalent attitude towards it among the general population, though there are sporadic reports of violence towards gays, and conservative İstanbullus frown upon open displays of affection between persons of the same sex.

Lambda (Map p107; ☎ 212-245 7068; www.lambda istanbul.org; Katip Çelebi Mah. Tel Sokak 28/6 Kat 5, Beyoğlu) is the Turkish branch of the international Gay, Lesbian, Bisexual and Transgender Liberation Group. It organises occasional events at its information centre (☎ 3-8pm weekdays, 1-8pm weekends).

The monthly *Time Out İstanbul* mag includes gay and lesbian listings. Kaos GL (www.geocities.com/kaosgl) is the country's only gay and lesbian magazine; it's published in Turkish only.

Pride Travel Agency (Map p50; ☎ 212-527 0671; www.travelagencyturkey.com; İncili Çavuş Sokak 33/11, Ateş Pasajı Kat 2, Sultanahmet) is a well-regarded gay-owned and gay-run travel agency specialising in booking accommodation and tours for gay travellers.

For more information about gay and lesbian issues in the city, see the boxed text, p183.

HEALTH
Food & Water

Travellers in Turkey experience a fair amount of travellers diarrhoea (the sultan's revenge) and it's possible that you'll pick up a bout in İstanbul, particularly if you eat street food (see the boxed text Fancy Some Bacteria with That?, p148).

DINING PRECAUTIONS

In lokantas choose dishes that look freshly prepared and sufficiently hot.

Beware of milk products and dishes containing milk that have not been properly refrigerated. If you want a rice pudding (süt-laç) or some such dish with milk in it, choose a shop that has lots of them in the window, meaning that a batch has been made recently. In general, choose things from trays, pots etc that are fairly full rather than almost empty. Eating some fresh yogurt every day can also help to keep your digestive system in good condition.

DRINKING PRECAUTIONS

Tap water in İstanbul is chlorinated, but is still not guaranteed to be safe (most locals don't drink it). Spring water is sold everywhere in 0.33L, 1.5L and 3L plastic bottles and is very cheap.

Illnesses
FOOD POISONING & TRAVELLERS DIARRHOEA

Food-poisoning symptoms are headaches, nausea and/or stomachache, diarrhoea, fever and chills. If you get food poisoning, go to bed and stay warm. Drink lots of fluids; preferably hot tea without sugar or milk. Chamomile tea (papatya çay) can ease a queasy stomach.

Simple things like a change of water, food or climate can all cause a mild bout of diarrhoea, but a few rushed toilet trips with no other symptoms is not indicative of a major problem.

Dehydration is the main danger with any diarrhoea, particularly in children or the elderly, as dehydration can occur quite quickly.

Gut-paralysing drugs such as loperamide or diphenoxylate can be used to bring relief from the symptoms, although they do not actually cure the problem. Only use these drugs if you do not have access to toilets, eg if you *must* travel. Note that these drugs are not recommended for children under 12 years.

If you experience diarrhoea with blood or mucus (dysentery), any diarrhoea with fever, profuse watery diarrhoea, persistent diarrhoea not improving after 48 hours or severe diarrhoea, antibiotics may be required. These symptoms suggest a more serious cause of diarrhoea and in these situations gut-paralysing drugs should be avoided. A stool test may be necessary to diagnose what bug is causing your diarrhoea, so seek medical help urgently.

Fluid replacement is important. Weak black tea with a little sugar, soda water, or soft drinks allowed to go flat and diluted 50% with bottled water are all good. You need to drink at least the same volume of fluid that you are

losing in bowel movements and vomiting. Urine is the best guide to the adequacy of replacement – if you have small amounts of concentrated urine, you need to drink more. Keep drinking small amounts often. Stick to a bland diet as you recover.

Other Health Risks

Turks smoke like chimneys. If you are asthmatic or allergic and have difficulty coping with cigarette smoke, you'll find İstanbul challenging because there are so few places to escape it. Nonsmoking restaurants and bars are almost unknown, taxi drivers smoke incessantly and few hotels have designated nonsmoking rooms.

Vaccinations

You need no special inoculations before entering Turkey unless you're coming from an endemic or epidemic area. However, do discuss your requirements with a doctor. Consider typhoid fever and hepatitis A and B vaccinations if you plan to travel off the beaten track in Turkey; also make sure that your tetanus/diphtheria and polio vaccinations are up to date (boosters are necessary every 10 years).

A rabies vaccination should be considered for those who plan to stay for a month or longer in Turkey, where rabies is common. Rabid dogs have been a problem in İstanbul in the recent past, but the council now vaccinates dogs (the yellow tag on the ear shows they've been vaccinated) and the danger seems to have been alleviated somewhat.

HOLIDAYS

The official Turkish calendar is the Gregorian (Western) one. Friday is the Muslim holy day, but it is not a holiday. The day of rest, a secular one, is Sunday.

Religious Holidays

Religious festivals, two of which (Şeker Bayramı and Kurban Bayramı) are public holidays, are celebrated according to the Muslim lunar Hejira calendar. As the lunar year is about 11 days shorter than the Gregorian one, Muslim festivals occur 11 days earlier each year.

Muslim days begin at sundown. Thus a Friday holiday will begin on Thursday at sunset and last until Friday at sunset.

For major religious and civic holidays there is also a half-day vacation for preparation, called *arife*, preceding the start of a festival; shops and offices close about noon, and the festival begins at sunset.

Day-to-day business in İstanbul shuts down during religious holidays, and roads and flights out of town are full of locals escaping to the coast or mountains. Hotels in town and flights into the city can be busy with people from other parts of Turkey and the Middle East who have decided to escape to İstanbul.

RAMAZAN (RAMADAN)
During the Holy Month of Ramazan, called Ramadan in other Muslim countries, a good Muslim lets *nothing* pass the lips during daylight: no eating, drinking or smoking.

The fast is broken traditionally with flat *pide* (bread). Lavish *iftar* (breaking of the fast) dinners are given and may last far into the night. Before dawn, drummers circulate throughout the town to awaken the faithful so they can eat before sunrise.

Although many İstanbullus observe the fast, most restaurants and cafés open to serve non-Muslims and locals who are not. It's polite to avoid ostentatious public smoking, eating, drinking and drunkenness during Ramazan.

Ramazan starts on 2 September 2008 and 22 August 2009. The 27th day of Ramazan is *Kadir Gecesi* (Night of Power) when the Quran was revealed and Mohammed appointed the Messenger of God.

Also see the boxed text Ramazan in the Hippodrome, p57.

ŞEKER BAYRAMI
This is a three-day festival at the end of Ramazan. *Şeker* (shek-*ehr*) is sugar or candy. During this festival children traditionally go door to door asking for sweet treats, Muslims exchange greeting cards and pay social calls, and everybody enjoys drinking lots of tea in broad daylight after fasting for Ramazan. The festival is a national holiday when banks and offices are closed, and hotels, buses, trains and planes are heavily booked.

KURBAN BAYRAMI
Called Eid al-Adha in Arabic countries, this is the most important religious holiday of the year. Meaning Sacrifice Holiday, it is a four-day festival commemorating Abraham's near-sacrifice of his son on Mt Moriah (Genesis 22; Quran, Sura 37). Right after the early morning prayers on the actual day of Bayram, the head of the household sacrifices a sheep. A feast is prepared, with much of the meat going to charity. Almost everything closes, including banks, and public transport is crowded with families heading for their ancestral homes, usually in the country.

Secular Holidays
Banks, offices and government services close for the day on the five secular public holidays per year. These are New Year's Day (1 January), National Sovereignty & Children's Day (23 April), Youth & Sports Day (19 May), Victory Day (30 August) and Republic Day (29 October).

INTERNET ACCESS
There are internet cafés all over İstanbul, usually filled with adolescents playing computer games. Look for internet cafés that advertise having an ADSL connection; other places can be frustratingly slow. Most hostels and hotels now also offer wi-fi internet access for their guests. For city hotspots, check www.ttwinet.ttnet.net.tr/eng.

When in a local internet café, you may have to use a Turkish keyboard, in which case you need to be aware that Turkish has two 'i's: the familiar dotted 'i' and the less-familiar dotless 'ı'. Unfortunately the one in the usual place is the dotless 'ı' on a Turkish keyboard; you will need to make sure you use the correct dotted 'i' when typing in a web or email address. To create the @ symbol, hold down the 'q' and the right-hand ALT keys at the same time.

The following places have relatively fast connections and staff who know what they're talking about.

Café Turka Internet Café (Map p50; ☎ 212-514 6551; Divan Yolu Caddesi 22/2, Sultanahmet; per hr YTL2.50; 🕙 9am-2am) This place is always full of backpackers and Sultanahmet locals, who come to check their email and drink tea while lolling on the beanbag chairs. It's on the 2nd floor above SDC Turizm.

Robin Hood Internet (Map p107; ☎ 212-244 8959; Yeni Çarşı Caddesi 24/4, Galatasaray; per hr YTL2; 🕙 9am-11pm Mon-Sat, 11am-10pm Sun) Opposite the Galatasaray Lycée, this friendly place has lots of terminals inside and wi-fi access on its balcony. Coffee, tea and sandwiches are available. It's on the 4th floor up a steep flight of stairs.

MAPS
Lonely Planet produces a handy, laminated *İstanbul* city map that includes a walking tour.

Free maps in several different languages are usually available from tourist information offices. English maps are sometimes available in the arrivals hall at Atatürk International Airport. For more detailed guidance, look for *Sokak Sokak İstanbul* (İstanbul Street by Street) in bookshops. It costs YTL50.

MEDICAL SERVICES

The fact that Turkey doesn't have reciprocal health-care arrangements with other countries means that having travel insurance is highly advisable.

For minor problems, it's customary to ask at a chemist/pharmacy *(eczane)* for advice. Sign language usually suffices to communicate symptoms and the pharmacist will prescribe treatment on the spot. Drugs requiring a prescription in Western countries are often sold over the counter (except for the most dangerous or addictive ones) and will often be cheaper, too. Ensure you know the generic name of your medicine; the commercial name may not be the same in Turkey. See the Language chapter for a list of medical terms; for a more comprehensive list, get a copy of Lonely Planet's *Turkish Phrasebook*. The word for hospital is '*hastanesi*'.

Most doctors in Turkey speak English and half of all the physicians in İstanbul are women. If a woman visits a male doctor, it's customary to have a companion present during any physical examination or treatment, as there is not always a nurse available to serve in this role.

If it's an emergency and you want to try a public hospital, consider Taksim Hastanesi (Emergency Hospital; Map p107; ☎ 212-252 4300; Sıraselviler Caddesi, Cihangir; ⏰ 24hr) The doctors speak English, and charges are the same whether or not you're a foreign visitor/resident or a Turkish citizen.

Though they are expensive, it's probably easiest to visit one of the private hospitals listed below if you need medical care when in İstanbul. The standard of care given by these places is generally quite high and you will have no trouble finding staff who speak English.

Alman Hastanesi (German Hospital; Map p107; ☎ 212-293 2150; Sıraselviler Caddesi 119, Taksim; ⏰ 8.30am-6pm Mon-Fri, 8.30am-5pm Sat) This hospital is a few hundred metres south of Taksim Square on the left-hand side. It has eye and dental clinics, German administration and English-speaking staff. A standard consultation costs YTL120. Credit cards are accepted.

American Hastanesi (American Hospital; off Map p115; ☎ 212-311 2000; Güzelbahçe Sokak 20, Nişantaşı ⏰ 24hr emergency department) About 2km northeast of Taksim Square, this hospital has a US administration (all doctors speak English) and a dental clinic. A standard consultation costs YTL140. Credit cards are accepted.

MONEY

The unit of currency is the *Yeni Türk Lirası* (New Turkish Lira; YTL). Coins come in amounts of 1, 5, 10, 25 and 50 kuruş and notes in 5, 10, 20, 50 and 100 lira.

In this book, we have cited prices for hotels and organised tours in euros, as this reflects the reality on the ground. All other prices are in YTL.

Also see the exchange-rate table in the Quick Reference section on the inside front cover.

ATMs

Automated teller machines (ATMs, cashpoints) are common in İstanbul. Virtually all of them offer instructions in English, French and German and will pay out Turkish liras when you insert your bank debit (cash) card. ATMs will also pay cash advances on Visa and Mastercard. The limit on cash withdrawals is generally YTL600 to YTL800 per day, though this varies from bank to bank.

All of the major Turkish banks and some smaller banks have ATMs; Akbank and Yapı Kredi are the most common. The specific machine you use must be reliably connected to the major ATM networks' computers via telephone lines. Look for stickers with the logos of these services (Cirrus, Maestro, Plus Systems etc) affixed to the machine. If the connection is not reliable, you may get a message saying that the transaction was refused by your bank (which may not be true) and your card will (hopefully) be returned to you.

Changing Money

There are 24-hour exchange bureaux (*döviz bürosu*) in the arrivals hall at Atatürk International Airport that offer rates comparable to those offered by bureaux in the city. Count the money you're given carefully and save your currency-exchange receipts (*bordro*), as you may need them to reconvert Turkish liras at the end of your stay.

US dollars and euros are easily changed at exchange bureaux. They are also often accepted as payment without being changed.

Rates are similar whichever bureau you go to, with the possible exception of those in the tourist precinct of Sultanahmet. Bureaux are open long hours (at a minimum, between 9am and 7pm). You will usually need to show your passport when changing cash.

As Turkish liras are fully convertible, there is no black market.

Credit Cards

Most hotels, car-rental agencies, shops, pharmacies, entertainment venues and restaurants will accept Visa and Mastercard; Amex isn't as widely accepted as the others and Diner's isn't accepted often. Budget hostels and hotels, and basic eateries such as lokantas, *pidecis*, *kebapçıs* and *börekçis*, usually accept cash only.

Travellers Cheques

If you have travellers cheques, you will have to change them at a bank or post office. Exchange bureaux do not handle them. You'll need to show your passport.

NEWSPAPERS & MAGAZINES

Local daily newspapers are in full lurid colour featuring scantily clad women squeezed between the advertisements. The journalistic content is best left unmentioned. Of prime interest to visitors is the Turkish Daily News (www.turkishdailynews.com.tr), an English-language daily newspaper published in Ankara and sold for YTL1.50 in İstanbul. It has some international news and an oversupply of self-important editorial opinion and is in hot competition with two newish English-language dailies: the New Anatolian (www.thenewanatolian.com; YTL1) and Today's Zaman (www.todayszaman.com; YTL1.50).

The *Guide İstanbul* is published bi-monthly and runs listings of restaurants, shops and other services. Features can be interesting, but often read as advertorial. It costs YTL5.50.

There are monthly Turkish and English editions of the Time Out İstanbul (www.timeout.com.tr) magazine. Like the *Guide İstanbul*, this has a large listings section. Its features are particularly interesting, and it is the best source of details about upcoming events in town. It costs YTL4. Time Out also publishes an annual shopping guide (in Turkish).

The glossy magazine *Cornucopia* has excellent restaurant reviews and articles on Anatolian arts, culture, history and literature. It's published three times per year and costs YTL20.

You can also buy the big international papers such as the *International Herald Tribune*, *Le Monde* and the *Guardian* from newsstands. Be sure to check the date on any international paper before you buy it. The best selection of international magazines can be found at the Remzi Kitabevi bookshops at Akmerkez and Kanyon (see p143).

ORGANISED TOURS

The following companies offer tours of the city:

Kirkit Voyage (Map p50; ☎ 212-518 2282; www.kirkit.com; Amiral Tafdil Sokak 12, Cankurtaran; tours €23-50; ⏰ 10am-8pm) This small agency in the middle of the main hotel district in Sultanahmet specialises in tailoring walking tours for groups of two or more. You can choose from its 'Classic İstanbul', 'Ottoman İstanbul', 'Byzantine İstanbul' and 'Old Pera: The Hills of Beyoğlu' half- and full-day tours, as well as specialised tours such as 'İstanbul: The Unusual Way', which explores *hans* (caravansaries) around the Grand Bazaar. Other tours visit sights by public transport and minibus. It can also organise private guides (€110 per day, €80 per half-day).

Les Arts Turcs (Map p50; ☎ 212-458 1318, 212-520 7743; www.lesartsturcs.com; İncili Çavuş Sokak 37, Kat 3, Sultanahmet; tours €35-85; ⏰ 10am-8pm) This friendly company, which has a strong arts and culture bias, organises a wide range of 'off-the-beaten-path walking tours' of neighbourhoods around the city. There are special tours of Jewish, Armenian and Greek neighbourhoods and to the Princes' Islands. It also runs a highly recommended tour to a Dervish ceremony in Fatih (see p109). At the time of research, the company was planning to relocate its office to İshakpaşa Caddesi 6, Cankurtaran, next to the entrance to Topkapı Palace (Map p63).

Senkron Travel Agency (Map p50; ☎ 212-638 8340; www.senkrontours.com; Arasta Bazaar 51, Sultanahmet; tours €25-60; ⏰ 8am-9pm) This professional outfit offers 10 different bus tours, including a day tour of the Bosphorus and Dolmabahçe Palace and one of the Christian highlights of the city.

POST

Post offices, marked by black-on-yellow signs, are traditionally known as PTTs (peh-teh-teh; *Posta, Telefon, Teleğraf*). İstanbul's Central Post Office (Merkez Postane; Map p63; Şehinşah Pehlevi Caddesi, Eminönü) is several blocks southwest of Sirkeci Railway Station. It has a section open 24 hours a day, where you can make phone calls, buy stamps and send and receive faxes.

There's a PTT booth (Map p50) outside Aya Sofya on Aya Sofya Meydanı in Sultanahmet, which is open 9am to 4pm Tuesday to Sunday. There are PTTs in the law courts (Map p50) on İmran

Öktem Caddesi in Sultanahmet; off İstiklal Caddesi at Galatasaray Square (Map p107); near the Galata Bridge (Map p103) in Karaköy; and in the southwestern corner of the Kapalı Çarşı (Map p78) near the Havuzlu Restaurant on Gani Çelebi Sokak.

The *yurtdışı* slot is for mail to foreign countries, *yurtiçi* is for mail to other Turkish cities, and *şehiriçi* is for mail within İstanbul. Mail delivery is fairly reliable. Postcards to Europe cost YTL1 and to all other destinations YTL1.10.

If you decide to ship something home, don't close your parcel before it has been inspected by a customs official. Take packing and wrapping materials with you to the post office. Parcels sent by surface mail to Europe cost YTL25 for the first kilogram, then YTL3.50 for every extra kilogram; mailing to the US and Australasia is more expensive.

The easiest way to send a parcel is by courier; there is a DHL office (☎ 212-444 0040) conveniently located on Cumhuriyet Caddesi just north of Taksim Square. Be prepared for a hefty charge, though.

SAFETY
Pedestrian Safety

As a pedestrian, give way to cars and trucks in all situations, even if you have to jump out of the way. The sovereignty of the pedestrian is recognised in law but not out on the street.

Police

Blue-clad officers are part of a national force designated by the words *polis* or *emniyet* (security). Under normal circumstances you will have little to do with them. If you do encounter them, they will judge you partly by your personal appearance. If you look tidy and 'proper', they'll be on your side. If you're dressed carelessly they may not be as helpful.

Other blue-clad officers with peaked caps are market inspectors (*belediye zabıtası*). You won't have much to do with them.

Racial Discrimination

Turkey is not ethnically diverse. Its racial mix is mostly among subgroups of the Caucasian group, with admixtures (sometimes ancient) of Asian races. Recent immigration has largely been from Russia and Eastern Europe. This means that travellers who are Asian or black stand out as being different and can be treated unacceptably as a consequence. As well as harassment, there have been isolated incidents of violence towards blacks, allegedly at the hands of individual members of the police force.

Theft & Robbery

Theft is not generally a big problem and robbery (mugging) is comparatively rare, but don't let İstanbul's relative safety lull you. Take normal precautions. Areas to be particularly careful in include Aksaray/Laleli, the city's red-light district; the Grand Bazaar (pickpocket central); İstiklal Caddesi in Beyoğlu; and Galipdede Caddesi in Tünel, where bag snatching sometimes occurs.

Traffic Accidents

It's worth mentioning that Turkey has one of the world's highest motor-vehicle accident rates. Drive very defensively. A massive safety campaign is under way, but its full effects will not be felt for some years.

TELEPHONE & FAX

If you are in European İstanbul and wish to call a number in Asian İstanbul, you must dial 0, followed by ☎ 216. If you are in Asian İstanbul and wish to call a number in European İstanbul use ☎ 212. Do not use a prefix (that is, don't use the 0 or 212/6) if you are calling a number on the same shore.

Country code (☎ 90)

European İstanbul (☎ 212)

Asian İstanbul (☎ 216)

Code to make an intercity call (☎ 0 + local code)

International access code (☎ 00)

Directory inquiries (☎ 118)

International operator (☎ 115)

Türk Telekom (www.telekom.gov.tr) has a monopoly on landline services, and it provides an efficient if costly service. You can direct-dial within Turkey and overseas with little difficulty.

If you're only going to make one or two local calls, it's best to look for a booth with a sign reading *kontörlü telefon* (metered telephone); after making your call here the phone's owner will read the meter and charge you accordingly. The cost of a local call depends on what the phone's owner charges for each *kontör* (unit).

Public phones are located outside PTTs, in most major public buildings, in public squares and in train and ferry stations. You'll need to buy a phonecard to use one (see below).

Fax

Most PTTs will send and hold faxes for you.

Mobile Phones

Mobile reception is very good in İstanbul and locals have embraced the technology whole-heartedly. All mobile numbers start with a four-figure code beginning with ☎ 05.

If you want to use your home phone here you should note that Turkey uses the stan-dard GSM network operating on 900Mhz or 1800Mhz. Most mobiles can connect with Turkcell (www.turkcell.com.tr), Telsim (www.telsim.com.tr) or Avea (www.avea.com.tr) networks. If you want to buy a prepaid SIM card *(hazr kart)* while you're here, we suggest you stick to these three big networks. To buy a SIM card you'll need to show your passport to the dealer and fill out an application form. The dealer will then send this through to the network provider so that your account can be activated.

Phonecards

There are two types of phonecard *(telefon kartı)*: the regular floppy version *(manyetik kart)* or a rigid 'smart kart'. They cost about the same and are both available at telephone shops or centres. To use these cards you call the national toll-free number, put in the PIN number on the card and make your call. Readily available phonecards usually come in denominations of 50-*kontör* (YTL3.75), 100-*kontör* (YTL7.50), 200-*kontör* (YTL15) and 350-*kontör* (YTL19). You'll need a 350-*kontör* card to make an international call. You can't use these cards with mobile phones. Reduced rates for international calls are in effect from 10pm to 9am and all day Sunday.

TIME

İstanbul time is East European Time, two hours ahead of Coordinated Universal Time (UTC, alias GMT), except in the warm months, when clocks are turned ahead one hour. Daylight-saving (summer) time usually begins at 1am on the last Sunday in March and ends at 2am on the last Sunday in October.

Turks use the 24-hour clock.

TOILETS

In most public toilets you must pay around YTL0.50. Instead of providing toilet paper, these toilets are equipped with a tap and receptacle for water or a little copper tube that spurts water where needed. Some toilets are tiled holes in the ground rather than sit-down numbers.

Basic public toilets can be found near the big tourist attractions and transport hubs. Some are dirty, others quite acceptable. Every mosque also has a toilet.

TOURIST INFORMATION

The Ministry of Culture & Tourism (www.kultur.gov.tr) runs the following tourist information offices:

Atatürk International Airport (☎ 212-573 4136; ⏱ 24hr) In the international-arrivals area.

Beyazıt Square (Hürriyet Meydanı; Map p78; ☎ 212-522 4902; ⏱ 9am-5pm Mon-Sat)

Elmadağ (Map p115; ☎ 212-233 0592; ⏱ 9am-5pm Mon-Sat) In the arcade in front of the İstanbul Hilton Hotel, just off Cumhuriyet Caddesi near Taksim Square.

Karaköy International Maritime Passenger Terminal (Map p103; ☎ 212-249 5776; ⏱ 9am-5pm Mon-Sat)

Sultanahmet (Map p50; ☎ 212-518 8754; ⏱ 9am-5pm) At the northeastern end of the Hippodrome.

All usually stock free maps and brochures. At the time of research, there was some talk that the Beyazıt Square office would close.

TRAVELLERS WITH DISABILITIES

İstanbul can be challenging for mobility-impaired travellers. Roads are potholed and pavements are often crooked and cracked. Fortunately, the city is making attempts to rectify this state of affairs.

Government-run museums are free of charge for disabled visitors and many have wheelchair access. Airlines and most four- and five-star hotels have wheelchair access and at least one room set up for disabled guests. All public transport is free for the disabled and both the LRT and *tramvay* (see p235) can be accessed by people in wheelchairs.

VISAS

At the time of research, nationals of the fol-lowing countries (among others) could enter Turkey for up to three months with only a valid passport (no visa is required): Denmark, Finland, France, Germany, Japan, New Zealand, Norway, Sweden and Switzerland.

Nationals of the following countries (among others) could enter for up to three months upon purchase of a visa sticker at their point of arrival (ie not at an embassy in advance): Australia, Belgium, Canada, Greece, Ireland, Italy, Netherlands, Portugal, Spain, UK and USA.

Nationals of Norway, Hungary and many Eastern European and Central Asian countries could enter for up to one month upon purchase of a visa sticker at their point of arrival.

Your passport must have at least three months' validity remaining, or you may not be admitted into Turkey. If you arrive at Atatürk International Airport, get your visa from the booth to the left of the 'Other Nationalities' counter in the customs hall before you go through immigration. You can pay in Turkish lira, euros or US dollars; customs officials sometimes insist on correct change. An ATM machine dispensing Turkish liras is next to the counter, but it's not always working. The fees change, but at the time of research Australians, Americans and Britons paid €15 and Canadians paid €45.

Visa Extensions

There are single- and multiple-entry visas. Single-entry visas are valid for three months from the day of entry; multiple-entry visas are valid for three-month blocks during a one-year period. Depending on your nationality, you may be able to extend your visa. Most visitors wanting to extend their stay for a few months avoid bureaucratic tedium by taking a quick overnight trip to Greece (Thessaloniki or Rhodes), returning to Turkey the next day with a new three-month stamp in their passports. See the website of the Ministry of Foreign Affairs (www.mfa.gov.tr) for the latest information.

WOMEN TRAVELLERS

Travelling in İstanbul as a female is easy and enjoyable provided you follow some simple guidelines. Tailor your behaviour and your clothing to your surrounds – outfits that are appropriate for neighbourhoods such as Beyoğlu and along the Bosphorus (skimpy tops, tight jeans etc) are not appropriate in conservative suburbs such as Balat and Fener, for instance. In general, we suggest you dress in a reasonably demure fashion; showing lots of bare leg and cleavage can lead to attention and occasional lewd behaviour on the part of local men.

Women should be careful when walking alone at night, especially in Aksaray/Laleli, Eminönü and Karaköy. It's a good idea to sit in the back seat of taxis rather than next to the driver. If approached by a Turkish man in circumstances that upset you, try saying *Ayıp!* (ah-*yuhp*), which means 'Shame on you!'

You'll have no trouble finding tampons, sanitary napkins and condoms in pharmacies and supermarkets in İstanbul. Bring a shawl to cover your head when visiting mosques.

WORK

After sampling the manifold delights of İstanbul, many travellers decide to stay. Jobs aren't all that easy to find (Turkey has a very high unemployment level) and most of these people end up teaching English at one of the many private colleges or schools; others get work as nannies (check www.anglonannies.com) or in the tourism industry.

If you want to get a job at one of the well-paid private language schools, you'll need to have a Teaching English as a Foreign Language (TEFL) certificate or equivalent, and a graduate degree (it doesn't matter what it's in).

Other jobs are advertised in the *Turkish Daily News* and on the expat websites www.mymerhaba.com, www.expatinturkey.com and http://craigslist.org.

For loads of practical information and advice about information on living, buying real estate, working and doing business in Turkey, get yourself a copy of Pat Yale's excellent *A Handbook for Living in Turkey,* published by İstanbul-based Çitlembik Publications and available in most of the city's English-language bookshops.

DEIK (www.deik.org.tr) is the Foreign Economic Relations Board of Turkey. Its website has useful links and economic and business information.

LANGUAGE

Turkish is the dominant language in the Turkic language group, and is distantly related to Finnish and Hungarian. In 1928, Atatürk did away with Arabic script and adopted a Latin-based alphabet that was better suited to easy learning and correct pronunciation. He also instituted a language-reform process to purge Turkish of Arabic and Persian borrowings, returning it to its 'authentic' roots. The result is a logical, systematic and expressive language with only one irregular noun, *su* (water), one irregular verb, *olmek* (to be) and no gender. It's so logical, in fact, that Turkish grammar formed the basis for the development of Esperanto, an ill-fated artificial international language. Word order and verb formation in Turkish are very different from what you'll find in Indo-European languages like English. Words are formed by agglu-

tination, meaning that affixes are joined to a root word – one scary example is *Avustralyalılaştıramadıklarımızdanmısınız?*, which means 'Are you one of those whom we could not Australianise?' This makes it somewhat difficult to learn at first, despite its elegant logic.

In Istanbul's tourist areas you'll usually have little trouble finding someone who speaks English, but a few words in Turkish will be very well received and bring just reward for your having made the effort. If you want to learn more Turkish than we've included here, pick up a copy of Lonely Planet's comprehensive but user-friendly *Turkish Phrasebook*.

PRONUNCIATION

Once you learn a few basic rules, you'll find Turkish pronunciation quite simple to master. Despite oddities such as the soft 'g' (ğ) and undotted 'i' (ı), it's a phonetically consistent language – there's generally a clear one-letter/one-sound relationship.

It's important to remember that each letter is pronounced; vowels don't combine to form diphthongs and consonants don't combine to form other sounds (such as 'th', 'gh' or 'sh' in English). It therefore follows that h in Turkish is always pronounced as a separate letter. For example, your Turkish friend Ahmet is 'ahh-met' not 'aa-met', and the word *rehber* (guide) is pronounced 'reh-ber' not 're-ber'.

Here are some of the letters in Turkish that may cause initial confusion:

â	a faint 'y' sound in the preceding consonant
İ, i	a short 'i', as in 'hit' or 'sit'
I, ı	a neutral vowel; as the 'a' in 'ago'
Ö, ö	as the 'e' in 'her' said with pursed lips (but with no 'r' sound)
U, u	as the 'oo' in 'book'
Ü, ü	an exaggerated rounded-lip 'you'
C, c	as the 'j' in 'jet'
Ç, ç	as the 'ch' in 'church'
G, g	always hard as in 'go' (not as in 'gent')
Ğ, ğ	silent; lengthens preceding vowel
J, j	as the 'z' in 'azure'
Ş, ş	as the 'sh' in 'show'

SOCIAL
Meeting People

Hello.
Merhaba.
Goodbye.
Allaha ısmarladık. (said by one departing)
Güle güle. (said by one staying)
Please.
Lütfen.
Thank you (very much).
Çok teşekkür ederim.
Yes/No.
Evet/Hayır.
Do you speak English?
İnglizce konuşuyor-musunuz?
Do you understand (me)?
Anlıyormusunuz?
Yes, I understand.
Anlıyorum.
No, I don't understand.
Anlamıyorum.

Could you please ...?
Lütfen ...?

repeat that	*tekrarlar mısınız*
speak more slowly	*daha yavaş konuşur musunuz*
write it down	*yazar mısınız*

Going Out

What's on ...?
... görülecek neler var?

locally	Yerel olarak
this weekend	Bu hafta sonu
today	Bugün
tonight	Bu gece

Where are the ...?
... nerede?

clubs	Klüpler
gay venues	Gey klüpleri
places to eat	Yemek yenilebilecek yerler
pubs	Birahaneler

Is there a local entertainment guide?
Buranın yerel eğlence rehberi var mı?

PRACTICAL

Question Words

Who?	Kim?
What?	Ne?
When?	Ne zaman?
Where?	Nerede?
How?	Nasıl?

Numbers & Amounts

1	bir
2	iki
3	üç
4	dört
5	beş
6	altı
7	yedi
8	sekiz
9	dokuz
10	on
11	on bir
12	on iki
13	on üç
14	on dört
15	on beş
16	on altı
17	on yedi
18	on sekiz
19	on dokuz
20	yirmi
21	yirmi bir
22	yirmi iki
30	otuz
40	kırk
50	elli
60	altmış
70	yetmiş
80	seksen
90	doksan
100	yüz
1000	bin
2000	iki bin
1,000,000	milyon

Days

Monday	Pazartesi
Tuesday	Salı
Wednesday	Çarşamba
Thursday	Perşembe
Friday	Cuma
Saturday	Cumartesi
Sunday	Pazar

Banking

I'd like to ...
... istiyorum.

cash a cheque	Çek bozdurmak
change money	Para bozdurmak
change a travellers cheque	Seyahat çeki bozdurmak

Where's the nearest ...?
... nerede?

ATM	Bankamatik/ATM
foreign-exchange office	Döviz bürosu

Post

Where is the (main) post office?
(Merkez) Postane nerede?

I want to send a ...
Bir ... göndermek istiyorum.

fax	faks
parcel	paket
postcard	kartpostal

I want to buy ...
... satın almak istiyorum.

an aerogram	Telsiz telgraf
an envelope	Zarf
a stamp	Pul

Phones & Mobiles

I want to buy a phone card.
Telefon kartı istiyorum.

I want to make ...
... istiyorum.

a (local) call	(Yerel) bir görüşme yapmak

reverse-charge/ collect call	Ödemeli görüşme yapmak

I'd like a/an ...
... istiyorum.

charger for my phone	Cep telefonum için şarj aleti
mobile/cell phone for hire	Cep telefonu kiralamak
prepaid mobile/ cell phone	Kontörlü cep telefonu
SIM card for your network	Buradaki şebeke için SİM kart

Internet

Where's the local internet café?
En yakın internet kafe nerede?

I'd like to ...
... istiyorum.

check my email	E-postama bakmak
get internet access	İnternete girmek

Transport

What time does the ... leave?
... ne zaman kalkacak?

bus	Otobüs
ferry	Feribot
plane	Uçak
train	Tren

What time's the ... bus?
... (otobüs) ne zaman?

first	İlk
last	Son
next	Sonraki

Is this taxi free?
Bu taksi boş mu?
Please put the meter on.
Lütfen taksimetreyi çalıştırın.
How much is it to ...?
... ne kadar?
Please take me to (this address).
Lütfen beni (şu adrese) götürün.

EMERGENCIES

It's an emergency!
Bu acil bir durum!
Could you please help?
Yardım edebilir misiniz lütfen?
Call the police/a doctor/an ambulance!
Polis/Doktor/Ambulans çağır(ın).
Where's the police station?
Polis karakolu nerede?

HEALTH

Where's the nearest ...?
En yakın ... nerede?

chemist (night)	(nöbetçi) eczane
dentist	diş hekimi
doctor	doktor
hospital	hastane

I need a doctor (who speaks English).
(İngilizce konuşan) bir doktora ihtiyacım var.

Symptoms

I have (a) ...
... var.

diarrhoea	Ishalim
fever	Ateşim
headache	Ibaş ağrısı
pain	Ağrım/sancım

FOOD

Can you recommend a ...
İyi bir ... tavsiye edebilir misiniz?

bar	bar
café	kafe
restaurant	restoran

Is service included in the bill?
Hesaba servis dahil mi?

For more detailed information on food and dining out, see p149.

GLOSSARY

Here, with definitions, are some useful words and abbreviations.

ada(sı) – island
aile salonu – family room; for couples, families and women in a Turkish restaurant
altgeçidi – pedestrian subway/underpass
arabesk – music that's a mix of folk, classical and fasıl traditions
aşik – Turkish troubadours
Asya – Asian İstanbul
Avrupa – European İstanbul
ayran – a yogurt drink

bahçe(si) – garden
balık – fish
banliyö treni (s), banliyö trenleri (pl) – suburban (or commuter) train
belediye – town hall
bey – 'Mr'; follows the name
birahane – beer hall
boğaz – strait
bordro – exchange receipt
börek – flaky pastry that can be sweet or savoury
börekçi – place selling pastries
büfe – snack bar
bulvarı – often abbreviated to 'bul'; boulevard or avenue
büyük tur – long tour

caddesi – often abbreviated to 'cad'; street
caïque – long, thin rowboat
çalışma vizesi – work visa
çamaşır – laundry; underwear
camii – mosque
çarşı(sı) – market, bazaar
çay bahçesi – tea garden
cicim – embroidered mat
çift – pair
çocuk – child
çorba – soup

darüşşifa – hospital
deniz – sea
deniz otobüsü – catamaran; sea bus
Dikkat! Yavaş! – Careful! Slow!
dolmuş – shared taxi (or minibus)
döner kebap – meat roasted on a revolving, vertical spit
dondurma – ice cream
döviz bürosu – currency-exchange office

eczane – chemist/pharmacy

ekmek – bread
emanet – left luggage
emniyet – security
eyvan – vaulted hall opening onto a central court in a *medrese* or mosque
ezan – the Muslim call to prayer

fasıl – energetic folk music played in taverns or *meyhanes*
fayton – horse-drawn carriage
feribot – ferry
fiş – electricity plug

gazino – open-air Turkish nightclub (not for gambling)
gece – night
gişe – ticket booth
göbektaşı – hot platform in Turkish bath
gözleme – Turkish pancake
gündüz – daytime

hamam(ı) – Turkish steam bath
harem – family/women's quarters of a residence
hat(tı) – route
hazır yemek lokanta – ready-made-food restaurant
hısar(ı) – fortress or citadel

ikamet tezkeresi – residence permit, known as 'pink book'
imam – prayer leader; Muslim cleric; teacher
imaret – soup kitchen
iskele(si) – landing place, wharf, quay

jeton – token (for telephones)

kadın – wife
kale(si) – fortress, citadel
kapı(sı) – door, gate
karagöz – shadow-puppet theatre
kat – storey (of a building)
KDV – katma değer vergisi; value-added tax (VAT)
kebapçı – place selling kebaps
kilim – pileless woven run
köfte – Turkish meatballs
köftecı – place selling grilled meatballs
köprü – bridge
köy(ü) – village
küçük tur – short tour
kürsü – prayer-reader's platform
kuru temizleme – dry cleaning

lahmacun – Arabic soft pizza
liman(ı) – harbour

lokanta – restaurant
lokum – Turkish delight

mahalli hamam – neighbourhood Turkish bath
mahfil – high, elaborate chair
Maşallah – Wonder of God! (said in admiration or to avert the evil eye)
medrese – theological shool
menba suyu – spring water
merkez postane – central post office
mescit – prayer room/small mosque
mevlevi – whirling dervish
meydan(ı) – public square, open place
meyhanes – wine shops, taverns
müezzin – the official who sings the *ezan*
müze(si) – museum

nargileh – water pipe

ocakbaşı – grill
oda(sı) – room
otel – hotel
otogar – bus station
otopark – car park
otostop – hitch
otoyol – multilane toll highway

padişah – Ottoman emperor, sultan
pastane – also pastahane; pastry shop, patisserie
pazar(ı) – weekly market, bazaar
pide – Turkish pizza
pidecı – pizzeria
polis – police
PTT – Posta, Telefon, Telğraf; post, telephone and telegraph office

rakı – aniseed-flavoured grape brandy

saz – traditional Turkish long-necked string instrument
sebil – fountain
sedir – low sofa
şehir – city; municipal area
sema – Sufic religious ceremony
servis ücreti – service charge
servis yolu – service road
sıcak şarap – mulled wine
şile bezi – an open-weave cotton cloth with hand embroidery
sinema – cinema
şiş kebap – grilled, skewered meat
sokak, sokağı – often abbreviated to 'sk' or 'sok'; street or lane
su – water
Sufi – Muslim mystic, member of a mystic (dervish) brotherhood
sultan – sovereign
sumak – flat-woven rug with intricate detail
sünnet odası – circumcision room

tabhane – hostel
tarikat – a Sufic order
tatıcı – specialist dessert place
TC – Türkiye Cumhuriyeti (Turkish Republic); designates an official office or organisation
telekart – telephone debit card
tuğra – sultan's monogram, imperial signature

ücretsiz servis – free service

valide sultan – queen mother

yardımcı – assistant
yeni otogar – new bus station
yıldız – star

yol(u) – road, way

BEHIND THE SCENES

THIS BOOK

This 5th edition of *İstanbul* was researched and written by Virginia Maxwell. Virginia also authored the 4th edition. The 3rd edition was revised and updated by Verity Campbell. The 1st and 2nd editions were written by Tom Brosnahan. The guide was commissioned in Lonely Planet's London office and produced by the following:

Commissioning Editor Will Gourlay

Coordinating Editors Michael Day, Helen Koehne

Coordinating Cartographers Hunor Csutoros, Jolyon Philcox

Coordinating Layout Designer Wibowo Rusli

Senior Editors Sasha Baskett, Helen Christinis

Managing Cartographer Shahara Ahmed

Managing Layout Designer Adam McCrow

Assisting Editor Carly Hall

Assisting Cartographers Anna Clarkson, Amanda Sierp

Cover Designer Marika Mercer

Project Manager Sarah Sloane

Thanks to Jennifer Garrett, Adriana Mammarella, Wayne Murphy, Paul Piaia, Celia Wood

Cover photographs Whirling dervishes, Lonely Planet Images (top); under the Çiçek Pasajı glass roof, Getty Images (bottom)

Internal photographs p5 (#5) Christian Baitg Schreiweis/Alamy; p9 (#3) Rebecca Erol/Alamy; p10 (#1), p12 (#3) Scott Barbour/Getty Images. All other photographs by Lonely Planet Images: p6 (#2), p12 (#2), p85, p87 (top left), p89 (left) Anders Blomqvist; p152 (bottom) Chris Mellor; p87 (bottom) Corinne Humphrey; p90 (top) Diana Mayfield; p2, p9 (#2), p12 (#1), p149, p151 (top), p152 (top), p154, p155 (left) Greg Elms; p156 (left) Hanan Isachar; p150 Holger Leue; p4 (#3), p6 (#1), p10 (#2), p11 (#2, #3), p86, p88 Izzet Keribar; p9 (#1), p156 (right) Jeff Greenberg; p5 (#4), p7 (#3) John Elk III; p90 (bottom) John Sones; p153 Margie Politzer; p91 Mark Avellino; p8 (#2) Mark Parkes; p3, p4 (#1, #2), p5 (#6), p6 (#3), p7 (#1, #2), p8 (#1), p10 (#3), p87 (top right), p89 (top right), p92, p151 (bottom), p155 (right) Phil Weymouth; p11 (#1) Simon Richmond; p8 (#3) Tim Hughes

All images are copyright of the photographer unless otherwise indicated. Many of the images in this guide are available for licensing from Lonely Planet Images: www.lonelyplanetimages.com.

THANKS

VIRGINIA MAXWELL

In İstanbul, many thanks to René, Ames, Tahir Karabaş, Nurdoğan Şengüler, Ann Uysel, Alison Tanik, Attila Pelit, Adem Basak and colleagues, Tina Nevens and the many locals who shared their knowledge and love of the city with me. Thanks also to Paul Kalina and Susan Charalambidis for their company in many of the city's restaurants, sites and bars. My good friend Pat Yale generously shared her great knowledge of the city and checked out restaurants, cafés and bars galore with me. Thanks Pat! And my sister Elizabeth was, as always, the perfect travelling companion and host. We've come a long way since North Balwyn.... At Lonely Planet, sincere thanks to Turkophile Will Gourlay for giving

THE LONELY PLANET STORY

Fresh from an epic journey across Europe, Asia and Australia in 1972, Tony and Maureen Wheeler sat at their kitchen table stapling together notes. The first Lonely Planet guidebook, *Across Asia on the Cheap*, was born.

Travellers snapped up the guides. Inspired by their success, the Wheelers began publishing books to Southeast Asia, India and beyond. Demand was prodigious, and the Wheelers expanded the business rapidly to keep up. Over the years, Lonely Planet extended its coverage to every country and into the virtual world via lonelyplanet.com and the Thorn Tree message board.

As Lonely Planet became a globally loved brand, Tony and Maureen received several offers for the company. But it wasn't until 2007 that they found a partner whom they trusted to remain true to the company's principles of travelling widely, treading lightly and giving sustainably. In October of that year, BBC Worldwide acquired a 75% share in the company, pledging to uphold Lonely Planet's commitment to independent travel, trustworthy advice and editorial independence.

Today, Lonely Planet has offices in Melbourne, London and Oakland, with over 500 staff members and 300 authors. Tony and Maureen are still actively involved with Lonely Planet. They're travelling more often than ever, and they're devoting their spare time to charitable projects. And the company is still driven by the philosophy of *Across Asia on the Cheap*: 'All you've got to do is decide to go and the hardest part is over. So go!'

me this repeat gig and to Shahara Ahmed for steering the mapping. I particularly enjoyed working with unflappable editor Michae+l Day, a fellow İstanbul devotee. And finally, my thanks and love to Peter and Max, who held the fort at home for 10 long weeks. It's my treat at Mikla next year!

OUR READERS

Many thanks to the travellers who used the last edition and wrote to us with helpful hints, useful advice and interesting anecdotes:

Frances Ambler, Florence Bannicq, Christine Barker, Clare Barman, Puneet Batra, Sabine Bauer, Brian Beary, Albert Blitz, Flo Boyko, Jean Buisson-Ramey, Zoe Bulmer, Sue Burt, Charles Carter, John Challen, Nicholas Daniels, Torene David, Alan Davies, Natali Del Conte, Sonja Demaï, Nilgun Demirkaya, Denis Donnelly, Jeffrey Dorfman, Nelson Duarte, Hakan Ersoy, Janet Evans, JKG Evens, David Fairservice, Fay Fishman, Pete Freeman, Frank Gauthier, Mia Green-Dove, Celine Guibe, Asaf Gurvitz, Penelope Hackett-Jones, Su Harada, Alison Herga, Constance Holden, Erik Hom, Carol Hopson, Natalie Hume, Rachael Hunter, Jerry Keita, Carolyn Kelley, Jeffrey Knight, Sandy Kobayashi, Iris Kokkelmans, Alex Kopp, Barbara Meli, Tassilo Lang, Elisabeth Lemoigne, Corinne Lennox, Julie Li, Jacqueline Linnane, Paul Lithander, Natalya Marquand, Derek McConnell, Hélio Medeira, George Miley, Colin & Robyn Mills, Beatrice Milmor, Sana Moazzam, Rebecka Molander, Dominic Moore, Michael Mueller, Yasmine Naga, Evi Papanagiotou, Andrea Patterson, Inga Petruschke, Achim Pfriender, Haris Pilidis, Cecile Popp, Mary L Pretz, Abi Robinson, John Rudolph, David Sabata, Deepak Sapra, Tom Seeberger, Lynn Sherriff, Helen Shin, Samu Slotte, Tamar Sommerstein, Joseph Stanik, Stan Steward, Daphne Tan, Layla Theiner, Jan Truyen, Turgay Turkucak, Colin Turnbull, Jessica van Campen, Andrew & Gabrielle van Nooten, Peter Verity, Maurice Vrolijk, Dagmar Wabel, Katarina Wihlborg, Daniëlle Wolbers, Tony Wright, Selcuk Yigit

SEND US YOUR FEEDBACK

We love to hear from travellers – your comments keep us on our toes and help make our books better. Our well-travelled team reads every word on what you loved or loathed about this book. Although we cannot reply individually to postal submissions, we always guarantee that your feedback goes straight to the appropriate authors, in time for the next edition. Each person who sends us information is thanked in the next edition – and the most useful submissions are rewarded with a free book.

To send us your updates – and find out about Lonely Planet events, newsletters and travel news – visit our award-winning website: www.lonelyplanet.com/contact.

Note: We may edit, reproduce and incorporate your comments in Lonely Planet products such as guidebooks, websites and digital products, so let us know if you don't want your comments reproduced or your name acknowledged. For a copy of our privacy policy visit www.lonelyplanet.com/privacy.

ACKNOWLEDGMENTS

Many thanks to the following for the use of their content:

Akşit Kültür Turizm Sanat Ajans (İstanbul): plan of Chora Museum (Kariye Müzesi) from *The Museum of Chora – Museum and Frescoes*, İlhan Akşit (2002).

Notes

Notes

Notes

Notes

Notes

INDEX

See also separate
indexes for:

Arts	p262
Drinking	p262
Eating	p263
Nightlife	p263
Shopping	p263
Sights	p264
Sleeping	p265
Sports & Activities	p265
Top Picks	p266

A

accommodation
197-209, *see also*
Sleeping *subindex*
Bazaar District 205
Beşiktaş & Ortaköy 209
Çanakkale 224
costs 198
Galata & Tophane 205-6
İstiklal & Around 206-8
Princes' Islands 222-3
styles 198
Sultanahmet 198-203
Taksim, Harbiye &
Nişantaşı 208
Topkapı Palace & Around
203-5
activities 191-6, *see also*
Sports & Activities
subindex
Adıvar, Halide Edib 30, 216
air travel 230
airlines 230
airports 230
telephone numbers, *see
inside front cover*
to/from airports 231
Akbank Jazz Festival 17
Akbank Short Film
Festival 18
ambulance 237
Anadolu Kavağı 219
Anniversary of Atatürk's
Death 17
al-Ansari, Ayoub 99
antiques 133, *see also*
Shopping *subindex*
Anzac battlefields 212, **214**
Gallipoli 223, 225-8, **226**

Anzac Day 226
apartments, *see* Sleeping
subindex
Aqueduct of Valens 82-3
architecture 85-92
area codes, *see inside front
cover*
Arnavutköy 216
art galleries 186-7, *see
also* Arts, Shopping,
Sights *subindexes*
artisans 53
arts 28, 185-90, *see also*
Arts *subindex*
carpets 28-30, 136-7
cinema 34-7, 187
dance 189-90
literature 30-2
music 32-4, 188
theatre 190
visual arts 37
Atatürk 27, 116, 118,
226, 227
Anniversary of Atatürk's
Death 17
reforms 27, 29, 30, 32,
40, 245
ATMs 240
Aya Sofya 49-53, 59, **52,
4, 89**
Ayoub al-Ansari 99

B

Balat 95
ballet 189-90
bargaining 132-3
bars, *see* Drinking *subindex*
Basilica Cistern 58-9, 61, **4**
bathrooms 243
battlefields
Anzac 212, **214**
Gallipoli 223, 225-8, **226**
Bazaar District 76-84, **78, 7**
accommodation 205
drinking 174
food 161-3
shopping 137-40
walking tour 83-4, **83**
bazaars, *see* Sights
subindex
beaches 192
Bebek 216-18

belly-dancing courses 236-7
Beşiktaş 116-20, **117, 11**
accommodation 209
drinking 177
food 169
Beyazıt Camii 80, 84
Beykoz 218
bicycle travel 222
Blue Mosque 54-5, 59, **4,
85, 90**
blues music festival 18
boat travel 231-2, **12**
books 20, 36, 134, *see
also* literature, Shopping
subindex
Sinan, Mimar 20, 87
börekçi, see Eating
subindex
Bosphorus tours 212-20,
215, 12
Bebek to Kanlıca 216-18
Eminönü to Ortaköy 215
İstinye to Sariyer 218-19
Kanlıca to İstinye 218
Ortaköy to Bebek 216
Sariyer to Anadolu
Kavağı 219
transport 217
boza 174
bridges, *see* Sights *subindex*
bus travel 232-3
city buses 232
intercity & international
buses 233
business hours 236, *see also
inside front cover*
shopping 132-3
restaurants 157
Büyükdere 219
Byzantine architecture
88-9
Byzantium 19-20

C

cable-cars 234
cafés, *see* Drinking, Eating
subindexes
cage life 53, 70
Çanakkale 223-5, **225**
car travel 233-4
driving licence 233
hire 233

carpets 28-30, 136-7, *see
also* Shopping *subindex*
scams 137
çay bahçesıs, see Drinking
subindex
cell phones 243
ceramics 133, *see also*
Shopping *subindex*
changing money 240-1
chemists 240
children, travel with 58, 236
Children's Day 16
Chora Church 93, 95, 100,
96, 8, 89
churches, *see* Sights
subindex
cinema 34-7, 187, *see
also* Arts *subindex*
Akbank Short Film
Festival 18
International İstanbul
Film Festival
circumcision 99
classical music 188
climate 236
change 230
clothing, *see* Shopping
subindex
clubbing 180-2, *see also*
Nightlife *subindex*
coffee 155
coffee houses, *see* Drinking
subindex
Constantinople 20-1
consulates 236
cooking courses 157
copper 133
costs 18, 157
accommodation 198
food 157
public transport 233
taxes 132-3
courses
belly-dancing 236-7
cooking 157
handicrafts 237
language 237
credit cards 241
Crimean War 26
Crusades 22-3
cultural centres 188-9, *see
also* Arts *subindex*

currency exchange 240-1
customs regulations 237
cycling 222

D

dance 189-90, *see also* Arts *subindex*
dangers & annoyances
    carpet bait & switch 137
    food poisoning 148, 238
    nightlife scams 184
    pedestrians 242
    theft 242
day trips 211-29, **213**
delicatessens, *see* Eating *subindex*
diarrhoea 238
disabilities, travellers with 243
Dolmabahçe Palace 116-18, **11**, **91**
dolmuş 234
drinking 155-6, 171-8, *see also* Drinking, Shopping *subindexes*
    Bazaar District 174
    Beşiktaş & Ortaköy 177
    Çanakkale 224-5
    Galata & Tophane 174-5
    İstiklal & Around 175-7
    Kadıköy 177
    Sultanahmet 172-3
    Topkapı Palace & Around 173-4
driving, *see* car travel
drugstores 240

E

earthquakes 38
Easter 16
eating, *see* food, Eating *subindex*
Efes Pilsen Blues Festival 18
Efes Pilsen One Love 16
economy 28
electricity 237
Electronica Global Gathering 17
embassies 236
emergencies 237, *see also inside front cover*
Eminönü 215
environmental issues 37-8

etiquette
    food 146
    hamam 194
exchange rates, *see inside front cover*
excursions 211-29, **213**

F

fashion 39-40
fax services 243
ferry travel 231-2, **12**
festivals 16-18
film, *see* cinema
fire services 237
Florence Nightingale Museum 124-5
folk dance 189
food 145-70, *see also* Eating, Shopping *subindexes*
    Bazaar District 161-3
    Beşiktaş & Ortaköy 169
    Bosphorus 219-20
    business hours 157
    Çanakkale 224-5
    costs 157
    etiquette 146
    Galata & Tophane 163-5
    İstiklal & Around 165-9
    Kadıköy 170
    Princes' Islands 223
    reservations 157
    self-catering 158
    Sultanahmet 158-60
    tipping 158
    Topkapı Palace & Around 160-1
    Üsküdar 169-70
    vegetarians & vegans 157
    Western Districts 163
food poisoning 148, 238
football 195-6
fortresses, *see* Sights *subindex*
fountains, *see* Sights *subindex*
fratricide 25, 53, 70
funiculars 234

G

Galata 102-5, **103**, **9**
    accommodation 205-6
    drinking 174-5
    food 163-5
    shopping 140
    walking tour 105, 105
Galata Bridge 74-5
galleries, *see* art galleries

Gallipoli 223, 225-8, **226**
    tours 224
gay travellers 183, 237
    bars 177
    hamams & saunas 193, 195
glassware 133, 142
government 38-9
Grand Bazaar 76-7, 79, 83, 138, 77, **7**, **156**
Great Byzantine Palace 56
Greek Patriarch of Fener 99
gyms 192

H

Hagia Sophia 49-53, 59, 52, **4**, **89**
hamams 192-5, *see also* Sights, Sports & Activities *subindexes*
    etiquette 194
handicrafts, *see also* Shopping *subindex*
    courses 237
Harbiye 114-15, **115**
    accommodation 208
    shopping 142-4
harems, *see also* Sights *subindex*
    cage life 53, 70
headscarves 40
health 237-8
    clubs 192
Hippodrome 56-7, 60, **5**
historic areas, *see* Sights *subindex*
historic buildings & structures, *see* Sights *subindex*
history 19-28, 70
    Bosphorus 214-15
holidays 238-9
homewares, *see* Shopping *subindex*
hospitals 240
hostels, *see* Sleeping *subindex*
hotels 198, *see also* Sleeping *subindex*

I

illnesses 238
insurance
    car 233
    health 240
International Design Week 17

International İstanbul Biennial 17
International İstanbul Film Festival 16
International İstanbul Jazz Festival 17
International İstanbul Music Festival 16-17
International İstanbul Theatre Festival 16
International Ülker Puppet Festival İstanbul 16
internet access 239
internet resources 18
Islamic Eclecticism 92
İstanbul Modern 102, 104, 105
İstiklal & Around 106-13, **107**, **10**
    accommodation 206-8
    drinking 175-7
    food 165-9
    shopping 140-2
    walking tour 111-13, **112**
İstinye 218-19
itineraries 15, 48, 212

J

jazz 182
    Akbank Jazz Festival 17
    International İstanbul Jazz Festival 17
jewellery 133-4, *see also* Shopping *subindex*
Justinian 21, 49, 54, 57

K

Kadıköy 126-7, **127**
    drinking 177
    food 170
    shopping 144
kahvehanes, *see* Drinking *subindex*
Kanlıca 216-18
kebapçıs, *see* Eating *subindex*
kebaps 152
Kemal, Mustafa, *see* Atatürk
köftecis, *see* Eating *subindex*
Kösem Sultan 25
Kumkapı 163

L

language 40-2, 245-9, *see also inside front cover*
    courses 237

leather 134, *see also*
    Shopping *subindex*
legal matters 133
lesbian travellers 183, 237
light rail transit 234
literature 30-2, *see also*
    books
    Nadel, Barbara 36, 95
    Pamuk, Orhan 3, 31, 41
lokantas, *see* Eating
    subindex
lokum 134, 155, **155**

M
magazines 241
malls 143
maps 134, 239-40
markets 143, *see also*
    Shopping, Sights
    subindexes
measures, *see inside front*
    cover
media 39
medical services 240
Mehmet the Conqueror
    23-4, 62, 69, 90, 96
Menderes, Adnan 27
metric conversions, *see*
    inside front cover
metro 234
meyhanes 167, *see also*
    Eating *subindex*
meze 151, **150**
Mimar Sinan, *see* Sinan,
    Mimar
mobile phones 243
monasteries, *see* Sights
    subindex
money 18, 240
mosaics 54
    Chora Church 93, 95,
        100, 96, **8, 89**
    Fethiye Camii 97
    Great Palace Mosaics
        Museum 55-6, 60
mosques, *see* Sights
    subindex
Murat III 25, 53, 68, 70
museums, *see* Sights
    subindex
music 32-4, 188, *see also*
    Nightlife, Shopping
    subindexes
music festivals
    Akbank Jazz Festival 17
    Efes Pilsen Blues Festival
        18
    Efes Pilsen One Love 16

Electronica Global
    Gathering 17
International İstanbul
    Jazz Festival 17
International İstanbul
    Music Festival 16-17
Rock'n Coke 17

N
Nadel, Barbara 36, 95
nargilehs 173, **9**
neighbourhoods, *see also*
    individual neighbourhoods
    Bazaar District 76-84,
        78, **7**
    Beşiktaş & Ortaköy
        116-20, **117, 11**
    Galata & Tophane 102-5,
        103, **9**
    İstiklal & Around 106-13,
        107, **10**
    Kadıköy 126-7, **127**
    Sultanahmet 49-61,
        50, **4-5**
    Taksim, Harbiye &
        Nişantaşı 114-15, **115**
    Topkapı Palace & Around
        62-75, 63, **6**
    Üsküdar 121-5, **122**
    Western Districts 93-101,
        94, **8**
Nevizade Sokak 111, **10**
Nevruz 16
newspapers 241
nightlife 179-84, *see also*
    Nightlife *subindex*
Nişantaşı 114-15, **115**
    accommodation 208
    shopping 142-4
Nurbanu, Valide Sultan
    25, 121

O
Obelisk of Theodosius
    21, 56-7
opera 188
Ortaköy 116-20, 215-16,
    117, 11
    accommodation 209
    drinking 177
    food 169
Orthodox Easter 16
Ottoman architecture 90-1
Ottoman Empire 23-6
Özal, Turgut 27-8

P
palaces, *see* Sights
    subindex
Pamuk, Orhan 3, 31, 41

parks, *see* Sights *subindex*
Paşa, İbrahim 57-8
Paşa, Rüstem 82
Paşabahçe 218
pastane, *see* Eating *subindex*
pedestrian safety 242
Pelit, Attila 126
performance venues 188-9,
    see also Arts *subindex*
pharmacies 240
phonecards 243
pideçıs, *see* Eating *subindex*
planning 16-18
police 242
politics 38-9, 41
postal services 241
Princes' Islands 220-3
    transport 221
puppetry festivals 16

R
racial discrimination 242
Ramazan 57, 239
reservations 157
restaurants, *see* food,
    Eating *subindex*
robbery 242
Rock'n Coke 17
Roxelana 53, 58, 59,
    69, 82
rugs, *see* carpets
Rule of the Women 24-5, 121
Rumeli Kavağı 219

S
Şafak, Elif 31
Sariyer 218-19
self-catering 158
Selim the Grim 24, 70,
    99, 100
Selim the Sot 24-5, 53, 121
shopping 131-44, *see also*
    Shopping *subindex*
    bargaining 132-3
    Bazaar District 137-40
    business hours 132-3
    Galata & Tophane 140
    İstiklal & Around 140-2
    Kadıköy 144
    malls 143
    markets 143
    shopping strips 134
    Sultanahmet 134-6
    Taksim, Harbiye &
        Nişantaşı 142-4
    Topkapı Palace & Around
        136-7

silk 134
Sinan, Mimar 24, 50, 90-1
    Atik Valide Camii 121,
        125
    Azapkapı Sokollu Mehmet
        Paşa Camii 104
    Baths of Lady Hürrem
        53-4, 59, **5**
    books 20, 87
    Caferağa Medresesi
        73, 75
    Çemberlitaş Hamamı
        193
    Gâzi İskender Paşa Camii
        218
    Mihrimah Sultan Camii
        (Edirnekapı) 96, 100
    Mihrimah Sultan Camii
        (Üsküdar) 121
    Mimar Sinan Çarşısı 121
    Rüstem Paşa Camii
        82, 84
    Şehzade Mehmet Camii
        81-2, 84
    Şemsi Paşa Camii 123,
        125
    Sokollu Mehmet Paşa
        Camii 58
    Süleymaniye Camii 80-1,
        84, **7, 86**
    Süleymaniye Hamamı
        193
    Topkapı Harem 68-70, **6**
sleeping, *see* accommoda-
    tion, Sleeping *subindex*
smoking 238
souvenirs, *see* Shopping
    subindex
spectator sports 195-6
Spice Bazaar 82, 84, **2, 7**
spices 134, *see also*
    Shopping *subindex*
Spoonmaker's Diamond
    67
sports 191-6, *see also*
    Sports & Activities
    subindex
Süleyman the
    Magnificent 24, 58, 59,
    69, 80-1, 91, 151
Süleymaniye Camii 80-1,
    84, **7, 86**
Sultanahmet 49-61, 50,
    4-5
    accommodation 198-203
    drinking 172-3
    food 158-60
    shopping 134-6
    walking tour 59-61, 60

swimming 192
synagogues, see Sights subindex

T
Taksim 114-15, 115
   accommodation 208
   shopping 142-4
Taksim Square 111
Tarabya 218
taxes 132-3
taxis 234-5
tea 155
tea gardens, see Drinking subindex
telephone numbers, see inside front cover
telephone services 242-3
textiles 134, see also carpets, Shopping subindex
theatre 190
   International İstanbul Theatre Festival 16
theft 242
Theodora 21, 22, 57
tickets
   nightlife 180
   transport 233
time 243, 259
tipping 158
toilets 243
tonics 139
Tophane 102-5, 103, 9
   accommodation 205-6
   drinking 174-5
   food 163-5
   shopping 140
Topkapı Palace 62, 65-8, 75, 64, 6, 87
Topkapı Palace & Around 62-75, 63, 6, 87
   accommodation 203-5
   drinking 173-4
   food 160-1
   shopping 136-7
   walking tour 75, 74
tourist information 243
tours 224, 241, see also walking tours
toys, see Shopping subindex
traffic accidents 242
train travel 235
trams 235
transport 230-5

000 map pages
000 photographs

travellers cheques 241
Troy 223, 228-9
   tours 224
   transport 223
Turkbalon 127
Turhan Hatice, Valide Sultan 25
Turkish delight 134, 155, **155**
Turkish music 182-4, see also Nightlife subindex
Turkish War of Independence 27

U
Üsküdar 121-5, 122
   food 169-70
   walking tour 125, 124

V
vacations 238-9
vaccinations 238
vegetarians & vegans 157
visas 243-4
visual arts 37, 186-7
   International İstanbul Biennial 17

W
walking tours
   Bazaar District 83-4, 83
   Galata & Tophane 105, 105
   İstiklal & Around 111-13, 112
   Sultanahmet 59-61, 60
   Topkapı Palace & Around 75, 74
   Üsküdar 125, 124
   Western Districts 100-1, 101
water 238
water pipes, see nargilehs
weather 236
weights, see inside front cover
Western Districts 93-101, 94, 8
   food 163
   walking tour 100-1, 101
whirling dervishes 106, 108, 109, **10**
women of the Ottoman Empire 24-5
Women, Rule of the 24-5, 121
women travellers 244
wood 133
work 244

Y
Yeniköy 218

ARTS
ART GALLERIES
Galerı Nev 186
Galerist 186
Platform Garanti Contemporary Art Centre 186
Proje4L/Elgiz Museum of Contemporary Art 186
santralistanbul 186
Schneidertempel Art Center 105, 187

CINEMAS
AFM Akmerkez 187
AFM Fitaş 187
Alkazar Sinema Merkezi 187
Atlas Sinemaları 187
Emek 187
Kanyon Mars Cinema 187
Rexx 187
Şafak Sinemaları 187

CULTURAL CENTRES & PERFORMANCE VENUES
Akbank Culture & Arts Centre 188
Atatürk Cultural Centre 188
Aya İrini 188
Borusan Arts & Culture Center 188
Cemal Reşit Rey Concert Hall 188
İş Art & Cultural Centre 189
Italian Cultural Centre 189
Lütfi Kirdar Concert Hall 189
Tarik Zafer Tunaya Kültür Merkezi 189

DANCE
Dance of Colours 189
Orient House 189

DRINKING
BARS
5 Kat 175
360 176
Ada 175
Anemon Galata Bar 175

Badehane 175
Büyük Londra Oteli Bar 175
Cheers Bar 172
Çırağan Palace Hotel Kempinski 177
Hotel Nomade Terrace Bar 172
James Joyce Irish Pub 175
Karga Bar 177
Keve 175
Kybele Hotel Bar 172
Leb-i Derya 175-6
Leb-i Derya Richmond 176
Leyla 176
Mikla 176
Nu Teras 176
Pano 176
Pasific House 176
Seven Hills Terrace Bar 172
Smyrna 176
Sultan Pub 172
Urban 176
Yalı Hanı 225
Yeşil Ev Garden Bar/Café 173

BOZA BARS
Vefa Bozacisi 174

CAFÉS
Ada 175
Fes Café 172-3
Java Studio 173
Kaffeehaus 177
Yeni Marmara 173

ÇAY BAHÇESIS (TEA GARDENS)
Balkan Türkleri Dayanışma ve Kültür Derneği 174
Café Meşale 173
Derviş Aile Çay Bahçesi 173
Erenler Çay Bahçesi 174
Haco Pulo 177
Lale Bahçesi 174
Set Üstü Çay Bahçesi 173-4
Türk Ocağı Kültür ve Sanat Merkezı İktisadi İşletmesı Çay Bahçesi 173

GAY BARS
Club 17 177

KAHVEHANES (COFFEE HOUSES)
Etham Tezçakar Kahveci 174
Şark Kahvesi 174

EATING

ANATOLIAN
Bab-i Hayat 162
Caferağa Medresesi 161
Çamlica Restaurant 170
Canim Ciğerim İlhan Usta 168
Cankurtaran Sosyal Tesisleri 160
Flamm 168
Galata Konak Patisserie Café 164
Hamdi et Lokantası 161-2
Havuzlu Restaurant 162
House of Medusa 159
Karaköyüm Café & Restaurant 164
Konyalı 160
Köy Evi 224
Meshur Kuru Fasülyeci 162
Niyazibey 169
Rami 159
Şehzade Mehmed Sofrası 162
Zinhan Kebap House at Storks 161

ASIAN
Banyan 169

BÖREKÇIS (PASTRY SHOPS)
Hafiz Mustafa Şekerlemeleri 161
Sebo Börek 165

CAFÉS
Büyükada Kültür Evi 223
Donjon 220
Hıdiv Kasrı Café 220
Il Porto 220
Mangerie 220
Sade Kahve 220

DELICATESSENS
Namli 164
Nimla Pastirmaci 162

GEORGIAN
Galata House 164

ICE CREAM
Mado 169

INDIAN
Dubb 159

INTERNATIONAL
360 165
Albura Café & Restaurant 159
Changa 165
House Café 167, 169
İstanbul Modern Cafe 163-4
Kafe Ara 167
Lokal 167
Mozaik 159
Müzedechanga 220
Zinhan Kebap House at Storks 161

KEBAPÇIS (KEBAP HOUSES)
Ayasofya Kebap House 160
Buhara Restaurant & Ocakbaşi 161
Develi 163
Karadeniz Aile Pide ve Kebap Salonu 160
Konak 168

KÖFTECIS (MEATBALL SHOPS)
Tarihi Sultanahmet Köftecisi Selim Usta 160

LOKANTAS (RESTAURANTS)
Çıya Sofrası 170
Güney Restaurant 164
Haci Abdullah 167-8
Helvetica Lokanta 168
İmren Lokantası 162-3
Kanaat Lokantesi 169-70
Lale Restaurant (Pudding Shop) 159-60
Sefa Restaurant 161
Subaşı Lokantası 162

MEDITERRANEAN
Lokanta 166
Mikla 165
Nu Teras 165-6

MEYHANES (TAVERNS)
Boncuk Restaurant 166-7
Krependeki İmroz Restaurant 166

Refik 166
Sofyali 9 167

MUHALLEBICIS (PUDDING SHOPS)
Saray Muhallebicisi 168-9

OTTOMAN
Asitane 163
Rami 159

PASTANES (PASTRY SHOPS)
Baylan Pastahane 170
Çiğdem Pastanesi 160
Galata Konak Patisserie Café 164
Hafiz Mustafa Şekerlemeleri 161
İnci Pastanesi 168
Karaköy Güllüglu 165
Saray Muhallebicisi 168-9

PIDEÇIS (PIZZERIAS)
Karadeniz Aile Pide ve Kebap Salonu 160
Konak 168

SEAFOOD
Alibaba Restaurant 223
Balikçi Sabahattin 158, **150**
Çınar 169
Giritli 158
Kör Agop Restaurant 163
Körfez Restaurant 219
Poseidon 220
Rumeli İskele 220
Sultanahmet Fish House 160-1
Tarıhı Karaköy Balik Lokantası 164

TURKISH
Albura Café & Restaurant 159
Cezayir 166
Hünnaphan 224
Leb-ı Derya 166
Mozaik 159
Rıhtım Restaurant 224
Teras Restaurant 158-9
Yücetepe Kır Gazinosu 223

VEGETARIAN
Saf' Organic Bistro 166
Zencefil Nature & Peace 168

NIGHTLIFE

CLUBS
Angelique 180
Araf 180
Babylon 180
Balans Music Hall 180-1
Blackk 180
Crystal 181
Déjá Vu 181
Depo 225
Gabile 181
Ghetto 181
Love Dance Point 181
Roxy 181
Sortie 181
Tonique 181-2

JAZZ
İstanbul Jazz Center 182
Jazz Café 182
Nardis Jazz Club 182
Q Jazz by Les Ottomans 182

TURKISH MUSIC
Andon 182-3
Cumhuriyet 183
Degustasyon 183
Despina 183
Garibaldi 184
Kokosh by Asmali 184
Levendiz Greek Meyhane 184

SHOPPING

ART & ANTIQUES
Anadol Antik 140
Artrium 140
Denizler Kitabevi 140
Design Zone 134
Galeri Alfa 140
Hikmet + Pinar 140
Şamdan 140
Sofa 136
Ziya Aykaç 137

BOOKS
Denizler Kitabevi 140
Galeri Kayseri 134-5
Greenhouse Bookshop Cafe 144
Homer Kitabevi 140

İstanbul Kitapçısı 141
Pandora 141
Robinson Crusoe 141

CARPETS & TEXTILES
A La Turca 142
Antique Objet 139
Azad Tekstil 139
Cocoon 135
Dhoku 139
Er & Ne & Met 135
Galeri Cengiz 135
Haseki Hamam Carpet & Kilim Sales Store 135
İpek 142
Mehmet Çetinkaya Gallery 135
Muhlis Günbatti 139
Semerkand Suzani 139
Şişko Osman 139
Yörük 139
Yörük Collection 136

CERAMICS
Beyoğlu Hali Evi 141
İznik Classics & Tiles 135
Yıldız Porselen Fabrikası 120

CLOTHING
art.i.choke 141
Bis 141
Gönül Paksoy 143
Leyla Seyhanli 141
Mavi Jeans 141
Mudo Pera 141-2
Sedef Çalarkan 141
Vakko 143
Vakko İndirim 136
Yargici 143-4

FOOD & DRINK
Ali Muhiddin Hacı Bekir 136-7
Ambar 142
Hafiz Mustafa Şekerlemeleri 137
Kurukahveci Mehmet Efendi Mahdumları 137-8
La Cave Wine Shop 142

000 map pages
000 photographs

264

GIFTS & SOUVENIRS
İstanbul Modern Gift Shop 140
Mudo Pera 141-2
Vakko 143
Yargici 143-4

GLASSWARE
Paşabahçe 142

HANDICRAFTS
Caferağa Medresesi 135
İstanbul Handicrafts Market 135

HOMEWARES
Abdulla Natural Products 138
Derviş 138

JEWELLERY
Ak Gümüs 138
Milano Güzeliş 138
Mor Taki 142
Necef 138
Sema Paksoy 144

LEATHER
Koç Deri 138-9
Küçük Köşe 139

MALLS
Akmerkez 143
Cevahir 143
Kanyon 143
Metrocity 143

MARKETS
Fatih Pazarı 143
Salı Pazarı 143

MUSIC
Elvis 142
Lale Plak 142
Mephisto 142

SPICES & TONICS
Mehmet Kalmaz Baharatçı 139

TOYS
Deli Kizin Yeri Junior 139-40

Ekincioğlu Toys & Gifts 140
Greenhouse Bookshop Cafe 144
İyigün Oyuncak 142

SIGHTS
ART GALLERIES
İstanbul Modern 102, 104, 105
Schneidertempel Art Center 105, 187

BAZAARS
Arasta Bazaar 59, **5**
Grand Bazaar 76-7, 79, 83, 138, **77**, **7**, **156**
Hasircilar Caddesi 84
Old Book Bazaar 79
Sahaflar Çarşısı 79, 83-4
Spice Bazaar 82, 84, **7**, **2**

BRIDGES
Bosphorus Bridge 215
Galata Bridge 74-5

CHURCHES
Aya Sofya 49-53, 59, **52**, **4**, **89**
Chora Church 93, 95, 100, **96**, **8**, **89**
Christ Church 109
Church of St George 99
Church of St Mary Draperis 112
Church of St Mary of the Mongols 97-8
Church of St Stephen of the Bulgars 98, 101, **8**
Church of SS Peter & Paul 105
Fethiye Camii 97
Küçük Aya Sofya Camii 57, 60

FOUNTAINS
Fountain of Sultan Ahmet III 65, **87**
Kaiser Wilhelm's Fountain 56

FORTRESSES
Anadolu Hisarı 217
Rumeli Hisarı 217, **90**
Yedikule Hisarı Müzesi 128

HAMAMS
Baths of Lady Hürrem 53-4, 59, **5**
Mimar Sinan Çarşısı 121
Süleymaniye Hamamı 193

HAREMS
Dolmabahçe Harem-Cariyeler 118
Topkapı Harem 68-70, **6**

HISTORIC AREAS
Avrupa Pasajı 111
Beyazıt Square 80
Çiçek Pasajı 110-11
Hippodrome 56-7, 60, **5**
İstanbul University 80
Mimar Sinan Çarşısı 121
Soğukçeşme Sokak 73, 75
Taksim Square 111

HISTORIC BUILDINGS & STRUCTURES
Anadolu Kavağı Kalesi 219
Aqueduct of Valens 82-3
Basilica Cistern 58-9, 61, **4**
Binbirdirek Cistern 59
Boğaziçi Üniversitesi 216
Botter House 113
British Consulate General 111-12
Caferağa Medresesi 53, 73, 75, 135, 161, 237
Çemberlitaş 59
Ecumenical Orthodox Patriarchate 99, 100
Egyptian consulate building 216
Ethem Pertev Yalı 218
Fethi Ahmet Paşa Yalı 215
Galata Tower 104, 105, **9**
Hıdiv Kasrı 218
Kamondo Stairs 104-5, **9**
Kıbrıslı Mustafa Emin Paşa Yalı 216
Kiz Kulesi 123
Köprülü Amcazade Hüseyin Paşa Yalı 218
Kuleli Military School 216
Netherlands Consulate General 112
Obelisk of Theodosius 21, 56-7
Patisserie Markiz 109-10, 113

Pera Palas Oteli 110
Royal Swedish Consulate
   113
Russian Consulate 113
Sirkeci Railway
   Station 73, **92**
Spiral Column 57

MARKETS
Balık Pazar (Fish Market)
   111
Fatih Pazarı 96

MONASTERIES
Hagia Triada Monastery
   221
Monastery of St George
   222

MOSQUES
Arap Camii 104
Atik Valide Camii 121, 125
Aya Sofya 49-53, 59, **52**,
   4, **89**
Azapkapi Sokollu Mehmet
   Paşa Camii 104
Beyazıt Camii 80, 84
Blue Mosque 54-5, 59, **4**,
   85, **90**
Çinili Camii 121, 125
Eyüp Sultan Camii & Tomb
   99-100, **8**
Fatih Camii 95-6
Fethiye Camii 97
Gâzi İskender Paşa Camii 218
Küçük Aya Sofya Camii
   57, 60
Mihrimah Sultan Camii
   (Edirnekapı) 96, 100
Mihrimah Sultan Camii
   (Üsküdar) 121
Nuruosmaniye Camii
   79-80, 83
Ortaköy Camii 120, **3**,
   11, **87**
Rüstem Paşa Camii 82, 84
Şehzade Mehmet Camii
   81-2, 84
Şemsi Paşa Camii 123, 125
Sokollu Mehmet Paşa
   Camii 58
Süleymaniye Camii 80-1,
   84, **7**, **86**
Sultan Selim Camii 99,
   100
Yeni Camii 73-4, 84

Yeni Valide Camii 123, 125
Zeyrek Camii 82, **88**

MUSEUMS
Askeri Müzesi 114
Aya Sofya 49-53, 59, **52**,
   4, **89**
Deniz Müzesi 118-19
Florence Nightingale
   Museum 124-5
Galata Mevlevihanesi 106,
   108-9, 113, **10**
Great Palace Mosaics
   Museum 55-6, 60
İstanbul Archaeology
   Museums 70-2, 75, **6**
Miniaturk 129
Museum of Turkish
   Calligraphic Art 80, 84
Museum of Turkish &
   Islamic Arts 57-8, 61
Pera Museum 110, 112
Rahmi M Koç Müzesi
   128-9
Sadberk Hanım Müzesi
   219
Sakıp Sabancı Müzesi
   218
Yedikule Hisarı Müzesi
   128
Yıldız Şale 119-20

PALACES
Beylerbeyi Palace 215-16
Çırağan Palace 119, **11**
Dolmabahçe Palace 116-18,
   11, **91**
Dolmabahçe Selamlik
   118
Great Byzantine Palace
   56
Küçüksu Kasrı 216
Tekfur Sarayi 96-7
Topkapı Palace 62, 65-8,
   75, **64**, **6**, **87**

PARKS
Büyük Çamlica 123-4
Gülhane Parkı 72, 75
Yıldız Parkı 119-20, **11**

SYNAGOGUES
Ahrida Synagogue 98
Neve Shalom Synagogue
   105
Yanbol synagogue 98

SLEEPING
APARTMENTS
Galata Residence Camondo
   Apartment Hotel 205-6
İstanbul Holiday
   Apartments 206
Side Hotel & Pension
   202-3
Triada Residence 207

BOUTIQUE HOTELS
Ajia 209
Hotel Kervansaray 224
Hotel Les Ottomans
   209
Hotel Nomade 201
Lush Hip Hotel 207
Sumahan on the Water
   209
Tan Otel 204

HISTORIC HOTELS
Büyük Londra Oteli 207

HOSTELS
Bahaus Guesthouse 203
Big Apple Hostel 203
Mavi Guesthouse 203
Orient International Hostel
   203
Sultan Hostel 203
World House Hostel 206
Yellow Rose Pension 224

HOTELS
Çanak Otel 224
Divan Taksım Suites 208
Efes Hotel 224
Hotel Akol 224
Hotel Armada 199
Hotel Daphne 200-1
Hotel Erboy 205
Hotel Hali 202
Hotel Niles 205
Hotel Residence 207
Maydos Hotel 224
Merit Halki Palace 222
Richmond Hotel 207
Riva Hotel 208
Side Hotel & Pension
   202-3
Splendid Palas 223
Taksim Square Hotel
   207

Vardar Palace Hotel
   207-8
World Park Hotel 204-5
Yenişehir Palas 208

LUXURY HOTELS
Bentley Hotel 208
Central Palace 208
Çırağan Palace Hotel
   Kempinski 209
Four Seasons Hotel
   Istanbul 199
Marmara İstanbul 206
Marmara Pera 206-7
Sofa Hotel 208

OTTOMAN BOUTIQUE HOTELS
Anemon Galata 205
Artefes Hotel 201
Ayasofya Konakları 204
Dersaadet Oteli 199-200
Eklektik Guest House 206
Hanedan Hotel 202
Hotel ALP Guesthouse
   202
Hotel Ararat 201
Hotel Empress Zoe 200
Hotel Peninsula 202
Hotel Poem 201-2
Hotel Şebnem 201
Hotel Sultan's Inn 202
Hotel Turkoman 200
Hotel Türkuaz 205
Hotel Uyan İstanbul 201
İbrahim Paşa Oteli 199
Konuk Evi 204
Kybele Hotel 204
Ottoman Hotel
   Imperial 204
Sari Konak Oteli 200
Tria Hotel İstanbul 200
Yeşil Ev 199

SPORTS & ACTIVITIES
GAY HAMAMS & SAUNAS
Ağa Hamamı 195
Aquarius 195
Çeşme Hamamı 195
Yeşildirek Hamamı 195

GYMS
Orsep Royal Hotel 192

HAMAMS
Ambassador Hotel Spa Center 192-3
Cağaloğlu Hamami 193
Çemberlitaş Hamamı 193
Süleymaniye Hamami 193

Tarihi Galatasaray Hamami 193

SWIMMING POOLS
Çırağan Palace Hotel Kempinski 192
Hotel Les Ottomans 192
Istanbul Hilton 192

Swissôtel İstanbul the Bosphorus 192

TOP PICKS
architecture 86
architecture books 87
arts venues 185
children 58

drinking 171
food 145
free activities 80
hotels 197
nightlife 179
shopping 131
sights 43
sports & activities 191

000 map pages
000 photographs

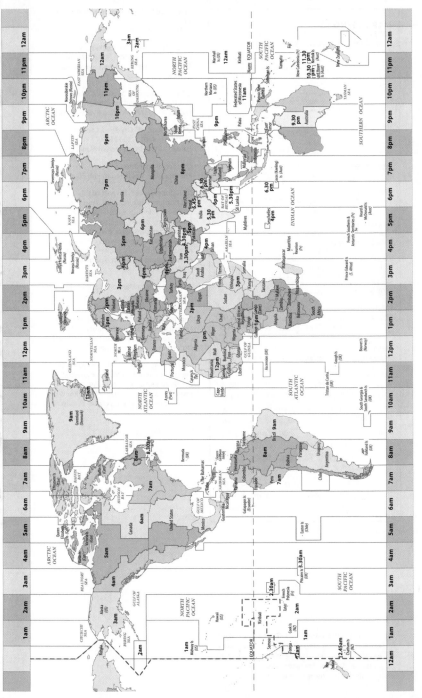

267

MAP LEGEND

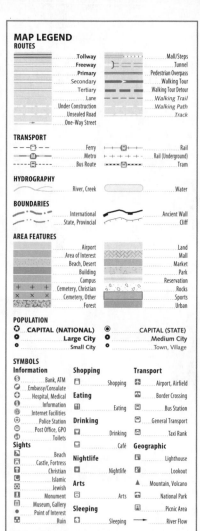

ROUTES

..........Tollway
..........Freeway
..........Primary
..........Secondary
..........Tertiary
..........Lane
Under Construction
Unsealed Road
One-Way Street

..........Mall/Steps
..........Tunnel
Pedestrian Overpass
..........Walking Tour
Walking Tour Detour
..........Walking Trail
..........Walking Path
..........Track

TRANSPORT

..........Ferry
..........Metro
..........Bus Route

..........Rail
Rail (Underground)
..........Tram

HYDROGRAPHY

..........River, Creek
..........Water

BOUNDARIES

..........International
State, Provincial

..........Ancient Wall
..........Cliff

AREA FEATURES

..........Airport
Area of Interest
Beach, Desert
..........Building
..........Campus
Cemetery, Christian
Cemetery, Other
..........Forest

..........Land
..........Mall
..........Market
..........Park
..........Reservation
..........Rocks
..........Sports
..........Urban

POPULATION

○ CAPITAL (NATIONAL)
● Large City
● Small City

◉ CAPITAL (STATE)
● Medium City
● Town, Village

SYMBOLS

Information
Bank, ATM
Embassy/Consulate
Hospital, Medical
Information
Internet Facilities
Police Station
Post Office, GPO
Toilets

Sights
Beach
Castle, Fortress
Christian
Islamic
Jewish
Monument
Museum, Gallery
Point of Interest
Ruin

Shopping
Shopping

Eating
Eating

Drinking
Drinking
Café

Nightlife
Nightlife

Arts
Arts

Sleeping
Sleeping

Transport
Airport, Airfield
Border Crossing
Bus Station
General Transport
Taxi Rank

Geographic
Lighthouse
Lookout
Mountain, Volcano
National Park
Picnic Area
River Flow

Published by Lonely Planet Publications Pty Ltd
ABN 36 005 607 983

Australia Head Office, Locked Bag 1, Footscray, Victoria 3011, ☎ 03 8379 8000, fax 03 8379 8111, talk2us@lonelyplanet .com.au

USA 150 Linden St, Oakland, CA 94607, ☎ 510 893 8555, toll free 800 275 8555, fax 510 893 8572, info@lonelyplanet.com

UK 2nd Floor, 186 City Road, London, ECV1 2NT, ☎ 020 7106 2100, fax 020 7106 2101, go@lonelyplanet.co.uk